On the Government of Rulers
De Regimine Principum

THE MIDDLE AGES SERIES

Ruth Mazo Karras, General Editor
Edward Peters, Founding Editor

A complete list of books in the series
is available from the publisher.

On the Government of Rulers
De Regimine Principum

Ptolemy of Lucca
with portions attributed to
Thomas Aquinas

translated by James M. Blythe

PENN

University of Pennsylvania Press

Philadelphia

Copyright © 1997 University of Pennsylvania Press
All rights reserved
Printed in the United States of America on acid-free paper

10 9 8 7 6 5 4 3 2 1

Published by
University of Pennsylvania Press
Philadelphia, Pennsylvania 19104-6097

Library of Congress Cataloging-in-Publication Data

Bartholomew, of Lucca, ca. 1236–1327.
    [De regimine principum. English]
    On the government of rulers : De regimine principum / Ptolemy of Lucca;
with portions attributed to Thomas Aquinas ; translated by
James M. Blythe.
        p.   cm. — (The Middle Ages series)
    Includes bibliographical references and index.
    ISBN 0-8122-3370-0 (alk. paper)
        1. Political science—Early works to 1800.   I. Blythe, James M., 1948–   .
II. Thomas, Aquinas, Saint, 1225?–1274. De regno, ad regem Cypri. English.
III. Title.   IV. Series.
JC121.B2813   1997
320.1′01—dc21   97-2015
                                                                        CIP

Contents

Preface

WHEN I WAS WORKING ON MY BOOK, *Ideal Government and the Mixed Constitution in the Middle Ages*, I was especially drawn to Ptolemy of Lucca (c.1236–c.1327), whose radical ideas were remarkable for his time, but about whom very little has been written, and I devoted a chapter to him.[1] I felt that a translation of his work was long overdue, considering its originality and the fact that it influenced much of the political thought of the later Middle Ages, the Renaissance, and the early modern period. Only a few professional medievalists have read Ptolemy's work in its scholastic Latin, but if it were available in English it could benefit all historians of political thought as well as many others interested in political theory, the history of ideas, and the history of constitutionalism. It could also be used in courses in political thought and in the medieval and early modern intellectual tradition. I have already used it in a graduate readings course in medieval history with excellent results. It might also begin to redress the serious undervaluation of Ptolemy's position in the history of ideas, reflected in what has been at best cursory treatment in general histories of political thought.

More than anyone else, Ptolemy combined the principles of northern Italian government with scholastic Aristotelian political theory. He was also the first of his time, or among the first, to state many ideas that were later to become commonplace. He is the first medieval political theorist not to endorse kingship as the best form of government . In fact, he attacks it as the moral equivalent of despotism, totally inappropriate for a virtuous and freedom-loving people. Believing this, he obviously cannot subscribe to the dominant medieval appreciation for the Roman Empire. Instead he glorifies Republican Rome and brands Julius Caesar as a tyrant and the Roman Empire as tyranny. These are remarkable assertions for someone writing around 1300,

---

1. James Blythe, *Ideal Government and the Mixed Constitution in the Middle Ages* (Princeton, N.J.: Princeton University Press, 1992), 92–117.

and the harbinger of a commonplace humanist view of the fifteenth century. Although he defends republicanism vigorously, he nevertheless believes that different circumstances, climates, and national characters may require different forms of government and that most are not suited to the best government, which includes the representation of the few and the many in a mixed constitution. Ptolemy was also the first to equate the standard Greek models of mixed constitution—Sparta, Crete, and Carthage—with the Roman Republic, biblical rule, the Church, and medieval government. Again anticipating the humanists, he was the first to suggest that the perfect republic could be so inwardly harmonious that it could transcend the normal imperatives of decay and ultimate destruction. He also began a debate on whether women should serve in the military.

One of the most remarkable things about Ptolemy's book is its wealth of examples, unique in scholastic works of his time. Almost everything he writes suggests some new example to him. Many of these come from the ancient or patristic classics, and these are unusual only in their number, their variety, and the use to which Ptolemy puts them. But he also makes many references to the history, customs, and attitudes of the Middle Ages. For example, mentioning that a king should be wealthy inspires him to discuss how coins are minted. After stating that climate determines national character, he demonstrates this with German immigrants to Sicily who soon became like the Sicilians. He analyzes northern Italian city-states and the struggles between popes and emperors and touches on such diverse topics as Totila the Ostrogoth, Tuscan battle formations, the hunting habits of the French and English kings, the procedure for secret ballots in Florence, and the exchange between Pope Innocent III and the king of Aragon over debased money.

I am convinced that Ptolemy today stands in much the same position Marsilius of Padua once did. He was mentioned briefly in some general works and a few scholars pointed out that several later writers referred to him, but even those who noticed him did not accord him any major importance. This all changed in the 1950s, when Alan Gewirth translated Marsilius's major work and wrote a book-length introduction to his thought.[2] Today, Marsilius is considered to be *the* great radical political thinker of the fourteenth century, and excerpts of his work appear in every historical anthology of western political thought. In his own way, Ptolemy was every bit as radical and influential as Marsilius, and I think that this translation of his major political work, *On the Government of Rulers*, perhaps supplemented in the future by a

---

2. Alan Gewirth, *Marsilius of Padua, the Defender of Peace*, 2 vols, Records of Civilization: Sources and Studies 46 (New York: Columbia University Press, 1951–1956; reprinted New York: Harper and Row, 1967).

translation of his other political treatise, *A Short Determination of the Juris-diction of the Roman Empire*, would contribute to Ptolemy achieving a major place in future histories of political thought.

Although Ptolemy did not write Book 1 and part of Book 2 of the treatise translated in this volume, I decided to translate the whole, since it has appeared in this form since the fourteenth century, and I wanted to show the difference between the two parts more clearly by providing a version that maintains a consistent terminology throughout. Whether the other author was Thomas Aquinas, as has been traditionally assumed, or another, as is now often argued, is of secondary concern in a volume centered on Ptolemy. In the next few pages I will discuss the first part and its author, but my main purpose is to introduce Ptolemy's thought and the contemporary events, conflicts, and intellectual trends and paradigms that shaped it. Of necessity, this introduction will be brief, but I hope to publish a book-length study of Ptolemy within the next few years.

Ptolemy supported papal supremacy, justified despotic kings for most peoples, and tied character to birth and geography, but he also began the theoretical attack against monarchy. Today, American and European peoples pride themselves on their "democracies," which reduce monarchy to at most a ceremonial post. At the same time, their governments sponsor tyrannies, massacres, and exploitation around the world and immiserate a growing segment of their own citizenry, yet with no sense of irony use "medieval" to mean "backward," "cruel," and "barbaric." Ptolemy and his successors may have begun to undermine the almost universal acceptance of monarchy, but the revolutions they eventually spawned created a resourceful new ruling class. In its dotage, this class has been able, to a degree not possible in the recent past, to rededicate itself to greed and the oppression necessary to sate its members' individual desires, thanks to the discrediting of egalitarian ideologies by totalitarian pseudo-socialist regimes. Almost miraculously it has been able to justify this to the masses as the essence of freedom. Aristotle and the medieval writers who followed him defined good government as that which promotes the common good. What these words mean has changed over the centuries, but the concept is sound and can never rationally mean the right of a few to monopolize and destroy the wealth of the earth for their own benefit. In that sense classical and medieval political thought still has relevance for us today.

The University of Memphis requires that the following statement be included: "This work was supported in part by a grant from the University of Memphis Faculty Research Grant Fund. This support does not necessarily imply endorsement by the University of research conclusions."

For advice on a few difficult passages, I thank Brian Tierney and James

John of Cornell University. I would also like to thank Cary Nederman of the University of Arizona for his many helpful comments, Antony Black of the University of Dundee for some information on the authorship of the treatise, Philip Grierson of Cambridge University for some help with passages about coins, and the two readers for the University of Pennsylvania press, who provided much useful advice and saved me from a few blunders. Thanks also to my Spring 1996 graduate seminar at the University of Memphis for pointing out some confusingly translated passages and for making several useful suggestions. Finally, thanks most of all to the great, but undiscovered, painter Sheila Martin, my companion and partner for more than twenty years, whom I torture by forcing her to read and critique all my writing. She has gone over the whole translation with me and helped to make it more readable.

A Note on the Text

My intention is to provide an idiomatic, readable translation, while being absolutely consistent with regard to political, theological, and philosophical terminology. While I have been rather free with syntax, voice, word order, and wording, I have regarded a specified terminology as sacrosanct and have listed or discussed the most important protected words at the end of the introduction. In the footnotes and indices, I refer to *On the Government of Rulers* simply by Book, chapter, and section numbers. For ancient and medieval works for which there are standard divisions, for example, Thomas Aquinas's *Summa Theologiae*, I do not cite a specific edition, even if I suggest a modern translation in the bibliography for those who cannot read these texts in the medieval version. The reason for this is that what Ptolemy cites does not necessarily agree completely with any particular modern edition, still less with any translation. I do, however, make note of significant discrepancies with standard Latin editions. I use an improved method of footnote references, which helps readers to decide whether they want to look at a note: I use plain text numbers for notes that give only a source references, boldface for notes that contain additional information, and italics for notes on the translation. Some note numbers may be both boldface and italics. Some notes provide information on the original Latin words that helps to clarify the text, especially in the case when Ptolemy is discussing etymologies. I have chosen to regard this as additional information (boldface) rather than a note on the translation (italics). Inevetably, there are some boarderline cases that could be handled in more than one way. For more information on conventions that concern only the translation, see the last section of the introduction.

Introduction

I. The Treatise *On the Government of Rulers*

On the Government of Rulers (*De Regimine Principum*) was very popular and influential in the Middle Ages, partially because it was often attributed to Thomas Aquinas (c.1225–1274). Actually, Thomas wrote at most only the first part, known also as *On the Kingdom, to the King of Cyprus*, and Ptolemy of Lucca continued it from the middle of Book 2, chapter 4. Some manuscripts have only the first part, a few end in the middle of Book 2, chapter 2, but many others contain all four Books. There were some medieval attributions of the second, larger part to Ptolemy, but this was not generally recognized until the twentieth century, and the whole treatise often appears among Thomas's collected works. Objective internal evidence dates Ptolemy's part at around 1300. The text mentions the emperor Albert I of Hapsburg (r.1298–1308) [1] and states that 270 years "or thereabouts" had elapsed since the crowning of the emperor Conrad II (1027, 1030 in Ptolemy's chronology).[2] More subjective reading suggests a date of 1301, but no later than 1303.[3]

The date of the first part is still in question. Assuming that Thomas was not the author, Walter Mohr has suggested dates ranging from 1218 to 1277.[4] Early dates pose some problems, including several unambiguous references to Aristotle's *Politics*, which was not available in Latin until around 1260. This part does have more references to the *Ethics*, which was available much earlier, and the references to the *Politics* could be interpolations or from portions known somewhat earlier, but this is unlikely. There are also passages similar

---

1. 3.20.2.
2. 3.19.1.
3. See Charles Till Davis, "Ptolemy of Lucca and the Roman Republic," *Proceedings of the American Philosophical Society* 118 (1974): 38: n. 45 for a bibliography and summary of the arguments for dating.
4. Walter Mohr, "Bemerkungen zur Verfasserschaft von *De Regimine Principum*," in *Virtus Politica*, ed. Joseph Müller and Helmut Koblenberger (Stuttgart and Bad Cannestatt: Frommann Verlag and Günther Holzboog, KG, 1974), 141–42.

to ones in Thomas's *Summa Theologiae* and *Summa contra Gentiles*, though this in itself proves neither Thomas's authorship nor the priority of his other works. All in all, the most likely dates for composition are the 1260s or 1270s.

The two parts are not attached seamlessly, and Walter Mohr sees a further problem with the connection between Book 1 and the early chapters of Book 2.[5] It would be difficult to describe an overall plan that includes Book 1, which states explicitly that its purpose is to discuss the kingdom and the king's office. It begins by proving the necessity of government and defining the good and bad kinds of government; later, it also gives arguments showing the advantages of republican rule. Nevertheless, the bulk of this Book is devoted to discussing the powers and responsibilities of a king and to proving that monarchy is the best and most natural form of government and that with the proper safeguards it will not degenerate into tyranny.

Book 1 can be read as a coherent and self-contained treatise on government. To Mohr the transitional statement at the end of Book 1: "These are the the things that pertain to the office of king, and I must now treat each of them more diligently,"[6] seems clumsy and betrays the absence of an organic connection with Book 2, which never fulfills this promise, instead moving on to other matters and quickly abandoning the pretense of considering kingdoms alone.[7] In my reading, though not in Mohr's, Books 2 through 4 do provide a unified, if incomplete, working out of an overall plan. Book 2 analyzes the factors necessary for a successful government, beginning with the geography and climate, then moving on to natural and manufactured wealth, governmental officials, defensive structures, roads, coinage, weights and measures, welfare, and religion. This last provides the transition to Book 3, which begins with a discussion of God's role in government, and then illustrates this role, most extensively with ancient Roman politics. At this point Ptolemy initiates an analysis of the various forms of human lordship, which takes up the rest of the treatise. There is one universal form, that which God gave to all humans over the natural world in the Garden of Eden, and four forms of lordship of human over human: one form that is both regal and sacerdotal, another purely regal (under which he includes imperial rule), political rule, and household rule. Ptolemy disposes of natural rule, regal and political rule, and regal rule in the remainder of Book 3 and devotes Book 4 to political rule. In the last paragraph of the treatise, he explains that household rule is so different from the other kinds that it deserves a separate treatise of its own, as

5. Mohr, "Bemerkungen," 129.
6. 1.16.8.
7. Mohr, "Bemerkungen," 129.

does the treatment of the particular virtues required for subjects and rulers. There is no evidence that he ever wrote either of these projected works.

II. Authorship of the Treatise

Everyone now agrees that *On the Government of Rulers* is the work of at least two authors. It is surprising that this fact was ever overlooked, since the second part of the work differs from the first in style, content, emphasis, organization, authorities cited, and choice of materials. Even more strikingly, the political beliefs are often contradictory, especially in the matter of kingship, which is praised in and stands at the center of Book 1 but is frequently criticized in Books 2 through 4. One controversy was to my mind definitively settled many years ago by Alfred O'Rahilly, who demonstrated that Ptolemy was the author of the second part and that his contribution began in the middle of 2.4.[8] The question of what parts, if any, Thomas wrote is still hotly debated, and Walter Mohr has even questioned some of the material O'Rahilly attributed to Ptolemy.[9] The questions whether the dedication to the king of Cyprus appeared in the original first part, and if so, to what king and on what occasion it was presented have also not been incontrovertibly answered.[10]

In *Political Thought in Europe, 1250–1550*, Antony Black takes it as fairly certain that Thomas wrote none of the treatise, with the possible exception of 1.1.[11] In a letter to me Professor Black says that he bases his opinion on "the fundamental differences in both literary (and indeed intellectual) style and opinion between *De Regimine Principum* and the work of Aquinas." Stylistically, this treatise *is* quite different from the great Summae and commentaries for which Thomas is chiefly famous, but it is a very different kind of work, and it would take a close analysis of Thomas's style and word usage, particularly in his authentic occasional pieces, to establish Black's intuition as a decisive argument. I may do this in the future.

Walter Mohr, who launched the most convincing attack on Thomas's authorship, based his conclusions both on an analysis of the manuscript tradition and on the ideological content of the treatise. Many of his points are

---

8. A. O'Rahilly, "Notes on St. Thomas: IV. *De Regimine Principum*"; "V. Tholomeo of Lucca, Continuator of the *De Regimine Principum*," *Irish Ecclesiastical Record* 31(1929): 396–410; 31(1929): 606–14.

9. Mohr, "Bemerkungen," 133.

10. See Mohr, "Bemerkungen," 140–42.

11. Antony Black, *Political Thought in Europe, 1250–1550*, Cambridge Medieval Textbooks (Cambridge: Cambridge University Press, 1992), 22.

perceptive and call Thomas's authorship seriously into question, but I do not believe that any are substantial enough to discount it entirely. I will take up this subject in detail in my book on Ptolemy; here I will summarize Mohr's arguments and my response. With regard to manuscript evidence, he points out that there was always confusion about authorship. Book 2 is even more questionable in that it lacks connection to Book 1, it is internally confused, and its very existence contradicts references to a single "Book" by Thomas on kingship. He concludes that it is most likely the work of several authors, and that Ptolemy's work begins only with Book 3. Books 3 and 4 form a coherent whole; Ptolemy never intended to continue an earlier work but to create an independent work, although he had Books 1 and 2 before him as he wrote.

Some of these points are more defensible than others. Early manuscripts and comments by Ptolemy and others about Thomas's writings do not decisively settle the question. Numerous manuscripts attribute this portion to Thomas, but Mohr's attempt to discredit these is plausible. Book 2 is somewhat confused and lurches awkwardly from topic to topic, but the chasm between it and Book 1 is not impassable. Contrary to Mohr's assertion, the last chapter of Book 1 does bring up the matter of Book 2 when it mentions the king's numerous duties in providing for the good life of the people.[12] While it would be natural for a modern writer to proceed directly to a more detailed analysis of government, the systematic scholastic mind might well feel it incumbent to begin with the basics: physical location, climate, natural resources, and the like. Later, the focus shifts away from kingship to government in general, but only where traditionally Ptolemy's part begins. This tendency intensifies progressively throughout Book 2. In my reading, any lurching and confusion result more from a new writer trying to graft his ideas onto an original that is not completely compatible and divert the treatise into his own schema.

I am convinced that Ptolemy wrote everything from the middle of 2.4 on. While Books 3 and 4 can be read as a complete and coherent work, this does not prove that it was not conceived as part of a larger work, and there is compelling evidence to suggest that it was. As O'Rahilly demonstrated, the terminology, word usage, and use of sources of the second part of Book 2 coincide with Ptolemy's, both in the rest of *On the Government of Rulers* and elsewhere, including some idiosyncratic usages that seem conclusively to link the work to Ptolemy.[13] Also, the political thought of this part accords with Books 3 and 4, though not with Book 1. The only alternative, as I see it, is that

---

12. 1.16.
13. O'Rahilly, "Notes on St. Thomas: V," 606–14.

Ptolemy both completed Book 2 and wrote a separate treatise, and that these were later joined. The manuscript evidence makes this unlikely, since Books 3 and 4 never appear by themselves. There are also two references to Book 1 in Book 4 and two probable references in Book 2, which treat it as an earlier part of the same work.[14]

With regard to ideological content, Mohr argues that the approach, assumptions, and conclusions of Book 1 are incompatible with those found in Thomas's indisputably authentic writings. His most telling point is that the emphasis on law and the linking of the common good to law, found in all Thomas's other works, is lacking here.[15] This is almost decisive, since it seems hardly credible that Thomas would leave out something so important to him in his only systematic political treatise. Another omission, which Mohr does not mention, is the distinction between regal and political power, which Thomas emphasized in his *Commentary on the "Politics"* and which Ptolemy modifies and makes central to his thought.

On the other hand, I believe that the kind of government for which the author of the first part argues is compatible with what Thomas advocates in *Summa Theologiae*, namely, a limited monarchy in which the king's power is "tempered" by that of others. For this reason, and because I am not yet convinced by the manuscript and stylistic evidence, despite the strong arguments based on content, I feel that the question of whether Books 1 and the beginning of Book 2 were written by the same person, and whether this person was Thomas Aquinas, is still open.

III. Political Thought of the First Contributor

The prologue to Book 1 puts it in the tradition of "mirror of princes" literature, a genre of advice books popular in the Middle Ages. Commonly these concentrated on the generic Christian virtues necessary for a good ruler and had little analysis of politics. Book 1, however, stresses the nature of the kingdom and the political duties of kings. It also considers other forms of government and what measures can ensure that a king does not become a tyrant.

The influence of Aristotelian political thought is evident from the beginning, when the author proves that government is necessary. In contrast to the standard Christian-Augustinian emphasis on government arising only as a result of sin and existing solely for repressing evil, the author invokes a

14. 4.1.2, 4.1.3, 2.8.1, 2.9.3.
15. Mohr, "Bemerkungen," 135–40.

naturalistic and positive justification: humans are naturally social and political animals who need each other in order to provide for the necessities of life, which leads to the necessity of government to guide society toward its common good.[16] In using the formulation "social and political animals" instead of simply "political animals," as Aristotle usually does, the first author, while not distorting Aristotle's meaning, shifts the emphasis from a natural need to participate in government to a natural need to live together in communities. This means that the common good can be the criterion for good government without the concomitant necessity of direct participation. This corresponds to Thomas's thought in other works.[17]

Aristotle wrote of simple forms of government (or polity, to use the Greek word the medieval Aristotelians commonly employed) based on two criteria: whether one, few, or many rule and whether the ruling group governs for the common good or for its own good. This gives rise to six possible forms: the three good forms of monarchy, aristocracy, and polity (confusingly the general term does double duty as a specific form; others call it "good democracy") and the three bad forms of tyranny, oligarchy, and democracy, which are corrupt versions of the good forms.[18] The first contributor argues forcefully that monarchy is the best form, while admitting that others may also be good.[19] This is not surprising in a treatise written for a king, and it also accords with what Thomas wrote elsewhere. The confusion that some historians have found in Thomas's writings stems from their failure to realize that for him the government of one does not preclude the participation or power of others in a mixed government and that he sometimes loosely uses "monarchy" to refer either to this mixed government or to the simple form of monarchy.[20]

The first contributor considers all the arguments for monarchy, then shows that the potential dangers of this form can be overcome, and finally that there is less danger in monarchy than in any other form. The last two points are necessary since he admits that tyranny, monarchy's perversion, is the worst possible form of government, which might mean that another form is best in practice.[21] His injunction that the dangers of monarchy can be overcome if the monarchy is "tempered" and his appeals to "public authority" suggest that the author has a mixed constitution in mind, although he does not use

16. 1.1.3–6.
17. Aristotle, *Politics*, 1.2.1253a.2–3, 7–8. See also *Ethics*, 1.7.1097b.11–12, 9.9.1169b.18; *History of Animals*, 1.1.488a.7, 10. In *History of Animals* Aristotle does call them "social animals." See also Thomas Aquinas, *Summa Theologiae*, 1.2.72.4.
18. Aristotle, *Politics*, 3.7.1279a.22–b.10.
19. 1.2.2–3 for the classification; arguments for monarchy are found throughout Book 1.
20. Blythe, *Ideal Government*, 39–59.
21. 1.4, 1.6.

the expression.[22] As I mentioned, what is missing compared with Thomas's other works is a direct emphasis on law as a restraining factor on the king.

In an apparent exception to his support of monarchy, the first author praises the Roman Republic,[23] which has led Ronald Witt to write that he is the only medieval author who "provides a rationale for the putative superiority of republicanism over monarchy."[24] This conclusion stems from a misunderstanding of the writer's purpose. Although he admires the Roman Republic, recognizes the benefits of a republic, and provides arguments for future republicans, in context he is not simply supporting republicanism. Rather, in a discussion of why monarchy is best, he pauses to discuss how tyranny is worst. To this end, he shows how the Romans were able to advance under a republic once they had expelled tyrannical kings. But he is equally at pains to point out the dangers of republican government: the Roman Republic collapsed in civil wars. Thus the first contributor is actually developing his preference for a "tempered" monarchy in which aristocrats and the people are given some share of government, both to prevent the monarch from becoming a tyrant and to give the people the feeling that they have a stake in the polity. Even under a king, this eliminates the perception that the common good is in the hands of one, which, the writer admits, is a problem of monarchy. He does not believe that the multitude can contribute positively to government, but their desire to have a part of political power reflects their nature as political animals. By satisfying this natural desire, without surrendering a destructive amount of control to the masses (something Thomas outlines most clearly in *Summa Theologiae*[25]), the best government, a mixed constitution, can overcome the problems of each individual form.

IV. The Life and Works of Ptolemy of Lucca

Ptolemy of Lucca, also known as Tolomeo da Lucca or Bartholomew of Lucca, was born to a middle-class family of Lucca, a republican city of Tuscany, around 1236. As a young man he joined the Dominican order, then studied under Thomas Aquinas at the University of Paris in 1261–1268, and subsequently traveled with him in Italy. They were together when Thomas died in 1274, and much of what we know of Thomas's life comes to us from

22. 1.7.2, 1.7.7.
23. 1.5.
24. Ronald Witt, "The Rebirth of the Concept of Republican Liberty in Italy," in *Renaissance Studies in Honor of Hans Baron*, ed. Anthony Mohlo and John A. Tedeschi (Dekalb: Northern Illinois University Press, 1971), 193.
25. Thomas Aquinas, *Summa Theologiae*, 1.2.105.1.

Ptolemy's writings. From the 1280s to the early 1300s Ptolemy served as prior in several Tuscan houses, including Santa Maria Novella in Florence, which was a key center for classical studies, republicanism, and "pre-humanism."[26] He spent much of the first two decades of the fourteenth century at the papal court in Avignon writing, doing research, and possibly serving as papal librarian. John XXII appointed him Bishop of Torcello, near Venice, in 1318 and protected him in a dispute with the Patriarch of Grado, who imprisoned him for a time. In 1323 Ptolemy was tried and acquitted of the patriarch's charges in Avignon, where he probably attended canonization ceremonies for his mentor in July 1323. In 1327 he died in Torcello at the age of about ninety. Besides the treatise translated here, Ptolemy wrote several other works including Tuscan annals, a history of the Church (*The Ecclesiastical Histories*), a commentary on the six days of creation (*The Hexameron*), and a treatise on the Roman Empire (*A Short Determination of the Jurisdiction of the Roman Empire*), an important question for Italian city-states struggling to remain independent of both pope and emperor.

Of these works, only *A Short Determination* has substantial political content. Written twenty years earlier, it is in many respects a complementary work to *On the Government of Rulers*.[27] The latter concerns itself primarily with the internal structure and functioning of government, the former with the relationship between government (especially the Roman Empire) and the Church. There are some obvious disagreements between the two, but a general similarity of conception. In spite of his apparent republicanism, Ptolemy, in both works, assigns primary authority in the world to the pope and is involved in the canon law debate over the nature of papal power that had been going on at least since the Gregorian Reform Movement of the eleventh century and was especially urgent in the later thirteenth and early fourteenth centuries, when papal rhetoric was becoming more strident while real power was in decline. It is remarkable that in one passage he describes the Church as a limited monarchy.

V. The Political and Ecclesiological Issues of Ptolemy's Time

To understand Ptolemy's ideas fully, one must consider them in the context both of medieval political theory and the controversies of his day, especially

---

26. See Davis, "Ptolemy of Lucca," for the connection of Dante Alighieri, Remigio de'Girolami, Nicholas Trevet, and others to this house.

27. Ptolemy of Lucca, *Determinatio Compendiosa de Juribus Imperii* (*A Short Determination of the Jurisdiction of the Roman Empire*), in *Fontes Iuris Germanici Antiqui*, ed. Marius Kramer (Hanover and Leipzig: Bibliopolius Hahnianus, 1909), c. 31, 63–64 (hereafter cited as *A Short Determination*).

those in which he was personally involved. As a northern Italian by birth and for a large part of his life by residence, Ptolemy would have been influenced by the volatile Italian political situation. As a student, academic, and papal functionary in Paris and Avignon, he would also have been exposed to the problems of the northern monarchies and the empire. As a cleric and supporter of the pope he would have been caught up in the current conflicts between church and state and internal conflicts within the church. Finally, as a scholastic thinker and a student of Thomas Aquinas he would have been schooled in and aware of the disputes about Aristotelian thought, canon law, and Roman law, which dominated their respective fields in the university. Before examining Ptolemy's work itself, I will say a few words about each of these.

ITALY

Northern Italy was unique in western Europe in that it consisted of many semi-independent city-states. Nominally a part of the Roman Empire, in practice the emperor was rarely able to control it. Occasionally, he would invade and hold the region for a short time, but as soon as he left the cities would reassert their independence. Until the Investiture Controversy of the later eleventh century, bishops and counts, appointed by the emperor but usually representing local noble interests, dominated city government. The turmoil of that period made possible the coming to power of the communes to supplant the authority of both emperor and bishops. Originally these were private organizations formed to protect the interests of nobles and some large businesspeople, but in the Consular Phase, named for the consuls who were the elected magistrates of the communes, which lasted from about 1080 to 1220, they became the chief governing group in all major cities of north and central Italy. Dissention among the rulers and a desire to have a more smoothly operating executive led in many places to the appointment of an outsider, usually a military figure from another city, to the position of podestà. He had great powers, but his term was limited, usually to one year, and at the end of his term he had to answer to the commune for his actions and expenses under threat of fine or imprisonment.

One of the distinguishing characteristics of northern Italy was the phenomenal growth of commerce from the eleventh century on. Italian merchants came to dominate European trade and banking. Genoa, Pisa, and Venice challenged Muslims for control of the Mediterranean, and eventually Italians supplanted both Muslims and Byzantines there and in Black Sea trade. Italian manufactured goods also became important in European and international trade. During the Consular Phase guilds arose throughout northern

Italy to represent the interests of the new commercial class, and eventually these guilds vied for and succeeded in gaining political power in many cities. At first the great magnates, some of whom were already represented in the communes, dominated the guilds, but over the "Period of the *Popolo*," which lasted in some cities into the fourteenth century, there was increasing, sometimes successful pressure from less prominent guilds and from less prominent members of guilds for extension of participation, resulting in many cities in a republicanism extending political power to a broader group of citizens than any since ancient Greece. Many also passed anti-magnate legislation, attempting to control the behavior and influence of great families.

This very period, however, also saw the growth of vicious factionalism, both between the guild government and those outside it on either side—the magnates fighting to regain their power, lower guildspeople asserting their right to equal participation, and sometimes even workers struggling against fierce guild opposition to form their own guilds and share power—and within society as a whole with the formation of the widespread Guelph and Ghibelline parties. Originally these were factions in the struggle between pope and emperor, but they took on increasingly local roles. In many cities there was an alternation of the parties in power with the losers often having their assets seized and their families exiled, leading them to seek allies to help them return and overthrow their rivals. Throughout the thirteenth and fourteenth centuries, northern Italy was rife with conflict, and in this atmosphere many cities abandoned republican government for despotism, although there is much disagreement as to why and how this happened. Even those cities that maintained a semblance of republican rule retained merely honorary republican offices and ceded effective power to a small elite.

Ptolemy grew up in the Tuscan city of Lucca, and he wrote *On the Government of Rulers* in Tuscany. It is to this city and region, then, that we should primarily look for Italian influences. Lucca was an ancient Roman city established by the second century B.C.E., and it was the seat of one of three Lombard dukes from the late sixth century until Charlemagne's conquest in 774. For a time in the ninth and tenth centuries, Lucca assumed great importance as the capital of Tuscany under the rule of dukes who became margraves of Tuscany, until it was supplanted by Florence. An initial supporter of the papacy in the Investiture Controversy, it went over to the empire and was rewarded with a charter of liberties, which soon resulted in the formation of a commune and conquests of the neighboring countryside; a series of wars with Pisa for access to the sea followed in the twelfth century. In the last decade of the twelfth century, the Luccans appointed their first podestà. Conflict with Pisa continued sporadically in the thirteenth century, but the Genoese defeat of Pisa in 1284 rendered Lucca the chief rival to Florence in Tuscany. These events were part of a Tuscan struggle for supremacy among Pisa, Florence, and Lucca, in which other cities merely attempted to preserve their independence. Florence eventually gained control of almost the whole region, but Lucca never lost its independence.

The thirteenth century also saw the increasing importance of Lucca as an industrial and banking center, the former largely based on a silk industry. As elsewhere, guilds vied with the commune for power, and they were victorious in the late thirteenth century. Their government eventually included several popular councils, a council of elders (*Anziani*), and an executive captain of the *Popolo*. It was only in Ptolemy's old age that Lucca followed most other cities on the path of despotism. Having long returned to being a Guelph city, it opposed Emperor Henry VII during his invasion of 1310–13, but it was conquered and subsequently ruled from 1316 to 1328 by the local Ghibelline military leader Castruccio Castracani, who was succeeded by a series of other lords, and it came for a time under the rule of the emperor. In 1368 it became one of the few cities to reestablish oligarchic, but republican, government. Thus in Lucca we see a city struggling with the same problems as other republics, and resolving them more successfully than most.

EUROPEAN MONARCHIES AND THE EMPIRE

Ptolemy's century was one of the most significant for European state building. Since many of the accomplishments of this time unraveled in a series of fourteenth-century disasters, it was also the period in which emerging national states reached their highest development until the late fifteenth-century "New Monarchies" of France, Spain, Portugal, and England. In all northern states, monarchs contended with nobles and the church to centralize and extend their rule and law. Although powerful states arose only where monarchs prevailed, they never become absolute rulers or overcame medieval principles of limited government.

Feudalism succeeded in reestablishing order in a tenth- to twelfth-century Europe torn by Viking, Magyar, and Muslim invasions and fragmented into a multitude of petty, quarreling lordships, but it also promoted another kind of decentralization. Bound to the higher lord only by a contractual feudal oath which promised strictly defined military aid and limited financial donations in return for protection, vassals felt themselves entitled to refuse all other aid and to govern their fiefs and subjects according to their own law and without royal interference.

Fiefdoms became hereditary; thus monarchs could not depend on the loyalty of their lords. One tactic they devised came into conflict with the increasing prestige and demands of the Roman Catholic Church during and after the Gregorian Reform Movement of the eleventh century. This was royal appointment (called "investiture") of bishops, who thereby became major fiefholders. The advantage was that priests did not have legitimate heirs, so the fief would revert to the monarch when the bishop died. The Church gladly accepted this earlier, but as the papacy sought to reform and gain control over the Church it came increasingly to oppose it. The Church also began to demand other rights, such as the right to try clergy and some lay offenders in its own courts. Around the time *On the Government of Rulers* was written, the king of France was engaged in a protracted struggle with the pope over the right of the state to tax the Church without its consent.

Thus, in order to build a powerful monarchy, the monarch had to limit the claims of both vassals and Church, although in the twelfth and early thirteenth centuries, as both church and state were trying to extend their authority, there were often times when monarch and pope could be allies in undercutting localism in both realms.

Although these general principles held true throughout northern Europe, they worked themselves out differently in different areas. England was a relatively small area conquered by Norman rulers, who were consequently able to upset the established order and institute a fairly centralized feudal monarchy from the start, in most cases with the cooperation of the Church. Likewise, in southern Europe—in southern Italy and Sicily—Norman conquerors were able to establish another centralized monarchy, one even more subject to the king's will. Although English kings promoted a common law for the kingdom as early as the twelfth century, they remained subject to the law and had to turn to their barons for exceptional taxation or legislation. By the early thirteenth century Magna Carta, originally only a restatement of traditional feudal rights in the minds of the barons who made King John sign it, established the principles that would shape English constitutional government. Ptolemy's life corresponded to the reigns of Henry III (r.1216–72), Edward I Longshanks (r.1272–1307), and Edward II (r.1307–1327), who struggled to maintain their authority against rebellious barons, in the process unintentionally laying the foundations of Parliament, at first simply a traditional word for meetings of the king with nobles. Henry III began also to summon representatives of local areas. Edward I was the first king to call such meetings often, in 1275 summoning both knights and burgesses "to take up the affairs of the kingdom together with the magnates of our kingdom."[28]

The French kings were in a much weaker position initially. Many of their

---

28. See Carl Stephenson and Frederick Marcham, eds., *Sources of English Constitutional History* (New York: Harper, 1937), 153.

nominal fiefs were controlled by the English kings or virtually independent lords; at times they ruled little more than the Royal Demesne around Paris, at other times even that was in jeopardy. Beginning in the twelfth century, a series of ambitious kings set out to assert their rule, but this process was not completed until the fifteenth century, and a common law was not even on the agenda. Ptolemy lived for some time in the France of Louis IX (r.1226–70), a monarch idealized in his own day and canonized in 1297, just before *On the Government of Rulers* was written. The nobility limited Louis's power more than the English king's, and it has been suggested that Thomas Aquinas based the mixed monarchy he defended in *Summa Theologiae* on Louis's government.[29] At the time that Ptolemy wrote, Philip IV the Fair (r.1285–1314) was king. He had more success in limiting feudal and ecclesiastical power than any previous French monarch, but France was also in the process of developing representative or restraining institutions, such as *parlements* (courts in France) and the Estates-General, which would much later topple the monarchy in the French Revolution. To gain support against Pope Boniface VIII, Philip called the first Estates-General in 1302.

Many other, smaller states also arose in this period and developed traditions of centralized, limited government, most notably Castile, one of several monarchies in the part of Spain not ruled by Muslims. The German Roman Empire was an anomaly, since of all European states only it and Italy failed to form a national state by the early modern period. At the time, this outcome would have seemed most unlikely, since the Empire was the strongest and most important state in Europe, with a long-established claim to rule all Christendom. What prevented its ultimate unification was the elective nature of the monarchy and the desire of various powers, both internal and external, to prevent any emperor from becoming too powerful. The German lords, particularly those especially prominent ones who would become the permanent electors, tended, unless there was a crisis requiring decisive action, to choose weak emperors who could not encroach on their authority. Ptolemy witnessed one of the major chapters in the medieval empire. The Hohenstaufen emperor, Frederick II (r.1215–50), used his strong position as king of Sicily to try to bring all of Germany and Italy under his sway. Frederick's ambitions dominated European politics for the first half of the thirteenth century, but ultimately he was unsuccessful, and for the rest of Ptolemy's life the Empire was in disarray, first from a power struggle, then under a series of weak emperors.

---

29. Marcel Demongeot, *Le Meilleur régime politique selon saint Thomas* (Paris: Ancienne Librairie Roger et Chernoviz, 1928), 205.

THE CRISIS OF CHURCH AND STATE

Popes and kings often cooperated in their attempts at centralization, but they were often at odds. The Investiture Controversy initiated a period of papal aggressiveness aimed at establishing the pope's supremacy over the Church and increasingly over the state. This language is somewhat anachronistic, since the prevailing view was that Christendom was one society, *within* which secular and clerical officials performed their duties. Many felt that as one body it should have only one head, in the words of the canonist Alanus, "or else it would be a monster."[30] In the early Middle Ages the emperor was most often seen as the natural head, but as papal prestige grew the admittedly more important spiritual function of the pope made hierocratic arguments the more credible, and the emperor and kings frequently retreated to a position of political dualism that maintained that each of the two spheres had duties and rights not subject to the interference of the other. The church came closest to realizing its ambitions in the reign of Pope Innocent III (1198–1216), but thereafter began to lose ground. During Ptolemy's life, papal pretensions were discredited through involvement in petty political maneuvers in the struggle against the Hohenstaufen and the use of officially sanctioned crusades for political purposes within Europe against orthodox Christians. Above all, the emergence of national states and a predominately secular attitude toward politics in the thirteenth century made a hierocratic papacy something of an anachronism. The papacy did not give up easily, and the pope at the time that Ptolemy wrote, Boniface VIII (1294–1303), made claims more extreme than any previous pope, stating in his bull *Unam Sanctam* (1302): "the temporal authority ought to be subject to the spiritual power. . . . Therefore, we declare, state, define, and pronounce that it is altogether necessary to salvation for every human creature to be subject to the Roman pontiff."[31]

Boniface issued this bull during a protracted struggle with Philip IV of France over the right to tax the church and try clergy for crimes. After Philip called the Estates-General in 1302, both the French nobles and commons wrote to the cardinals refusing to acknowledge Boniface as true pope and asking for their support. The French clergy did not feel they could reject the pope, but even they wrote to state their disapproval of his actions and ask to be excused from a council that Boniface had called. Ultimately, Boniface was humiliated when French agents kidnapped him for several days. He died soon afterward, and the next pope but one, Clement V (1305–14), the first of a

---

30. Alanus, Commentary on Gratian's *Decretum*, Distinctio 96.6, translated in Brian Tierney, *The Crisis of Church and State, 1050–1300* (Toronto: University of Toronto Press, 1988), 123.
31. Boniface VIII, *Unam Sanctam*, translated in Tierney, *Crisis of Church and State*, 189.

line of French popes, publicly and retroactively approved Philip's actions and policy, moved the papal seat to Avignon, and arguably submitted to French royal domination. This "Babylonian Captivity," which lasted until 1378, and the Great Schism that followed (1378–1415) permanently undermined papal hopes for universal authority. The breakaway Bohemian Hussite church in the fifteenth century and the Protestant Reformation of the sixteenth delivered the coup de grâce.

Conflicts Within the Church

Papal hierocracy had also to contend with the lower clergy. As political appointees, bishops often sided with their national government against the pope. Beyond this, they asserted their independent authority within the Church as the successors of the Apostles, to whom, they argued, Jesus gave the same powers as he did to Peter. They did not dispute the pope's position as head of the church, but they denied that this relegated the bishops to the place of mere underlings.

With the rise of the universities in the twelfth and thirteenth centuries, popes and bishops both also had to deal with another segment of recalcitrant clergy—the university masters (professors), who came to see themselves as arbiters of philosophical and theological belief. They also promoted a new conceptualization of society that made scholars one of three fundamental divisions: *regnum* (secular functions), *sacerdotum* (priestly functions), and *studium* (intellectual functions).

Fusion of Aristotelian philosophy with a new approach to learning, the dialectical or scholastic method, developed by Peter Abelard (1079–1142) and his followers and involving the active confrontation of apparently contradictory texts, became the hallmark of university "scholasticism." Early efforts to slow the pace of Aristotelian studies in the university, because of possible conflicts with Christian dogma, failed, and by 1255 the University of Paris made lectures on the complete Aristotelian corpus mandatory. Thomas Aquinas and others tried to show that there could be no contradiction between reason, epitomized by Greek philosophy, and the revelation of Christian theology. A few, such as Siger of Brabant (c.1240–84), argued that both must be true, but they could lead to contradictory results. Such ideas scared orthodox clergy, and in 1270 Etienne Tempier, the bishop of Paris, condemned 13 of Siger's propositions and in 1277, 219 more, including around 20 held by Thomas Aquinas. Thus, when Ptolemy was writing, Thomas's controversial grand synthesis was under assault, and intellectual assumptions were in a period of transition. Optimism waned that Greek and Christian thought were compatible and the divine knowable through reason, and this was accelerated by the economic, agricultural, social, political, religious, and demographic crises that characterized the fourteenth century, but in this same period, the power of the university in society and its ability to govern itself grew.

The thirteenth century was also a period of intense struggle between orthodoxy and dissent. The Albigensian Crusade called by Innocent III in 1208 against the Cathar heretics of southern France went on until 1244, and prosecutions continued throughout Ptolemy's life and beyond. A proliferation of heresies led to increased prosecutions. Gregory IX's decree *Ille humani generis* of 1231 marks the beginning of a formal papal inquisitorial process, and, perceiving an increased threat, the church began to give greater powers to prosecutors, for example, allowing them to use secret witnesses. Boniface VIII, in his contribution to the body of canon law, the *Sixth Book* of 1298, allowed inquisitors to get confessions through torture, keep charges secret, and question suspects without bringing charges. The fact that the assets of heretics could be seized led Philip IV of France with forced papal complicity to declare the Knights Templar heretics and witches in the years 1307–1312, and both he and Edward I of England expelled Jews in order to rob them. As with the crusades, inquisitions were sometimes instruments of political power.

Ptolemy was a member of the Dominican Order, noted for providing papal inquisitors. The constitution of this order was a model of limited monarchy, and this undoubtedly influenced both Thomas and Ptolemy. The Dominicans remained relatively untroubled by dissent in this period, unlike the other major mendicant order—the Franciscan—which was also a major rival of the Dominicans in the university, where the two orders came to play a decisive role in scholarship after a joint struggle with the secular masters of the University of Paris over the right of mendicants to hold professorial chairs.

The Franciscans were founded by Francis of Assisi (1182–1226) as an order of begging preachers with no personal or corporate property, but even before Francis's death, and much to his distress, the realities of administering and disciplining a large and growing group had made the strict enforcement of these principles impossible. The popes, who became major patrons of an order they felt could help them by keeping the poor within the church, undercutting the power of bishops, and supporting the papal position within the universities, devised legal fictions to allow mainstream Franciscans to believe they were remaining true to their ideal, but there were always those who fought for a return to their original condition. From the 1250s these Spiritual Franciscans adapted the millennial views of Joachim of Fiore (c.1145–c.1202) to their own doctrine of apostolic poverty, and the mixture proved to be explosive. Lay followers of Peter John Olivi (1248–98) rose in open rebellion to the Church in Provence, and throughout the last half of the thirteenth and beginning of the fourteenth centuries the order was in schism, despite efforts of the approved (Conventual) Franciscans and the papacy to suppress the Spirituals. The sanctioning of Spiritual ideals by Pope Celestine V (1294), a pious but aged and inept hermit who resigned after five months, during which he established an order of Poor Celestines for the disaffected Spirituals, only exacerbated the conflict, until Pope John XXII (1316–34) felt that it was necessary to condemn the very idea of apostolic poverty as heretical; he proceeded to crush the Spirituals and the Conventual leadership, which could not accept this. The resignation of Celestine also weakened his successor Boniface VIII in the struggle to defend the Church's power described above, since both the king of France and the Spiritual Franciscans refused to accept the resignation, and consequently Boniface's election, as valid.

THE ROLE OF THE CLASSICS, ARISTOTLE, CANON LAW, AND ROMAN LAW

Although many classical sources that are well known today, such as most of Plato and Cicero's *On the Republic*, were not available in thirteenth-century Europe, the classical revivals from the "Carolingian Renaissance" on had provided far more of them than had once been realized. The twelfth-century humanist movement in particular promoted the writings of Latin and Greek antiquity, and Ptolemy and the other author were able to use many of them, as can be seen in the list of sources provided at the end of the section "Sources," later in this introduction. Beginning in the eleventh century, there was a steady flow of Latin translations of the works of classical antiquity into western Europe. Usually made in cooperation with Muslim or Jewish scholars in Spain or other border areas of the Christian and Muslim worlds from Arabic translations of the Greek, these often came with Muslim or Jewish commentaries attached.

Most influential was Aristotle. The earlier Middle Ages had known only some of his minor logical works, but by the late thirteenth century the complete corpus was available. Despite the problems of reconciling Aristotelian thought with Christianity (or Islam or Judaism for that matter), the comprehensive, logically coherent schema it offered for analyzing and understanding the world made it compelling to medieval scholars. Obviously, the most important of these texts for political thought was the *Politics*, whose influence led Walter Ullmann and others to speak of an Aristotelian revolution representing the watershed between medieval and modern politics.[32] This view has been discredited in recent years by showing that medieval writers adapted Aristotle to medieval political thought, that feudal concepts and ones from canon and Roman law were equally influential, and that other classical writers such as Cicero exercised a profound effect, but Aristotle was very important and provided the basis for much scholastic political speculation.

Since the *Politics* did not exist in an Arabic translation, it did not become available until the Fourth Crusade of 1204 gave western Europe access to the original Greek, and it was only in 1260 that William of Moerbeke, a Flemish cleric and friend of Thomas Aquinas, translated it in its entirety.[33] The translation was made more difficult by the lack of a Muslim or Jewish commentary and the alienness of the subject, and many words common today are simply transliterations of the Greek William chose when there were no Latin equivalents—words (in English) such as "politics," "aristocracy," "monarchy," and "democracy." On the one hand this made the text more difficult to understand, but on the other it made it easier to adapt Aristotle to medieval thought. The *Politics* never attracted as many commentators as Aristotle's logical and philosophical works, and most of these at first were from an interconnected group of scholars including Thomas, Peter of Auvergne (1240s–1304), Albert the Great (c.1193–1280), John of Paris (c.1250–1304), Giles of Rome (c.1243–1316), and Ptolemy, all of whom studied at the University of Paris. In the fourteenth century interest spread farther—most notably to England, Germany, and Italy, but there was still quite often some connection to the University of Paris or to Thomas Aquinas.

Many of Aristotle's ideas became important, but none more so than the very notion of political science. Earlier medieval writers such as John of Salisbury (c.1115–1180) had written on politics, and John explained why kingship accorded with nature and the divine. He is especially noted for his organic view of society, which influenced Ptolemy, Marsilius of Padua, and others, and which made analogies between organs of the human body and society. John and others, particularly other English writers, also stressed the importance of law and that the ruler was under law. Nevertheless, no medieval writer before 1260 wrote a systematic work of political science analyzing a variety of governments; almost all were concerned primarily with expounding the virtues and duties of a good ruler. This purpose generated the "mirror-of-

32. See, for example, Walter Ullmann, *A History of Political Thought: The Middle Ages* (Baltimore: Penguin Books, 1965), 159.

33. Aristotle, *Politicorum Libri Octo cum vetusta translatione Guilelmi de Moerbeke*, ed. Franciscus Susemihl (Leipzig, 1872).

princes" genre, which began in antiquity and continued beyond the rediscovery of the *Politics*; Machiavelli's *The Prince* (c.1513) is, in effect, an anti-mirror
of princes. Aristotle introduced the Middle Ages to the notion that politics
could be analyzed objectively, broken down into the various kinds of governments and purposes for which governments were instituted, using historical
examples to demonstrate how each worked and how each could fail. He raised
the question of what form of government was best absolutely, best in practice, best for most people, or best in certain circumstances or for certain types
of people. He distinguished simple types of government and discussed each
of these separately and in mixtures. He developed the idea that humans were
naturally political animals drawn to live in states and participate in government in a form quite distinct from Cicero's idea that this instinct did not lead
to government until humans were persuaded to abandon the state of nature,
where they lived as beasts. He investigated the nature of law and questioned
whether the best government was that of the best person or the best laws.
While we must not underestimate the influence of Cicero, since he continued
to provide the basis for the understanding of the origins of society for writers
such as John of Paris and Marsilius of Padua,[34] who were also influenced by
Aristotle, the ideas I have mentioned here entered medieval political discourse
in this form through the *Politics*, and many writers took them up in the late
thirteenth century and beyond.

Perhaps as important to medieval political thought was the influence of
canon and Roman law. Both were given new life in twelfth-century Bologna,
and both, particularly canon law, which dealt with both political and ecclesiological issues, went on to have a profound effect on emerging political ideas
and institutions. In both fields, the new scholastic or dialectical method, used
in almost all scholarly activities until the Renaissance, ensured that the study
of law would not simply be a codification of statutes but an active analysis of
principles, ambiguities, and contradictions. There was also an interpenetra-
tion of secular and ecclesiological ideas; although influence went both ways,
most commonly ideas developed to solve problems of church government
would eventually find their way into debates about secular government.[35] This
went on well into the modern period, but during and after the Reformation
and Renaissance, Protestant and humanist theorists were loath to reveal their
Catholic or nonclassical inspiration, which led an earlier generation of historians of political thought seriously to underplay the medieval contribution.

34. For this subject, see Cary Nederman, "Nature, Sin, and the Origins of Society: The
Ciceronian Tradition in Medieval Political Thought," *Journal of the History of Ideas* 49 (1988):
3–26.

35. See Brian Tierney, *Religion, Law, and the Growth of Constitutional Thought* (Cambridge:
Cambridge University Press, 1982).

There had been many collections of church laws during the early Middle Ages, but around 1140 the monk Gratian founded the new science of canon law in his *Concordance of Discordant Canons* (usually referred to as the *Decretum*). This became the standard text for the study of canon law, and also, with several additions over the next 200 years, the authoritative codification of canon law until the twentieth century.[36] Gratian's title indicates his approach: on any issue he collected all the church laws he could find, including decisions of popes, bishops, and councils, together with appropriate opinions of popes and Church Fathers. He then would try to make sense of the usually inconsistent statements. If possible he would show an underlying unity, if not he would decide what most probably was correct; at times this would remain open. Over the centuries numerous decretists (commentators on the *Decretum*) continued to rehash these issues, in the process bringing in new material and arguments. The dialectical method of the *Decretum* ensured that canon law would not become ossified, but remain at the center of ecclesiological, and eventually political, debates. Among the issues debated that would have an effect on secular political thought are the nature of law, the source and meaning of power and jurisdiction, the idea of consent, the election of officials, limitation of papal power, and the constitution of the Church (including ideas of mixed government). After 1260, in all of these areas there was also cross-fertilization from Aristotelian political thought.

The century after Gratian was one of the most fruitful for the study of canon law. Its influence was also immense, since there was an almost unbroken string of lawyer popes who sought to increase the power and prestige of the papacy, in part by expanding and standardizing the application of canon law. So much new law was promulgated in this period and in the succeeding ninety years that coincided with Ptolemy's life that four new and final additions were added to what came to be called the *Body of Canon Law*: a collection of papal letters (decretals), the *Decretals* (or *Extra Book*) in 1234; a further updating by Boniface VIII, which included several hundred of his own decretals, the *Sixth Book*, in 1298; the Decrees of the Council of Vienne in 1311; and the Decrees of Pope John XXII (1316–34).[37] In Ptolemy's time decretists were joined by decretalists, who analyzed the *Decretals*. Although there are almost no direct citations of canon law in *On the Government of Rulers*, Ptolemy was

---

36. There is an English translation of the first part of the *Decretum* together with its "Ordinary Gloss" (the standard medieval gloss by Joannes Teutonicus and some others in the thirteenth century): Gratian, *The Treatise on Laws (Decretum DD. 1–20)*, trans. Augustine Thompson (Washington, D.C.: Catholic University Press, 1993).

37. The most commonly used text of *The Body of Canon Law* is Emil Friedberg, ed., *Corpus Iuris Canonici*, 2 vols. (Leipzig: Tauchnitz, 1879; reprinted Graz: Akademische Druck- und Verlagsanstalt, 1959).

quite conversant with it, as shown by his extensive citations of it in *A Short Determination of the Jurisdiction of the Roman Empire*.

While less influential on Ptolemy or the other contributor than canon law, Roman (civil) law was a prominent part of the political thought of the time, and the authors cite it several times, often without acknowledgment.[38] Irnerius (c.1050–c.1130) initiated the renewed study of Roman law around 1100. The *Body of Civil Law* consisted of four books issued by the emperor Justinian in the years 529–533: the *Codex*, a code of laws, the *Digest* (*Pandects*), a collection of jurists' opinions, the *Institutes*, a law handbook for students, and the *Novels*, a collection of new laws of Justinian. Medieval civil law thus differed from canon law, but both kinds of legal experts used similar techniques and assumptions in their work, particularly in trying to resolve contradictions and adapt earlier rulings to modern situations. Both also largely worked by glossing their texts. Legists were also similar to Aristotelian scholars, in that both studied and interpreted already-existing classical works. In Ptolemy's time, modified Roman law was in the process of becoming the standard civil law of most states and remains so today. Even England, which developed its own common law, was significantly influenced by Roman law principles.

VI. Ptolemy of Lucca's Political Thought

All these influences helped to shape Ptolemy's thought, but four factors were of greatest significance: Aristotelian political theory, Italian republicanism, Augustinian theology, and papal hierocratic theory. Some of these exerted contradictory influences on him, which led him to a not-always-successful intellectual struggle for a consistent theory. In some ways it is this struggle that is the most fascinating aspect of Ptolemy's thought. I will begin with his classification of political authority using distinctions derived from Aristotle, to which he sometimes gave an original interpretation.

KINDS OF GOVERNMENT

In any analytic political theory one of the first tasks is to classify the different kinds of government, and Aristotle approached this in several distinct ways, of which I mention only two. Most often he used a variation of the sixfold schema, found previously in Herodotus and Plato, which I have already men-

38. 2.3.6, 4.1.3, 4.3.8, 4.25.3.

tioned, based on whether the ruling group is one, few, or many and if it rules
for the common good or for its own private good.[39] Sometimes Aristotle distinguishes between these forms of rule and what I have called modes of rule,
which refer to the way the ruling group exercises power. In the first chapter
of the *Politics*, Aristotle lists political, regal, household, and despotic rule.[40]
Although he never precisely defines them, he usually associates political rule
with alternation of office among a free and equal people, regal rule with the
absolute rule of one person over a free but unequal people, and despotic rule
as absolute rule over natural slaves. Political and regal rule exist to benefit the
subjects, despotic rule does so incidentally but exists primarily for the benefit
of the master. Household rule, a general name for rule within a family, is not
really a mode at all. In fact, particular family relationships exemplify the other
modes of rule: the rule of master over slave is despotic, the rule of husband
over wife is political, and the rule of father over child is regal.[41]

Ptolemy uses both these schemata, but emphasizes the modal one. He
never formally itemizes Aristotle's six forms, although he uses the terms and
refers to the first author's classification of them.[42] He seems to find a distinction of modes to be more basic, and, as we shall see, he had a conceptual problem in distinguishing monarchy, tyranny, and despotism. Ptolemy derived his
modes from Aristotle, but they are somewhat different: he identifies what he
calls four kinds of lordship: sacerdotal and regal, regal alone, political, and
household.[43] Aristotle warned that his modes should not be taken to apply
simply to communities of different sizes, but Ptolemy ignores this warning
and develops a hierarchy: sacerdotal and regal rule for the world, regal rule (in
general) for the kingdom or province, political rule for the city, and household rule for the home.[44] As an exception, Ptolemy often supports political
rule for a large polity. Above all is the divine and universal lordship of God.

Ptolemy quickly treats sacerdotal and regal rule, his name for the universal authority of the pope in both religious and secular matters, and then
ignores it.[45] And only in his concluding paragraph does he mention household rule again, and then only to say that he will write a separate work on
the subject, something he apparently never did.[46] Here he is interested in the

---

39. Aristotle, *Politics*, 3.7.1279a. There is a similar schema in the *Ethics*, VIII.10.1160a–b,
where polity is also called "timocracy."
40. Aristotle, *Politics*, 1.1.1252a.
41. Aristotle, *Politics*, 1.3, 5, 6, 7, 12, 3.4.1277b, 3.6.1278b. See also James Blythe, "Family,
Government, and the Medieval Aristotelians," *History of Political Thought* 10 (1989): 1–16.
42. 2.8.1, 4.1.1, referring to 1.2.2–3.
43. 3.10.1.
44. 4.2.1, 3.10.
45. 3.10.2–3.11.
46. 4.28.10.

organization of actual political communities, which directly concerns only the regal and political modes, even though he has no doubts that the pope properly exercises the highest human lordship.

What is missing in Ptolemy's modal classification is Aristotle's despotic rule, and this omission is the key to understanding his concept of government. For Ptolemy, despotic rule is indistinguishable from regal rule, and consequently kingship can never be an acceptable option for a free people. He writes that although Aristotle sometimes uses a more complex classification of government, at other time he simply uses the two categories of political and despotic.[47] Elsewhere he writes that regal is included in the term "despotic," and that the Bible shows that despotic rule can be "reduced" to regal rule.[48] To understand this, we must clarify the meaning of these terms. Despotic rule is the rule of master over servant, which makes it similar to regal government, in which a king rules by laws that he himself determines, and unlike political government, in which the ruler or rulers govern according to laws that the citizens themselves impose. These are the essential characteristics, but Ptolemy does not bind himself narrowly to them; rather he associates a complex of characteristics with each. Political rule includes citizen-made law, but also plurality of rulers, alternation of rulers, election, judgment of past rulers, mild rule, and salaries for the rulers. Regal rule is based on the ruler's will, but also includes the rule of one, permanence of ruler, inheritance of rule, immunity of the ruler, harsh rule, and no salary for the ruler.[49] Not every regime shares all the criteria, so that it can vary more or less from the model regime. Ptolemy thinks that the characteristics associated with each mode go together naturally and will normally be found together, but he is quite willing to recognize exceptions. For example, imperial rule has some characteristics of each: since office is elective and open to all, it is political; since emperors have jurisdiction like that of kings, are crowned, make law, and have arbitrary power over their subjects, it is regal.[50] More simply, since the power of the emperor depends on the many, rule is political, but since he rules by will, it is regal.

A strict definition would be more comprehensive and less ambiguous, but it would also be less empirical, forcing existing governments into an a priori framework. Ptolemy is more flexible and shows greater concern for the actual historical development. In effect, he has largely replaced the various schemata of the Aristotelian theorists with a twofold classification in which all forms dependent on multiplicity—the rule of one who depends on others,

47. 2.8.1
48. 4.8.4, 2.9.1.
49. See, e.g., 2.8, 4.1, 4.7.
50. 3.20.1, 4–8. See also *A Short Determination*, c. 30, 61.

aristocracy, polity, oligarchy, and democracy—represent political rule, and all forms dependent on one alone—monarchy, despotism, and tyranny—represent regal rule.

Ptolemy repeats Aristotle's distinction between regal and despotic, but since his key to classifying government is whether or not it is by the will of the ruler or the power of the many he found it difficult conceptually to separate two forms that depend on will. Sometimes he unconsciously interchanges the two. For example, he writes that Aristotle distinguished two kinds of rule, political and despotic, and then goes on: "Political rule exists when a region, province, city, or town is governed by one or many according to its own statutes . . . in *regal* lordship . . . the rulers, not being obligated by the laws, may judge by what is in their hearts."[51] Later I will show how Ptolemy tries to resolve this conflict by saying that the coming of sin into the world resulted in regal government becoming oppressive. But this leads to even more problems.

The conclusion that political rule is the only good form for human beings seems inevitable. Indeed, Ptolemy shows no enthusiasm for any other kind of government, and he is often treated, if at all, as an unabashed republican.[52] It is reasonable to suppose that Ptolemy's experience in republican Italy combined with his fear for its continued existence in troubled times, made him fervent to preserve popular political rights and especially hostile to one-person rule.

Yet things are not so simple, and this picture depends on selective quotation. In the case of papal power in church and state, Ptolemy is a dedicated monarchist. A closer look at his writings shows that the situation is more complex with regard to secular rule as well. Although he is enthusiastic about republican government, he often says that monarchy is necessary for most peoples and occasionally enumerates the abstract benefits of monarchy. He often starts a passage with a withering attack on kingship, but ends up by restricting the suitability of political rule to a few regions or peoples.

I do not think that Ptolemy's contradictory statements can be resolved, since they reflect insoluble internal conflicts, especially between the Aristotelian and republican influences of his education and upbringing, which portray good government as the implementation of natural instincts to promote the common good, and the Augustinian and biblical arguments for the corrupt nature of humanity, which makes all government a form of oppressive servitude, necessary to restrain sin. Ptolemy never admits a conflict between

51. 2.8.1, 2.8.6. The italics are mine, and the ellipses separate rather distant passages, but I believe the point is valid.

52. See, for example, Charles Till Davis, "Roman Patriotism and Republican Propaganda: Ptolemy of Lucca and Pope Nicholas III," *Speculum* 50 (1975): 413.

Augustine and Aristotle, but I read his work as a valiant but unsuccessful attempt to resolve the contradictory paradigms.[53] Ptolemy's writings contain all the elements for a radical critique of monarchy, both secular and papal, but Ptolemy himself never takes this step, which later, more radical thinkers do.

Ptolemy's dilemma is epitomized by two biblical passages presenting dramatically divergent views of kingship. Moses prescribed the form that Israelite kingship would take: the king will neither enrich himself nor oppress his people, and he will carefully study and obey God's law. But according to Samuel the future king will impress the people to his service and seize land and money for his own use, until the people cry out for relief. Ptolemy never doubts that both these passages concern the true nature of kingship, so he could not accept Thomas Aquinas's interpretation that Samuel's king is not a true king and that Samuel only predicts, but does not recommend, the future tyrant. Both sections of the Bible ostensibly describe "regal laws," and the kings foretold were established and anointed by God in the person of His prophet.[54] So how can we explain the difference? Ptolemy's answer follows a circular path that recurs often in his writing. He begins confidently with an Aristotelian distinction between regal and despotic rule, with the latter sometimes being necessary, but then Augustinian ideas bring him back to the conclusion that the two cannot be separated.

In Deuteronomy, Ptolemy says, God established a king for the common benefit, the proper function of any legitimate ruler. In contrast, the king of 1 Kings is concerned only with his own well-being, making him a tyrant and despot. God approved this despotism because the Jews were ungrateful for what they had and failed to understand the benefits of good government. In such a case tyranny becomes expedient for divine justice and harsh rule necessary.[55] Ptolemy claims that both Aristotle and Augustine agree. This is a half-truth, since the two did not mean the same thing when they justified oppressive rule. Aristotle supported some despots because he believed that natural slaves were incapable of self-government, but that, unlike tyranny, despotism benefits the governed. For Augustine all rule is from God, who often supports a tyrannical rule for the forcible repression of a naturally sinful humanity. Since all government is a form of servitude, there is really no theoretical difference among the different forms that would make one preferable to the others.

53. For another view, see R. A. Markus, "Two Conceptions of Political Authority: Augustine's *De Civitate Dei*, XIX, 14–15, and Some Thirteenth Century Interpretations," *Journal of Theological Studies* n.s., 16 (1965): 96–97.

54. 2.9.2, 3.11.1; Deuteronomy 17.14–20; 1 Kings 8.11–18; Thomas Aquinas, *Summa Theologiae*, 1.2.105.1.ad 5.

55. 3.11.1, 9.

In either case it is the people's nature that legitimizes despotism. Is this nature characteristic of only some people, as Aristotle believed, or is it basic to all humanity, as Augustine taught? Ptolemy tries to have it both ways, using two incompatible notions of sin: the original sin of Adam and Eve and the particular sins of certain peoples. He writes that despotic government is reduced to regal by original sin, but almost immediately adds that in certain "ill-tempered regions despotic rule is necessary for kings."[56] The first statement implies that although regal and despotic rule have different natures in themselves, in post-lapsarian times the kings rule despotically. This is what is meant by the one form being "reduced" to the other. The second qualifies this conclusion and suggests that some peoples may be sufficiently virtuous to escape servitude. Ptolemy uses actual examples of nondespotic government in the Bible, in Aristotle, and in later history as illustrations. This contradicts standard Christian-Augustinian thought, and Ptolemy's flawed resolution of this problem is one of his most original contributions. Ultimately he replaces original sin with local and contingent sin, and in so doing implicitly rejects the Augustinian theory of government by misrepresenting it.

One obstacle in making Augustine an Aristotelian is the nature of society in the Garden of Eden. If humans are naturally political animals, as Aristotle wrote, government must have existed there; if government came about only as a result of sin, as Augustine thought, it should not. This brings up another problem. If it is sin that makes regal government despotic, where is the place for nondespotic regal government in the Augustinian schema? Only in the realm of platonic ideas, since there was no government before sin.

Ptolemy tries to have it both ways. He begins by arguing that Aristotle, the Bible, and Augustine all agree that the first humans naturally possessed lordship over the lower species and that the rule of human over human existed in Eden in a noncoercive sense of deliberating about and directing human activity. He justifies this with Aristotle's view of humans as social and political animals and Aquinas's principle that any society must be ordered and have something directing it. Such an order implies inequality and lordship, even if in paradise there is no natural superiority. Thus, he concludes, "the lordship of human over human is natural, lordship exists even among the Angels, it existed in the First State, and it exists even now."[57]

There is not even a place for ideal regal government in Eden, since

political government is placed ahead of royal government for two reasons. First, if we refer lordship to the integral state of human nature, called the State of Innocence, in

56. 3.11.9, 4.8.4.
57. 3.9.7.

which there was political, not regal lordship, there was no lordship then that involved servitude, but rather preeminence and subjection existed according to the merits of each for disposing and governing the multitude, so that whether in influencing or receiving influence each was disposed proportionately according to its own nature.[58]

Despite his disclaimer that it is sin which converts regal rule to despotic, it is clear that Ptolemy thinks of regal rule as invariably implying servitude—it is in the nature of the rule itself, not in the character of either the ruler or the ruled.

A common medieval argument for kings was that, as universal statements, laws cannot fit all particulars. A regal king, restricted only by reason, can best handle changing circumstances. Ptolemy makes this point as well,[59] but before the Fall this problem did not exist. In its natural state everything acts according to natural law, and therefore the law cannot fail in particulars. This is what Ptolemy means when he writes that "each was disposed proportionately according to its own nature." So not only would a regal ruler have imposed servitude in Paradise, there would not have been compensatory benefits.

How was government changed by sin? Ptolemy agrees with Augustine that sin is the cause of servitude, but not to the extent of saying that political authority is by its nature servitude. If sin made servitude necessary, how can any group of sinful human beings escape it? If not, how does the Fall affect human government? Ptolemy may not give satisfactory answers, but he unambiguously asserts that fallen humans may aspire to the virtue necessary for a paradisiacal type of government free from servitude and that this government would be political, since regal rule necessarily involves servitude.

Ptolemy cites at least one people that has already achieved these aspirations—the pagan Romans! To do this he must twist the views of Augustine, Aristotle, and the Bible to base an Aristotelian polity comparable to that of the Garden of Eden on secular virtue alone. "Therefore," he writes, "political government was better for wise and virtuous persons, such as the ancient Romans, since it imitated this state of nature."[60] Original sin has become a sin like any other that people of sufficiently good character can overcome through secular virtue. Ptolemy attempts to equate true virtue, which for Augustine can be nothing less than harmony with God, with the political virtue of people living in the best community. For Augustine the perfect City of God was a mystical community of the saved that existed unchanged in eternity, never institutionalized on earth or by human agency. But Ptolemy's polity,

58. 2.9.4
59. 2.9.4.
60. 2.9.4.

when properly constructed, can be like the City of God in its harmony, virtue, felicity, and permanence. Though the product of time-bound and imperfect humans, this polity cannot decay because of its internal harmony, there being no contradictions to cause its collapse.[61]

What of Samuel's king? All Ptolemy's reasoning has led him to conclude that this despotic rule is the natural form for kingship, irrespective of original sin. So he must accept Samuel's king as a legitimate king, and his "regal laws" as God's will for controlling an unvirtuous people unsuited for good rule, that is, political rule. But this only creates a new problem—there now is no place in the real *or* platonic world for the beneficent king of Aristotle and Deuteronomy. If a people is virtuous, it deserves and is best served by a political government. If it lacks virtue it can only be restrained by the rigors of regal rule, but because of that people's sinful nature, regal rule is inevitably despotic. That this is so is confirmed by Ptolemy's discussion of the political rule of the judges among the Jews: "Samuel," he writes, ". . . said to them when he wanted to show that his government had been political and not regal . . . 'Speak of me in the presence of the Lord and his Christ and say whether I have taken anyone's cow or ass, whether I have slandered anyone, whether I have oppressed anyone, whether I have accepted a gift from anyone's hands,'" which, Ptolemy adds, "those who have royal lordship do."[62]

Ptolemy is not simply using the term "regal" loosely, sometimes in the technical sense of one ruling without any laws, which he condemns, sometimes as a synonym for king, who could be good. This is proved by his failure to attach the "regal laws" of Deuteronomy to any actual or hypothetical kings. He does not, for example, follow Aquinas and identify Moses as a king.[63] And when he encounters in Aristotle an official called "king" in a polity of which he approves, he interprets his rule as aristocratic, that is, political, and not monarchical.[64] None of his distinctions can save Ptolemy from his underlying belief that regal and despotic rule are essentially the same. He cannot accommodate the virtuous king working for the common good either to the Augustinian insistence on corrupt humanity or to his own belief that at least some peoples can overcome their corruption. This, finally, is why he says that regal and despotic governments can be reduced to each other.

Had he been willing to follow up on this thought, Ptolemy could have insisted that since all kingship is despotic, every people should work for its overthrow and the establishment of a political government under the con-

---

61. 4.23.4.
62. 2.8.72; 1 Kings 12.3.
63. Thomas Aquinas, *Summa Theologiae*, 1.2.105.1.
64. 4.19.4.

trol of the whole people. This would have made him the earliest of the radical Aristotelian proponents of republicanism. What is more, the same arguments could just as easily apply to the papacy. Medieval writers often wrote analogously of church and state government, and certainly we would expect Ptolemy to think that if any people were virtuous, or at least could aspire to virtue, it would be the Christian people. This last possibility does not even occur to him, since it is obvious to him that the papacy was established by God himself on the model of his own rule in the universe. God as king is another factor that makes it difficult for him to reject kingship absolutely, since it is a commonplace that art imitates nature and also that the earthly should imitate the heavenly. And the fact is that, as a practical matter, he does little to discourage monarchy in the secular world either. True, after much equivocation, Ptolemy in theory discounts the role of original sin in the transformation of regal into despotic government. Original sin becomes a necessary but not sufficient condition for servitude and coercion. But, in practice, this seemingly liberating revision of Augustinian doctrine renders political rule by a virtuous people the exception to the rule, something we can expect only rarely. Original sin predisposes people to sin and to despotic rule—which they can transcend only through virtue. The Fall, far from changing the nature of regal rule, created the rationale for its existence and its justification for most peoples. As Ptolemy writes: "But because 'the perverse are corrected with difficulty and the number of fools is infinite,' as is said in Ecclesiastes, in corrupt nature regal government is more fruitful, because it is necessary for human nature to be disposed in such a way to, as it were, restrain its flux within limits. . . . In this respect regal lordship excels."[65]

Not every people can even aspire to virtue. There are many uncontrollable contingencies that make despotic rule more appropriate. Among these are the nature and character of the people, which Ptolemy ascribes largely to astrological factors, climate, and environment. For example, only the people in temperate regions, such as Italy and Athens, can have the temperament for political rule. Even some temperate regions, such as Greek islands and Sicily, have always had tyrants because of the nature of their peoples.[66] When it comes to his native Italy, or cities anywhere, Ptolemy is a champion of republicanism. But in most places for most peoples and for large kingdoms, he favors regal rule. This is not an afterthought justifying the status quo, it is basic to his theory of sin. Only the exceptional community blessed with a favorable climate, a fortunate configuration of stars, and great virtue can profit from political rule. Others need the rigor that only regal rule can provide.

65. 2.9.5; Ecclesiastes 1.15.
66. 3.11.9, 3.22.6, 2.8.4.

Ptolemy goes beyond Aquinas in two significant areas, but not ones that support the theory that Ptolemy is radically anti-king: his development of a natural basis for political rule and his rejection of regal rule in the Aristotelian sense of the good rule of one over a free people. Ptolemy's recognition of the inseparability of servitude from regal rule has been mistaken for a rejection of nonpolitical rule and a more consistent Aristotelianism than that of Aquinas,[67] whereas Ptolemy actually believes that servitude is best for most people. His ideas can be used to express radical republican values more easily than Thomas's, but in themselves they are neither more Aristotelian nor more republican. It is their revolutionary potential that makes Ptolemy the most interesting political theorist of his time. For those not bound by Ptolemy's uneasy synthesis of Aristotle and Augustine, there would be no reason to tolerate an inherently despotic king or even a pope. Ptolemy's answer, that most people are incapable of self-rule, would not impress all who were drawn to the hostility toward monarchy that he was the first to show.

Historical Governments

Aristotle examined many contemporary and historical governments in Greece and nearby lands in order to derive the principles of government, to understand how institutions worked in practice, and to collect data for deciding what kinds of governments are best. Since scholasticism generally proceeded by deduction from a priori principles, such close analysis of real-world entities was not as common. The few examples generally came either from the same ancient polities cited by Aristotle, from the Bible, or from ancient Rome. The contemporary political situation often was the inspiration for political writing, but direct discussion of it was less common. Ptolemy is an exception in that he did refer to specific medieval conditions, but since he also spent much more time on the other kind of examples, I will begin with them.

Ancient Greek Government

Much of Book 4, which Ptolemy dedicates to political government, is given over to a close look at several ancient Greek governments. Three real and three ideal republics, all but one of which Aristotle analyzed, come in for especially close scrutiny. In this, Ptolemy is interested not merely in what we would call the constitutional arrangements in these polities, but also in their social assumptions and ways of life.

---

67. For example, Davis, "Ptolemy of Lucca," 47, 50; "Roman Patriotism," 416, 423.

Of the ideal republics, the one Plato described in his dialogue *The Republic*, is best known to modern readers. Like most of Plato's writings, it uses Socrates as an interlocutor, in this case to defend an aristocracy of "guardians" or "philosopher-kings." The *Republic* was not available in the Middle Ages; Ptolemy derived information about what he calls "the polity of Socrates and Plato" largely from Aristotle. Ptolemy is critical of Aristotle's version and accuses him of misrepresenting Plato and Socrates by attributing to them a view that he says would be impossible for men so devoted to virtue: that women and children should be held in common. Ptolemy argues that all they really advocate is the Christian principle of loving one's neighbors and sharing with them, and points out that others had reproached Aristotle for not always fairly reporting others' positions.[68]

Aristotle also said that Plato advocated a community of possessions. This proposition is not subject to a similar moral objection, especially since it could be said that Jesus' Apostles held their goods in common, but both medieval practice and the explosive situation in the Franciscan Order, called for rejecting it. Ptolemy's answer follows the common explanation of the time that communalism was suited only for the spiritually perfect, among whom, Ptolemy adds, are included the Socratics and Platonists. The rest of us need property to avoid quarrels.[69]

Ptolemy's most original discussion of the platonic republic concerns women warriors. Aristotle's brief reference to this is ambiguous and the translation makes it more so. Plato wanted women to share in all education insofar as they are capable, and he stressed warfare and athletics. What could Ptolemy make of such an idea? Would the idea of women soldiers not seem preposterous in a society dominated by male knights? In some ways this was less unthinkable for medieval people than for those raised in America until recently, where nearly all responsible positions outside the home and traditionally female occupations were occupied by men. In the Middle Ages, although men were favored, in the absence of a suitable male heir a woman could become the lord of a fief and enjoy all the rights and power of that position. Male vassals of female lords might try to take advantage of their lord's sex, but they rarely displayed the extreme reluctance of many modern males to have a female superior. And since the essence of the lord-vassal relationship was military service, a female lord would be expected to provide a complement of knights to her lord and to direct her own knights and those of her vassals, even if she herself rarely took part in the actual fighting. Some women did fight, and many others commanded troops in battle.

68. 4.4.6.
69. 4.5.10–11.

The two chapters that Ptolemy devotes to this question is one of the few places where he follows strict scholastic form, with arguments for the thesis that women should be instructed in war followed by arguments against and answers to the arguments for. He supports it with three kinds of evidence: analogy with the natural world, the physical nature of women, and historical practice. However, he finds contrary arguments to be decisive, and these, remarkably, resemble objections we still hear too often today about the place of women in the home and family, their physical weakness, and the demoralizing and divisive effects they would have on men.[70]

As for governmental structure, Ptolemy notes that Plato and Socrates wanted all officials to have lifetime tenure, and uses this as an occasion for a general discussion of whether it is better to have changing or permanent magistrates. His conclusion is that so long as the people is virtuous and rulers rule according to law, it is much better periodically to change the rulers. It is only in the regal form that permanent rulers are best. Ptolemy criticizes Plato both for advocating what would be a repressive government and for confusing forms in instituting permanent rulers in a republic.[71]

One reason I have spent so much time on this one example is to show how many of Ptolemy's most interesting ideas come up almost as asides in attempts to deal with specific points. In the course of reacting to one proposal for a government, he has taken a position on property and apostolic poverty, discussed the nature of women, and analyzed the nature of political office. He takes up other issues in considering the ideal polities of Hippodamus and Pythagoras,[72] the second of which is not found in Aristotle, but I will turn now to the real three ancient Greek governments that Ptolemy discusses at length—Sparta, Crete, and Chalcedonia. "Chalcedonia" corresponds to Aristotle's "Carthage," but Ptolemy and most other medieval writers were misled by William of Moerbeke's mistranslation.

These three states were frequently cited examples of mixed constitutions incorporating aspects of monarchy, aristocracy, and democracy. Aristotle criticized aspects of each of them, but it could be argued that he favored mixed constitutions in general.[73] Ptolemy comments that "the three polities of the Spartans, Cretans, and Chalcedonians were the most famous among the

---

70. 4.5–4.6. I am currently completing an article on this topic, and on other medieval authors who discussed it, entitled "Women in the Military: A Medieval Debate." This is based on a paper I presented at the 30th International Congress on Medieval Studies, Kalamazoo, Michigan, 1995.

71. 4.7–4.8.

72. 4.11–13, 4.21–22.

73. See Blythe, *Ideal Government*, 18–24.

Greeks, because, more than others, they were ordained according to virtue,"[74] but he criticizes the first two for their social problems and political institutions. But he almost always praises the Chalcedonian government, and his reasons reveal a lot about his ideal state.[75] It chose a council of 104, the Gerousia, from among the better people to elect and advise the king. If a worthy person was poor, they allocated a salary to remove the temptation of bribery, but they also gave the rich a role by picking five wealthy men for the important council of Pentacontarchs. They did not always select the king from the same family, and any important action that king and Gerousia took required the consent of the whole people. Whereas Aristotle believed that Carthage was basically oligarchical, Ptolemy commends Chalcedonia for having aristocratic, oligarchic, and democratic aspects. What both ignore is the monarchical aspect, and in fact Ptolemy regards the joint action of king and Gerousia as aristocracy, and by implication the king as merely an executive officer comparable to the consuls of Rome. His reasons for this are not obvious. Part of his criticism of Sparta was that the kings were not elected for a life term, and he does not explain why he calls the Spartan magistrates true kings and not the Chalcedonian ones. In his analysis of Rome Ptolemy suggests an explanation: the consuls (and by analogy the Chalcedonian kings) were not regal but political because they were elected, their power, however great, depended on the many, and they were not always nobles.[76] Thomas Aquinas would have characterized this situation as political kingship, but Ptolemy has no room for such an entity and must therefore consider the kings not to be monarchs at all. Ptolemy explicitly compares the Chalcedonian government with the Roman Republic, although not directly on this point. But he compares the relationship of king and people to that of consuls and Senate.[77]

Rome

The Roman Republic is the only polity for which Ptolemy has unbounded admiration, and so his evaluation of it most clearly reveals the characteristics of his ideal government. In his influential *The Crisis of the Early Italian Renaissance*, Hans Baron argued that it was only the rise of "civic humanism" in Florence around 1400 that allowed a revision of earlier concepts of classical Rome that had seen the Empire as part of a theological schema and down-

74. 4.19.1.
75. 4.19–20.
76. 3.20, 2.8, 4.1.
77. 4.19.4, 4.19.5.

played the Republic. He admitted that Ptolemy was an early isolated instance of advocacy of the Republic, but felt that he lacked a coherent historical critique of the Empire in terms of the decline of virtue, which for Baron came only with the civic humanists.[78] But this is precisely what Ptolemy does.

Ptolemy believed that political rule was better for those suited to it—and above all this applied to Romans, whose virtue caused them always to find kingship intolerable. As Charles Till Davis has demonstrated, Ptolemy converts Augustine's ambivalent appreciation of Roman qualities in *The City of God* into the highest praise.[79] Among the many virtues that, according to Ptolemy, made them worthy of God's grant of good government and lordship are humility, moderation, lack of hate or jealousy, the willingness to care for the Republic with their own wealth, patriotic zeal, piety toward the laws, and civil benevolence.[80]

Ptolemy often discusses the development of Roman government. His chronology is not always accurate, but he consistently singles out the period from the expulsion of the kings until the time of Julius Caesar for praise.[81] He uses biblical and classical sources to show how Roman government developed gradually, adding institutions when necessary. The Senate came into existence under Romulus, the two annual consuls after the kings were expelled, the dictator because of the Sabine threat, and the tribunes when the people, felt themselves to be oppressed by the consuls and the senate.[82] All these institutions worked together for the harmony of the Republic, and Ptolemy is particularly fond of citing the Jews' admiration for Rome in the Book of Maccabees:

No one wore a diadem or assumed the purple so as to be glorified by those things, and they took care to consult daily with the 320, always taking counsel about matters concerning the multitude so that they might do those things that were worthy. They committed their magistracy to one person to exercise lordship over all the lands for a single year, and all obeyed that one, and there was neither ill-will nor jealousy among them.[83]

Here a consul and the Senate are described in what presumably is Rome at its best, but Ptolemy characterizes the entire course of Republican history as political, moderate, and good. The consuls depended for their power on the many, who could judge even the greatest, such as Scipio Africanus.[84]

---

78. Hans Baron, *The Crisis of the Early Italian Renaissance* (Princeton, N.J.: Princeton University Press, 1966), 55–57.
79. Davis, "Ptolemy of Lucca."
80. 3.4–3.6, 2.8. See also *A Short Determination*, c. 21, 42–45.
81. 2.9, 4.19.4–5.
82. 4.26, 2.10.
83. 3.6.3, 1 Machabees (Maccabees) 8.14. See also 2.8.4, 3.20.3, 4.1.4, and *A Short Determination*, c. 21, 46.
84. 2.8.1, 4.1.6.

Ptolemy does not use the word, but he is describing Republican Rome as a mixed constitution of the kind that Polybius described and Machiavelli would later describe as the naturally evolving variety. They saw Rome this way and contrasted it with the mixed constitution laid down all at once by a single lawgiver, like Lycurgus of Sparta.[85] Since Polybius's work was not known in Latin until the sixteenth century, this cannot have been Ptolemy's source, and, in the tempering effect of each organ on the others, his mixed constitution also shares some characteristics with the Thomist model of the first part of this treatise and the *Summa Theologiae*, where Thomas described Moses' government as a mixed constitution of monarchy, aristocracy, and democracy. Ptolemy may be following up Thomas Aquinas's earlier but incomplete comparison of the Jewish and Roman governments, when he described the Jewish polity as a mixed constitution, but failed to say more about Rome.[86]

Ptolemy's explanation of Roman institutions clarifies the mixed constitutional structure: a government of a few virtuous ones, like that of the consuls after the kings' expulsion, is aristocracy, a government of many, like that of the consuls, dictator, and tribunes in the later period, is polity.[87] Since Ptolemy had already said that the rule of the consuls alone depended on the many, he is saying something new here. Any political rule depends on the many, but not every political rule *is* the rule of the many. Since the consuls still existed, what happened was not that rule was turned over completely to the many, but that a democratic element (the tribunes) was added to the aristocratic government, producing a mixed government of the type most common in Aristotle's *Politics*: the mixture of the few and the many.

This is precisely how Ptolemy evaluates the situation in another key passage:

First the two consuls were created, then, as the histories tell us, the Dictator and the Master of Equites, to whom belonged the whole civil government, and so Rome was governed by an aristocratic rule. Later, tribunes were set up to favor the plebeians and the people, so that the consuls and the others I mentioned could not exercise government without them, and in this way democratic rule was appended. In the course of time the senators took over the power of governing. Romulus first established the senators when he divided the whole city into three parts: senators, knights, and plebeians. Then, when there were kings in Rome, the senators held the place of the elders called Ephors in Sparta, Kosmoi in Crete, or Gerousia in Chalcedon, as I made clear above. And because the senators were principally from the multitude, the rule of the Romans was called political. But when the polity was corrupted through the might of some, in the time when the civil wars arose, it was governed by an oligarchic rule.[88]

85. Polybius, *Histories*, 6.10; Machiavelli, *Discourses*, 1.2.
86. 1.5; Thomas Aquinas, *Summa Theologiae*, 1.2.105.1
87. 4.1.2.
88. 4.19.5.

The word "appended" definitely suggests a Polybian mixed constitution, and the officials Ptolemy mentions were from the very polities that Aristotle used as examples of mixed constitutions. Beside confirming that Rome under the Republic was a mixed constitution, we have the even more remarkable suggestion here that Rome even under the kings was to some degree a mixed government, a mixture of monarchy and aristocracy. Nonetheless, Ptolemy generally refers to the government by the name of the most powerful element of the mixed constitution: kingship, aristocracy, polity (here meaning good democracy), oligarchy. This is also a Polybian idea: as the mixed constitution attempts to temper one group with another there is a perpetual struggle for balance; only when there is perfect balance (and in the case of Rome this was never achieved) will there be stability.[89]

Rome acquired its empire under the Republic, which was a sign of the greatness of that rule. Ptolemy has a much more negative view of the period of emperors, which he conceives as the end of political rule. Virtue declined, authority became concentrated in fewer and fewer hands, and finally one man, Julius Caesar, usurped power to rule tyrannically.[90] In his view of the end of the Republic, if not of its evolution, Ptolemy follows the author of the first Book in seeing its root in the conversion of the common good to the good of the few.

Ronald Witt has made the excellent point that one should be careful of equating anti-Caesarist comments with anti-imperialism, since the former was usually personal and not a reflection on the empire as an institution or the line of true emperors beginning with Augustus.[91] To some extent we can see this in Ptolemy, although I do not think that Witt's comment that Ptolemy's criticism of the Empire is "too vague to be significant" is accurate. Further, as I will explain, Ptolemy identifies Caesar's "usurpation of Empire" with the end of Rome's role as a world monarchy, and in this sense Augustus can be no other than Caesar's successor, whose rule represents the destruction of the true polity of the Roman Republic. Ptolemy was by no means a consistent thinker, and he sometimes supports the empire as the political arm of the papacy, but what is significant is that he provides a coherent critique of the Empire in terms of the decline of virtue and the incompatibility of any monarchy, including the Empire, with the needs of any "virile" people.[92] He himself would perhaps see no inconsistency, since he could have argued that

---

89. 4.19.5; Polybius, *Histories*, 6.10 and passim in Book 6.

90. 4.1.4. Ptolemy, as he often does, equates tyranny and despotism in this passage.

91. Witt, "Republican Liberty," 193–94; "The *De Tyranno* and Coluccio Salutati's View of Politics and Roman History," *Nuova Rivista Storica* 53 (1969): 443–50.

92. 4.8.4.

with the loss of virtue among the ancient Romans came the inability to govern themselves and the necessity of a monarchy like the Empire, even though this would inevitably mean oppression.

One of Hans Baron's charges about the Middle Ages is that it maintained a theological and eschatological view of the Roman Empire.[93] I have argued elsewhere that this is far from true,[94] but it is interesting that Ptolemy of Lucca, the author most devoted to republican ideas and most hostile to monarchy, also has a greater teleological component to his thought with regard to Rome than any other scholastic political writer. As in other areas, Ptolemy cannot reconcile all the contradictory viewpoints to which he is committed. He provides arguments for removing teleology from secular politics, but he does not ultimately reject it. In particular, he conceives history as a series of world empires, through a variant of a common interpretation of Nebuchadnezzar's vision in the Book of Daniel of a statue, whose parts are understood to refer to four great empires: the Assyrian, the Medean and the Persian, the Greek, and the Roman. After these, according to Ptolemy, a fifth kingdom, the Roman Church, will rule forever.[95] Although Daniel mentioned an eternal kingdom, most world-empire theories delayed this until the end of the world and left Rome in charge until then; identifying it with a fifth earthly empire and the Church is original with Ptolemy. By "monarchy" Ptolemy does not mean the usual idea of the rule of one person, but rather the rule of one nation or church over all peoples. This is clear since the Fourth Monarchy does not refer to the period of formal Empire, but rather the preceding Republic, particularly the period of widest participation, the Rome of 1 Maccabees.[96]

After Julius Caesar, the Fifth Monarchy of the Church took over. As Davis pointed out, Augustus served as a vicar for Christ until Christ Himself took command,[97] but this was justified only because of the decline in Roman virtue that made the continuance of the Republic impossible. Ptolemy says that the Republic's monarchy (in the sense of Fourth Monarchy) lasted up until Caesar's "usurpation of empire."[98] Thus, Augustus is at most a place holder or regent for Jesus and not a legitimate ruler in his own right. Ptolemy

---

93. Hans Baron, "A Defense of the View of the Quattrocento First Offered in The Crisis of the Early Italian Renaissance," in Baron, *In Search of Florentine Civic Humanism* (Princeton, N.J.: Princeton University Press, 1988), vol. 2, 195–97.

94. In a paper, " 'Civic Humanism' and Medieval Political Thought," written for a conference on the legacy of the concept of civic humanism sponsored by Harvard University and the University of Colorado in August 1995. The procedings of this conference are currently in press.

95. 3.10; Daniel 2.37–45. Daniel interprets the dream somewhat in this manner, but does not specify what particular empires are signified.

96. 3.6, 3.12.

97. Davis, "Ptolemy of Lucca," 42–43.

98. 3.12, 4.1.

does not subscribe to the common theory that God acknowledged the legitimacy of the Roman Empire through the birth of Christ there, on the contrary, this indicates a transfer of universal power to the Church. Ptolemy may be arguing for an inversion of this theory. If Roman virtue had continued, would it have been right for God to take away its empire? Since all power is from God, he could not properly be faulted, but perhaps he came to earth and established the Fifth Monarchy at this time precisely because Rome no longer governed the world by right, so the Fifth Monarchy would not be perceived as a usurpation. It may be, as Davis claims, that Ptolemy makes the Republic a precursor to Christ and thereby increases its importance, but I think that the reverse is also true and more in line with Ptolemy's argument—Rome deserved this position because of the great virtue manifest in its republican government. In any case, from one point of view, the result of the final transfer of Monarchy removes any theological component from secular government, which now must stand or fall solely on the goodness of its institutions. God's will is expressed through the Universal Church; there is no longer any need for a universal secular monarchy, and so each state must govern itself in the best way possible, with no religious concerns other than obedience to the Roman Church.

Ptolemy cannot bring himself to make this final break, and he sometimes supports the Empire as an adjunct to the papal monarchy, which may be interpreted as bringing back a theological component to the Empire. Ptolemy is at pains to show that most emperors after Constantine subordinated themselves to the pope in both secular and theological matters and helped to advance the Christian cause.[99] He shows how the pope transferred the Empire from the Greeks to the Franks, from the Franks to the Saxons, and finally from the Saxons to the Germans, as this became necessary for the defense of the Church.[100] But he is aware that there is no necessity for the emperor to subordinate himself to the Church, and that he has not always done so. This suggests that Ptolemy's support is practical rather than teleological; indeed, he never uses teleological language in speaking of the medieval Empire. Since Ptolemy is concerned with the Church above all, he can justify overlooking his arguments critical of monarchy in secular government even when it is made necessary by evil subjects, if this will help to advance the Church. To some extent he justifies this by saying that imperial rule is midway between regal and political. But this still gives emperors the powers that Ptolemy believes make regal government inherently tyrannical: government by the will of the ruler instead of law and lack of plurality in government.[101]

99. 3.17–18.
100. 3.19.
101. 3.20.

He never says this, but he could justify himself by arguing that, unlike other rulers, emperors are completely subordinate to the pope. The pope's monarchy is different from all secular ones in that it was divinely ordained and guided, and therefore it is not subject to the problems of regal government. It follows from Ptolemy's principle that the powers of lesser officials are determined by and coordinate with the dominant mode of government that the pope's functionaries must have subordinate monarchical powers.[102] This situation would still leave room for independent republics for those peoples virtuous enough to have them, even within the Empire, under the overall direction of the Church and its imperial agent. It is notable that many humanist republicans could also justify giving the Roman Empire a universal role in establishing a peace under which republics could flourish.

Medieval Governments

Most often Ptolemy cites biblical, Greek, or Roman models, but he mentions contemporary examples more than other scholastic writers. Most of these concern Italy, and the way he presents them confirms the suspicion that analysis of ancient states was at least partially directed toward defending Italian republicanism. For example, after defining political rule as government according to the statutes of a community, he mentions that this often holds true in Italy,[103] and that because they are ruled politically, contemporary Italian polities pay salaries to their officials.[104] Frequently a reference to northern Italy turns up in a discussion of ancient Rome to show either that the governments are similar or that the peoples of Italy can only be effectively governed by political rule.[105] Given that ancient Rome is Ptolemy's key example of a state suited to a "virile and virtuous people," linking contemporary Italy with Rome shows a strong preference for the kind of political life found there.

Since many peoples are not suited to political rule, Ptolemy must do more than simply link ancient republics and modern Italy; he must show that the modern Italians require and are capable of it. This partially explains his insistence on astrological factors that predispose certain regions to political rule.[106] Ptolemy is aware of the migrations that have occurred in Europe since ancient times, and so he wants to show that a new location transforms the nature of a people originally from a place where political rule is impossible. This, I think, is the point of his remarks on how successive waves of immi-

102. 3.22.
103. 2.8.1.
104. 2.10.2.
105. 3.22.6, 4.1.2, 4.1.5, 4.8.4.

grants to Sicily from Gaul were transformed in short order to the Sicilian character.[107] In fact, he follows this up immediately with a statement that it is difficult to subjugate Italians, who strongly desire political rule.[108]

This leads to one last, equally futile attempt to reconcile Ptolemy's contradictory views of kingship. If a people desires political rule, it can only be subjected through tyranny. Ptolemy explains that this is why Sicily, Sardinia, and Corsica always had tyrants and why perpetual rulers in Lombardy were always tyrants.[109] The alternative is for rulers who normally would rule monarchially to act politically to avoid tyranny, such as counts in Italy.[110] A seeming exception was the doge (duke) of Venice, but, Ptolemy notes, Venice had a temperate government.[111] He does not explain this further, but possibly Ptolemy viewed the doge as an aristocratic element after the Chalcedonian model. The idea that the nature of a freedom-loving people converts regal to tyrannical rule does not work any better that his previous suggestion that original sin did it. In that case, it became impossible to understand how any people could avoid oppressive government; in this case there is no reason why a regal government in a less favored region would be inherently oppressive, "reduced" to despotic rule.

Most of Ptolemy's references to northern Italy are general, but he also alludes specifically to Tuscany. After comparing the governments of Chalcedonia and ancient Rome, to the effect that both incorporated aristocratic, democratic, and oligarchic institutions, Ptolemy comments that Italian cities, especially in Tuscany, do the same.[112] Various scattered statements illuminate his views on how they designed their mixed constitutions. As with the Roman consul, one person, the podestà, exercised annual power in Tuscan cities, and as in Rome his was an aristocratic, not a regal authority, since his power rested on the many.[113] The consent and counsel of the whole people was required for choosing rulers.[114] The position of the *Anziani* (Lucca and elsewhere) or priors (Florence) is a little less clear. Ptolemy calls them "elders,"[115] which suggests an aristocratic or oligarchic role, but elsewhere he compares them to the Roman tribunes, originating to represent democratic interests.[116] He also

106. 2.8.4, 2.9.6.
107. 4.8.3.
108. 4.8.4
109. 4.8.4.
110. 3.22.6.
111. 4.8.4.
112. 4.19.4.
113. 4.1.5.
114. 4.18.3, 4.13.6.
115. 4.13.3.
116. 4.26.3.

compares medieval judges to ancient Roman censors.[117] Most interestingly, he describes the method whereby the Tuscans use different color beans or coins as secret ballots for voting on policy and deciding criminal cases.[118]

Most of Ptolemy's references to contemporary non-Italian governments other than the Empire are to the various officials found there and not to the governmental structure per se, except to note that officials in general exercise the same kind of rule as the government they serve,[119] which in northern Europe was uniformly monarchic. He argues that even there, cities are governed politically, mentioning the cities of Germany, Spain, Scythia, and Gaul specifically.[120] Except in those places especially suited to political rule, such as Italy, he thinks that regal rule is most natural for entities larger than cities.[121] But he mentions rebellions in Spain, Hungary, Egypt, and the lands of the Tartars against monarchic excess, made necessary since monarchs are not subject to regular examination, as are political rectors.[122]

In his contemporary examples of monarchy we find once again the profound ambivalence discussed in the theoretical sections. While it is inherently oppressive, it is necessary in most places. There are degrees of oppressiveness: if it is relatively mild it should be endured, except in freedom-loving regions; if it is nonhereditary, as in the Empire or in Egypt, where new rulers are chosen from slave boys, there is less danger of violence, ambition, or excessive tyranny.[123]

VII. Ecclesiology and the Papacy

Ptolemy showed no hostility to one monarchy alone—the papacy, established by Jesus in imitation of divine rule with full power over the Church and secular rulers. Such hierocratic ideas were common among papal apologists from the late eleventh century on, but it is rare to find them being expressed by a strong supporter of republicanism. More typically hierocrats see human monarchy, whether ecclesiastical or secular, as the reflection of divine rule and as one element of a great Neoplatonic Chain of Being. As Ptolemy's contemporary Giles of Rome (c.1243–1316) put it, since the universe is ruled regally by God, and the human being regally by reason, so too should polities, which

117. 4.26.5.
118. 4.13.4.
119. 2.10.3, 3.22.6.
120. 4.1.5, 4.16.1.
121. 4.2.1, 4.16.1.
122. 4.1.6.
123. 4.1.7.

are hierarchically located between these two, be ruled regally.[124] The first contributor's part of *On the Government of Rulers* repeats many of the metaphysical arguments commonly given in support of monarchy.[125]

Ptolemy's problem is that he supports republican government for a virtuous people, and although it would be possible to argue that because of original sin, no people is virtuous, he does not do so. It would seem that if the pagan Romans and fractious northern Italians qualified, the Christian people would at least potentially be sufficiently virtuous. Ptolemy's solution is to create a separate category of rule specifically for the papacy—regal and sacerdotal rule—set above all other rule and giving all other rule legitimacy.

Ptolemy repeats many common arguments for papal authority, such as the example of popes who had deposed kings and emperors, the Donation of Constantine, the coronation of Charlemagne,[126] the dictum of Pope Gelasius that the emperor depends on the pope's judgment,[127] the translation of the Empire,[128] the subordination of emperors to ecumenical councils,[129] the vicarate of Christ, and the pope's fullness of power.[130] Although he states that the pope has power over all secular rule by these last two principles, almost all of his arguments concern the empire and the pope's special relationship to it.

Ptolemy's original contribution to hierocratic theory concerns the eschatological role of the Church as the Fifth Empire, as discussed above. Despite his extreme views on the papacy, Ptolemy does recognize some limits. The pope, though vicar of Christ and successor to Christ's secular and sacerdotal power, does not share in all of Christ's power, that which he calls Christ's "excellent" power. The pope must operate within the framework that Christ established; the pope could not found another Church, or save without baptism, or change the nature of the sacraments.[131] And he must act for the common good.[132]

Ptolemy does not say what happens when the pope does not work for the common good. This was an ongoing debate among canonists, who were re-

---

124. Giles of Rome, *De Regimine Principum Libri III (On the Government of Rulers)* (Frankfort: Minerva, 1968; reprint of the Rome, 1556 edition), 2.1.14.154v. Ptolemy, 3.19.3, also compares rule to God in the universe and the spirit in the body, but, unlike the first author (1.13.3) does not conclude from this that secular rule should be regal.

125. 1.3.4, 1.4.4, 1.13.3.

126. 3.10.8.

127. 3.17.1, 3.

128. 3.17.3.

129. 3.17, 18.

130. 3.19.2.

131. 3.10.10.

132. Implied in 3.10.9, where Ptolemy says that the Church's Empire shall last if it directs itself to feeding the flock.

luctant to impose restraints on the pope, but who realized that the pope could commit heresy or another serious crime. Suggestions ranged from leaving it up to God, to saying that by heresy the pope deposed himself, to appealing to a General Council (though who was authorized to call one against a pope was unclear), to arguing that in case of notorious crime, anyone could judge a pope. Ptolemy proposed no solution here, but in *A Short Determination*, he implies that he favors a mixed constitution for the Church as well as the state, in this case including a monarchical element. Referring to Moses and his "co-adjutors" Aaron and Hur, Ptolemy writes:

[Moses] said to the elders of Israel, according to Exodus 24 [.4]: "You have Aaron and Hur with you, and if any question should arise, refer it to them." By this we are shown that those assigned to the salutary councils that I have mentioned ought to help and support the leaders of the faithful. On the one hand, the Aaronites, that is, the cardinals and other major prelates of the churches, ought to support the ecclesiastical leader, for which reason they were long ago instituted. On the other hand, the Hurites, that is, the princes and barons, ought to strengthen the civil leader, whether he be a king, or emperor. For this reason they established parliaments, which ought to set themselves to the end of taking counsel to profit the leader's government, otherwise, if by chance something should be decided incautiously with hasty counsel, what comes from the throne of buffoons may easily be revoked by their successors, as in fact we see. . . . The ancient Romans, as is clear from what I said above, are especially commended for this in the period in which the Republic flourished. For he to whom they had committed its magistracy or consulate for a year, as the Book of Maccabees relates, took counsel daily with the senate concerning the multitude, so that they might do those things that are worthy. The Roman Church acts in the same way today, for the highest pontiff takes counsel with the cardinals, who hold the position of the senators.[133]

This is from a much earlier work, and Ptolemy's political thought had not yet reached its final form. In the 1270s and 1280s he was probably working under the influence of Thomas Aquinas's conception of moderate or tempered monarchy, in which a king is not invariably a despot acting without bounds imposed by others or the law. When he compares the Church, the Roman Republic, and secular kingdoms, he is extending and completing Thomas's view of ancient Hebrew kingship under Moses.[134] The Roman Senate, the College of Cardinals, and national parliaments share in the rule of their respective polities, just as councils of Jews ruled jointly with Moses. Most of these are called monarchies, because the single ruler is the most important and visible official, but the other parts share in the rule and must be consulted in important matters. In identifying the Senate with the College of

---

133. *A Short Determination*, c. 31, 63–64.
134. Thomas Aquinas, *Summa Theologiae*, 1.2.105.1.

Cardinals Ptolemy followed an important current of contemporary canonistic thought, which insisted that the pope was required to consult the cardinals and that the College of Cardinals or the congregation of all the faithful could depose or restrict the pope in case of dire necessity.[135] But in bringing together these disparate elements and in comparing the Church to Mosaic kingship and the Roman Republic, Ptolemy anticipated a new conception of the Church as a mixed constitution that was to surface in the next few decades in the writings of Peter John Olivi and John of Paris.[136] This concept would later assume great importance in the conciliar response to the Great Schism in the Church during the fourteenth and fifteenth centuries. In *On the Government of Rulers* Ptolemy backs off from the implications of this analogy; there, neither a king or a pope is bound to share power, and such a sharing goes against against the nature of monarchy.

One question medieval political thinkers faced was whether Aristotle's concepts could apply to the Church. As an association united by a common belief and requiring leadership to advance the common good of the faithful, it would seem to fit the definition of an Aristotelian polity. It also fit Augustine's definition of city, which Ptolemy was fond of quoting: "a multitude of human beings bound together by one chain of society."[137] Ptolemy even describes the Church in these terms, as "one body distinguished in parts but united by the chain of charity."[138] The canonists and Thomas Aquinas began the assimilation of the two types of society; later, John of Paris, William of Ockham, and Nicole Oresme took the process further.[139] Ptolemy also treated church and state as analogous in *A Short Determination*, although he gave the pope final power over any state. In *On the Government of Rulers* Ptolemy lessens the analogy by creating a special mode of rule for the Church alone, although it retains a connection to political monarchy. The problem is that Ptolemy believes that Jesus established papal government once and for all, and so it becomes difficult to apply the principles developed in the later treatise to it. Ptolemy's advocacy of political rule for a virtuous people and hostility to monarchy could not be extended to the Church without destroying

---

135. See Brian Tierney, "A Conciliar Theory of the Thirteenth Century," *Catholic Historical Review* 36 (1950–1951): 415–40; Davis, "Roman Patriotism," 423. Peter Damian, in the eleventh century, may have been the first to refer to the cardinals as "senators." See Stefan Kuttner, "Cardinalis: The History of a Canonical Concept," *Traditio* 3 (1945): 174.

136. Peter John Olivi, *De renuntiatione papae Coelestini (On the Resignation of Pope Celestine)*, ed. V. P. Livarius Oliger, in *Archivum Franciscanum Historicum* 11 (1918): 354–57; John of Paris, *Tractatus de Potestate Regia et Papali*, in *Johannes Quidort von Paris: Über kö nigliche und päpstliche Gewalt*, ed. F. Bleienstein (Stuttgart: E. Klett, 1969), c. 19, 175; translated by John A. Watt as *On Royal and Papal Power* (Toronto: Pontifical Institute of Mediaeval Studies, 1971).

137. Augustine, *The City of God*, 15.8; see 4.2.8, 4.4.9, 4.18.3, 4.23.1.

138. 4.23.2, citing 1 Corinthians 12, especially 12–14.

139. See Blythe, *Ideal Government*, 149–57, 166–70, 180–83, 205, 233–37.

papal monarchy, which would have gone against Ptolemy's most fundamental beliefs. The only solution was to deny that the Church was an Aristotelian polity.

VIII. Ptolemy of Lucca's Influence on Later Political Thought

Since many manuscripts of *On the Government of Rulers* survive and are listed in numerous and widespread library catalogues, and since it was attributed to Thomas Aquinas, we may reasonably infer that it was widely read, and not simply by those interested primarily in political thought. Ptolemy's formulations of concepts of the Empire, of regal and political rule, of political rule as especially suited to cities, and of the determinative importance of local conditions on government had considerable impact on contemporary and future writers. They were also of importance in the development of ideas of civic humanism. Charles Till Davis was thinking of Ptolemy in part when he wrote of the matrix of Tuscan thinkers of the late thirteenth and early fourteenth centuries: "Here streams of classical influence flowed together, and all dealt with subjects that concerned the Roman Republic. Perhaps it is at this point that we find the 'rediscovery of pre-imperial Rome' which Baron defers until Petrarch, and in regard to Cicero, until Coluccio Salutati." [140] And *A Short Determination* had at least an indirect influence on fourteenth- and fifteenth-century conciliarism. Since medieval political writers rarely gave a direct reference to their peers, and still less were Renaissance and Protestant thinkers willing to credit despised medieval and Catholic sources, it is difficult always to identify direct influence, but the use of Ptolemy's ideas seems clear to me in the works of many important writers, including Dante Alighieri, Engelbert of Admont, Nicole Oresme, Claude de Seyssel, and Nicolò Machiavelli. There are also two cases where the influence is both clearly demonstrable and profound in the consequences for early modern political ideas, and I will concentrate on them.

John Fortescue (c.1394–c.1476), an English jurist who served as Lord Chief Justice of the King's Bench under Henry VI, was a key figure in the late medieval development of English constitutionalism and an important bridge between medieval and early modern mixed constitutionalism. He was also very influential for theoreticians of the Tudor and Stuart monarchies.

Believing himself to be following Thomas Aquinas, Fortescue revived Ptolemy's formulation of regal and political rule and made a combination of

---

140. Davis, "Ptolemy of Lucca," 41.

the two the basis of good government. Whereas Ptolemy used these categories to contrast rule by a king with that by the many, Fortescue applied both to kings. The distinction then becomes one of the modes by which law is made, and he normally considers political rule only in combination with regal rule: lordship is regal if the king rules by laws he makes himself, it is regal and political if he can make law only with the consent of the people.[141] Thus, "regal" can either serve as a synonym for "monarchical," since a king is regal even if he needs consent for law, or it can refer to the ability to make law without consent. Fortescue never defines "political" rule in isolation, since he takes kingship for granted, but logically, as in Ptolemy, it would be the people ruling by its own law.

What Fortescue calls regal and political rule is similar to what Thomas defined as political rule in *Summa Theologiae* and his *Commentary on the "Politics"*, although not in *On the Government of Rulers*. Felix Gilbert has shown that this can be explained by Fortescue's adoption of Ptolemy's view of the Roman Empire as both regal and political: regal in that the emperor makes law, political in that he is elected. This is clear in Fortescue's changing terminology: originally he used "regal and political" to refer to any government that shared some features with regal rule and others with political rule, but eventually he came to use only the criterion of how law was made. Gilbert argues that this change was related to Fortescue's needs in defending the hereditary but limited Lancastrian monarchy.[142]

Fortescue uses Ptolemy's categories for a quite different purpose than Ptolemy intended—to defend monarchy. But in some ways Fortescue develops Ptolemy's ideas and helps to resolve issues Ptolemy could not. Fortescue writes that pure regal rule could arise only by force, since the people would never give it their voluntary consent, without which the king has no legitimate claim. This implies that pure regal rule is never legitimate. Fortescue writes that the only distinction between the privileges of a regal and a regal and political king is that the former has the capacity to do harm, which is more impotency than potency.[143] In some ways this is more radical in practice than Ptolemy, who argued that most peoples needed regal rule. Thus, Fortescue resolves some of the contradictions inherent in Ptolemy's thought by combining regal and political power in a constitutional monarchy appropriate for everyone.

141. John Fortescue, *The Governance of England: Otherwise Called The Difference between an Absolute and Limited Monarchy*, ed. Charles Plummer (Oxford: Clarenden Press, 1885), c. 1, 109.

142. Felix Gilbert, "Sir John Fortescue's 'Dominium Regale et Politicum,'" *Mediaevalia et Humanistica* 2 (1943): 88–97.

143. John Fortescue, *De Laudibus Legum Angliae (On the Praise of the Laws of England)*, ed. S. B. Chrimes (Cambridge: Cambridge University Press, 1942), c. 14.

Fortescue's use of Ptolemy's ideas to describe a government in which power is divided between a king and the people played an important part in the development during the succeeding two centuries of the "classical theory" of England as a mixed constitution of a king limited both by law and a Parliament consisting of a House of Commons and House of Lords.

Fortescue also appropriated Ptolemy's analysis of ancient Israel and Rome. Taking Ptolemy's comments on the judges and interpreting them in light of his own theory of kingship, he transforms Ptolemy's purely human political rule to a regal and political regime, a political theocracy to be precise.[144] He does not completely explain his vision, but it seems that God rules as king through the judges, while the councils, described in Deuteronomy as by and from all the people, made laws. This is quite close to Savonarola's scheme for Florence in the 1490s, also greatly influenced by Ptolemy.

Fortescue's comparison of the Roman Senate to the English Parliament, as a council of over 300, suggests Ptolemy's frequent allusions to the Book of Maccabees. However, Fortescue praises Rome for a longer period: from the time of the early kings until Nero destroyed the Senate. In support of this he cites Ptolemy's anomalous comment that Rome enjoyed political rule even under the kings.[145] Like Ptolemy, Fortescue views the consuls as aristocrats restricted by the power of the Senate. He has a favorable opinion of the Republic, but it pales in comparison to his perfect monarchy, and he argues that it was precisely the lack of a king that ultimately led to its downfall during the period of civil wars until it was transformed into an even better mixed constitution of emperor and Senate. Worried that the War of the Roses may have the same destructive effect on English government as Nero had on the Roman, he called for a return to well-chosen councils.

In contrast to Fortescue's use of Ptolemy for monarchical purposes, the Dominican preacher Girolamo Savonarola (1452–1498), the key figure in Florentine politics in the first years after the devastating French invasion of 1494, generally continues Ptolemy's republicanism, although he also feels that a Thomas's limited king is good for some peoples. Born in Ferarra, but a Florentine resident from 1482, he played an important part in the republican revolt against the Medici in 1494. He never became a public official, but he dominated the new republic until he fell out of favor and was executed for sedition and heresy in 1498. Ptolemy's part of *On the Government of Rulers*, particularly his distinction between regal and political power, is a constant

144. Fortescue, *Governance*, c. 16, 150; c. 1, 110–11; *De Laudibus*, c. 9.
145. 4.19.5; John Fortescue, "Example What Good Counseill Helpith and Advantageth, and of the Contrare What Folowith," Appendix A in *The Governance of England*, 347–48. See also *Governance*, c. 16.

presence in his political sermons and writings. Even in an early work of the 1480s, "On the Polity and Kingdom," before Savonarola showed much interest in politics, he repeats almost verbatim Ptolemy's view that Italians and others who had intelligence and an independent spirit are suited only for political rule, and he also tends to equate despotism and regal rule. He also repeats Ptolemy's counterexample of the doge of Venice to the observation that in Italy all those who try to become permanent monarchs end up as tyrants.[146] Savonarola was also influenced by the first writer's part of the treatise and by Thomas's other writings, especially Thomas's praise of good monarchy. Like Thomas, Savonarola supports a political, not a regal, monarchy and, using the first author's own word, argues that the community should "temper"the king's power to prevent him from becoming a tyrant.[147] In his later writings, Savonarloa tends to make the monarchical element of a good government metaphysical by installing Christ as king of an earthly republic. Even in his early writings, he followed Ptolemy in favoring limited or mixed government except for servile peoples and republican government for the best.[148]

When he wrote *Treatise on the Constitution and Government of Florence*, not long before his fall, Savonarola transformed the basis of Thomas and Ptolemy's political science, by incorporating the question of best government in an eschatological schema of God's elevation of Florence to the role of "New Jerusalem," the epicenter of a New World Order. Savonarola's vision is a new, republican version of the earlier teleological schemes of history, such as the four-empire theory. In this new framework, the questions of Aristotelian politics about the most beneficial ordering of various peoples become trivial, and the virtues of Florentines and their particular constitutional arrangements acquire universal significance.[149] Yet Savonarola still bases the political aspect of this largely on Ptolemy and Thomas. Even some of what appear to be internal contradictions comes not from Savonarola's religious vision but from them. Monarchy is suitable only for the cowardly and servile, the worst choice for a contentious people, and intolerable for an intelligent and vital people like the Florentines.[150] Florence may have a privileged position, but the same argument holds anywhere. Savonarola uses similar arguments to dis-

---

146. 4.8.4; Girolamo Savonarola, *"De Politia et Regno* (On the Polity and the Kingdom)," in *Compendium Totius Philosophiae* (Venice, 1542), 585. See Donald Weinstein, *Savonarola and Florence: Prophecy and Patriotism in the Renaissance* (Princeton, N.J.: Princeton University Press, 1970), 292–93.

147. Savonarola, *"De Politia et Regno,"* 588. See Weinstein, *Savonarola and Florence,* 291.

148. Weinstein, *Savonarola and Florence,* 295, presents a different view of Savonarola's political development.

149. Girolamo Savonarola, *Treatise on the Constitution and Government of Florence,* in *Humanism and Liberty,* ed. R. N. Watkins (Columbia: University of South Carolina Press, 1978).

150. Savonarola, *Constitution of Florence,* 234–36.

credit aristocracy, which leads him to conclude that a virtuous people must have a republic, a "civil government."

Savonarola lived at a crucial transitional time in European history. The "New Monarchies" of northern Europe were shifting the balance of power and culture; northern European explorations were beginning to transform the world economy as well; the Reformation was about to begin. The invasion of 1494, which has been called the dividing line between the medieval and modern worlds, was the first of many that would reduce Italy to a minor and dependent position. Savonarola influenced the political thought, such as that of Machiavelli, that was produced in response to the political crises, and exercised directly and indirectly an influence on what Pocock called the "Atlantic Political Tradition," stretching from England to America.[151]

Through his confusion with Thomas Aquinas, Ptolemy was able to exercise an influence beyond what would have been likely under his own name. Although there were many other important factors, modern ideas of both constitutional monarchy and what we now call "democracy" rest partially on Ptolemy's ideas. What I have written here is only the beginning of an appreciation of Ptolemy's influence. Much remains to be done in identifying specific influence and lines of transmission.

IX. Sources

The authors used a great number of sources, many of which they acknowledged. At the end of this section I list seventy-two sources they explicitly cited. These represent a wide variety of patristic and classical Greek and Latin literature and a smaller selection of medieval writers. Ptolemy used all of these, with the exception of the two marked "first author only" there, and I will concentrate on him. Following a common medieval style, Ptolemy normally gave a citation to the author, usually to the work, and sometimes to the Book. Variations in quotations and misattributions suggest that he often made citations from memory, another typical practice in a time when many, especially biblical, texts were known by heart and libraries were small. Ptolemy is rarely critical toward his sources, but on the other hand, he mainly uses them for illustration of his points and so he can be selective, choosing to cite only supportive material or material that can be interpreted as supportive. One major exception to this is Aristotle's *Politics*, which serves to struc-

---

151. J. G. E. Pocock, *The Machiavellian Moment: Florentine Political Theory and the Atlantic Republican Tradition* (Princeton, N.J.: Princeton University Press, 1975).

ture his argument, and so he cannot be as selective, and he does occasionally criticize it. For the most part, though, he resorts to selective citation and creative interpretation to enforce agreement and dissents only when neither of these strategies is possible.

The other problematic source is Augustine. While it would be possible to dispute Augustine's views, his authority was enormous, so this could be only a last resort, and, practically, only if his views contradicted Scripture. As the only Church Father who wrote much about politics, he could not be ignored, even though his thought was antithetical to Aristotle's. Besides which, his views were such a part of medieval consciousness that they were regarded almost as common sense. And so Ptolemy resorted to systematic, often strained distortion. As discussed above, he valiantly but unsuccessfully tried to make Augustine into an Aristotelian and misrepresented Augustine's position on Rome.

With the Bible, dissent is not an option, but neither does Ptolemy prove his arguments by biblical citation. Rather, it is used to illustrate a point or to serve as a stimulus to a rational argument. For, example, Ptolemy's musing on seemingly contradictory biblical models of kingship leads to a purely secular discussion of the nature of monarchy.[152] With such a varied source, produced by many authors over many centuries, it is always possible to find apt and supportive quotations.

Ptolemy's minor sources are mostly classical and early Christian. Although he was clearly influenced by medieval ideas, particularly those of his teacher Thomas Aquinas, the only major medieval source of secular political thought that he cites explicitly is the twelfth-century writer John of Salisbury, whose *Policraticus* was one of the most important medieval political treatises before the translation of Aristotle's *Politics*. Ptolemy cites him primarily for his organic metaphor in which the organization of society is compared to the human body, whereas the first contributor mentions his defense of regicide against a tyrannical king and his comparison of the king on earth to God in the universe.[153]

For his information about ancient history, Ptolemy relied on Aristotle, the Bible, and Augustine above all, but also on a number of late classical historians popular in the Middle Ages: Valerius Maximus, Eutropius, Vegetius, Justin the Spaniard, Sallust and, to a lesser extent Suetonius and Livy. The first four are not as well known today as they were in the Middle Ages, so let me say a few words about them. One reason that their reputations have suffered

152. 3.11.
153. 3.7.7, 4.26.7, 1.7.5, 1.10.5.

is that all four wrote late compendia of earlier works or knowledge making no claim for originality, and this made them especially useful to medieval writers.

Valerius Maximus wrote his *Memorable Deeds and Sayings* around 31 C.E., intending it to be used in teaching rhetoric. There are quite a few errors, and connoisseurs of classical Latin find it awkward and unorganized, in spite of which it was widespread in the Middle Ages. Like much medieval thought, it praises republican heroes while being pro-imperial.

Eutropius was a fourth-century bureaucrat and administrator in imperial service under the Christian emperors Constantius II, Jovian, Valens, and Theodosius, as well as the apostate Julian. His *A Brief History of Rome (Breviarium)* is dedicated to Valens, probably in 369 C.E. The emperor commissioned this work so that he and his colleague Valentinian, as well many top officers, who were of Germanic origins or low estate, could learn enough Roman history to satisfy the older aristocracy. Another purpose was to glorify the wars of Rome so as to generate patriotic support for the current conflict with the Persians. Eutropius himself may have also wanted to show how the Senate had had an important part in directing policy, so as to moderate imperial absolutism.[154] Paul the Deacon (c.720–c.799), famous for his history of the Lombards and his place in the intellectual circle around Charlemagne, wrote a continuation and expansion of Eutropius, *Roman* (or *Mixed*) *History*, that was widely known in the Middle Ages, and Ptolemy used it as well.

Though little is known for certain of his life, Vegetius was also probably a Christian bureaucrat in imperial service. He also dedicated his *On the Military* to an emperor, but since it cannot be dated with certainty and since he does not mention the emperor's name, it is not sure whether he is Theodosius I (379–395), Honorius (393–423), or Valentinian III (425–455). Vegetius also had a practical purpose: to summarize what had been written about the organization of the military and the practice of warfare in a period when the Roman Empire was under attack. He sets out to propose solutions to what he sees as the deficiencies of the contemporary military.[155] Accounts of historical events are purely incidental, and medieval authors used it for knowledge of how the greatest empire fought.

Marcus Junianus Justinus (Justin the Spaniard) lived in the third century C.E., but nothing is known of his life. He is remembered for preserving

154. There is a recent paperback English translation: Eutropius, *Brevarium (A Brief History of Rome)*, trans. H. W. Bird, Translated Texts for Historians 14 (Liverpool: Liverpool University Press, 1993). The purposes I have listed are developed in the introduction to this edition, xviii–xxxiii.

155. There is also a recent paperback English translation of this: Vegetius, *Epitome of Military Science (On the Military)*, trans. N. P. Milner, Translated Texts for Historians 16 (Liverpool: Liverpool University Press, 1993).

material from the lost *Philippian Histories* of Pompeius Trogus in his *Philippian Histories of T. Pompeius Trogus*. Pompeius Trogus was a late first-century B.C.E. Roman historian from Gaul. In his work, known only from a surviving table of contents and Justin's epitome, he centers on the Macedonian Empire founded by Philip of Macedon, father of Alexander the Great, and the Hellenistic monarchies that followed, but also treats the ancient Assyrian and Persian empires, as well as the governments of Parthia, Rome, Gaul, and Spain.

Two other important classical sources are Seneca (c.4 B.C.E.–65 C.E.) and Cicero (106–43 B.C.E.). Ptolemy and other medieval writers knew Seneca's moral and philosophical works, including his letters, but not the plays. Although he was a pagan, patristic writers, including Augustine, Jerome, Lactantius, and Tertullian, all praised his life and morality, believed wrongly that he had corresponded with the Apostle Paul, and felt that he was at least close to being a Christian, even if he did not actually convert. Although no such qualification could be manufactured for Cicero, his influence in moral matters was second to no other pagan writer. The once common belief that Cicero was of minor importance until the rise of humanism from the fourteenth century on has long been discredited. More recently, Cary Nederman has shown how the political ideas of Cicero, particularly with regard to the origin of human society and government and the union of eloquence and government, were pervasive in the Middle Ages, forming the basis for the theories of John of Paris and Marsilius of Padua, among others, in these matters.[156]

Following are the sources cited directly in *On the Government of Rulers* that the authors probably used. They also used many others, some of which are suggested in the notes, but these are the only ones that can be listed with confidence. On the other hand, direct reference does not necessarily prove anything; for example, Ptolemy cites Cicero's *On the Republic*, which he only knows second hand (mostly from Augustine) and Plutarch's "The Instruction of Trajan," which is not known outside of John of Salisbury, who may have forged it himself. In neither case does Ptolemy acknowledge his actual source. Ptolemy undoubtedly knew some sources, such as a letter of Innocent III, from *The Body of Canon Law*, and some items of this sort may still be listed.

The Bible
The Body of Canon Law
The Body of Civil Law

---

156. Nederman, "Nature, Sin"; "The Union of Wisdom and Eloquence Before the Renaissance: The Ciceronian Orator in Medieval Thought," *Journal of Medieval History* 18 (1992): 75–95; *Community and Consent: The Secular Political Theory of Marsiglio of Padua's "Defensor Pacis"* (New York: Rowman and Littlefield, 1994). What changed with the humanists was their emphasis on Cicero as a stylist.

Aimoinus Floriac, *History of the Franks*

Aristotle, *Ethics, Metaphysics, On Sense, On the Generation of Animals, On the Heavens, On the Spirit, Physics, Politics, Rhetoric*

Pseudo-Aristotle, *Household Management, Problems*

Augustine, *The City of God, On Order, On the Heptateuch, On the Immortality of the Spirit, On the Literal Meaning of Genesis, Regulation for the Servants of God, Sermons*

Aulus Gellius, *Attic Nights*

Boethius, *The Consolation of Philosophy*

Cassiodorus, *Tripartite History*

Cicero, *On Duties, On Friendship, On Laws, Philippics, Tusculan Disputations*

Claudianus, *On Eutropius*

Pseudo-Dionysius the Areopagite, *On the Divine Names, On the Celestial Hierarchy*

Eustratius, *On "The Ethics"*

Eutropius, *A Brief History of Rome*

Gregory I the Great, *Pastoral Regulation*

Hilary, *Commentary on Matthew*

Isidore, *Etymologies*

Jerome, *Against Jovinian, Apology against the Books of Rufinus, Commentary on Ecclesiastes, Commentary on Daniel, Commentary on the Gospel of Matthew, Commentary on the Prophet Isaias, Letters*

John Damascene, *Exposition of the Orthodox Faith*

John of Salisbury, *Policraticus*

Josephus, *Antiquities of the Jews, Wars of the Jews* (first author only)

Julius Caesar, *The Gallic War*

M. Justinus Hispanus, *Philippian Histories of T. Pompeius Trogus*

Livy, *History of Rome*

Macrobius, *Commentary on Scipio's Dream*

Origen, *On First Principles*

Palladius Palatinus, *Country Matters*

Paul the Deacon, *Roman* (or *Mixed*) *History*

Peter Comestor, *Scholastic History*

Pseudo-Plutarch, "The Instruction of Trajan,"

Ptolemy, *Almagast, Centiloquium, Quadripartus*

Sallust, *The Jugurthine War, The War with Cataline*

Seneca, *Letters to Lucilius; On the Providence of God; On the Shortness of Life, to Paulinus; On the Tranquility of the Spirit, to Serenus*

Simplicius, *On "On the Heavens"*

Suetonius, *The Twelve Caesars*

Valerius Maximus, *Memorable Deeds and Sayings*

Vegetius, *On the Military*
Vergil, *Aeneid*
Vitruvius, *On Architecture* (first author only)

X. The Translation

There are two modern editions of the Latin text of Ptolemy's portion of *On the Government of Rulers*. Although I have used both, the better one, and the one on which I primarily relied, is that of R. P. Joannes Perrier in Thomas Aquinas, *Opuscula Omnia necnon Opera Minora*, Tomus Primus: *Opuscula Philosophica* (Paris: P. Lethielleux, 1949). The other is that of Joseph Matthis in Thomas Aquinas, *Politica Opuscula Duo* (Marietti, 1949, reissued 1971). Although the portion attributed to Thomas is also included in these, I have used the more recent edition of Roberto Busa in Thomas Aquinas, *Opera Omnia* (Stuttgart-Bad Cannstatt: Frommann Verlag and Günther Holzboog, KG, 1980).

Sections of the part attributed to Thomas have been translated into English many times before, most recently in Cary Nederman and Kate Forhan, eds., *Medieval Political Theory—A Reader* (London: Routledge, 1993). Gerald B. Phelan and I. T. Eschmann have translated it in its entirety; this translation has appeared in two versions: *The Governance of Rulers, To the King of Cyprus* (Toronto: Pontifical Institute of Mediaeval Studies, 1934) and *On Kingship* (Toronto: Pontifical Institute of Mediaeval Studies, 1949). J. G. Dawson also did a complete translation in A.P. d'Entrèves, ed., *Aquinas: Selected Political Writings* (Oxford: Blackwell, 1948). Cambridge University Press is also considering a new edition. I have chosen to retranslate this part in order to publish a complete and internally consistent edition of the entire treatise as it has traditionally appeared.

I am very conscious of the distortions that can result when a translator does not consistently translate key words. For example, the common practice of considering the words for "regal" and "monarchic" to be equivalent has led to the confusion of an important distinction. As a result I am very careful always to translate technical words in politics, philosophy, and theology in the same way and always to use a different English equivalent for each one. In some cases this has resulted in a word seeming awkward in places, but I felt that this was preferable to concealing the underlying term. In the few cases in which I felt I must depart from my consistent practice, I have indicated this in a note. Occasionally, English usage will require different English equivalents for the same Latin word, but I never use the same English word for different Latin terms. I list the most important equivalents at the end of this section.

Given this precision, I have been more relaxed in the language I use for everything else, since my intention is to provide an idiomatic, readable translation that preserves the meaning. Scholastic Latin can be stultifying in literal translation, and I have tried to make it less so. For example, I have mostly eliminated the passive voice and the proliferation of virtually meaningless connective words that start many sentences. I have used the first person more often than the authors do. I have broken down long sentences and combined short ones, according to English usage. To make the meaning more clear, I often use a noun where the author uses a pronoun, but only when he has recently used this specific noun and I can reasonably assume it is the referent. The same considerations control my occasional addition of clarifying words or phrases—I only repeat what the author has already said or implied. I have tried not to change the intent of his words (even when he is not using technical language), but I have felt free to use idiomatic English rather than literal translation. I almost never alter his order (on two occasions I interchanged two sentences and indicated my reasons in a note).

I think that it is important to annotate extensively, especially since I anticipate that this translation will be read by a wide variety of readers, not all of whom will have an extensive background in classical and medieval history and political thought. As far as possible, I have identified all references, explicit or implicit, to other works and to other parts of the treatise. As far as I was able, I identified proper names (other than some biblical ones) and historical references and have tried to clarify puzzling formulations and indicate alternative translations and problematic readings. Although I have found almost all direct references, a few still escape me, and I would appreciate hearing from anyone who recognizes any or has spotted some blunder of mine. Because of the vast number of references to Aristotle and Augustine, I have left out Ptolemy's textual references to the particular work or book number of these authors unless I felt this was important. I have of course identified these in the notes, and have indicated when Ptolemy's reference was wrong. It is always possible to tell when Ptolemy is making an explicit reference, since I have not deleted the reference to the author in the text.

I follow the New American Bible, a modern Roman Catholic Bible, for the spelling of biblical names of people and places. I also use the modern name for books of the Bible (in the text only) if the only difference is in spelling. I do all this only to avoid unfamiliar spellings like "the Queen of Saba" instead of "the Queen of Sheba," but the standard for both the medieval authors and me is the Latin Vulgate, and all references are to it, and all translations of it into English are my own. Where the names of books of the Bible or the chapter and verse numbers differ between the New American Bible and the Vulgate, I use the Vulgate name or numbers and give the alternative in parentheses in the footnote.

The Vulgate Old Testament often contains the word "*Christus*," which I translate as Christ, despite the fact that this distorts the original meaning. "Χριστός" is Greek for "anointed," and when Jerome translated the Bible into Latin, all references to "anointed" became "*Christus*." Whether or not they were aware of this, medieval people could not avoid seeing this as reference to Jesus.

There are some choices I made in translation that require more explanation. One of the most difficult problems was the elimination of sexism not present in the text (I have, of course, faithfully reproduced the sexism that *does* appear in the text), but which still often shows up in English translation. For example, "*homo*," "human being," is traditionally translated as "man," and indeterminate pronouns as masculine. I have tried to avoid unnecessary sexism as unobtrusively as possible, using "human being," "human," or "person" for "*homo*," substituting plurals for singulars so as to be able to use "they," using "one," and so forth, but I confess to occasionally using a third person singular "they" and to feeling free to use "he" with "king." There will be no really satisfactory solution until we have a non-sex-specific third person singular pronoun.

I also could not use "people" for the plural "*homines*," since this was reserved to translate "populus." The choices for *homo* and *populus* contribute to a problem with *gens* and *natio*. Gens can mean a number of things, including "a people" or "nation" or even any well-defined group of people — Ptolemy refers, for example, to the "priestly *gens*" (4.12.2) and the "plebeian *gens*" (4.19.4). So even the somewhat confusing expedient of using "a people" for "*gens*" and "people" for "*populus*" would not solve the problem. I have decided to use "nation" or "nationality" for "*gens*" and "country" for "*natio*," even though there is some awkwardness with the first and some potential misunderstanding with the second, since "*natio*" does not correspond to the modern meaning of "country."

The Greek equivalent of "*servus*" means "slave," and this meaning was also possible in Latin. On the other hand, it could also mean "servant," or even "serf." Although it is usually impossible to determine which Ptolemy actually had in mind, "servant" seemed to fit most contexts best, and so I have used this word throughout. However, one should bear in mind the other meanings.

"*Lex*" and "*ius*" are both often translated as "law." "*Ius*," however is a stronger, more complex concept that can mean "right," the proper relationship between things or actions inherent in the nature of things, or it can refer to conventional agreement to certain standards. In either case it can be either a norm (objective right) for action or an internal faculty to some claim (subjective right), although Thomas, the first writer, and Ptolemy normally mean the former. This is a complex issue, and any word choice would be bound to imply a modern connotation missing in the original.[157] I use "right" whenever possible, but often this doesn't work and "law" is the only alternative. In these cases, I have always included a note to alert the reader. Similarly, although I translate "*ius gentium*" as "law of nations," I always give a note to distinguish this from "*lex gentium*," which also occurs.

While "*dominium*" can mean "lordship," and this is the word I have used for it, it implies a sense of ownership missing in English.

By "Ἀρετή," Aristotle meant action in accordance with true ends or functions, primarily of the soul, but to a lesser degree of the body. See, for example, *Ethics*, 1.13. This is the word usually translated into English or Latin as "virtue" or "*virtus*," but in Latin (and to some degree in English) "virtue" has a different range of common meanings. It can have the moral sense of "virtue," or the more neutral meaning of "force," and I have used whichever one seemed appropriate in context.

Finally, the word "*simpliciter*," which I have rendered "simply" or "speaking simply" has a technical sense in scholastic Latin not present in English. It refers to what would be the case if we consider something without qualification, without contingent factors. So, something that is best "simply" may not be best in all circumstances.

What follows is a list of important equivalents I used for technical political terms and other significant words not already discussed. The reader will note that there are a great number of words that mean "government," more or less, and I had to stretch to find distinct English equivalents for each. This more than anything else causes awkwardness in places, especially since the same English equivalent does not always sound appropriate in every context. But I felt consistency in this matter overrode concerns of euphony. Since the same Latin word can give rise to several English words, though not the reverse, there are some duplications in this list so that the reader can find the Latin equivalent for a given English translation easily. I ignore certain minor words, such as the "to" of an infinitive, in alphabetizing.

• to assist in a ministry—*subministro*; • assistance—*subventio*; • association—*collegium*; • to attend to—*intendo*; • to be in charge, have precedence—

---

157. The question of natural rights in the Middle Ages has been much discussed in recent years. For an introduction, see Brian Tierney, "Origins of Natural Rights Language: Texts and Contexts, 1150–1250," *History of Political Thought* 10 (1989), 615–46.

praeesse; • be in the military—*milito*; • by birth—*genere*; • to care, have the responsibility—*cura habeo*; • castle, camp, town—*castrum*; • chief, provincial governor—*praeses*; • civility, civic entity—*civilitas*; • to come before, place in front or ahead, put in charge—*praepono*; • command, empire—*imperium*; • to command—*imperare*; • compatriots—*populares*; • concede (the legitimacy of)—*consedere*; • custom—*mos*; • to decree—*jubeo*; • defense, protection—*praesidium*; • degree, grade, gradation, rank, hierarchy—*gradus*; • to direct—*dirigo*; • direction—*moderamen*; • dispute, litigation—*litigium*; • dominance—*dominatio*; • domination —*dominatus*; • dominator—*dominator*; • duke, leader—*dux*; • duty, office—*officium*; • to elevate, take up—*assumo*; • empire, command—*imperium*; • exalted rank—*fastigium*; • to exercise governance, guide—*gubernare*; • to exercise lordship, lord over—*dominari*; • exercise lordship from the start—*praedominari*; • fatherland—*patria*; • function, mode of operation, operation—*operatio*; • genus, stock, kind—*genus*; • to give precepts, order—*praecipere*; • to go before—*praeeo*; • to govern—*rego*; • governance—*gubernatio*; • governing (in the first author's part only)—*regativa*; • government—*regimen*; • governor, pilot—*gubernator*; • grade, gradation, rank, degree, hierarchy—*gradus*; • governorship—*gubernaculum*; • to guide, exercise governance—*gubernare*; • to have precedence, be in charge—*praeesse*; • to have the responsibility, care—*cura habeo*; • hegemony—*potentatus*; • hierarchy, grade, gradation, rank, degree—*gradus*; • household—*familia*; • (pertaining to) household management—*oeconomicus*; • judgment—*judicium*; • kind, genus, stock—*genus*; • king—*rex*; • kingdom—*regnum*; • knight—*miles*; • to lead—*duco*; • leader, duke—*dux*; • leadership—*ducatus*; • litigation, dispute—*litigium*; • lord—*dominus*; • to lord over, exercise lordship—*dominari*; • mandate—*mandatum*; • to mandate—*mandare*; • might, mighty one—*potens*; • might, potency, potentiality—*potentia*; • to minister—*ministro*; • ministerium, ministry—*ministerium*; • mode of operation, operation, function—*operatio*; • morality—*mores*; • name, title—*nomen*; • to occupy, take possession of—*occupo*; • office, duty—*officium*; • operation, mode of operation, function—*operatio*; • ordain—*ordino*; • order—*praeceptus*; • to order, give precepts—*praecipere*; • people—*populum*; • persona, personage—*persona*; • pilot, governor—*gubernator*; • to place in authority—*praeficere*; • to place in front or ahead, come before, put in charge—*praepono*; • potency, potentiality, might—*potentia*; • political—*politicus*; • polity—*politia*; • poll tax—*census*; • to preside—*praesedere*; • prince, ruler—*princeps*; • protection, defense—*praesidium*; • as a provincial governor, in the manner of one presiding—*praesidialiter*; • provincial governor, chief—*praeses*; • to put in charge, place in front or ahead, come before—*praepono*; • rank, grade, gradation, degree, hierarchy—*gradus*; • regal—*regalis*; • to regulate—*regulo*; • regulation—*regula*; • to reign—*regnare*; • royal—*regius*; • to rule—*principari*; • rule, ruling position—*principatus*; • ruler, prince—*princeps*; • to stand in the place of—*gerit vices*; • state, status—*status*; • stock, genus, kind—*genus*; • subdue, subject—*subdo*; • subject to—*deserviens*; • to surpass—*praecello*; • sway—*dictio*; • to take possession of, occupy—*occupo*; • to take up, elevate—*assumo*; • taxes—*vectegalia*; • title, name—*nomen*; • town, castle, camp—*castrum*; • usage—*consuetudo*; • village—*villa*.

Book I

Attributed to Thomas Aquinas

Prologue

When I was pondering what I could offer that would be worthy of Your Royal Highness and suitable to my profession and office, it occurred to me that what I could best offer a king was to compose a book about the kingdom. In it, to the best of my ability, I would diligently bring to light the origin of the kingdom and what pertains to the office of king, according to the authority of divine scripture, the teaching of philosophers, and the examples given by those who praise rulers, relying for the beginning, progress, and consummation of this work on the aid of the one who is King of Kings and Lord of Lords; through whom kings reign: God, Great Lord, and Great King above all gods.[1]

Chapter 1

Something must govern human beings who live together.

[1] To begin to fulfill my intention, I must explain how we should understand the title "king."

[2] There needs to be something that directs all things ordained to an end, which might be achieved in various ways, so that they might achieve the due end by a direct path. A ship, impelled by changing winds, moves in various directions, and it could not arrive at its destined end unless the industry of a pilot directed it to port. There is an end for human beings, to which their

---

1. Psalms 94.3 (95.3), Apocalypse (Revelation) 17.14.

whole lives and actions are ordained, since they act through the intellect, which characteristically and manifestly works toward an end. Humans proceed in various ways toward their intended end, which the diversity of human endeavors and actions demonstrates, and so they need something directing them to their end. The light of reason is implanted naturally in all human beings, and it may direct them in their acts toward their end.

[3] If it were suitable for humans, like many other animals, to live alone, they would need nothing else to direct them to their end, and all would be kings to themselves under God, the highest king, in that they all would direct themselves in their acts through the divinely given light of reason. But, more than for any other animal, it is natural for human beings to be social and political animals,[2] living in a multitude, as natural necessity requires. Nature has prepared food for all other animals, hair to cover them, and defenses, such as teeth, horns, or claws, or at least speed for flight. But human beings were established with nothing of the sort prepared for them by nature. In place of all of these things reason was given to them, through which they could prepare all these things for themselves by the use of their hands.[3] One person acting alone is not enough to obtain a sufficient life, so it is natural for human beings to live in the society of many.

[4] Other animals also have natural diligence implanted in them by which they know what things are useful or harmful. For example, a sheep naturally judges a wolf to be an enemy. From this natural diligence some animals also recognize medicinal herbs and other necessities for their lives. But human beings have only a general cognition of the necessities of life, in that by reasoning from universal principles they can achieve a cognition of the individual things that are necessary for human life. It is not possible for individual human beings to attain all things of this sort through their own reason. It is therefore necessary for humans to live in a multitude, so that one might help another and different ones might be occupied in finding out different things. For example, one could study medicine, another something different, and still another something else.

[5] This is most clearly shown by the fact that it is characteristic of human beings to use speech, through which individuals can completely express their

2. Aristotle, *Politics*, 1.2.1253a.2–3, 7–8. See also *Ethics*, 1.7.1097b.11–12, 9.9.1169b.18; *History of Animals*, 1.1.488a.7, 10, and the introduction under "Political Thought of the First Contributor."

3. Aristotle, *On the Parts of Animals*, 4.10.687a.19.

own concepts to others.[4] Other animals express their own passions to each other only in general, as when a dog shows anger by barking, or other animals display their own passions in various ways. Human beings are more communicative to each other than any other animal that seems to be gregarious, such as the crane, the ant, or the bee.[5] Considering this, Solomon says in Ecclesiastes: "It is better that there be two than one. For they have the advantage of their mutual society."[6]

[6] If, therefore, it is natural for human beings to live in the society of many, it is necessary that among human beings there be that through which the multitude may be governed. For if there were many persons and all individual persons provided only that which was suitable for themselves individually, the multitude would be broken up and dispersed unless there were something to take care of what pertained to the good of the multitude. Likewise, the body of a human or of any animal would dissipate unless there were some general governing strength in the body to attend to the common good of all the members. Considering this, Solomon says: "Where there is no governor, the people will be scattered."[7]

[7] This is rational, since that which is individual is not the same as that which is in common. They differ by their individual characteristics, but they are united by what they have in common. But different things have different causes. Therefore, it is necessary for there to be something which impels to the common good of the many beyond that which impels to the particular good. For this reason, one finds something governing all things ordained to one end.[8] In the physical universe the first body, namely the celestial body, governs the other bodies through the order of divine providence, and all bodies are governed by rational creatures.[9] In individual human beings the spirit governs the body, and among the parts of the spirit, the irascible and concupiscible are ruled by reason.[10] Likewise, among the members of the body one

---

4. The emphasis on speech as the characteristic act of human beings probably derives from Cicero.

5. Aristotle, *History of Animals*, 1.1.488a.10.

6. Ecclesiastes 4.9.

7. Proverbs 11.14.

8. Aristotle, *Politics*, 1.5.1254a.28–31. Aristotle says that all wholes made up of parts have ruling and subject elements.

9. See Thomas Aquinas, *Summa contra Gentiles*, 3.78, 3.23. In the first reference Thomas explains more clearly that divine providence rules through a universal hierarchy reaching from God to the lowest creatures, and that of all creatures the intellectual ones are highest. Therefore, all are under rational creatures. In 3.23 he explains that the motion of the heavens, that is, the first body, must itself be moved by an intellectual substance above it.

10. See, for example, Thomas Aquinas, *Summa Theologiae*, 1.81.3, ad 2; 1.2.9.2, ad 3; 1.2.17.2 in 2; and passim. In the first place cited, Thomas repeats Aristotle's statement that the rule of

is principal, like the heart or head, and this moves all others.[11] Therefore, it is necessary that there be something that governs in every multitude.

Chapter 2

Distinctions among the various forms of lordship or government.

[1] In the case of certain things that are ordained to an end it is possible to proceed either rightly or not rightly. There is also both a right approach and one that is not right in the government of a multitude.[12] It is directed rightly when it is led to a suitable end, not rightly when it is led to a unsuitable end. But the end suitable for a multitude of the free is different than that for a multitude of servants, since the free exist for their own sake, while servants are servants for the sake of another.[13] If, therefore, the one governing ordains a multitude of the free to the common good of the multitude, the government will be right and just, as is suitable for the free. But if the government is ordained to the private good of the one governing, the government will be unjust and perverse.[14] The Lord threatens such rectors through Ezekiel, saying: "Woe to the shepherds who feed themselves," that is, those who seek their own profit, "should not the flocks be fed by the shepherds?"[15] Shepherds certainly ought to seek the good of the flock, and all rectors should seek the good of the multitude subject to them.

[2] Therefore, one alone who brings about an unjust government by seeking individual profit from the government, and not the good of the mul-

---

spirit over body is despotic, in the sense that the will need only command the movement of any part subject to the will and it will immediately respond, without any ability to resist. The spirit, however, is different from the body in that it is free and its parts must consequently be able to resist. The irascible and concupiscible tendencies of the spirit, not being slaves, are able to resist their ruler, reason, which rules regally but not despotically. See Blythe, *Ideal Government*, 44–45.

11. Aristotle, *Metaphysics*, 5.1.1013a.5–6, where, however, Aristotle explains that the heart or head, like the foundation of a house, is an imminent part, from which a person, like a house, takes its beginning, and in fact contrasts this usage of "beginning" with that when we refer to that whose will determines motion, such as the magistrates in cities.

12. Aristotle, *Politics*, 3.6.1279a.17–21. Aristotle expresses this idea frequently in both the *Politics* and the *Ethics*.

13. Aristotle, *Metaphysics*, 1.2.982b.25–27.

14. The classification of government according to the number of rulers and whether or not they serve the common good comes from Aristotle, *Politics*, 3.7.1279a.22–b.10, and the writer takes most of what he says in the next few paragraphs from this. In *Ethics*, 8.10,1159b.31–1160a.23, Aristotle gives the same classification, but also calls polity "timocracy," and characterizes it by a property qualification.

15. Ezechiel (Ezekiel) 34.2

titude subject to that rector, is called a tyrant. This name is derived from
"fortitude,"[16] because a tyrant oppresses through might instead of governing through justice, which is why mighty ones were called tyrants among the
ancients. But if more than one, although still a few, bring about an unjust
government, it is called "oligarchy," that is, the rule of the few. This occurs
when a few oppress the plebs for the sake of riches, and they only differ from
a tyrant by their plurality. But if the many exercise an unjust government it is
named "democracy," that is, hegemony of the people. This occurs when the
plebeian people oppresses the rich through the might of the multitude. Then,
the whole people will act as if it were a single tyrant.

[3] I must distinguish just governments in a similar way. If some multitude
administers the government, it is called by the common name "polity"; for
example, when a multitude of warriors exercises lordship in a city or province.
But if a few virtuous ones administer a government of this kind, it is called
"aristocracy," that is the best hegemony, or hegemony of the best, and for this
reason the few are called "optimates."[17] But if one alone is involved with just
government, that one is properly called "king." The Lord says through Ezekiel: "My servant David will be king over all, and there will be one shepherd
of all of them."[18] This shows clearly that the very idea of king is one who
presides, and that he should be a shepherd seeking the common good of the
multitude and not his own profit.

[4] Since it is appropriate for human beings to live in a multitude, because
as solitary individuals they are not self-sufficient with respect to the necessities of life, it follows that the more perfect the society of the multitude is,
the more it will be self-sufficient with respect to the necessities of life. There
is, no doubt, some sufficiency for life in one household living in one home—
that which pertains to natural acts of nutrition, giving birth to offspring,
and other things of this kind—and in one neighborhood with respect to the
things pertaining to one craft. But in a city, which is the perfect community,
there is sufficiency with respect to the necessities of life, and it is even more
present in a province, since there is a necessity of fighting together and giving
mutual aid against the enemy.[19]

16. Isidore of Seville, *Etymologies*, 9.19. See also Augustine, *The City of God*, 5.19, where Augustine explains that the word "tyrant" in its ancient meaning signified a man of power.
    17. "Best" is "*optimus*" in Latin. "Optimate" was a common term for the powerful in the
northern Italian city-states of the author's day.
    18. Ezechiel (Ezekiel) 37.24.
    19. Most of this discussion comes from Aristotle, *Politics*, 1.2.1252b.9–30, but the author of
this book adds the part about a province in order to bring Aristotle's scheme of the completion
of a political entity in the city-state more into line with medieval kingdoms—to say, in effect, that

[5] Therefore, one who governs the perfect community, that is a city or province, is called by the epithet "the king,"[20] but one who governs a home, is called "paterfamilias" and not king. Nevertheless, he is similar in some ways to a king, and for this reason kings are sometimes called fathers of their peoples.

[6] Therefore, it is clear from what I have said that a king is one who governs the multitude of one city or province for the common good. As Solomon says in Ecclesiastes: "The king commands all the land serving him."[21]

Chapter 3

*It is more useful to the multitude of human beings living together
to be governed by one than by many.*

[1] Now that I have set out these introductory points, I must ask whether it is more expedient for a province or a city to be governed by many or by one. This can be considered with respect to the end of government. The intention of those who govern should be directed to this, in order to procure the health of that which they undertake to govern. It is the pilot's job to conduct a ship unharmed to the well-being of the port by preserving it against the dangers of the sea. But the good and well-being of a multitude joined in society is that its unity should be preserved, and this is called peace.[22] If this is taken away, the utility of social life perishes, and, moreover, the dissenting multitude becomes onerous to itself. Therefore, a rector of a multitude ought especially to attend to this, so as to procure the unity of peace.

[2] Rectors do not rightly take counsel about whether to make peace within the multitudes subject to them, just as doctors do not take counsel about

---

although the city may be complete, the kingdom is more complete. Aristotle also speaks of the village as less complete than the city, whereas the writer here speaks of the neighborhood. The word used, "*vicus*," could refer to either, but the writer has in mind the medieval arrangement of a city in which each quarter, street, or neighborhood was associated with a trade.

20. The author says that such a one is called "the king" antonomastically, that is, by the figure of speech whereby an epithet is substituted for a person's or thing's proper name, e.g., "His Holiness" for the pope, or "the City" for Rome, or conversely whereby a proper name is applied to another, e.g., "an Einstein." The former mode is used when the epithet is considered to belong to the one to which it is applied in an essential way, although it may be used for others generically.

21. Ecclesiastes 5.8.

22. Augustine, *The City of God*, 19.12. See also Thomas Aquinas, *Summa contra Gentiles*, 4.76.4. In the Latin version of the *Ethics* that Thomas used, the word "εὐνομια," (3.3.1112b.13–14) the observance of good laws, is translated as "*pax*," peace, which allowed him to claim an Aristotelian ancestry for his position.

whether to cure the sick committed to them.[23] No one ought to take counsel about an end to which they are obliged to attend, but rather concerning those things which lead to that end. This is why Paul says, after commending the unity of the faithful people: "You should be solicitous to preserve the unity of the spirit in the chain of peace."[24] Therefore, the more effective a government is in preserving the unity of peace, the more useful it will be. For we say that that which leads to the end is more useful. It is evident that what is one in itself can better bring about unity than can many,[25] just as the most effective cause of heat is that which is hot in itself. Therefore, the government of one is more useful than that of many.

[3] It is also evident that the many could in no way preserve the multitude if there were total dissent among them. A certain unity among the many would be required for them to govern at all; many could not pull a ship in one direction unless they were joined together in some way.[26] But many are said to be united to the degree that they approach to one. So it is better for one to govern than many, who only approach to one.

[4] Besides, those things which are in accord with nature are best, for nature operates for the best in individuals. But all natural government is by one. Among the multitude of members there is one which moves all of them, namely the heart, and among the parts of the spirit one strength principally presides, namely reason. There is also one king among the bees,[27] and in the whole universe one God, maker and rector of all. This is in accord with reason, since every multitude derives from one. So, if those things which exist by art imitate those things that are from nature, and if a work of art is better the closer it comes to that which is in nature,[28] it follows necessarily that a human multitude is best governed by one.

[5] This is also apparent from experience. Provinces and cities that are not governed by one labor under dissentions and are tossed about without peace, so that what the Lord bewailed through the prophet seems to be fulfilled: "Many shepherds have demolished my vineyard."[29] On the contrary, prov-

---

23. Aristotle, *Ethics*, 3.3.1112b.13–14.
24. Ephesians 4.3.
25. Thomas Aquinas, *Summa contra Gentiles*, 4.76.4; *Summa Theologiae*, 1.103.3.
26. Aristotle, *Politics*, 3.4.1276.b.20–27 makes a similar analogy about the different functions of sailors.
27. A common misconception in ancient times and the Middle Ages. See, e.g., Aristotle, *History of Animals*, 5.21.553b.6.
28. Aristotle, *Physics*, 2.2.194a.21–22.
29. Jeremias (Jeremiah) 12.10.

inces and cities that are governed by one king rejoice in peace, flourish in justice, and are gladdened by their affluence. This is why, as a great gift, the Lord promised his people through the prophets that he would put in place one head for them and that there would be one ruler in their midst.[30]

Chapter 4

Many reasons and arguments prove that just as the lordship of one, so long as it is just, is best, so its opposite is worst.

[1] Just as the government of a king is best, so the government of a tyrant is worst. Democracy is opposed to polity, each being a government exercised by many, as is apparent from what I have said;[31] oligarchy is opposed to aristocracy, each being exercised by a few; and kingdom is opposed to tyranny, each being exercised by one. I have already shown that a kingdom is the best government.[32] If, therefore, the worst is opposed to the best, it follows that tyranny is necessarily the worst.[33]

[2] Moreover, a united force is more efficacious in producing its effect than is a dispersed or divided force. Many gathered together can pull what separate individuals working individually could not pull. Therefore, just as it is more useful for a force working for good to be more one, so that it may work for the good more effectively, so it is more harmful if a force working for evil is one, than if it is divided. But the force of one presiding unjustly works to the disadvantage of the multitude, and such a one twists the common good of the multitude to that one's own good alone. Just as, if the government is just, a kingdom is better than aristocracy and aristocracy better than polity, since the more the governing element is one, the more the government will be useful; so, conversely, if the government is unjust, the more the ruling element is one, the more harm it will do. Therefore, tyranny is more harmful than oligarchy, and oligarchy is more harmful than democracy.

[3] Further, a government becomes unjust when it spurns the common good of the multitude and seeks the private good of the governing element. The more it recedes from the common good, the more it is an unjust government.

30. Jeremias (Jeremiah) 30.21; Ezechiel (Ezekiel) 34.23, 37.25.
31. I.2.2–3.
32. I.3.
33. Aristotle, *Ethics*, 8.10.1160b.9.

But it recedes more from the common good in oligarchy, in which it seeks the good of a few, than in democracy, in which it seeks the good of the many, and it recedes even more from the common good in tyranny, in which it seeks the good of one alone: for the many is closer to the whole than the few is, and the few are closer than one alone. Therefore the government of tyranny is the most unjust.

[4] Likewise, this is apparent to those who consider the order of divine providence, which disposes all things for the best. Good arises in things from one perfect cause in which everything which can help to effect the good is united, but evil arises from any individual defect.[34] No body possesses beauty unless all its members are properly disposed, but ugliness is present when any member is improperly disposed. Thus, ugliness arises from many causes and in different ways, but beauty arises only in one mode and from one perfect cause. This is the way it is with all good and evil things, as if God provided this so that the good, arising from one cause, should be stronger, but evil, arising from many, should be weaker. Therefore, it is expedient for just government to be of one alone, so that it will be stronger. But if it should decline into unjust government, it is more expedient for it to be of many, so that it will be weaker, and so that the many will mutually impede each other. Therefore, among the unjust governments democracy is more tolerable, and the worst is tyranny.

[5] This is especially apparent if you consider the evils that arise from tyrants. The consequence of tyrants having contempt for the common good and seeking their private good is that they burden their subjects in various ways, depending on the various passions to which they are subject for obtaining certain goods. Those controlled by the passion of cupidity snatch away the goods of their subjects. As Solomon says: "A just king will build up the earth, but an avaricious man will destroy it."[35] One who is subject to the passion of wrath will shed blood for nothing, so that, as Ezekiel says: "Its rulers in its midst are like wolves snatching their prey to shed blood."[36]

[6] Therefore, we must flee this government, as the Wise One warns, saying: "Keep far away from persons who have the power to kill,"[37] because they kill

---

34. Pseudo-Dionysius the Areopagite (or Dionysius the pseudo-Areopagite), *On the Divine Names*, 4.30. Dionysius was a fifth- or sixth-century Christian Neoplatonist who was incorrectly believed in the Middle Ages to be the same as Dionysius the Areopagite, an Athenian follower of Paul (Acts 17.34). He was immensely influential in the Middle Ages.

35. Proverbs 29.4.

36. Ezechiel (Ezekiel) 22.27.

37. Ecclesiasticus (Sirach) 9.18.

not for justice but use their power to satisfy the lust of their will. Therefore, there will be no security, for all things are uncertain when there is deviation from what is right, and nothing can be made firm that depends on the will of others, still less on their lust. Such ones not only burden their subjects in temporal things, they also impede their spiritual goods. Since those who have precedence desire that which profits them, they impede all progress of their subjects, suspecting any excellence among their subjects to be prejudicial to their own iniquitous dominance. Tyrants "suspect the good more than the evil, and they always dread another's virtue."[38]

[7] These tyrants attempt to prevent those subjects who become virtuous from acquiring the spirit of magnanimity and not putting up with their iniquitous dominance, and to keep their subjects from joining in a compact of friendship and mutually rejoicing in the advantage of peace. For if their subjects have no trust in one another, they can not take any concerted measures against their lordship. For this reason they sow discord among their subjects, they nourish the discord that has arisen, and they prohibit those things which promote human association, such as marriages and common meals, and other similar things which commonly generate familiarity and trust among human beings.[39] They also try to keep their subjects from becoming mighty or rich. Conscious of their own evil, they suspect others; they fear that just as they use their might and riches for harm, the might and riches of their subjects might become harmful to them. As is said in Job about tyrants: "The sound of dread is always in their ears, and when there is peace," that is, when no one intends evil against them, "they always expect treacheries."[40]

[8] The result is that few virtuous ones are found under tyrants, since those presiding, who ought to lead their subjects to virtue,[41] instead despicably envy the virtue of their subjects and impede it as much as they can. In Aristotle's opinion, brave men are found among those who honor those who are most brave.[42] And as Cicero says, those things of which everyone disapproves are

38. Sallust, *The War with Cataline*, 7.2. The author of this part does not acknowledge that he is quoting anyone. The only difference in this sentence, and it is a interesting one, is that Sallust writes "kings," meaning any king, instead of "tyrants."

39. Aristotle, *Politics*, 5.11.1313a.39–1313b.21, except for the prohibition of marriage. In medieval society, upper-class and many other marriages were arranged, most often in an attempt to increase the power and prestige of a family. Naturally a tyrant would be suspicious of this and perhaps the writer here also had in mind large marriage feasts that would bring potentially powerful rivals together. Obviously he does not mean that tyrants would ban marriage altogether, but simply try to prevent disadvantageous unions and encourage ones to their own benefit.

40. Job 15.21.

41. Aristotle, *Ethics*, 2.1.1103b.3–6.

42. Aristotle, *Ethics*, 1.3.1095b.28–30, 3.8.1116a.20–21.

always neglected and flourish too little.[43] It is also natural that persons who are nourished by fear degenerate and develop a servile spirit, and that they become fainthearted in performing all manly and difficult work. Experience shows this clearly in provinces that were under tyrants for a long time. As Paul says in Colossians: "Fathers, don't provoke your children to indignation, lest they become weak in spirit."[44]

[9] Considering these harmful effects of tyranny, king Solomon says, "When the ungodly reign, it is the ruin of persons,"[45] because through the wickedness of tyrants subjects abandon the perfection of virtues. He also says: "When the ungodly take up rule, the people will groan,"[46] having been led, as it were, into servitude. And again he says: "When the ungodly rise up, persons will hide,"[47] so that they might evade the cruelty of the tyrants. We should not wonder at this, because persons who preside without reason according to the lust of their souls differ in no way from beasts. As Solomon says: "An ungodly ruler over a poor people is like a roaring lion or a hungry bear";[48] for that reason, persons hide themselves from tyrants just as from cruel beasts, and it seems that to be subject to a tyrant is the same thing as to be placed under a raging beast.

Chapter 5

How lordship varied among the Romans. Sometimes their Republic grew more under the lordship of many.

[1] Since the best and the worst subsist in monarchy, that is in the rule of one, the royal dignity is rendered odious to many because of the evil of tyrants. While some desire the government of a king, they fall under the cruelty of tyrants, and many rectors exercise tyranny under the pretext of the royal dignity.

[2] There is a good example of this in the Roman Republic. After the people had expelled the kings, whose royal, or rather tyrannical, arrogance they could not bear, they wanted to change the kingdom into an aristocracy and so instituted for themselves consuls and other magistrates. These began to govern

---

43. Cicero, *Tusculan Disputations*, 1.2.
44. Colossians 3.21.
45. Proverbs 28.12.
46. Proverbs 29.2
47. Proverbs 28.28.
48. Proverbs 28.15.

and direct them, and, as Sallust reports: "It is incredible to relate how the Roman city grew in a short time once liberty had been obtained."[49]

[3] It often happens that persons living under a king strive for the common good rather sluggishly, inasmuch as they reckon that that which they devote to the common good does not benefit themselves but the king, under whose power they see the common goods to be. But when they see that the common good is not in the power of one, each attends to it as if it were their own, not as if it were something pertaining to someone else. For this reason experience seems to show that one city administrated by rectors chosen for a year can sometimes do more than one king who has three or four cities, and small services that kings exact weigh more heavily than great weights imposed by the community of citizens.

[4] This was true throughout the course of the Roman Republic. Plebeians were signed up for the military and paid for being in the military, and when the public treasury did not suffice for the payroll, private wealth came into public use, so much so that even the senate itself kept no gold except that each senator kept his ring and *bulla*, the insignia of his dignity.[50]

[5] But when they were worn out by the continual dissensions which escalated into civil wars—during which, liberty, for which they were very zealous, was ripped from their hands—they came under the power of the emperors. From the beginning the emperors were unwilling to be called kings, because this title was odious to the Romans. Some of them procured the common good faithfully, as is the true royal custom, and through their zeal the Roman Republic was increased and preserved. But most of them were tyrants to their subjects yet idle and feeble toward their enemies, and these led the Roman Republic to naught.

[6] There was a similar process among the Hebrew people. First, while the judges governed them, their enemies ravaged them on all sides. For they did "what was good in their own eyes."[51] But when kings had been divinely given

---

49. Sallust, *The War with Cataline*, 7.3. See also Augustine, *The City of God*, 5.12.

50. Augustine, *The City of God*, 3.19; Livy, *History of Rome*, 36. The *bulla* is an amulet worn by freeborn males. Augustine says that individuals gave the symbols of their rank—rings, *bullae*, etc., and that even senators had nothing left. Livy says that each senator kept only a ring for himself and family members, a *bulla* for his son, and an ounce of gold each for his wife and daughters. Both mention pay for the military.

51. 1 Kings (1 Samuel) 3.18. This quote actually refers to the Judge Samuel's comment about God: "Let him do what is right in his own eyes." See below 2.8–9 for Ptolemy's very dif-

to them at their own insistence,[52] they fell away from the cult of the one God because of the kings' evil and were finally led into captivity.

[7] Therefore, dangers threaten from either side; either they fear a tyrant and avoid a king's lordship, which is best, or, when they do take this into consideration, the royal power changes into tyrannical evil.

Chapter 6

Tyrannical lordship comes about more often in the government of the many than from the government of one; for that reason, the government of one is better.

[1] When there are only two choices, and each poses a danger, it is better to choose the one from which less evil follows. But less evil follows from a monarchy that is converted into tyranny, than from the government of the many best, when that is corrupted. Dissension, which usually follows from the government of many, is contrary to the good of peace, which is the chief good in the social multitude.[53] Tyranny does not remove this good, rather it partially impedes the good of individual persons, unless there is an excessive tyranny that rages against the whole community. Therefore, the government of one is more desirable than that of many, although dangers follow from both.

[2] Further, it seems that we ought to flee more that from which greater dangers are more likely to follow. But the greatest dangers to the multitude more often follow from the government of the many than from the government of one. It more often happens that one of the many will depart from the intention of the common good than that one alone will do so. When any one of the many who preside turns from the intention of the common good, the danger of dissension threatens among the multitude of subjects. When the rulers dissent, dissension follows among the multitude. But those who preside alone often look to the common good, and if they do avert their attention from the common good, it does not necessarily follow that they attend to the oppression of their subjects, for this is an excessive tyranny, which represents the greatest degree of evil in government, as I showed above.[54] Therefore we

---

ferent evaluation of the Judges—as political rulers whose excellent rule came to an end because the people foolishly preferred a king.
  52. 1 Kings (1 Samuel) 12.13–15.
  53. See above, 1.3.
  54. 1.4.

should flee the dangers that originate from the governance of many more than from those originating from the governance of one.

[3] Further, the government of the many turns into tyranny not less, but perhaps more frequently, than that of one. After the government of many has led to dissention, it often happens that one of them gets the upper hand over the others and alone usurps lordship over the multitude. We can clearly see this from what has happened through the course of time. The government of all the many has usually ended in tyranny, as appears clearly in the case of the Roman Republic. After it had long been administered by many magistrates, rivalries, dissensions, and civil wars arose, and it fell under the cruelest tyrants. If you diligently consider past deeds and the contemporary situation everywhere, you will discover that more have exercised tyranny in lands governed by many, than in those guided by one.[55]

[4] It might seem that the government of kings, which is the best government, should be especially avoided on account of tyranny; in fact, a tyrant is not less, but more, likely to arise under the government of the many. So, it remains simply that it is more expedient to live under one king than under the government of many.

Chapter 7

Conclusion: The government of one is the best simply. The multitude ought to act toward that one so as to take away the occasion for tyrannizing, but even if this should happen it should tolerate that one to avoid a greater evil.

[1] As is clear from what I have said, we should prefer the government of one, which is best, although it may be converted into tyranny, which is worst. Thus, we need to work out with diligent zeal how to provide a king for the multitude yet keep it from falling under a tyrant.

[2] First, it is necessary for those to whom it pertains to promote a king to choose someone of such a condition that makes it unlikely that he will de-

55. Aristotle, *Politics*, 5.10.1310b.14–16. Aristotle says that most tyrants were demagogues who took power by getting popular support against the notables. By "contemporary situation" the author of this part no doubt has in mind northern Italian cities, some of whose despots came from popular leaders or especially from "captains of the *popolo*," supposedly representing the "democratic" power of the guilds. In the author's time members of the Della Torre family in Milan and Mastino della Scala in Verona, for example, had used this office to achieve great personal power.

cline into tyranny. When, in 1 Kings, Samuel praises the providence of God with respect to the institution of a king, he says: "The Lord has sought a man according to his own heart, and the Lord has ordered him to be a leader over his people."[56] Thereafter, the governance of the kingdom must be so disposed as to remove the occasion of tyranny from the king who has been instituted. At the same time his power should also be tempered, so that he can not easily decline into tyranny.[57] In what follows I will consider how these things may come about.

[3] Finally, care should be taken for what could happen if a king is diverted into tyranny. If it is not excessive, it is more profitable to tolerate a slack tyranny for a time than to go against the tyranny and become involved in many dangers, which are more serious than the tyranny itself. It could happen that those who act against the tyrant do not prevail, and the provoked tyrant might rage all the more. Even if someone could prevail against the tyrant, the most serious dissensions often arise among the people from this very thing; either while they are rising up against the tyrant or after the tyrant has been overthrown, when the multitude divides into parts with regard to the ordination of the government.

[4] It also sometimes happens that someone who helps the multitude to expel a tyrant takes power, seizes tyranny, and fearing to suffer the same thing from someone else, oppresses the subjects with a heavier servitude. It customarily happens in tyranny that the later tyranny is heavier than that the former, and new tyrants do not abandon the preceding oppression but contrive new forms of it from the evils of their own hearts. Once in Syracuse when everyone desired Dionysius's death, a certain old woman prayed continually that he should be unharmed and outlive her. When the tyrant learned this he asked her why she did it. She replied: "When I was a little girl we had a harsh tyrant, and I desired his death, but when he had been killed one somewhat harsher succeeded. I greatly desired his lordship to end as well, but then we had a third one as rector who was even more unfit: you. So, if you were taken away, a worse would succeed in your place."[58]

[5] It seems to some that if there were an intolerably excessive tyranny, it would be virtuous for brave men to kill the tyrant and expose themselves to

56. 1 Kings (1 Samuel) 13.14.
57. Thomas Aquinas, *Summa Theologiae*, 1.2.105.1, ad. 2.
58. Valerius Maximus, *Memorable Deeds and Sayings*, 6.2.ext 2. See also John of Salisbury, *Policraticus*, 7.25.

the dangers of death for the liberation of the multitude.[59] There is even an example of this in the Old Testament. A certain Ehud killed Eglon, king of Moab, who was oppressing the people of God with a heavy servitude, by thrusting a dagger into his thigh, and he was made a judge of the people.[60] But this does not agree with the apostolic teaching. Peter teaches us to be reverent subjects of lords, not only to the good and moderate ones, but even to those of bad temper: "This is grace: for someone through conscience toward God to endure harshness, suffering unjustly."[61] The great multitude of nobles and the people who were converted to the faith when many Roman emperors tyrannically persecuted the faith of Christ were praised not for resisting but for enduring death patiently and with courage on Christ's behalf. This is clear in the case of the sacred legion of Thebians,[62] and so Ehud must be judged more as one who killed an enemy than a rector of the people, even though he was a tyrant. Also in the Old Testament we read that those who killed Joash, king of Judah, were killed and their children saved according to the precept of the law, even though Joash had abandoned the cult of God.[63]

[6] It would be dangerous to the multitude and its rectors if from their private presumption some should attempt to bring about the death of those who preside, even if they are tyrants. The evil more than the good commonly risk dangers of this kind, for to them the lordship of kings is customarily no less heavy than that of tyrants. According to Solomon's statement in Proverbs: "A wise king scatters the impious."[64] Therefore, this kind of presumption threatens more danger from the loss of a king than remedy from the removal of a tyrant.[65]

[7] It also seems that proceeding against the cruelty of tyrants should pertain to public authority rather than to the private presumption of some. First, if it pertains to the right of some multitude to provide a king for itself, the same

---

59. John of Salisbury, *Policraticus*, 8.18–20.

60. Judges 3.14–22. See also John of Salisbury, *Policraticus*, 8.20.

61. 1 Peter 2.18–19.

62. See, e.g., Jacob de Voragine, *The Golden Legend*, part 2, September 22 (Saint Maurice and His Companions). See also *Acta Sanctorum*, September, vol. 6, p. 308. The story relates that the emperor Maximian (r.286–305, 306–308 C.E.), sent by Diocletian (r.284–305) during his persecution of Christians, ordered the Theban Legion, led by Maurice, to sacrifice to idols. When they refused, all but a few were slain.

63. 4 Kings (2 Kings) 14.5–6.

64. Proverbs 20.26.

65. But see Thomas Aquinas, *Summa Theologiae*, 2.2.42.2, ad 3, where Thomas argues that unless worse harm is caused by rebelling it is not sedition to overthrow a tyrant; rather, it is the tyrant who is seditious.

multitude can, not unjustly, depose a king that they instituted or bridle his power, if he should abuse the royal power tyrannically. Nor should such a multitude be thought to be acting unfaithfully when it abandons the tyrant, even if it had previously subjected itself to him in perpetuity, because he deserved to have his subjects not preserve their pact with him by not behaving faithfully in the government of the multitude, as the office of king demands.

[8] Thus, the Romans ejected Tarquin the Proud, whom they had elevated as king, from the kingdom, because of his tyranny and that of his sons, and substituted a lesser power, namely the consular power.[66] Thus also the Roman Senate killed Domitian, who succeeded his father, Vespasian, and brother, Titus, very moderate emperors, when he exercised tyranny.[67] Through a *senatusconsultum*[68] they justly and beneficially revoked and made void all the things that he did perversely to the Romans. By this same *senatusconsultum* the Blessed John the Evangelist, the beloved disciple of God, whom Domitian had relegated to exile in Patmos, was allowed to go back to Ephesus.

[9] But if it pertains to the right of a superior to provide a king for a multitude, they must wait for a remedy for the worthlessness of the tyrant from that superior. This happened to Archelaus, who had already begun to reign in Judea in place of his father, Herod, and was imitating his father's evil, when the Jews took a complaint to Caesar Augustus against him. First, his power was diminished by taking the royal name away from him and by dividing half of his kingdom between his two brothers; then, when this did not curb his tyranny, Tiberius Caesar exiled him to Lyons, a city of Gaul.[69]

66. Augustine, *The City of God*, 5.12. Lucius Tarquinius the Proud (r.534–510 B.C.E.) was, according to Roman legend, the last of the seven kings of early Roman history. See note at 4.26.1.

67. Vespasian (r.69–79 C.E.), Titus (r.79–81), and Domitian (r.81–96) were the three Flavian emperors of Rome. Augustine, *The City of God*, 5.21, mentions Vespasian and Titus as good and Domitian as evil, but does not mention the assassination or the Senate. See also Eutropius, *A Brief History of Rome*, 7.23, which correctly states that he was killed in a palace conspiracy, although his actions against them had earned the hatred of the senators, who applauded his downfall. Domitian was especially reviled by Christians because of the intense persecution he sponsored, which according to legend resulted in the exile of the Apostle John.

68. A decree of the senate.

69. Josephus, *The Wars of the Jews*, 2.6–7. According to Josephus (and historically), it was Augustus (not Tiberius (r.14–37 C.E.)) who exiled Archelaus to "Vienna, a city of Gaul" (not Lyons). Herod Archelaus (r.4 B.C.E.–6 C.E.) was the fourth son of Herod the Great (r.37–4 B.C.E.), under whom Jesus was born according to the Bible. Herod the Great was the Roman-supported king of Judaea and Samaria as well as other territories including Galilee. Archelaus succeeded to the kingship, while two other sons became tetrarchs of Herod's other territories. A cruel ruler, he was denounced by Jews and Samaritans, as a result of which Augustus banished him and converted Judaea into a Roman province. The order of events here is misleading. According to Josephus, the Jews complained to Rome at the start of the reign and again nine years later, but the author of the first part compresses these events. Augustus approved Archelaus's rule

[10] Certainly, if human aid against a tyrant is not to be had, recourse must be made to God, the king of all, who is, "a helper in due time in tribulations."[70] For his might can convert the heart of a tyrant from cruelty into gentleness, according to Solomon's statement in Proverbs: "The heart of a king is in the hand of God, and it will go wherever he has willed."[71] He turned the cruelty of King Ahasuerus, who was preparing death for the Jews, into gentleness.[72] It was he who converted cruel King Nebuchadnezzar so that he proclaimed the divine might: "Now, therefore, I, Nebuchadnezzar, praise and magnify and glorify the king of heaven, because his works are true and his ways judgments, and he can make humble those who are walking in pride."[73]

[11] He can also take away from their midst those tyrants whom he reputes unworthy of conversion or he can reduce them to the lowest state, according to the statement of the Wise One: "God has destroyed the seats of the proud leaders and made the gentle to sit in their place."[74] It is he who, seeing the affliction of his people in Egypt and hearing their clamor, threw the tyrant pharaoh and his army into the sea.[75] It is he who not only ejected Nebuchadnezzar, who had been full of pride, from the throne of his kingdom, but also ejected him from the fellowship of human beings by changing him into the likeness of a beast.[76]

[12] Nor is his hand shortened, so that he cannot liberate his people from tyrants.[77] For he promised his people through Isaiah that rest would be given to them from their labor and confusion, and from the harsh servitude in which they had previously served.[78] And through Ezekiel he says: "I will liberate my flock from their mouth,"[79] that is, from the mouth of the shepherds who feed themselves. But for the people to deserve to obtain this benefit from God, it ought to cease from its sins, for divine permission gives rule over the impious

---

from the start only on the condition that he did not take the title of king, but rather "ethnarch," and the division of Herod's kingdom also occured immediately after his death and according to his will. Thus, Augustus never took the regal title away from him.

70. Psalms 9.10 (9–10A.10).
71. Proverbs 21.1.
72. Esther 15.11 (D.8) and passim.
73. Daniel 4.34.
74. Ecclesiasticus (Sirach) 10.17.
75. Exodus 14.23–28, 15.1, 4.
76. Daniel 4.28–30. Nebuchadnezzar II (d.562 B.C.E.), king of the neo-Babylonian empire, conquered Judah, including Jerusalem and exiled many of the Jewish elite to Babylon, the so-called "Babylonian Captivity."
77. Isaias (Isaiah) 59.1.
78. Isaias (Isaiah) 14.3, 58.11.
79. Ezechiel (Ezekiel) 34.10.

as vengeance for their sin,[80] as the Lord says through Hosea: "I will give you a king in my anger";[81] and in Job it is said: "He makes a hypocrite reign because of the sins of the people."[82] Therefore, its fault must be taken away so that the plague of tyrants might cease.

Chapter 8

Opinions and conclusions in the matter of whether honor or glory
ought especially to motivate a king in his governing.

[1] Since according to what I have said it pertains to a king to seek the good of the multitude, the office of king would be exceedingly onerous if it did not produce some good for him alone. Therefore, we must consider what the suitable reward for a good king should be. To some, this seems to be nothing other than honor and glory. Cicero, in *On the Republic*, declares that the ruler of a city should be nourished with glory,[83] and Aristotle seems to give as a reason for this that, "the ruler to whom honor and glory does not suffice becomes a tyrant."[84] For it inheres in everyone's spirit to seek their own good. Therefore, a ruler who was not content with glory and honor would seek to fulfill desires for pleasure and riches and be thus converted to robbing and injuring the subjects.

[2] If we should accept this opinion, several unsuitable consequences would ensue. First, it would be harmful to kings to endure such great labor and solicitude for so fragile a wage. Nothing in human affairs seems more fragile than the glory and honor of human favor, since it depends on human opinion, than which nothing is more mutable in human life. So the prophet Isaiah calls glory of this kind, "hay flower."[85]

[3] Then also, the desire for human glory detracts from greatness of spirit. Those who seek the favor of human beings must necessarily serve their will in all that they say or do, and, being zealous to please all, they become everyone's servant. For this reason Cicero says in *On Duties* that we must guard

---

80. Isidore of Seville, *Etymologies*, 3.48.11; Gregory I the Great, *Morals in Job*, 25.16.34, on Job 34.30.
81. Osee (Hosea) 13.11.
82. Job 34.30.
83. Cicero, *On the Republic*, 5.7.9; reported in Augustine, *The City of God*, 5.13.
84. Aristotle, *Ethics*, 5.6.1134b.7.
85. Isaias (Isaiah) 40.6.

against the desire for glory. It snatches away the liberty of the spirit, from which all the contentment of great-spirited men ought to come.[86] But nothing is more fitting to a ruler instituted for the pursuit of good things than greatness of spirit. Therefore, the reward of human glory is insufficient for the office of king.

[4] Having such a reward for rulers is also harmful to the multitude. The duty of a good man demands that he be contemptuous of glory, as of other temporal goods. For, on behalf of justice, the virtuous and brave spirit is characteristically contemptuous of glory, as also of life. From this something odd ensues: that because glory follows virtuous acts, but glory itself is condemned by the virtuous, from contempt of glory a person is rendered glorious. According to Fabius's statement, the one who spurns glory will have true glory,[87] and as Sallust said about Cato, the less one seeks glory, the more one will attain it.[88] Even the disciples of Christ showed themselves as ministers of God "through glory and obscurity, through ill-fame and good report."[89] Therefore, glory, which the good condemn, is not a suitable reward for a good man. If, therefore, this good alone were established as a reward for rulers, it would follow that good men would not take up rule, or if they should take it up they would be unrewarded.

[5] Further, dangerous evils come from the desire for glory. Many who have immoderately sought glory in war ruined themselves and their armies and brought the liberty of their fatherland under a hostile power. Torquatus, a Roman ruler, in an example of avoiding this risk, "killed his son, who, when provoked, attacked the enemy with youthful ardor against his father's command, so that the evil resulting from this example of contempt for command would not be greater than the good from the glory of crushing the enemy."[90]

[6] There is another vice intimately associated with desire for glory, and that is simulation. Because it is difficult to achieve true virtues, and few succeed in

---

86. Cicero, *On Duties*, 1.20.68.
87. Livy, *History of Rome*, 22.39. Fabius Maximus (d.203 B.C.E.) was consul, censor, dictator, and army commander. He is famous for avoiding defeat by Hannibal in the Second Punic War by the "Fabian" strategy of quick strikes against the enemy and backing away from major battles.
88. Sallust, *The War with Cataline*, 54.6, reported in Augustine, *The City of God*, 5.12. Cato the Younger (95–46 B.C.E.), a Stoic philosopher, tribune, military praetor, and quaestor, opposed Cataline and Caesar, and committed suicide after Caesar's victory.
89. 2 Corinthians 6.8.
90. Augustine, *The City of God*, 5.18. Titus Manlius Imperiosus Torquatus was a fourth-century B.C.E. Roman general, dictator, and consul who fought against the Gauls. While consul, he killed his son in 340.

it, although it is this alone to which honor is due, many who desire glory become simulators of virtues. As Sallust says: "Ambition has compelled many mortals to become false, to have one thing shut up in their breast, another ready on the tongue, and to have a better appearance than nature."[91] Our Savior also calls them hypocrites, that is simulators, who do good works in order to have persons see them doing them.[92] Therefore, just as it is dangerous to the multitude if rulers seek pleasures and riches for a reward, since they may become insolent and robbers, so also is it dangerous when glory is reserved as a reward, since rulers may become presumptuous and simulators.

[7] It is apparent that it was not the intention of the wise ones mentioned above to have decided on honor and glory as a reward because kings' intentions ought principally to be directed to them, but because it is more tolerable for them to seek glory than to desire money or pleasure. And, actually, this vice is close to being a virtue, since the glory that persons desire is, as Augustine says, nothing other than "the judgment of persons when they think well of other persons."[93] The desire for glory has some vestige of virtue, at least when it seeks the approbation of the good and refuses to displease them. Therefore, since few achieve true virtue, it seems to be more tolerable if someone be preferred for government who fears human judgment and thus is restrained from manifest evils.

[8] One who desires glory either tries for human approval in the true way through the works of virtue, or at least contends for it by fraud and deceit.[94] But someone who does not have the desire for glory who desires to exercise lordship will not fear to displease those who judge well and will usually seek to obtain what is desired by the most open crimes. Such a one surpasses the beasts in the vices of cruelty and indulgence. A clear example is Nero Caesar, who "was so indulgent that," as Augustine says: "it would be thought that there was nothing virile to be feared from him; yet, so great was his cruelty it would be thought that he was not soft at all."[95] Aristotle expresses this quite well in what he says about the magnanimous—that they do not seek honor and glory as a great thing, which could be a sufficient reward for virtue, but

---

91. Sallust, *The War with Cataline*, 10.5.
92. Matthew 6.5.
93. Augustine, *The City of God*, 5.12.
94. Sallust, *The War with Cataline*, 11.1–2; reported in Augustine, *The City of God*, 5.12, 5.19.
95. Augustine, *The City of God*, 5.19. The rule of the emperor Nero (r.54–68 C.E.) began well, but he was soon noted for his cruelty and profligate life style. He was reviled by Christians for instituting the first major persecution of their religion.

that they demand nothing more than these from humans.[96] For, of all earthly things, what seems to come first is that humans testify to the virtue of others.

Chapter 9

What kind of true end does a king have, which ought to motivate him to govern well?

[1] Since, therefore, worldly honor and human glory is not a sufficient reward for the royal solicitude, it remains to inquire what sort of reward is sufficient. It is suitable for kings to expect their reward from God, for ministers expect the reward for their ministry from their lord, but kings, by exercising governance over their people, are ministers of God. Paul says that all power is from the Lord God,[97] and that "they are ministers of God, avengers in wrath against those who act badly,"[98] and also in the book of Wisdom kings are described as ministers of God.[99] Therefore, kings ought to expect the reward for their government from God.

[2] God sometimes compensates kings for their *ministerium* with temporal goods, but such rewards are common to the good and the bad.[100] As the Lord says in Ezekiel: "Nebuchadnezzar, king of Babylon, made his army serve under great servitude against Tyre . . . and there is no wage given to him or to his army for Tyre, for the servitude by which he rendered service to me against it,"[101] namely for that servitude by which powers, according to Paul, "are the ministers of God, avengers in wrath against those who act badly."[102] Afterward, the Lord does mention a reward: "Therefore, the Lord God says: 'Behold, I will send Nebuchadnezzar, king of Babylon, into the land of Egypt, and he will plunder its spoils, and it will be the wage of his army.'"[103]

[3] If, therefore, the Lord compensates iniquitous kings with such a great wage for fighting against the enemies of God, although not with the intention of serving God but pursuing their own hatreds and desires, that he gives

---

96. Aristotle, *Ethics*, 4.3.1124a.16–19.
97. Romans 13.1.
98. Romans 13.4.
99. Wisdom 6.5.
100. Augustine, *The City of God*, 1.8.
101. Ezechiel (Ezekiel) 29.18.
102. Romans 13.4.
103. Ezechiel (Ezekiel) 29.19.

them victory over their enemies, subjects kingdoms to them, and provides spoils for them to plunder, what will he do for good kings, who with pious intention govern the people of God and attack his enemies? Instead of a terrestrial wage, he promises them an eternal one in no one other than himself, as Peter says to the shepherds of the people of God: "Feed the flock of God among you, so that when the Ruler of Shepherds comes," that is, the King of Kings, Christ, "you will receive a never-fading crown of glory."[104] Concerning this, Isaiah says: "The Lord will be a garland of exultation and a diadem of glory to his people."[105]

[4] Moreover, this is manifest by reason, for it is implanted in the minds of all who use reason that beatitude is the reward of virtue. Any virtue can be described as that which makes the thing that has it good and renders its work good. Moreover, everyone strives by working well to achieve that which is especially implanted in the desire. This is to be happy, which no one can not want.[106] Therefore, one may suitably expect as a reward that which makes a person blessed. But if to work well is the work of virtue, and the work of a king is to govern his subjects well, that also will be the reward of a king which will make him blessed.

[5] I must now consider what this is. We say that beatitude is the ultimate end of our desires. The motion of desire can not continue infinitely; otherwise, natural desire would be in vain, since we can not transverse infinities.[107] Since the desire of an intellectual nature is for universal good, that good alone could make one truly blessed by which, once it is obtained, there is no good remaining to be further desired. For this reason beatitude is called the perfect good, since it, as it were, comprehends all desirable things in itself.[108] But no

---

104. 1 Peter 5.2, 4.
105. Isaias (Isaiah) 28.5.
106. Aristotle, *Ethics*, 2.6.1106a.15–24. As noted above (1.4.2n.), Aristotle defines virtue as action in accordance with true ends or functions, that is, any excellence at all. Thus, it can apply to inanimate as well as animate objects. The example he gives at this point is the virtue of the eye, which makes both the eye and its work good, since it is through the eye's virtue that we see well. See also Thomas Aquinas, *Summa Theologiae*, 1.2.1.6.7. For the question of human happiness see Thomas Aquinas, *Summa contra Gentiles*, 3.27–37 and *Summa Theologiae*, 1.2.2.
107. Thomas Aquinas, *Summa contra Gentiles*, 3.25.9. This statement is rather confusing unless we understand the Aristotelian notion of teleological causation. The final cause, that is, the end, of any created thing imparts a natural inclination (or desire) in the thing that draws it to that end. In this sense natural desire is seen as a motion toward a proper end. If this end could not be realized in a finite time or in a finite number of steps (which, not understanding the idea of a convergent infinite sequence, Aristotle and the medieval thinkers believe amounts to the same thing), the final cause would be an unreachable one, and this contradicts the belief that nature does nothing in vain.
108. Aristotle, *Ethics*, 1.1.1094a.18–22.

earthly good is such, for those who have riches desire to have more, and the same thing is apparent with other goods. Even if they do not seek more, they desire that those things be permanent, or that other things succeed in their place. Nothing permanent is found in earthly things, so nothing earthly can quiet desire. Therefore, nothing earthly can make one blessed, and so no such thing can be a suitable reward for a king.

[6] Further, the final perfection and complete good of anything depends on something superior, because even corporal things are made better when better things are added, but worse, if they are mixed with worse things. If gold is mixed with silver, the silver is made better, but it is made impure from an admixture of lead. It has been established that all earthly things are beneath the human mind, and that beatitude is the final perfection and complete good of a human, which all desire to achieve. Therefore, there is nothing earthly that could make a person blessed; nor, therefore, is there anything earthly which is a sufficient reward for a king. As Augustine says:

> We do not call Christian rulers happy because they have commanded for a long time, or because after a peaceful death they have left their children as emperors, or because they have tamed the enemies of the Republic, or because they were able both to be on their guard against and oppress citizens rising up against them; rather, we call them happy if they command justly, if they prefer to command their desires than any nation, if they do all things not on account of empty ardor for glory, but because of the love of eternal felicity. Such Christian emperors we call happy, at present in hope, afterward in the thing itself in that future when that which we expect will have arrived.[109]

[7] Neither is there some other created thing that might make a person blessed and so could be chosen as a reward for a king. For the desire of anything at all tends to its origin, from which comes the cause of its being.[110] But the cause of the human mind is nothing other than God, who makes it after his own image. Therefore, it is God alone who can quiet the desire of a person, make a person blessed, and be a suitable reward for a king.

---

109. Augustine, *The City of God*, 5.24.

110. Thomas Aquinas, *Summa contra Gentiles*, 3.25.10–11. Here Thomas explains that in a series of causes, the end of the first cause must be the end of all. Therefore, we naturally desire, as our final cause, to know the first cause. Since the first cause of all is God, our final cause is to know God.

[8] Further, the human mind has knowledge of the universal good through the intellect and desire of it through the will, but the universal good is found nowhere but in God. Therefore, there is nothing that could fulfill desire and make a person blessed except God, about whom it is said in the Psalms: "He fulfills your desire with good things."[111] The king, therefore, ought to seek his reward in this. In regard to this, King David said: "What is in heaven for me, and what do I want on the earth other than you?"[112] Afterward, he adds, responding to this question: "It is good for me to adhere to God and to place my hope in the Lord God."[113] For it is he who gives salvation to kings; not only temporal salvation, by which he saves persons and beasts of burden alike, but even that salvation about which he says through Isaiah: "But my salvation will be everlasting,"[114] by which he saves human beings and leads them to equality with the angels.

[9] It can thus be verified that the reward of a king is honor and glory. What worldly and transitory honor can be similar to this honor, that a person should be a citizen and a member of the household of God[115] and, being counted among the children of God, obtain the inheritance of the heavenly kingdom with Christ? This is an honor which King David desired and wondered at, saying: "Your friends are exceedingly honorable, God."[116] Besides, what glory of human praise can be compared to this, which is not proffered by the false tongues of flatterers and deceived human opinion, but is produced from the testimony of interior conscience and confirmed by the testimony of God, who promised in return to those who confess him that he will confess them in the glory of the father in the presence of the angels of God?[117] Those who seek this glory find it, and they also achieve the human glory that they do not seek, as the example of Solomon shows. Not only did he receive wisdom, which he sought, from the Lord, but he was also made glorious above other kings.[118]

---

111. Psalms 102.5 (103.5).
112. Psalms 72.25 (73.25).
113. Psalms 72.28 (73.28.).
114. Isaias (Isaiah) 51.6.
115. Ephesians 2.19.
116. Psalms 138.17 (139.17, although the New American Bible refers to preciousness of design rather than honorableness of friends).
117. Matthew 10.32; Luke 12.8.
118. 3 Kings (1 Kings) 10.23.

Chapter 10

Many reasons and examples show that the reward of kings and rulers raises them to the highest rank of heavenly beatitude.

[1] It remains to consider that those who execute the royal office worthily and laudably will obtain both eminence and rank in heavenly beatitude. If beatitude is the reward of virtue, it follows that a greater degree of beatitude is owed to a greater virtue. Moreover, it is a special virtue by which persons can direct not only themselves but also others,[119] and the more it governs many, the more special it is. This is also true of bodily force, for those are reputed to be more forceful to the extent that they can conquer many or lift more weights. Therefore, greater virtue is required for governing the domestic household than for ruling oneself, and much greater for the government of a city or kingdom. Exercising the office of kings is, therefore, an exceptional virtue, to which an exceptional reward of beatitude is owed.

[2] Further, in every art[120] and potency, those are more laudable who govern others well than those who conduct themselves well according to another's direction. In speculative matters, it is greater to pass on the truth to others by teaching than to be able to grasp that which is taught. In crafts, an architect who designs a building is deemed greater, and receives a greater reward, than an artisan who implements the architect's design manually. In matters of war, the prudence of the leader leads to greater glory in the victory than the fortitude of the knight. But rectors of the multitude are in a similar position with regard to those things which are to be done by individuals according to virtue as professors in the academic disciplines, architects in building, and leaders in wars. The king is, therefore, worthy of a greater reward, if he guides his subjects well, than any of his subjects, if they conduct themselves well under the king.

[3] Further, if it is characteristic of virtue to render the work of a person good, it seems as if working a greater good would be characteristic of a greater virtue. But the good of a multitude is greater and more divine than the good of one.[121] Sometimes someone's evil is endured if this results in the good of the

---

119. Aristotle, *Ethics*, 5.1.1129b.31–1130a.1; *Rhetoric*, 1.9.1366b.3–5.

120. Some versions have "*actibus*," "acts," instead of "*artibus*," "arts," which seems to make the two items more consistent.

121. Aristotle, *Ethics*, 1.3.1094b.7–10; Thomas Aquinas, *Summa contra Gentiles*, 3.71.7. Aristotle says that the end of a polity is greater than that of a single person, and Thomas that the good of the whole is greater than the good of the part.

multitude, just as a thief is killed to give peace to the multitude. God himself would not permit evils to exist in the world unless he could elicit good things from them for the utility and beauty of the universe.[122] It pertains to the office of a king zealously to procure the good of the multitude, so a greater reward is owed to a king for a good government than to a subject for good action.

[4] This will become more obvious if we consider some more particulars. Private personages receive human praise, and God reckons them to be worthy of reward, if they assist the needy, if they pacify the discordant, if they snatch the oppressed from the more potent; in short, if they confer help or counsel on others in any way whatever for their well being. How much more, therefore, must those who make a whole province rejoice in peace, who hinder violence, who serve justice, who with their laws and precepts determine what persons should do receive human praise and be rewarded by God?

[5] Here the magnitude of royal virtue is apparent, which is similar to that of God, doing in the kingdom what God does in the world.[123] For this reason, the judges of the multitude are called gods in Exodus.[124] The Roman emperors were also called gods. But the more something is acceptable to God, the more it approaches imitation of him. As Paul warns: "Be, therefore, imitators of God, as most dear children."[125] If, according to the statement of the Wise One, "every animal loves one similar to itself,"[126] since causes are to some degree similar to that which is caused, it follows that good kings are most acceptable to God and are to be most rewarded by him.

[6] At the same time, if I may use the words of Gregory:

> What is a tempest at sea but a tempest of the mind? When the sea is quiet, even someone who is unexperienced directs the ship correctly, but when the sea is stirred up from the waves of a tempest, even the experienced sailor is confounded. It is also often true in the occupation of government, that the practice of good work is lost, which was preserved in periods of tranquility.[127]

---

122. Thomas Aquinas, *Summa contra Gentiles*, 3.71.7.

123. John of Salisbury, *Policraticus*, 8.17 is only one example of this common doctrine which goes back to Hellenistic political thought. See below 1.13.3.

124. Exodus 22.9.

125. Ephesians 5.1.

126. Ecclesiasticus (Sirach) 13.19.

127. Gregory I the Great, *Pastoral Regulation*, 1.9. There are several textual variants to "*tempestas maris*," tempest of the sea: "*sublimitas regis*," "height of a king," or "*potestas culminis*," "sum-

As Augustine says, it is extremely difficult for them not to be "puffed up amidst the tongues of those who puff up and honor them, and the obsequiousness of those who greet them with exceptional humility, but to remember that they are human beings."[128] And in Ecclesiasticus: "Blessed is the man who does not turn aside after gold, nor put his hope in hordes of money; who could transgress with impunity and does not transgress; who could do evil and does not do it."[129] Having been proved, as it were, in the work of virtue, he is found to be faithful, according to the proverb of Bias: "Rule shows the man."[130] Many who arrive at the summit of rule abandon virtue, who, when they were in a low state, seemed to be virtuous. Therefore, the very difficulty of acting well that threatens rulers makes them worthy of a greater reward. If sometimes they should sin through weakness, they are rendered more excusable among human beings and may be promised indulgence more easily by God, as long as, as Augustine says, they do not neglect to bring as an offering for their sins to their own true God the sacrifice of their humility, mercy, and prayer.[131] As an example of this the Lord said to Elijah about Ahab, king of Israel, who had sinned much: "Because Ahab was humbled, I will not introduce this evil in his days."[132]

[7] Divine authority confirms what reason shows—that kings are owed an excellent reward. It is said in Zechariah[133] that on that day of beatitude in which the Lord will be the protector of those living in Jerusalem, that is in the vision of eternal peace, the houses of others will be as the house of David, which means that all will be kings and will reign with Christ, as members with the head. But the house of David will be as the house of God, because just as he had carried out the office of God among the people by governing faithfully,

---

mit of power." The clauses are in a different order from that found in Gregory. Although the first line (which comes last in Gregory) seems confusing at first, it makes perfect sense if we take the tempest as an allegorical representation of mental torment. For a similar and interesting analogy between real and mental tempests, with reference to Apuleius's comments on the self-torments of demons, see Augustine, *The City of God*, 9.3.

128. Augustine, *The City of God*, 5.24.

129. Ecclesiasticus (Sirach) 31.8, 10. A slight variation from the Vulgate text, which says: "Blessed is the rich one" and does not include "with impunity."

130. Aristotle, *Ethics*, 5.1.1130a.1–2. Bias was a sixth-century B.C.E. political figure in Priene in Ionia. Only a few of his political aphorisms survive, which suggest that he was a political pragmatist. He was one of the Seven Wise Men of ancient Greece, whom Plato lists as Thales, Pittacus, Bias, Solon, Cleobulus, Chilon, and Myson of Chen, but there are many variations, especially Periander instead of Myson.

131. Augustine, *The City of God*, 5.24.

132. 3 Kings (1 Kings) 21.29.

133. Zacharias (Zechariah) 12.8. Zechariah, of course, says nothing about beatitude, eternal peace, or Christ.

so in his reward he will be closer to God and will cleave more closely to him. The gentiles also somewhat understood this as in a dream, when they thought that the rectors and preservers of their cities were transformed into gods.

Chapter 11

The king and ruler ought to be zealous for good government because this is good and useful for themselves, but the opposite follows from tyrannical government.

[1] Since kings are offered such a grand reward of celestial beatitude if they conduct themselves well in governing, they ought to watch themselves diligently, so that they do not change into tyrants. Nothing should be more acceptable to them than to be translated from the royal honor, by which they are elevated in their lands, to the glory of the celestial kingdom. But tyrants who go astray for the sake of terrestrial convenience abandon justice and are deprived of the great reward that they could have acquired by governing justly. No one but a fool or an infidel could be ignorant that it is foolish to lose the greatest and sempeternal goods for the sake of trivial, temporal things of this sort.

[2] I must also add that even these temporal conveniences, for which tyrants abandon justice, accrue to the advantage of kings when they serve justice.

[3] Among all worldly things there is nothing which seems worthy of being preferred to friendship. It is this which unites the virtuous and conserves and promotes virtue. It is this which all need to transact any of their affairs; it does not inflict itself importunely on them in prosperity, nor desert them in adversity. It is this which produces the greatest pleasure, so much so that whatever is delectable becomes tedious without friends. Whatever is harsh, love makes easy and seem almost like nothing; nor is there any tyrant, however cruel, who is not delighted by friendship. When Dionysius, once tyrant of Syracuse, wanted to kill one of two friends called Damon and Pythias, the one who was to be killed asked for a delay to go home and order his affairs, and the other friend gave himself to the tyrant as a surety for the other's return. When the promised day approached, and the friend had not returned, everyone accused the surety of foolishness. But he proclaimed that he had no fears for his friend's constancy, and at the very hour in which he was to be killed his friend returned. The tyrant approved the spirit of both, remitted the penalty

because of the faith of their friendship, and asked that they should receive him as a third in the ranks of their friendship.[134]

[4] Although tyrants desire the good of friendship, they cannot get it. Since they do not seek the common good, but their own, there is little or no communion between them and their subjects, but all firm friendships depend on some communion.[135] We see that friendships are entered into by those who have something in common, either natural origin, similarity of customs, or communion in any society. Therefore, there is little, or rather no, friendship between a tyrant and a subject, and when subjects are oppressed by tyrannical injustice and feel themselves to be despised, not loved, there can be no love at all. Nor do tyrants have any reason to complain about their subjects if they are not loved by them, because they do not show themselves to be such that they ought to be loved by them. But the many love good kings who zealously intend the common profit, since the subjects feel that they receive many benefits from this zeal and since the kings demonstrate that they love their subjects. It would be a greater evil than is possible if a multitude viewed their friends with hatred and paid back the good of their benefactors with evil.

[5] As a result of this love the kingdom of good kings is stable, since their subjects do not refuse to expose themselves to any dangers for them. Suetonius reports a clear example of this in Julius Caesar, who loved his knights so much that when he heard that some of them had fallen, he did not cut his hair or shave before he had avenged them. By such things he made his knights exceptionally devoted to him and vigorous, so that when captured many of them refused to save their own life on the condition that they would be willing to serve in the military against Caesar.[136] So much did his subjects love Octavian Augustus, who was very moderate in his use of command, that when they were dying many of them mandated an immolation of sacrificial victims to give thanks that he had survived them.[137] Therefore, it is not easy

134. Cicero, *Tusculan Disputations*, 5.63; Valerius Maximus, *Memorable Deeds and Sayings*, 4.7, ext. 1. See below 3.7.2, 4.22.2. The Damon and Pythias (more correctly, Phintias) story usually specifies the tyrant as Dionysius I (r.c.430–367 B.C.E.), not Dionysius II (r.367–345), but Valerius, to whom Ptolemy specifically refers below, does not.

135. Aristotle, *Ethics*, 8.9.1159b.25–35.

136. Suetonius, *The Twelve Caesars*, "Julius Caesar," 67–68. Gaius Julius Caesar (100–44 B.C.E.) was a Roman consul, general, dictator, and historian. He was assassinated by senators who feared his increasing power. He is considered the founder of the Roman Empire, even though Augustus was the first official emperor.

137. Suetonius, *The Twelve Caesars*, "Augustus," 59. Octavian (r.27 B.C.E.–14 C.E.; Augustus was an honorary title bestowed later) was the adopted son of Julius Caesar and the first Roman Emperor.

to perturb the lordship of a ruler whom the people love so consensually. As Solomon says: "The throne of the king who judges the paupers with justice will be made firm in eternity."[138]

[6] But the lordship of tyrants can not last long, since it is odious to the multitude. For what is repugnant to the wishes of the many can not long be preserved. One can scarcely go through the present life without enduring some adversities. In a time of adversity the occasion cannot be lacking to rise up against the tyrant, and where the occasion is present there will not be lacking one of the many who will use it. The people will ardently follow the one who rises up, and that which is attempted with the favor of the multitude will not easily be without effect. Therefore, it can scarcely happen that the lordship of a tyrant be extended for a long time.

[7] This is also completely apparent if one considers how a tyrant's lordship is preserved. It is not preserved by love, since there is little or no friendship between a subject multitude and a tyrant, as is clear from what I said above. Nor can tyrants trust in the faith of their subjects. For no multitude has such great virtue that the virtue of fidelity would restrain it from shaking off, if it could, the yoke of undeserved servitude. And perhaps in the opinion of many it is not contrary to fidelity to resist tyrannical wickedness in any way at all. What is left, therefore, is that the government of tyrants is sustained by fear alone, which is why they take care with all their intention to be feared by their subjects.

[8] But fear is a weak foundation. If the occasion arises in which they can hope for impunity, those whom fear subdues rise up more ardently against those who preside the more they were restrained against their will by fear alone, just as if water is kept in forcefully, it will flow more impetuously when it finds an opening. Fear itself is not without danger, since many fall into desperation from excessive fear, and despair of well being makes one hasten to try anything. Therefore, the lordship of a tyrant cannot be long-lasting.

[9] This is as apparent from examples as it is from reason. If we consider the deeds of the ancients and modern events, we would almost never find that the lordship of any tyrant was long-lasting. Aristotle lists many tyrants and demonstrates that each one's lordship was limited to a short time, and that those

138. Proverbs 29.14.

who were in charge longer lasted only because theirs was not a very excessive tyranny, but in many things imitated regal moderation.[139]

[10] This becomes still more clear when we consider divine justice. As is said in Job: "He makes a hypocrite reign because of the sins of the people."[140] But there is no one more truly a hypocrite than one who assumes the office of king and shows himself to be a tyrant. For one is called a hypocrite who portrays the persona of another, as was customary in theatrical spectacles. Therefore, God permits tyrants to be placed in authority to punish the subjects' sins. This punishment is customarily called "the wrath of God" in Scripture. As the Lord says through Hosea: "I will give you a king in my anger."[141] But unhappy is the king who is conceded to the people through the anger of God. His lordship can not be stable, because "God will not forget to be compassionate, nor will he hold back his compassion in his wrath";[142] rather, as is said through Joel: "He is patient with much compassion and exalted over evil."[143] Therefore, God does not permit tyrants to reign for long, but after they bring a tempest to the people, he introduces tranquility by casting them down. As Wisdom says: "God destroys the seat of proud leaders and makes the meek sit in their place."[144]

[11] It is also apparent from experience that kings acquire more riches through justice than tyrants do through robbery. Because the tyrants' lordship is not pleasing to the subjected multitude, it is necessary for them to have many attendants to keep them safe from their subjects, for which they must spend more than they can rob from their subjects.[145] But the lordship of kings, which pleases their subjects, is guarded by all the subjects acting as attendants, for which they must spend nothing; and sometimes, when it is necessary, they give more things to kings of their own accord than tyrants could seize. Thus is fulfilled what Solomon says: "Some," namely kings, "divide their own possessions," for benefiting their subjects, "and become richer; others," namely tyrants, "seize what is not their own, and are always in need."[146] In the same way, by the just judgment of God, those who unjustly gather riches dis-

---

139. Aristotle, *Politics*, 5.12.1315b.11–39. Aristotle says that those who lasted showed moderation, but does not associate this with regal rule.

140. Job 34.30.

141. Osee (Hosea) 13.11.

142. Psalms 76.10 (77.10).

143. Joel 2.13.

144. Ecclesiasticus (Sirach) 10.17.

145. Aristotle, *Politics*, 3.14.1284a.25–27 says that tyrants use mercenaries for guards.

146. Proverbs 11.24.

perse them uselessly, or else their riches are justly taken away from them. As Solomon says: "One who is avaricious will not be fulfilled by money, and one who loves riches will harvest no fruit from them."[147] Rather, as Proverbs says: "Those who eagerly pursue avarice disturb their own house."[148] But God increases the riches of kings who seek justice, as with Solomon, who received the promise of abundant riches when he sought wisdom for doing justice.[149]

[12] It seems superfluous to speak about fame. For who would doubt that good kings live in human praise and are longed for, not only in life, but also in a certain way after death, but that the names of the evil either immediately disappear, or if they were exceptionally evil, are remembered with detestation? As Solomon says: "The just are remembered with praise, but the name of the impious will rot,"[150] because it either disappears or remains with a stench.

Chapter 12

Even worldly goods, such as riches, power, honor, and fame, accrue more to kings than to tyrants, and tyrants fall into evils even in this life.

[1] It is obvious from these arguments that stability of power and riches, honor and fame accrue more from the wishes of kings than of tyrants, and it is through getting these things undeservedly that a ruler declines into tyranny. For no one declines from justice unless they are drawn by the desire of some advantage.

[2] In addition, a tyrant is deprived of the exceptional beatitude owed to kings as a reward, and what is more serious, the greatest torment of punishments befalls them. If those who rob, drive into servitude, or kill a single person deserve the greatest penalty—a human judgment of death and the judgment of God of eternal damnation—how much worse a punishment do tyrants deserve, who rob everyone everywhere, who labor against the liberty of all, who, at the pleasure of their will, kill anyone? Besides, such ones are rarely penitent; they are inflated with the wind of pride, and since they are deservedly deserted by God for their sins and besmeared with human adulation, they can

---

147. Ecclesiastes 5.9.
148. Proverbs 15.27.
149. 3 Kings (1 Kings) 3.9–13, 2 Paralipomenon (2 Chronicles) 1.10–12.
150. Proverbs 10.7.

rarely make worthy satisfaction. When will they restore all those things which they have taken away beyond what justice owes them? Yet no one doubts that they are obliged to restore them. When will they pay back those whom they have oppressed and harmed unjustly in various ways?

[3] Their lack of penitence increases, since they reckon that whatever they can do with impunity and without resistance is licit for them; so that not only do they not bustle about making amends for the bad things that they did, but, taking their usage for authority, they transmit the boldness of their sinning to those who come after them. Thus, not only are they responsible before God for their own misdeeds, but also for the misdeeds of those to whom they provided the occasion of sin.

[4] Their sin is aggravated because of the dignity of the office that they have undertaken. Just as an earthly king punishes his own ministers more severely if he discovers that they are opposed to him, so God punishes those whom he made executors and ministers of his government more if they do badly, converting God's judgment into bitterness. In the book of Wisdom it is said to iniquitous kings:

> Since, when you were ministers of his kingdom, you did not judge rightly, nor guard the law of justice, nor walk according to the will of God, he will appear to you terrifyingly and quickly, since a most severe judgment will accrue to those who are in charge. For mercy is granted to the lowly, but the mighty will be afflicted mightily with torments.[151]

And through Isaiah it is said to Nebuchadnezzar: "You will be dragged down to hell, to the depths of the pit. Those who see you will turn to you and look at you,"[152] that is, as one who is more deeply submerged in punishment.

[5] If, therefore, an abundance of temporal goods accrues to kings, and God prepares an exceptional degree of beatitude for them, but tyrants are frustrated in acquiring the temporal goods which they commonly desire and are subjected to many dangers besides, and, what is more, they are deprived from having eternal goods and the most severe penalties are reserved for them, then those who take up the office of governing must be especially zealous to offer themselves to their subjects as kings, not as tyrants.

151. Wisdom 6.5–7.
152. Isaias (Isaiah) 14.15–16.

[6] I have now said a great many things about a king: what he is, that it is expedient for the multitude to have a king, and also that it is expedient for the chief one to show himself to the subject multitude as a king, not as a tyrant.

Chapter 13

The king's office: by nature he is in his kingdom just as the spirit is in the body and God is in the world.

[1] We must now consider what the office of king is and what sort of person a king ought to be. Since art imitates nature,[153] which teaches us how to work according to reason, it seems best to take up the office of king by looking at the form that natural government takes.

[2] We find both universal and particular government in the nature of things. The universal is that according to which all things fall under the government of God, who by his own providence exercises governance over the universe of things. The particular is a government especially similar to divine government. It is found in the human species, which is called the microcosm,[154] because the form of universal government is found in it. For reason governs the members of the body and the spiritual strengths, just as the divine government includes the universe of corporal creatures and all spiritual virtues. Thus, in a certain way reason holds the same place in the human species as God does in the world. But because, as I showed above,[155] a person is naturally social and lives in a multitude, something similar to divine government is found among humans, not only because each person is governed through reason, but also because the multitude is governed by the reason of one person, which is especially the case with the office of king. In certain other animals that live socially, we can also find something similar to this government; for example, it is said that there are kings among the bees.[156] This is not because government among them is through reason, but because the Highest One who governs, the Author of nature, has imparted a natural instinct in them.

---

153. Aristotle, *Physics*, 2.2.194a.21–22.

154. Ptolemy does not actually use this word, but rather "lesser world." See Aristotle, *Physics*, 8.2.252b.24–28, where Aristotle says that what happens in the lesser world can also happen in the greater. See also Gregory I the Great, *Homilies on the Gospels*, 2.29.

155. I.I.

156. A common misconception in ancient times and the Middle Ages. See, e.g., Aristotle, *History of Animals*, 5.21.553a.25.

[3] Therefore, let the king know that this is the office that he has taken up, that he in his kingdom is as the spirit in the body and God in the world.[157] If he diligently reflects on this, two things will happen. On the one hand, zealousness for justice will be kindled in him when he considers that he was put in this position so that he might exercise judgment in his kingdom in the place of God. On the other hand, he will acquire the gentle qualities of mildness and clemency, when he reckons individuals under his government as his own members.

Chapter 14

The king bases his mode of government on this similarity, so that just as God distinguishes all things by their order and in their proper function and place, so does the king with regard to his subjects in the kingdom. The spirit acts in the same way.

[1] We must, therefore, consider what God does in the world; from this it will become clear what a king should strive for. There are two works of God in the world as a whole for us to consider, one by which he founded the world, the other by which he exercises governance over the world that he founded. The spirit also effects these two works in the body. First, the body is given form by virtue of the spirit, which then governs and moves the body.

[2] Of these, the second more properly pertains to the office of king. Governance pertains to all kings, and the very name "king" comes from the government associated with governance.[158] But the first work is not suitable for all kings. Not all found the kingdom or city in which they govern, but, rather, they devote themselves to the care of the government of a city that has already been founded. Nevertheless, we must consider that unless one had come before to found the city or kingdom, governance of the kingdom would not be possible. Under the office of king we must therefore also include the founding of a city or kingdom. Some kings founded the cities in which they reigned, such as Ninus who founded Nineveh[159] and Romulus Rome.[160] It also per-

157. See above, 1.10.5.
158. Isidore of Seville, *Etymologies*, 1.29.3; 9.3.1, 4, 6; 7.12.14. "*Rex*" is "king," and every form of this word other than the nominative singular begins with the letters "*reg*"; "*regimen*" is "government."
159. Ninus was the legendary first king of Assyria and builder of Nineveh. According to Augustine, *The City of God*, 16.17, Ninus was an older contemporary of Abraham. See also Isidore of Seville, *Etymologies*, 8.11.
160. Romulus (r.753–717 B.C.E., according to legend) was the mythical founder of Rome and its first king.

tains to the office of governance to preserve the things over which governance is exercised and to use them for that which they are constituted. Therefore, one cannot fully know the office of governance, if the raison d'être for foundation is not understood.

[3] The raison d'être for the foundation of a kingdom must be taken from the example of the foundation of the world. First, we must consider the production of things, then the ordained distinction of parts of the world. We see that diverse species of things are distributed in various parts of the world, such as stars in the sky, birds in the air, fish in the water, and animals on the earth, and that the things that individuals need seem to be divinely provided in abundance. Moses has subtly and diligently expressed this raison d'être of foundation. First, he set out the production of things, saying: "In the beginning God created the heaven and the earth."[161] Then, he declares that all things were divinely distinguished according to a suitable order, namely day from night, the lower from the higher, and the sea from the dry land. Then, he reports that the sky was adorned with lights, the air with birds, the sea with fish, and the earth with animals. Finally, lordship of the earth and of animals was assigned to human beings, and he declares that divine providence gave them and the other animals the use of plants.[162]

[4] The one who founds a city or a kingdom cannot produce human beings and places for them to inhabit and other things to support their lives all over again, but must use those things preexisting in nature, just as the other arts take the material of their operation from nature. So, for example, in the practice of their art a metal worker uses iron or a builder wood and stone. Therefore, first of all it is necessary for the one who founds a city or a kingdom to choose a suitable place that will preserve the inhabitants by its healthfulness,[163] will suffice for their sustenance by its fruitfulness,[164] will delight them by its pleasantness,[165] and will render them safe by protecting them.[166] If it should lack any of these advantages, the place will be more suitable to the extent that it has more of the necessities that I mentioned or the more important of them.

161. Genesis 1.1.
162. Genesis 3.30.
163. See below 2.1–2.2.
164. See below 2.3.
165. See below 2.4.
166. Ptolemy does not have a separate section on this, although it is implicit and explicit in much of what he writes. The sections on the first three necessities are the last sections attributed to Thomas; Ptolemy completes the section on pleasantness, but does not follow the first author's scheme from there on.

[5] Then, it is necessary that the one who founds a city or a kingdom distinguish the parts of the chosen place according to the exigencies of those things which the perfection of the city or kingdom requires. So that if a kingdom is to be founded, it is necessary to decide what places are suitable for constituting cities, what for villages, what for castles, where the studies of letters should be constituted, where the knights should exercise, where business should be conducted, and so on for all the things that the perfection of the kingdom requires. But if the work of foundation is for a city, it is necessary that the the one who founds it decide what place should be appointed for sacred matters, what for handing down the law,[167] what for individual artisans. Further, it is necessary to gather together the persons who are to be assigned to suitable places according to their duties. Finally, one must provide for necessities to be at hand for individuals according to their individual constitutions and states; otherwise, the city or kingdom could never last.

[6] I give only a summary of those things which pertain to the office of king in the foundation of a city or a kingdom, and I have chosen them for their similarity to those in the foundation of the world.

Chapter 15

The mode of exercising governance suitable for a king is that of divine governance, and this mode of exercising governance arises from the governance of a ship.[168] A comparison of sacerdotal and regal lordship.

[1] Just as the foundation of a city or kingdom can be suitably derived from the form of foundation of the world, so also we must derive the raison d'être of governance from the governance of the world.

[2] At the outset we must consider that to exercise governance is to lead that, over which governance is exercised, suitably to its proper end. Thus, for example, governance is said to be exercised over a ship when the industry of the sailor conducts it unharmed on a correct route to the port. If, therefore, something is ordained to an end beyond itself, as a ship to a port, it pertains to the office of governance not only to preserve the thing safe in itself, but

---

167. *Ius.*
168. A reference to the etymology of "*gubernatio*," "governance," but also "piloting of a ship." "*Gubernator*" in its original and primary meaning means pilot.

also to conduct it to its end. If there is something whose end is not beyond itself, the intention of the governor should be directed solely to preserve that thing safe in its perfection.

[3] Although there are no such things except God himself, who is the end of all things, many things in many ways obstruct the care of that which is ordained to an external end. Perhaps someone has the responsibility of preserving something in its being, and someone else of having it achieve a higher perfection. This is completely apparent from the example of the ship, which shows the raison d'être of governance. The carpenter has responsibility for repairing anything in the ship that has fallen into ruin, but a sailor must be solicitous to conduct the ship to port. It is the same with human beings: a physician has the responsibility of preserving their healthful life, a steward of supplying their necessities of life, a professor of taking care that they know the truth, and someone who institutes morality that they live according to reason.

[4] If human beings were not ordained to another, external end, the responsibilities just mentioned would be enough for them. But there is a certain good extrinsic to human beings as long as we are in this mortal life, namely the final beatitude, to which we look forward after our death in the enjoyment of God. As Paul says: "As long as we are in the body, we are absent from God."[169] For this reason Christian persons, for whom Christ won that beatitude through his blood, and who accept the pledge of the Holy Spirit in order to pursue that beatitude, need spiritual care through which they may be directed to the port of eternal salvation. This care is shown to the faithful by the ministers of the Church of Christ.

[5] We must make the same judgment about the end of the whole multitude as we do of one person.[170] If, therefore, the end of a person were some good existing in that one alone, and the ultimate end of the multitude to be governed were similar in that the multitude should acquire such a good and preserve it, and if indeed such an ultimate end were a corporal one, either of one person or of the multitude, then the life and health of that body would be the duty of a physician. If the ultimate end were affluence and riches, a steward should be king of the multitude. If the good of knowing the truth were of the kind which the multitude could attain, the king would have the same duty as a professor.

---

169. 2 Corinthians 5.6.
170. Aristotle, *Politics*, 7.2.1324a.5–8; 1325b.31–32.

[6] It seems that the end of a multitude gathered together is to live according to virtue.[171] Human beings gather together so that they may live well together, which a single person living alone could not do.[172] A good life is one lived according to virtue; therefore, a virtuous life is the end of human congregation. A sign of this is that only those who share with each other in living well are parts of a congregated multitude. For if human beings gathered together only for the sake of living, animals and servants would be a part of the civil congregation.[173] If human beings gathered together for the sake of acquiring riches, all those who did business together would be parts of one city.[174] But we see that only those who are directed in living well by the same laws and the same government are reckoned to belong to one multitude.

[7] Because by living according to virtue human beings are ordained to a further end, which lies in divine enjoyment, as I said above, it is necessary for a human multitude to have the same end as one person. It is not, therefore, the ultimate end of a congregated multitude to live according to virtue, but through virtue to arrive at divine enjoyment.

[8] If it could attain this end by virtue of human nature, the office of king would necessarily include directing human beings to this end. For we assume that the king is the one to whom the highest government of human affairs is committed. A government is more sublime to the degree that it is ordained to a higher end. For the one to whom the highest end pertains is always found to command those whose job deals with the things that are ordained to the highest end,[175] just as a pilot, to whom it pertains to arrange for navigation, commands someone who builds a ship as to what kind of ship to make to be suitable for navigation, and just as a civil governor who uses arms orders the metal workers to make certain kinds of of arms. But because humans do not attain the end of divine enjoyment through human virtue, but through divine virtue, according to what Paul says: "By the grace of God, eternal life,"[176] to lead to that end will not pertain to human government, but to divine.

[9] Therefore, government of that kind pertains to that king who is not only a person, but also God, namely to our Lord Jesus Christ, who by making

171. Aristotle, *Ethics*, 2.1.1103b.3–6, *Politics*, 3.9.1280b.5–11.
172. Aristotle, *Politics*, 1.2.1252b.27–30; 3.9.1280b.33–35.
173. Aristotle, *Politics*, 3.9.1280a.31–34.
174. Aristotle, *Politics*, 3.9.1280a.25–28.
175. Aristotle, *Ethics*, 1.1.1094a.10–15.
176. Romans 6.23.

human beings children of God led them to heavenly glory. This is the government given to him "which will not be corrupted";[177] which is why the Sacred Scriptures call him not priest alone but also king. As Jeremiah says: "The king will reign, and he will be wise."[178] Therefore, a regal priesthood derives from him, and, what is more, all the faithful of Christ, insofar as they are his members, are called kings and priests.[179]

[10] So that spiritual things might be distinguished from earthly things, the ministry of this kingdom was committed not to earthly kings, but to priests, and especially to the highest priest, the successor of Peter, the Vicar of Christ, the Roman Pontiff, to whom it is necessary that all kings of the Christian people be subject, just as to the Lord Jesus Christ himself. For those responsible for antecedent ends should be subject to and directed by the command of him with responsibility for the final end.

[11] Since the priesthood of the gentiles and their whole cult of divine beings only existed for seeking temporal goods ordained for the common good of the multitude, which falls under the responsibility of the king, the kings suitably subjected the priests of the gentiles. Likewise, since in the Old Law the true God, not demons,[180] promised that earthly goods would be delivered to religious people,[181] we read that priests were subject to kings. But in the New Law there is another priesthood, through which human beings are led to heavenly goods; so, by the law of Christ, kings ought to be subject to priests.

[12] For this reason Divine Providence wonderfully provided that in the Roman City, which God had foreseen would be the principal see of the Christian people, the custom grew little by little that the rectors of the city[182] should be subject to priests. As Valerius Maximus reports: "our city always placed religion before everything else, even those things in which it wanted the splendor of the highest majesty to be seen. For this reason the imperial did not hesitate to serve the sacred, reckoning that if they had attended well and constantly on the Divine Might they would be able to maintain the government of human affairs."[183] And because it also would come to pass that the religion of the

---

177. Daniel 7.14.

178. Jeremias (Jeremiah) 23.5.

179. 1 Peter 2.9; see also Hebrews 7. References to Christ, the pope, and Christians as both priests and kings are common in the medieval pro-papal polemical tradition.

180. As many dualists, such as the Manicheans, and the Waldensians believed.

181. Thomas cites Leviticus 26 and Deuteronomy 28 in *Summa Theologiae* 1.2.114.10.ad 1 and *On the Epistle to the Romans* 9.1.

182. The Latin text in the modern editions is actually "*civitatum*," "of the cities," but some manuscripts do have "*civitatis*," "of the city," which seems more likely to me.

183. Valerius Maximus, *Memorable Deeds and Sayings*, 1.1.9, but the quote is not exact.

Christian priesthood would be especially strong in Gaul, the Gauls' gentile priests, whom they called Druids, were given divine permission to define the law[184] of all Gaul, as Julius Caesar reports in the book he wrote on the Gallic war.[185]

Chapter 16

In seeking the mediate end, as for the ultimate end, the king must dispose his subjects to live according to virtue. Those things which ordain to living well and those things which impede it. A king ought to provide a remedy for these impediments.

[1] Just as the life by which human beings live well here is ordained to the end of the life which we hope will be blessed in heaven, so also all particular goods procured by human beings, whether riches, profits, health, eloquence, or learning, are ordained to the end of the good of the multitude. If, as I said, those who have responsibility for the ultimate end ought to have precedence over those who have responsibility for things ordained to that end and ought to direct them with their command, what I have said makes it apparent that the king ought to have precedence over all human offices and order them by the command of his government, just as he himself ought to be subject to the lordship and government administered by the office of priest.

[2] Those for whom it is incumbent to do something that is ordained to something else as an end ought to make sure that their work is suitable to that end, just as the metal worker makes a sword to be suitable for fighting and a builder arranges a home to be appropriate for habitation. Therefore, since heavenly beatitude is the end of the life that we live well at present, it pertains to the office of king to procure the good life of the multitude to make it suitable for attaining heavenly beatitude, that is, he should order those things which lead to heavenly beatitude and forbid their contraries, as far as possible.

[3] From divine law we know the way that leads to true beatitude and the things that are impediments to it, the teaching of which pertains to the office of priests. As Malachi says: "The lips of the priest will guard knowledge, and they will seek the law from his mouth."[186] In Deuteronomy the Lord orders:

---

184. *Ius.*
185. Julius Caesar, *The Gallic War*, 6.13.
186. Malachias (Malachi) 2.7.

> After the king sits on the throne of his kingdom, he will copy this law of
> Deuteronomy into a volume, taking the copy from a priest of the Leviti-
> cal tribe, and he will keep it with him and read it all the days of his life,
> so that he might learn to fear the Lord his God and guard his words and
> ceremonies, which were ordered in the law.[187]

Therefore, instructed by this divine law, he ought especially to be zealous
to attend to how the subject multitude might live well. This zealousness has
three parts: first, to institute a good life among the subject multitude; second, to preserve that which was instituted; and third, to move from what has
been preserved to something better.

[4] Two things are required for a person to have the good life. The principal
thing is working according to virtue, for virtue is that by which we live well;[188]
the secondary and, as it were, instrumental thing is the sufficiency of temporal goods, the use of which is necessary for an act of virtue.[189] Nature causes
the unity of the human species, but the unity of the multitude, which is called
peace, must be procured through the industry of that which governs. Therefore, to institute the good life of the multitude three things are required. First,
the multitude must be constituted in the unity of peace. Second, the multitude united by the chain of peace must be directed to acting well. For just as a
person cannot do well unless there is unity in that person's parts, a multitude
of persons that lacks the unity of peace is impeded from acting well while it
fights within itself. Third, a sufficient abundance of necessities for living well
must be present through the industry of that which governs.

[5] Consequently, when the office of the king establishes the good life among
the multitude, he should attend to its preservation. There are three things
which do not allow the public good to endure, one of which arises from
nature. The good of the multitude ought not to be instituted only for a particular time, but perpetually. But since human beings are mortal, they can not
live forever. Nor, while they live, do they always have the same vigor, because
human life is subject to many variations, and so human beings are not suited
to perform the same offices equally through their entire life. Another impedi-

---

187. Deuteronomy 17.18–19. The title of the biblical "Deuteronomy" comes not from the
Hebrew but from the Greek Septuagint version. The translators rendered the Hebrew words
meaning "copy of the law" in the cited verse as "Deuteronomy" and took this word as the title
of the book. The words in Latin are actually "the Deuteronomy of this law."
188. Augustine, *On Free Will*, 2.19.
189. Aristotle, *Ethics*, 1.8.1099b.1–2; 1.9.1099b.26–29.

ment to preserving the public good comes from within and subsists in the perversity of human will, so that persons either are indolent when it comes to doing those things that the republic requires, or they harm the peace of the multitude when they disturb the peace of others by transgressing justice. The third impediment to preserving the republic comes from outside, when the incursion of enemies dissolves the peace and sometimes demolishes the kingdom or city to its foundation.

[6] A king has a threefold responsibility involving these three impediments. First, he must take care for human succession in replacing those who are in charge of various offices. He must do this so that just as the divine government provided for corruptible things, since they can not always remain the same, that through the process of generation some things would succeed in the place of others and thus preserve the integrity of the universe, so also through the zealousness of the king the good of the subject multitude would be preserved, when he solicitously takes care for the succession to the places of those who can no longer fill their office. Second, he should compel those subject to him to avoid iniquity and lead them to virtuous works by his laws and precepts, penalties and rewards, following the example of God, who gave law to humans, handing out a reward to those who observe it and punishments to those who transgress it. Third, the king is responsible to render the multitude subject to him safe from its enemies, for there would be no profit in avoiding internal dangers if the multitude could not be defended from external ones.

[7] The third factor pertaining to the office of king in instituting a good multitude remains is that he should be solicitous for its advancement. He does this in the individual things that I have mentioned if he corrects what is inordinate, if he supplies what is lacking, if he is zealous to do whatever can be done better. This is why Paul warns the faithful always to strive for the better gift.[190]

[8] These are the the things that pertain to the office of king, and I must now treat each of them more diligently.

190. 1 Corinthians 12.31.

Book 2

Attributed to Thomas Aquinas to mid-2.4.7

Chapter 1

It pertains to the king to found cities or castles for attaining glory, and he ought to choose temperate places for these. What conveniences and inconveniences result from this.

[1] First, I must explain the office of a king in founding a city or kingdom. As Vegetius says: "the mightiest nations and most renowned rulers could seek no greater glory than either to start new cities or to transfer those started by others into their name and improve them."[1] This certainly accords with the documents of Sacred Scripture, for the Wise One says in Ecclesiasticus: "The building of a city will confirm a name,"[2] and the name of Romulus would be unknown today had he not founded Rome.

[2] In the founding of a city or kingdom the king must first of all choose a temperate region, if there are a number of possibilities, for the inhabitants receive many advantages from the temperateness of a region. First, human beings derive soundness of body and length of life from the temperateness of the region. Since health consists of a certain temperateness of the bodily fluids,[3] health will be preserved in a temperate place—for like is preserved by like. If there is an excess of heat or of cold, the quality of the body will neces-

---

1. Vegetius, *On the Military*, 4, prologue.
2. Ecclesiasticus (Sirach) 40.19.
3. Aristotle, *Physics*, 7.3.246b.4–20. This refers to the ancient and medieval theory of the bodily fluids, or humors, which were felt to be responsible for the health and disposition of each person. Like all other things the fluids' properties were determined by the qualities of moist and dry, cold and warm—the components of the four elements. There are four fluids, which correspond to the four elements: blood (hot and moist, air), phlegm (cold and moist, water), choler or yellow bile (hot and dry, fire), and melancholy or black bile (cold and dry, earth). The next several paragraphs all refer to this theory.

sarily be changed according to the quality of the air. Thus, by natural industry certain animals move to a warm place during a cold period, going back again to the cold place during a warm period,[4] in order to attain temperateness from the contrary disposition of each place at the particular time.

[3] Again, since an animal lives through warmth and moisture, if heat is too intense, natural moisture is quickly dried up and life fails, just as a lantern is extinguished if the fluid poured into it is quickly used up when the fire is too great. Thus, in certain very hot regions of Ethiopia, humans are not able to live more than thirty years. But in regions that are excessively cold, natural moisture is easily congealed and natural heat is extinguished.

[4] Then too the temperateness of a region is very advantageous for war, by which human society is made safe. As Vegetius reports:

> All nations that are near the sun and are dried up by the excessive heat are said to be more wise but to have less blood, and, therefore, they do not have constancy and confidence for close fighting, for those who know they have little blood fear wounds. On the contrary, peoples of the north, who are far away from the burning sun, are more imprudent but are overflowing with abundant blood, and so they are always ready for war. But those who live in temperate zones are supplied with an abundance of blood, so they are contemptuous of wounds and death, but they do not lack prudence, and this serves modesty in the camps and profits counsel in combat.[5]

[5] Finally, a temperate region is of benefit to political life. As Aristotle says:

> The nations that live in cold places are full of courage but deficient in intellect and art. For this reason they persevere more in their liberty, but they do not live politically, and they cannot govern their neighbors on account of their lack of prudence. Those who live in hot places are intellectual and accomplished in spirit, but without courage, on account of which they become subjected and remain subjected. But those who live in moderate places share in both courage and intellect, on account of which they persevere in freedom, they are especially suited to live politically, and they know how to govern others.[6]

4. Aristotle, *History of Animals*, 7.12.596b.23f.
5. Vegetius, *On the Military*, 1.2.
6. Aristotle, *Politics*, 7.7.1327b.23–33. This is not an exact quotation. Aristotle especially points to the people of Europe as sharing the characteristics of those from a cold climate. He does

[6] A temperate region should therefore be chosen for the foundation of a city or kingdom.

Chapter 2

Kings and rulers ought to choose regions for founding cities or castles in which the air is healthful. How and by what signs one can recognize such air.

[1] After choosing the region, it is necessary to choose a suitable place to build the city, and it seems that a search for healthful air should be the first concern. For natural life comes before civil intercourse, and healthful air safeguards this.

[2] As Vitruvius tells us, the most healthful place will be: "an elevated place, not foggy, not frosty, and facing regions of the sky that are neither hot nor cold. Finally, it should not be near swamps."[7] A place's elevation generally confers healthfulness to the air, since an elevated place is open to the blowing of the winds, by which the air is made pure. Also, the vapors, which by virtue of the sun's rays are freed from the earth and the waters, are more prevalent in valleys and in sunken places than in high ones, so that in high places the air is found to be more subtle. Moreover, the subtlety of air of this kind, which is of much benefit to free and pure breathing, is impeded by fogs and frosts, which habitually abound in places that are very damp, so that places of this kind are found to be contrary to healthfulness. And because swampy places abound with extreme dampness, it is necessary for the place where a city is constructed to be far away from swamps:

> For when the morning breezes arrive at that place as the sun rises, and the fogs that rise from the swamps are added to them, they will scatter the breaths of the venomous beasts of the swamps mixed with the fogs and make the place pestilential. . . . Nevertheless, if the walls are constructed in swamps near the sea and face north, or thereabouts,[8] and if

not refer to the climates where the other two kinds of people live, but describes the inhabitants of Asia in the same way as Ptolemy here describes those living in a hot climate, and he says that the Greeks, who live between the other two, would be able to rule the world if they could be unified.

7. Vitruvius, *On Architecture*, 1.4. The quotations of Vitruvius in this chapter are close but not exact.

8. Vitruvius says: "or between the north and east."

these swamps are more elevated than the seashore, they would seem to be rationally constructed, for, if trenches are built, the water will be able to drain out to the shore, and when in tempests the sea flows back into the swamps it will not permit swamp animals to be born. And if some animals come from higher places, they will be killed by the unaccustomed salinity.[9]

[3] It is also necessary for the place destined for the city be temperately disposed to heat and cold according to how it faces the various zones of the sky. "It will not be healthful if the walls, especially those built near the sea, face south."[10] Places of this kind will be cold in the morning, because the sun does not shine on them, but at noon they will be burning hot because of the sunshine. Places that face west are cool or even cold when the sun rises, but are warm at noon and burning hot in the evening because of the continuous heat and sunshine. Those that face east will be moderately warm in the morning, since the sun is directly opposite; at noon the heat will not be much increased, since the sun does not shine directly on them; but in the evening they will be cold since the rays of the sun are completely opposite. From the converse of what was said about those facing south, there will be the same or similar temperatures when the site of the city faces north. By experience we may learn that it is unhealthful to move to a warmer place: "Bodies which are brought from cold places into warm ones cannot last, but are dissolved, since the heat dissolves their natural virtues by sucking up their vapor," so that even in healthful places "summer makes bodies infirm."[11]

[4] Since bodies need suitable food for their health, it is necessary to confer about the healthfulness of the place chosen to build the city with regard to food, so that by the condition of the food we may find out about those who are born in the land. The ancients used to investigate this through the animals nurtured there.[12] Since both humans and other animals commonly use what they find in the land for their nutrition, it follows that if the viscera of killed animals are found to be exceptionally vigorous,[13] humans could be healthfully nourished there. But if the members of killed animals should appear to be diseased, it can reasonably be assumed that living in that place would not be healthful for humans either.

9. Vitruvius, *On Architecture*, 1.4.

10. Vitruvius, *On Architecture*, 1.4.

11. The part attributed to Thomas ends at this point in a few versions, but modern authorities reject this. See the introduction for an explanation.

12. Vitruvius, *On Architecture*, 1.4.

13. Vitruvius, *On Architecture*, 1.4, but Vitruvius mentions the liver in particular.

[5] In addition to a temperate atmosphere healthful water is required, for the health of human bodies especially depends on the things are used most often. Obviously, every day, in order to live, we must constantly inhale air by breathing, which means that its healthfulness will especially contribute to the good condition of our bodies. Likewise, nothing except the purity of its air is more pertinent to the healthfulness of a place than the healthfulness of its water, because among the things that we consume for nourishment we use water most often, both as drink and food.

[6] There are other signs that a place is healthful—the faces of persons who live there appear to have a good color, their bodies are robust and their members well disposed, their children are many and lively, and there are many who are old. Conversely, if the faces of persons appear to be deformed, if their bodies are feeble, if their members are exhausted or diseased, if their children are few and sick, and if there are rather few who are old, there can be no doubt that the place is deadly.

Chapter 3

The king must construct a city to have a copious amount of food, since without it a city cannot be perfect. There are two ways to do this, of which the first is more commendable.

[1] Moreover, the place chosen for constructing a city must be one that not only preserves the inhabitants in good health, but also suffices for a plentiful sustenance.[14] It is not possible for a multitude of humans to live where a copious supply of food is not at hand. Vitruvius reports that when the architect Dinocrates, a man of extraordinary skill, demonstrated to Alexander of Macedon that he could construct a city of distinguished appearance on a certain mountain, Alexander asked him whether there were fields that could provide a copious amount of grain to the city. When he found out that these were lacking, he responded that anyone who built a city in such a place would deserve to be censured: For: "just as a newborn infant could not be fed nor induced to grow without the milk of a wet-nurse, a city without an abundance of food cannot support a throng of people."[15]

14. Vitruvius, *On Architecture*, 1.5.
15. Vitruvius, *On Architecture*, 2, prologue. The "certain mountain" is Mt. Athos. Ptolemy calls the architect "Xenocrates." Alexander III the Great (r.336–323 B.C.E.), king of Macedonia, established the largest empire of antiquity, stretching from north Africa to India. He was also

[2] There are two ways through which a profusion of things can be present in any city. One is through the fertility of the region, which brings forth abundantly all things necessary for human life. The other is through the practice of mercantile transactions, through which the necessities of life are transported from various other places.

[3] It can be demonstrated that the first way is manifestly more suitable. The more worthy something is, the more it is found to be self-sufficient, since that which lacks something is deficient. But a city is more fully self-sufficient if it has a surrounding region that suffices for the necessities of life, whereas a city that lacks something receives these through mercantile transactions. A city is more worthy if it has an abundance of things from its own territory than if it has abundance through mercantile transactions since the first way seems to be more secure—because of the fortunes of war and the various hazards of the roads, transportation of food can easily be impeded and the city oppressed through a lack of food.

[4] It is also more useful for civil intercourse. A city that needs a multitude of mercantile transactions for its own sustenance must endure continual interaction with foreigners. According to the doctrine of Aristotle, this commonly corrupts the customs of citizens because foreigners, nourished on other laws and usages, necessarily act in many ways that differ from the customs of the citizens.[16] When their example provokes the citizens to act in similar ways, civil intercourse is disturbed.

[5] If the citizens themselves are devoted to mercantile transactions, the door to many vices is thrown open. Since the enthusiasm for business especially involves striving for gain,[17] cupidity is led into the citizens' hearts. The result is that all things in the city become venal; when faith is gone the place is thrown open to deceptions; when the public has contempt for the good, everyone is devoted to their own profit and enthusiasm for virtue ceases, and everyone prefers reward to the honor that comes from virtue. It follows that in such a city civil intercourse will necessarily be corrupted.

---

the subject of many medieval legends and romances. Dinocrates of Rhodes was his favorite architect, who designed the third temple of Artemis at Ephesus, the largest temple in Greece, and was one of two principle designers of the city of Alexandria in Egypt. He proposed to carve the mile-high Mt. Athos into a colossal statue of Alexander, but never began the project.

16. Aristotle, *Politics*, 5.3.1303a25ff.; 7.6.1327a.13–15. Diversity was not a medieval virtue.

17. Aristotle, *Politics*, 1.9.1257b.21–22.

[6] For the most part, the practice of business does more harm to military activity than do most occupations.[18] Businesspeople rest in the shade without laboring, and while they enjoy delights their spirits grow soft and their bodies become feeble and unsuitable for military labor. This is why according to the civil law knights are forbidden to take part in business.[19]

[7] Finally, a city is usually more peaceful if its people rarely gathers together and if few reside within the city walls. The frequent concourse of persons provides the occasion for disputes and the matter for seditions. According to Aristotle's doctrine, it is more useful for the people to be employed outside the cities than to remain constantly within the city walls.[20] But if the city is given over to mercantile transactions, it is especially necessary for the citizens to reside within the city and practice their mercantile transactions there.

[8] Therefore, it is better that there be a copious amount of food at hand for a city in its own fields, than that it be completely open to business. Nevertheless, it is not necessary to exclude businesspersons from the city altogether, because a place can not easily be discovered which abounds in all those things necessary for life and which does not stand in need of things brought in from another place. It is also true that those things which are especially abundant in a particular place become harmful to many if they cannot be transferred to another place through the office of merchants. For this reason it is necessary for the perfect city to practice mercantile exchanges in moderation.

Chapter 4

The region that a king chooses for a city or castle should be instituted to have amenities. The inhabitants should be made to use these moderately, since they are often a cause of dissolution, from which the kingdom is destroyed.

[1] A place should be chosen for building a city that will delight its inhabitants with its pleasantness. A multitude of inhabitants will not readily desert

18. Vegetius, *On the Military*, 1.3 uses almost the same words as those that follow to commend the suitability of rustics for military activity.

19. That is, according to the *Body of Roman Law. Codex* 1.12.34.

20. Aristotle, *Politics*, 6.4.1318b.10–16. Aristotle says that in a democracy it is best if the majority of people live by agriculture or herding, since these will have no leisure to attend the assembly, will not covet the property of others, and will prefer what they do to ruling. The writer probably misread *"congregationes facere,"* "to gather together (in assemblies)," as "to crowd together in the city."

a pleasant place, nor will it readily flock to an unpleasant place, since without pleasantness a person's life cannot long endure. For this pleasantness there should be large fields in the plains, fruitful trees, conspicuous nearby mountains, and agreeable glades, and it should be well-irrigated with water.

[2] Undoubtedly, too much pleasantness allures persons to enjoy delights unnecessarily, and this is especially harmful for cities. Thus, delights should be enjoyed moderately, first of all because persons devoted to delights become dull in their senses. The sweetness of the delights immerses their spirits in sensations, so that they cannot have free judgment about the delightful things. Aristotle's opinion is: "Pleasures corrupt prudence in judgments." [21]

[3] Superfluous pleasures also cause a fall from upright virtue, for nothing leads more completely than pleasure to immoderate increase, through which the middle way of virtue is corrupted. One reason is that the nature of pleasure is to be insatiable, so that one who has taken moderate pleasure is precipitated into the allurements of filthy pleasures, just as dry wood is kindled by a moderate flame. Another reason is that pleasure does not satisfy the appetite; on the contrary, a pleasure once tasted induces a thirst for more. Therefore, it pertains to the office of virtue to see that persons abstain from superfluous pleasures, for by shunning superfluity, one arrives more easily at the middle way of virtue.

[4] Consequently, those given over to superfluous delights grow weak in spirit and become fainthearted in attending to any arduous matter, in putting up with labor, and in standing up to danger. So also, for the most part, delights harm the practice of war, because as Vegetius says: "Those who know that they had fewer delights in their life fear death less." [22]

[5] Those who are unbridled in their enjoyment of delights usually grow sluggish, and, neglecting necessary studies and the affairs to which they ought to attend, they turn their attention to delights alone, in the course of which, being extravagant, they squander what others previously gathered. Thus, when they have been reduced to the condition of paupers, since they cannot do without the delights to which they have become accustomed, they embark on a course of theft and rapine so that they might have that through which they may sate their voluptuousness.

21. Aristotle says this in essence, though not in these words, at *Ethics*, 6.5.1140b.13–20.
22. Vegetius, *On the Military*, 1.3.

[6] It is, therefore, harmful for a city to abound in superfluous delights, whether these come from the disposition of the place or for another reason.

[7] Therefore, a modicum of pleasures is suitable in human intercourse, to provide spice, as it were, so that the human spirit may be restored,[23] since, as Seneca says in *On the Tranquility of the Spirit, to Serenus*, "relaxation should be given to spirits."[24] When they are refreshed, they rise up better and more fit, as if it profits the spirit to use delights temperately, just as salt used in cooking makes food pleasant, but added excessively ruins it.

[8] Moreover, if something that is a means to an end is sought as an end in itself, the order of nature is upset and destroyed. It is as if a craftsperson should search for a hammer, or a carpenter for a saw, or a doctor for medicine for its own sake, instead of for the proper end to which each is ordained. In a city, the end for which a king should strive through his government is living according to virtue. One should use other things as means to this end and to the extent necessary for pursuing this end. This is not the case for those things that rest superfluously on pleasures, since such pleasures are not ordained to the stated end; on the contrary, they seem to be sought as an end in themselves. The impious, who according to the book of Wisdom do not think rightly, seem to want to use pleasures in this manner, as Scripture witnesses: "Come, let us enjoy the good things that are here," which pertains to an end, and "let us use the creature quickly, as in youth,"[25] and likewise in what follows. Scripture shows that the immoderate use of things delightful to the body is characteristic of juveniles and rightly criticizes it. Aristotle makes an analogy between using things delightful to the body and using food,[26] which ruins the health of someone who eats too little or too much, but both preserves and improves the health of someone who takes food in the proper proportion. The same is true of virtue with regard to human pleasures and delights.

---

23. According to modern authorities Ptolemy's work begins only at this point.

24. Seneca, *On the Tranquility of the Spirit, to Serenus*, 17.5. Seneca continues, "so that, rested, they might rise up better and sharper."

25. Wisdom 2.6.

26. Aristotle, *Ethics*, 3.11.1119a.

Chapter 5

It is necessary for a king, or any other lord, to have an abundance of those temporal riches that are called "natural." The reasons for this.

[1] Now that I have itemized the things that are necessary for the substantial being of any civic entity, whether it is a polity or a regal government (and a king ought principally to attend to instituting and having foresight for these things), I must take up those things that pertain to the relationship between a king and his subjects, by means of which he guides his government with greater tranquility. To some extent I touched on this this topic generically already, but now I must treat it specifically by declaring more fully what a ruler should do.

[2] First, a ruler must act to ensure that the individual parts of the government have an abundance of natural riches—a term Aristotle used either because they occur naturally or because a person needs them by nature[27]—things such as farms, vineyards, groves, forests, and preserves of various animals and birds. Palladius Palatinus, a count of the emperor Valentinian, gave an ample lesson to the emperor about this in a most splendid style, exhorting him to provide these things.[28] And King Solomon, when he wanted to show how magnificent his government was, said: "I built houses for myself; I planted vineyards; I made gardens and orchards and planted them with every kind of tree; I constructed reservoirs for myself for irrigating the forest of sprouting trees."[29]

[3] I can give three reasons for this. The first comes from considering the use of a thing. It seems that it is more delightful to use one's own thing than that of another, since one is more united to it. Unity is a property of love, as Dionysius tells us,[30] and pleasure follows love, since the presence of what is loved brings pleasure. In addition, consider what diligence in work is required for such a thing, and that a person rejoices more if the work is more difficult, for as Aristotle says, we love the results more when the undertaking is not easy.[31] For this reason we love our children and anything of our own making in

27. Aristotle, *Politics*, 1.8.1256a.
28. Palladius Palatinus, *Country Matters*, 14. Palladius Palatinus was a fourth-century C.E. writer whose work on agriculture was widely read in the Middle Ages. Little is known of his life. There were two fourth-century emperors named Valentinian: Valentinian I (r.364–75) and his son Valentinian II (r.375–392).
29. Ecclesiastes 2.4–6.
30. Pseudo-Dionysius the Areopagite, *On the Divine Names*, 4.15.
31. Aristotle, *Ethics*, 10.6.1177a1–5 and various other places imply this.

proportion to the amount of work we put into it. Therefore, by being solicitous for one's own natural riches, they become more agreeable than those of another, and, being more agreeable, we will call them more delightful.

[4] The second reason comes from considering the king's officials. When it is necessary for them to obtain their lord's necessities of life from their fellow villagers, scandals may arise either among the subjects themselves or as a result of commercial activities. Avarice, which accompanies buying and selling, may cause harm, or fraud may lead to a disturbance. Proverbs says: "all buyers say: 'it is a calamity,' but once they have gone away they boast,"[32] which implies that they have outmaneuvered the seller by fraud. In Ecclesiasticus we are warned to beware: "of the corruption of buying and of businesspersons,"[33] as if this were characteristic of those who carry on trade. Commerce also leads to familiarity with women, and incautious speech, looks, or gestures causes jealousy among the citizens, who then become stirred up against the government.

[5] The third reason comes from considering the things that are for sale, and this confirms our conclusion. Food that is sold is not as effective for nourishment as it should be, since it is often adulterated. As Solomon says in Proverbs: "Drink water from your own cistern,"[34] which includes all nourishment, but especially drink, because it can more easily be adulterated, and being less removed from its own nature and purity, it more quickly reveals its malice. There is greater security in using one's own food, since outsiders can more easily poison something not kept in its proper storehouse or pantry, and it is more likely to be harmful. For this reason, the prophet Isaiah says in exalting the recompense of a just man: "Bread is given to him, and his waters are sure,"[35] as if it were more secure for him to use his own food and drink.

Chapter 6

It is expedient for a king to have other natural riches, such as herds and flocks, and without these lords cannot govern the earth well.

[1] The things that I have just said are pertinent not only to natural riches, but also to the various kinds of living things—and for the same reasons and causes

32. Proverbs 20.14.
33. Ecclesiasticus (Sirach) 42.5.
34. Proverbs 2.5.
35. Isaias (Isaiah) 33.16.

that I have given above. The Lord gave the privilege of governing and exercising lordship over living things to the first father, as if to all human nature for exercising lordship from the start, as is written in Genesis: "Increase and multiply and fill up the earth, and exercise lordship over the fish of the sea and the birds of the sky and all living things that move on the earth."[36] Thus, it pertains to the regal majesty to use and to have an abundance of all these things, and to the degree that it exercises lordship over them, its rule is similar to that of the first lord, since all things were deputed to human use at the beginning of creation.

[2] For this reason Aristotle says that the hunting of the animals of the forest is naturally just, because by it humans claim for themselves what belongs to them.[37] Something similar can be said about fishing and fowling, which is why nature provides rapacious birds and dogs to perform duties of this kind. But because fish do not have the aptitude for such ministries, human beings invented nets as substitutes for dogs and birds. Therefore, a king needs the things mentioned above to supply and adorn his kingdom.

[3] Some of them he needs for his use and to eat, such as fish, birds, herds of oxen, and flocks of sheep, of which Solomon had an abundance so as to display his magnificence, as is written in Ecclesiastes and in 3 Kings.[38] The king needs other animals in his ministry as well, so that horses, mules, asses, and camels are deputed to various ministries according to regional usage. Therefore, as much as possible a king ought to have a large number of living things deputed either for eating or to his ministry, for the reason I have already shown above in the case of other natural riches, which is that one's own things are more delightful, and that the more delightful they are the more they have of the raison d'être of life and hence are more similar to the divine, which is the greatest cause of love.

[4] What I have said suggests other reasons why it is expedient for a king to have abundant possessions of this kind. First, we see that nature, which delights in its own work, encourages this, when we consider the continually new ways living things develop through nature's actions, whether in living, in procreating, or in giving birth. Admiration arises in lords from these things, and

36. Genesis 1.28.
37. Aristotle, *Politics*, 1.8.1256b.15–26.
38. Ecclesiastes 2.7: "I had herds of oxen and great flocks of sheep . . ."; 3 Kings (1 Kings) 8.5: "Solomon . . . sacrificed sheep and oxen that could not be counted or numbered"; 3 Kings (1 Kings) 8.63: "Solomon slew . . . 22,000 oxen and 120,000 sheep . . ."

from admiration, pleasure. That there may be a nutritive cause of love and consequently of pleasure is clear in Exodus, where Pharaoh's daughter caused Moses to be suckled. Later in the same passage it is added that after he suckled she adopted him as her own son.[39] For the same reason the Lord made his affection known to the people in Hosea by saying: "I was like a tutor to Ephraim."[40]

[5] Moreover, hunting forest or other animals, for the sake of which rulers and kings submit their children and expose themselves to physical training, is effective for acquiring bodily strength, preserving health and invigorating the force of the heart, so long as they do it temperately, as Aristotle tells us,[41] and during periods of peace with their enemies. The kings of France and England are accustomed to doing this, and Aimoinus wrote the same thing about the Germans in *Deeds of the Franks*.[42]

[6] Equity also leads to this, since kings should be well furnished for embellishing the kingdom and defending it against its enemies, and they are more suited to and prepared for this if they have their own herds of horses, as is the custom for eastern kings and rulers. For instance, 3 Kings says that Solomon flourished in his prosperity, having "40,000 stalls of chariot horses and 12,000 of riding horses,"[43] which the prefects of this king guarded.

[7] If we consider living things ordained for eating, then it is more suitable to have one's own quadrupeds and reptiles, that is, fish. A person has more delight in using them in this case, since they are better nourished and more suitable for eating, both because we are happier when we use a known thing, and because they are more securely and freely offered to us for eating. This act is more proportionate to our nature, and so it is more delightful. The reason that I mentioned above also applies, namely to avoid commerce with the citizens, which could give rise to scandal. The king's officials should be on guard against this. Also, the king's magnificence requires these things for a more plentiful and bountiful administration of food and drink, which can be accomplished more expeditiously if kings have abundant flocks and herds.

---

39. Exodus 2.5–10.

40. Osee (Hosea) 11.3. In Latin, *"nutricius,"* "tutor," is simply the masculine form of the word for "nurse," and is closely related to the words nursing," *"nutritio,"* and "nutritive," *"nutritivus,"* used in this same passage.

41. Ptolemy refers to the *Ethics*, but the closest passage seems to be *Politics*,1.8.1256b.15–26, where Aristotle says that animals exist for the sake of humans and classifies hunting and warfare under the art of acquisition. On the other hand, he has just referred correctly to this same passage.

42. Aimoinus Floriac, *History of the Franks*, preface, chapter 2.

43. 3 Kings (1 Kings) 4.26.

[8] Therefore, I conclude that natural riches are necessary for a king, so that he might have his own things in different regions for the defense of his government and kingdom.

Chapter 7

It is necessary for a king to have an abundance of artificial riches,
such as gold and silver and the coins minted from them.

[1] A king also needs artificial riches, such as gold, silver, other metals, and the coins minted from them, to defend his government. If we suppose that by nature association is needed to constitute a rule or polity, and, consequently, a king or other lord to govern the multitude, we must also accept any consequences about the treasury that derive inevitably from this supposition, such as that a king cannot exercise his government adequately and favorably without gold, silver, and the coins minted from them. I can show this in many ways.

[2] The first way becomes obvious when we consider the king. A person uses gold, silver, or coins as an instrument for making exchanges. Aristotle says that a coin is, as it were, a surety for future necessity, because it incorporates any kind of work in determining prices.[44] Therefore, if anyone needs these things, the king needs them even more, because if something is true simply, it also applies to him as an individual, and even more so if it applies to him more than to others.

[3] Likewise, virtue is proportionate to nature, and work to virtue. The nature of the regal status has a certain universality, because it is common to the people subject to it; therefore, the same is true of its virtue and work. So, if the status of lords according to their nature is communicative, so is their virtue and mode of operation. This cannot happen without coins, just as there can be neither a craftsperson or carpenter without the appropriate instruments.

[4] Likewise, according to Aristotle, the virtue of magnificence involves great expenses, and great expenses pertain to the magnanimous, which the king is, as Aristotle mentions in the same passage.[45] It is written in Esther that when

44. Aristotle, *Ethics*, 5.5.1133a18–b.10–13. Aristotle believes that money primarily equates things according to the law of demand, but says that it also serves to equate different kinds of labor.

45. Aristotle, *Ethics*, 4.2.1122.b.2f., 10f. That is, Aristotle says great expenses pertain to the magnanimous, but he does not mention a king here.

Ahasuerus, who exercised lordship in 127 provinces of the east, gave a feast he ministered to the princes of his kingdom with food and drink as the king's magnificence demanded.[46] Since this could not be done without the instrument of life—that is, coins minted from gold or silver—we reach the same conclusion as before.

[5] Therefore, I conclude that when we consider the king, a treasury containing artificial riches is a necessity.

[6] The second way comes from considering the people generally or specifically, since the king ought to have an abundance of money so that he can provide what is necessary for his home and come to the aid of his subjects when necessary. As Aristotle tells us, the king ought to be to his people as a shepherd to his sheep or a father to his children.[47] As is written in Genesis, pharaoh acted in this way toward the whole land of Egypt, for through Joseph's foresight, he bought grain for the public stores, which he distributed when famine struck, so that his people would not die of starvation.[48] And in *The War with Catiline* Sallust relates Cato's opinion that the Republic was profitable to the Romans when the public stores thrived in Rome, but that after they had been abandoned the Republic reached a low point, as is said to have happened in the time of Cato himself.[49]

[7] Further, there is an analogy between any kingdom, city, camp, or association and the human body, as Aristotle and the *Policraticus* tell us.[50] In the latter, the common store is compared to the king's stomach, so that just as food is received by the stomach and distributed to the members, so also the king's store is filled with a treasury of money, which is shared and distributed to pay for the things that are necessary for the subjects and kingdom.

[8] This same thing also happens in specific cases. Borrowing for the expenses of the king or kingdom is foul and greatly detracts from the subjects' rever-

---

46. Esther 1.1–8.

47. Aristotle, *Ethics*, 8.10.1160b, where Aristotle says that a king rules for the interests of his subjects and compares the king to a father, but he does not mention a shepherd.

48. Genesis 41.33–57. Actually Joseph sold the grain which he had stored up as Pharaoh's agent.

49. Sallust, *The War with Catiline*, 52. The "low point" presumably refers to the civil wars, followed by Caesar's coming to power. Cato the Younger (95–46 B.C.E.), a Stoic philosopher, tribune, military praetor, and quaestor, opposed Cataline and Caesar, and committed suicide after Caesar's victory.

ence for what is regal. Moreover, when a king is subjected to a loan, the lords restrain him, with the result that his subjects or others may make undue exactions against the kingdom and weaken its state.

[9] Likewise, in borrowing one often suffers scandal, since by the nature of borrowing it is difficult to repay a loan. Bias, one of the Seven Wise Men, is said to have held the following opinion: "When a friend has borrowed money from you, you lose both the friend and the money."[51] Therefore, for the reasons I have mentioned, it is necessary for the king to accumulate artificial riches in order to provide for the people either generally or specifically.

[10] The third way to prove the same thing comes from considering the situation and the personages not under the king's lordship. There are two kinds of situation. One is when these personages are enemies, and to oppose these the king's public store must be full—first, to take care of the expenses of his household; second, to pay his tenants' knights when he moves his army against the enemy; and third, to repair and establish defenses to prevent the enemy from crossing the border and invading his kingdom. The other kind of external situation might actually lead to the enlargement of the king's kingdom, but for this he needs a treasury. It sometimes happens that regions are oppressed by poverty, either because of the weight of their debts or their enemies, and they then have recourse to the king's assistance. By coming to their aid with the instrument of life—that is gold, silver, or any kind of coinage—he may subject them, and thereby increase his kingdom.

[11] Therefore, it is apparent from what I have said that for these three reasons artificial riches are necessary to conserve the king's government. Thus, it is written in Judith that when Holofernes, a prince of Nebuchadnezzar, invaded the regions of Syria and Cilicia with a great army, "He took a vast quantity of gold and silver from the king's home,"[52] that is, as provisions for the expedition against his enemies. In the passage of Ecclesiastes that I mentioned above, the same thing is written about Solomon, among his other acts of regal magnificence: "I have heaped up gold and silver and the fortune of kings and provinces for myself,"[53] calling the treasuries of coins he and his father David exacted as tribute "fortune," as is clear in 2 and 3 Kings.[54] This

50. John of Salisbury, *Policraticus*, 5.2.
51. For Bias and the Wise Men, see note at 1.10.6.
52. Judith 2.10.
53. Ecclesiastes 2.8.
54. For example, at 2 Kings (2 Samuel) 20.24 and 3 Kings (1 Kings) 10.25.

is because, according to Aristotle, these things are the instruments of human life, as I said above.[55]

[12] This does not contradict the divine precept about kings and rulers of the people that the Lord gave us through Moses in Deuteronomy, where the law written for a king says that he should not have "an immense amount of gold or silver."[56] We must understand this as referring to regal ostentation or arrogance. The histories relate that Croesus, king of Lydia, suffered ruin for that reason, when Cyrus, king of the Persians, captured him and affixed him nude to a gibbet on a high mountain.[57] But for assisting the kingdom, riches certainly are necessary for the reasons I have given.

Chapter 8

Ministers are necessary for the government of a kingdom or any
other lordship. An incidental distinction between two lordships—
political and despotic—and many reasons to show that political
lordship must necessarily be mild.

[1] The king must be strengthened with ministers as well as with wealth. In speaking about this in Ecclesiastes, the great king Solomon said: "I possessed servants and maids and an exceedingly great household."[58] But that which is possessed seems to be under the lordship of the one who possesses it, and so I must incidentally make the following distinction about lordship. Although in Book 5 of the *Politics* Aristotle supposes that there are many forms of rule, which I have already described and will discuss again, elsewhere in the same work he supposes that there are only two, political and despotic,[59] each of which has its own distinctive ministers. Political rule exists when a region, province, city, or town is governed by one or many according to its own stat-

---

55. Aristotle, *Ethics*, 5.8.1133b.10–12. What Aristotle actually said, which Ptolemy quotes above, is that money is a surety for future necessity.

56. Deuteronomy 17.17.

57. Ptolemy writes of "Crassus," probably confusing Croesus (r.560–546 B.C.E.) with one of several famous Romans. In Herodotus's account Croesus was twice condemned to death and twice spared, but neither time was a gibbet involved, nor was his wealth a factor.

58. Ecclesiastes 2.7. Douay-Rheims translates "*familiam*," which I have rendered as "household" as "family." But *familia* as generally used included servants.

59. Aristotle, *Politics*, 1.3.1253b.18–21. Book 5 does discuss a variety of governments in regard to the different kinds of revolutions that may arise in them and how to avoid them, but Books 3.6–4.10 would seem to be a better reference. This is where Aristotle gives an extensive analysis of the different kinds of government. In 1.2, the author of the first part repeated Aristotle's six-fold classification of polities from *Politics*, 3.7.1279a, and it is probable that this is what Ptolemy means when he says that he has already discussed it.

utes, as happens in regions of Italy and especially in Rome, which for the most part has been governed by senators and consuls ever since the city was founded. Political lordship is more suitable for producing a certain civility in governing, because in it there is an uninterrupted alternation of government over citizens and foreigners alike, as 1 Maccabees says about the Romans: "they annually commit their magistracy to one person, who exercises lordship over all their land."[60]

[2] There are two reasons why the subjects of political lordship cannot be rigidly corrected, as they could be under a regal lordship. One reason has to do with the part that governs. Its government is temporary, and when it considers that its lordship will end after such a brief time it is less anxious to be harsh with those subject to it. This is why the judges of the people of Israel, who judged politically, were more moderate in their judgments than the succeeding kings. Samuel, who judged these people for a time, said to them, when he wanted to show that his government had been political and not regal (although the people had now chosen the latter): "Speak of me in the presence of the Lord and his Christ and say whether I have taken anyone's cow or ass, whether I have slandered anyone, whether I have oppressed anyone, whether I have accepted a gift from anyone's hands."[61] Those who have royal lordship do all of this, as I will make clear below and as this prophet shows in 1 Kings.

[3] Moreover, the mode of governing in those places where lordship is political is mercenary, since lords are employed for pay. When wages are fixed ahead of time for an end, lords are not as intent on governing their subjects, and, in consequence, the rigor of correction is tempered. The Lord refers to these things in John: "Mercenaries, and those who are not shepherds, who do not have the obligation of caring for the sheep," because they are put in charge of them only for a time, "see a wolf and flee. And mercenaries flee because they are mercenaries,"[62] as if the wages were the end of rule in themselves and the subjects a secondary matter. For this reason ancient Roman leaders, such as Marcus Curius, Fabricius, and many others, as Valerius Maximus writes,[63]

60. 1 Machabees (Maccabees) 8.16.
61. 1 Kings (1 Samuel) 12.3.
62. John 10.12–13.
63. Valerius Maximus, *Memorable Deeds and Sayings*, 4.3.5 (Curius), 4.3.6 (Fabricius), 4.8 (on liberality). Gaius Fabricius Luscinus was a third-century B.C.E. Roman general and consul. He negotiated with Pyrrhus after the Roman defeat in 280, eventually establishing a peace, and defeated the Samnites, Lucanians, and Bruttians. He won a reputation for scrupulous honesty by refusing large bribes. Manius (not Marcus) Curius Dentatus was a contemporary of Fabricius and also a general and consul noted for his simple life and devotion to Rome.

took care of the Republic with their own riches, which made them more bold and more solicitous for the care of the polity, as if their whole intention and inner disposition were directed to that. This verifies Cato's opinion, which Sallust relates in *The War with Catiline*: "The Republic, which had once been small, was made great because they displayed industry at home, just command abroad, a free spirit in counseling, and were addicted neither to lust nor transgressions."[64]

[4] The second reason why political lordship must be moderate and be exercised with moderation comes from its subjects, since, by nature, their disposition is suited to such a government. Ptolemy proves in his *Quadripartus*[65] that the various constellations divide human beings into distinct regions with respect to the government of mores, and that the lordship of the stars above always circumscribes human command of will. The Roman regions are situated under Mars, and so they are not as easily subjected as others. For the same reason, the Roman nation is not accustomed to be satisfied with its boundaries, and it can only be subjected when it cannot resist. Because it is unable to endure a foreign will, it is grudging of any superior. As is written in 1 Maccabees, of those who presided among the Romans: "no one wore a diadem or assumed the purple," and the effect of such humility is that "there is neither ill will nor jealousy among them."[66] Therefore, they exercised governance with a certain forgiving spirit, as the nature of that region's subjects requires. As Cicero relates in his *Philippics*, they needed no protection from those with arms, but only the love and benevolence of the citizens, for it is this, not arms, which fortifies the ruling element.[67] Sallust reports Cato's opinion of the ancient Roman Fathers, which is to the same effect.[68]

[5] Likewise, the subjects of a political government develop confidence from being released from the lordship of kings and from exercising lordship themselves at suitable times, and this makes them bold in pursuing liberty, so as not to be forced to submit and bow down to kings. For this reason political government must necessarily be mild.

[6] Moreover, this is a sure mode of governing because it is according to the form of the laws of the commune or the municipality, to which the rector

64. Sallust, *The War with Catiline*, 52.21. See above and below 3.4.3, 3.20.5, 4.23.5.
65. Ptolemy, *Quadripartus*, 2.3–4.
66. 1 Machabees (Maccabees) 8.14.
67. Cicero, *Philippics*, 2.41.
68. Sallust, *The War with Catiline*, 52.21.

is bound. But for this reason the ruler's prudence is not free, and, therefore, it is more remote from the divine and imitates it less. Although laws originate in natural law, as Cicero proves in his treatise *On Laws*,[69] and natural law derives from divine law, as the prophet David declares: "The light of your countenance is signed on us, Lord";[70] nevertheless they fail in particular acts, for which legislators cannot provide, since they are ignorant of future events. Thus, political government results in a certain weakness, since political rectors judge the people by the laws alone. This weakness is eliminated in regal lordship since the rulers, not being obligated by the laws, may judge by what is in their hearts,[71] and they therefore more closely follow divine providence "which has care of all things," as is said in the Book of Wisdom.[72]

[7] All this makes clear what sort of rule political rule is and its mode of governing. Now I must consider despotic rule.

Chapter 9

What despotic rule is and how it is reduced to regal rule. An incidental comparison of political and despotic rule in different regions and times.

[1] Here let me note that what is called despotic rule is the relationship of a lord to a servant. This title comes from the Greek, and to this day lords of that province are called despots. We can reduce that rule to regal rule, as Sacred Scripture makes clear.

[2] Someone may object that Aristotle contrasts regal and despotic rule.[73] I will explain this in the next book, when I have assembled the material necessary to understand it, but for now it will suffice to prove what I have said using divine Scripture. Samuel, a prophet of the Israelite people, handed down regal laws, and these were the laws that introduced servitude. The people had petitioned Samuel for a king, since he was in his declining years and his sons were not exercising just lordship in a political mode, as the other judges of this people had done. When Samuel consulted the Lord, he answered:

69. Cicero, *On Laws*, 1.15.
70. Psalms 4.7. The New American Bible says "Lord, show us the light of your face."
71. *The Body of Civil Law: Codex* 6.23.19.1 (law is in the ruler's heart); *Digest* 1.3.31, 32.1.23; *Codex* 6.23.3; *Institutes* 2.17.8 (the ruler is free of the laws).
72. Wisdom 12.13.
73. Aristotle, *Politics*, 1.5.1254b.2–5.

Hear the voice of the people in those things which they say. . . . But call them to witness and preach the law of a king to them: . . . "He will take away your sons and put them in his chariots and he will make for himself chariots and horsemen and those to run before his teams of horse . . . and appoint plowmen for his fields and reapers for his crops and forgers for his arms; he will also make your daughters into maids, perfumers, and bakers of bread."

1 Kings also relates other conditions that pertain to servitude,[74] with the intention of showing that political government, which Samuel's government and that of the other judges had been, was more fruitful to the people.

[3] Nevertheless, I showed the contrary above.[75]

[4] To clear up this contradiction I need to let you know that political government is placed ahead of royal government for two reasons. First, if we refer lordship to the integral state of human nature, called the State of Innocence, in which there was political, not regal lordship, there was no lordship then that involved servitude, but rather preeminence and subjection existed according to the merits of each for disposing and governing the multitude, so that whether in influencing or receiving influence each was disposed proportionately according to its own nature. Therefore, political government was better for wise and virtuous persons, such as the ancient Romans, since it imitated this state of nature.

[5] But because "the perverse are corrected with difficulty and the number of fools is infinite," as is said in Ecclesiastes,[76] in corrupt nature regal government is more fruitful, because it is necessary for human nature to be disposed in such a way to, as it were, restrain its flux within limits. This gives rise to the exalted royal dignity, of which it is written in Proverbs: "The king who sits on the throne of judgment scatters all evil with his gaze."[77] Therefore, the rod of discipline, which everyone fears, and rigor of justice are necessary in the governance of the world, because through them the people and the uneducated multitude are better governed. This is why Paul said in Romans, speaking of the rectors of the world: "they do not bear the sword without cause . . . they are avengers in wrath against those who act badly."[78] And Aristotle says that

74. 1 Kings (1 Samuel) 8.7–17. The quote is an abridgement of 7–13.
75. Presumably a reference to Book 1, which praises kingship.
76. Ecclesiastes 1.15.
77. Proverbs 20.8.
78. Romans 13.4.

the penalties imposed by laws were instituted to serve as medicine.[79] In this respect regal lordship excels.

[6] The second reason political government is placed ahead of royal government has to do with how the land is situated with respect to the stars. This disposes the region in various ways, as I said above,[80] so we see that certain provinces are suited to servitude and others to liberty. This is why Julius Caesar and Aimoinus, in describing the deeds of the Franks and Germans, attributed mores and deeds to them which still characterize them today.[81] Roman citizens at one time lived under kings, for a period of 264 years from Romulus to Tarquin the Proud, as the histories relate.[82] But since, for the reasons already given, the Roman region was more suited for political government, the Romans governed it in that way for 444 years until the time of Julius Caesar through consuls, dictators, and tribunes.[83] During this time, as I said above, the Republic profited greatly from such a government. Thus also the Athenians after the death of King Codrus lived under magistrates, because they lived in the same climate.[84] This should make clear what considerations I use in placing a polity before a kingdom and regal lordship before a polity.

Chapter 10

Now that the two lordships have been distinguished, ministers can be distinguished according to the different kinds of lords, but certain kinds of ministers are common to all lords. A proof that servitude is natural for some.

79. Aristotle, *Ethics*, 10.9.1180b.23–28.
80. 2.8.4.
81. Julius Caesar, *The Gallic War*, 6.11–24; Aimoinus Floriac, *History of the Franks*, preface, chapter 2.
82. The seven legendary king of early Rome and their legendary dates were: Romulus (r.753–717 B.C.E.), the mythical founder of Rome, Numa Pompilius (r.715–673), Tullus Hostilius (r.673–641), Ancus Marcius (r.641–616), Lucius Tarquinius Priscus (r.616–578), Servius Tullius (r.578–534), and Lucius Tarquinius the Proud (r.534–510). On Tarquin the Proud, see note at 4.26.1.
83. From the traditional founding of Rome in 1 A.U.C.=753 B.C.E. to the traditional end of the monarchy in 510 B.C.E. is only 243 years but from then to 44 B.C.E., the year of Julius Caesar's death when many republicans felt he first went beyond constitutional forms, is another 466 years, so the total is correct within one year. Eutropius, *A Brief History of Rome*, 1.8, which Ptolemy used, gives 243 years. Perhaps Ptolemy used a corrupt manuscript and then fudged to get the correct total.
84. I have moved this sentence for the sake of clarity. It actually should appear after "from Romulus to Tarquin the Proud, as the histories relate." Codrus was the legendary eleventh-century B.C.E. king of Athens, who died heroically fighting the Dorian invaders. After his death the Athenian nobles abolished the kingship and instituted the office of Archon. But this also carried a life term and was hereditary. The first archon was Codrus's son.

[1] Now that I have introduced these matters, I must consider ministers, because they are the complement of government, and without them no lordship at all can exist, since it is through them that offices are exercised, works distributed, and necessities administered, whether in a kingdom or in any republic, according to the ranking of personages and the merits of those concerned with these things. For this reason, as Exodus makes clear, Moses, the first leader of the Israelite people, was justly reproved by his relative Jethro because he was attempting to satisfy his people by himself without ministers: "That people which is with you will be consumed through your foolish work, which is beyond your strength, and you will not be able to bear it. . . . Provide mighty men who fear God and hate Mammon, and constitute from them tribunes and centurions and ones set over fifty and ten who will judge the people."[85] We find the same thing among the Romans, since when there was no longer a government of kings in Rome, Brutus was made consul and governed the City alone, taking too little counsel, but when the Sabines instigated a war against Rome the Senate appended a dictator who was higher than the consuls in dignity. The first of these was named Lartius. At the same time the Master of Equites, who obeyed the dictator, was appended. The first of these was Spurius Cassius. After this, but at more or less the same time, tribunes were instituted, to act in favor of the people.[86] All this is said to show that the government of any association, province, city, or town cannot be well governed without a ministerium of diverse officials.

[2] We still must distinguish among ministers of the various governments, because they must necessarily be conformed to the lords of each government, like members to the head. Thus, political government requires ministers who accord with the quality of that polity. For this reason, today in Italy all ministers, like the lords, are mercenaries and therefore act for their own gain, like those contracted for a wage who have determined from the start that their end is the wage itself, not the utility of the subjects. But when they acted as ministers for free, as the ancient Romans did, their solicitude was fixed on the republic as their end and so were of profit to it. For example, Valerius Maximus relates that Camillus begged that if any god felt that Roman happiness was too great, that god's ill-will should be sated to his detriment and not that of the Republic.[87]

---

85. Exodus 18.18, 21–22. The quote is not exact; in particular, Exodus says "avarice" instead of Mammon. Ptolemy quotes this four times, and each time with slight variations. Jethro was Moses' father-in-law, the father of his wife Zipporah.
86. Eutropius, *A Brief History of Rome*, 1.12–13. For these officials, see note at 4.26.2.
87. This story is not found in Valerius Maximus or Eutropius, but one like it is in Livy, *History of Rome*, 5.21. Livy, however, says that he prayed that if any god or human thought his or Rome's luck was too great, he might be allowed to appease them without harm to Rome and

[3] Others are ministers of a regal government deputed to a lifetime office of ministering to a king for his profit and that of his people. Counts, barons, and simple knights are of this sort, feudatories who in themselves and their successors are obliged in perpetuity to the governorship of the kingdom by virtue of their fiefs. From this it is clear both that ministers are necessary in any lordship and that ministers ought to be established according to the situation of that which exercises lordship. This is why it is said in Ecclesiasticus: "As is the judge of the people, so also are its ministers; and as is the rector of a city, so also are its inhabitants."[88]

[4] Aristotle distinguishes four other types of ministers, who can be considered to have a connection to government.[89] First, there are some whom the civic entity or each government considers to be necessary to exercise the low offices of the lords, and for these nature provides a rank among human beings, as among other things. We see that among the elements there is a lowest and a highest, and that even in a mixture there is always one element that predominates. Certain plants are deputed for human food, others for fertilizer. The same modes hold in animals, and in humans there is something analogous among the members of the body. We may consider that this same thing holds in the relation of the body to the spirit and even in the very potencies of the spirit compared to each other, because certain of them are ordained to command and move, such as the intellect and the will, and others to serve those things according to their rank. The same is true among humans, and this proves that there are some who are servants by nature. Moreover, it happens that some are deficient in reason on account of a defect of nature, and such ones need to be induced to work in the servile mode because they cannot use reason—this is called natural justice. Aristotle touches on all these things in the passage cited.

[5] There are also ministers, such as those subjugated in war, who are deputed to the same kind of office for a different reason. Not without reason, human law established this to incite warriors to fight more strongly for the republic, since those who are conquered may be made subject to the victors by right, which Aristotle calls "legal justice."[90] Such ones may excel in reason; nevertheless, they are reduced to the state of servants by a certain military law for

---

with minimal harm to himself. Marcus Furius Camillus was a fourth-century B.C.E. general and dictator, who saved Rome from the Gauls.

88. Ecclesiasticus (Sirach) 10.2.

89. Aristotle, *Politics*, 1.6.1255a–b. Here Aristotle discusses the natural slaves and the taking of slaves in war, but does not distinguish four types of slave.

90. Aristotle, *Politics*, 1.6.1255a–b.

inciting the hearts of warriors. The Romans followed this mode. The histories relate that a man of as great eloquence as Titus Livius was reduced to
servitude when the Romans captured him, but that Livius, a most noble Roman, under whose sway he had been placed, emancipated him on account of
his probity. Taking his cognomen from him, he was called Titus Livius, after
Livius granted him his freedom for instilling the liberal arts in his children,
although the statutes of the rulers had not previously allowed this. The divine
law also ordered this, as Deuteronomy makes clear.[91]

[6] There are also two other kinds of ministers who assist in the household:
those who serve for the wage of contractors and those who do it out of benevolence and love of serving, to increase their own honor or advance their
virtue, such as those who minister to rulers in their domestic homes — in military affairs, in fowling, in hunting, or in other household matters of the home.
I will say nothing now about particular examples of these, through which one
seeks the love or grace of lords, or earns a wage, or receives praise for virtue.
Thus, as is said in Proverbs: "an intelligent minister of the kingdom is wel-
comed,"[92] and in Ecclesiasticus: "Let a faithful servant be to you as your own
spirit."[93]

[7] I conclude that for fulfilling the kingdom and supporting the government,
the ruler ought to be fortified with the riches and ministers that I discussed
above. For this reason Aristotle says: "he is not a king who is not self-sufficient
and who does not greatly excel in all his goods."[94] King Solomon had a great
abundance of all these things, as 3 Kings makes clear, but especially of ornament and the order of his ministers, which astonished the Queen of Sheba:
"Your wisdom," she said, "exceeds what I heard about through rumor. Blessed
are your men and your servants, who stand always in your presence and hear
your wisdom."[95]

91. Deuteronomy 15.12–18 mandates the freeing of a Hebrew slave after six years of servitude. It places no limit on slavery for non-Hebrews. Titus Livius (59 B.C.E.–17 C.E.), the historian,
certainly does not conform to Ptolemy's biography. He was a Roman citizen, albeit a provincial
from Padua from birth, and his life was quiet and devoted to writing. Ptolemy is mixing up the
more famous Livy with the playwright Lucius Livius Andronicus. Born in Tarentum, he came to
Rome as a war prisoner, possibly at the surrender of Tarentum in 272 B.C.E., and when freed he
took his master's name. For some unreliable stories about his life, see Livy, *History of Rome*, 7.2.
    92. Proverbs 14.35.
    93. Ecclesiasticus (Sirach) 33.31.
    94. Aristotle, *Ethics*, 8.10.1160b.3–4.
    95. 3 Kings (1 Kings) 10.7–9.

Chapter 11

It is necessary for kings or any lords to have especially strong fortifications in their jurisdictions. The many reasons for this.

[1] In addition, strong lordship, whether regal or political, needs fortifications, and the king or his domestics should devote themselves to providing them. We find a proof of this in King David who took Mount Zion for his defense after he captured Jerusalem. He built a fortress there, with the pipes of the houses being laid as far as Millo, and he called this fortress his city.[96] Kings everywhere follow the practice of keeping a specially defended area or fortress within their cities and castles, where their household and officials spend their time. There are many reasons for this.

[2] One has to do with the rulers themselves. It is expedient for them to be in a safe place in order to be more secure in governing, correcting, and exercising governance and more bold in executing justice. For this reason the Roman consuls and senators chose a very safe place, namely the Capitoline Hill, where, the histories tell us, they remained unharmed when the whole Roman city was occupied by its enemies.[97]

[3] Moreover, the king and his family's[98] great repute demands this so that their majesty is not vilified in the sight of their people through intercourse with their subjects. It also demands this to prevent the king's people from becoming indignant or the king himself and his family taking the occasion of dishonoring themselves among their subjects through appearing incautiously when the greatest modesty is required (it is with just such modesty that the elders of the Trojan people interacted with Helen, as Aristotle says).[99] King David himself fell into error in just such a case involving the wife of Uriah, Joab's shield bearer, whom he saw bathing from the terrace of his royal home, as is written in 2 Kings.[100]

96. 2 Kings (2 Samuel) 5.7–9. Millo was a part of Jerusalem associated in later parts of the Bible with defense and the fortress.

97. Eutropius, *A Brief History of Rome*, 1.19.

98. The word I translate here in this passage as family, *"familia"* I usually render as "household." This is more accurate, but in a few case I felt that "family" more reasonably conveyed Ptolemy's thought.

99. Aristotle, *Ethics*, 2.9.1109b.8–11; Homer, *Iliad*, 3.156–60. Aristotle says that we need to guard against pleasure because it is hard to judge it impartially, and so we should feel toward pleasure as the elders of the people felt toward Helen.

100. 2 Kings (2 Samuel) 11.2.

[4] The second reason has to do with the people, which is motivated more by its sensibilities than by reason. When they see the magnificent expenses that kings incur for fortifications, their admiration more easily inclines them to obey and to submit to the kings' mandates, as Aristotle says.[101] Also, they then have less reason to rebel or subject themselves to the enemies when they are attacked vigorously, for when the kings' ministers are present at the fortifications, the people are stirred up to a bolder defense. After he conquered Zion, Judas Maccabeus also built strong fortifications by surrounding the heights with very strong walls and high towers for the defense of the fatherland against its enemy. Similarly, he built up very strong fortifications in Beth-Zur to oppose Idumea.[102]

[5] Another argument is that fortifications are necessary for rulers to conserve their riches, which they should have in abundance, as I said above, and so that they and their household can use them more freely. In this situation ministers are more inclined to take care of necessities, since doing so is more delightful and honorable in a domestic home. For the proper ordering of human actions characteristically produces the appearance or beauty that comes from something that is proportionate and commensurate in its parts, and from this a certain spiritual joy arises in us that becomes, as it were, a feeling of awe. The Queen of Sheba, it seems, experienced this from the sight of the ordering of the ministers of Solomon's court, as I showed earlier.[103]

Chapter 12

For the good government of the kingdom or any other lordship,
the highways and other roads in the region or province should be
secure and free.

[1] Fortifications are also ordained for another necessity to which the king must attend for the good government of his kingdom, that is, to make the highways secure and suited for travel by foreigners, natives, or his own regal household. Roads are common to all by natural right and the laws of nations, for which reason no one is allowed to take possession of them, for no one can acquire a right to them by prescription or passage of time. Thus, in the book of Numbers a public road is called "the royal road"[104] to signify this commu-

---

101. Aristotle, *Politics*, 6.7.1321a.31–40.
102. 1 Machabees (Maccabees) 4.60–61.
103. 3 Kings (1 Kings) 10.4–9.
104. Numbers 21.22.

nity. In his gloss on this passage Augustine explains these words by saying that it is called this because, by the nature of human society, a road ought to be free to whomever passes through without causing harm.[105] For this reason it is also written in the same passage of Numbers that when the Amorites refused to allow the children of Israel to pass through their region, even though they promised to walk only on the royal road, that is, without any harm to the region, the Lord mandated that the Amorites be destroyed.[106]

[2] To ensure that the highways in their community should be free and secure to those who pass through, rulers have the right to collect tolls. So also, in serving these rulers, officials can legitimately demand tolls from travelers, and those who depart are rightly obliged to pay them.

[3] Moreover, it is fruitful for the government of a kingdom to see to the security of its roads, because merchants and their goods will then flow into the kingdom and increase its riches. The Roman Republic prospered because of its roads, which the Romans took pains to keep free. The highways were called "Roman" so that persons might feel more secure in transporting their goods on them, and, as the chronologists write, the Romans deceived bandits by the crafty feint of altering the dates on the calendar so that they would not know the time when the market days were being celebrated in Rome. The Roman rulers also instituted markets outside the City and gave these markets their names, to give them greater security and to make these places safer for foreigners, and they have kept these names down to the present in many provinces and regions. One example is the Market of Julius.[107]

[4] Various Roman consuls and senators also established highways that extended into various provinces, and their names seem to have authenticated them to ensure freer or more secure access to the City or to make their memory more celebrated. Some examples are the Aurelian Way, named for the ruler Aurelius, and the Appian Way, named for senator Appius. The first leads toward Reate, where the histories place the Aurelian province, while the second progressed through Campania. It is the same for other individual consuls

---

105. Augustine, *On the Heptateuch*, 4.44, on Numbers 21.22.

106. Numbers 21.22–24.

107. The name mentioned here is "Forum of Julius." A number of market towns were named "*Forum*," or market, including *Forum Julii*, a town in Gallia Narbonensis colonized by the eighth legion and afterward called Frejus. The Latin is more easily read to mean that there are many Fori of Julius that retain that name, but my reading makes more sense. I have not been able to identify the "crafty feint."

or senators, such as Flaminius or Aemilius, who gave their names to highways or provinces for the same reasons.[108]

[5] Free access to roads also increases the divine cult, because persons are then more ready to show reverence for the divine by traveling to seek an indulgence or for the festival of a saint. It was a particular motive of the Romans in making their highways secure to serve the divine cult, that is, the cult of idols, for which the Republic was very zealous, as Valerius Maximus wrote.[109] And Sacred Scripture reports in Esdras that enemies in the surrounding area impeded the restoration of the temple and slowed down its rebuilding.[110] It was in reference to this that it was said to the Lord in John: "This temple was built in forty-six years, and you will rebuild it in three days?"[111]

Chapter 13

A kingdom or other lordship should have its own coinage. What great good comes from this and what inconveniences if it is lacking.

[1] Now that I have finished with these matters, I must take up the issue of coins, the use of which regulates a person's life and consequently all lordship, but especially a kingdom on account of the various products it obtains with coins. For this reason, the Lord asked the Pharisees who were deceptively tempting him: "Whose image and inscription is this?" When they had responded, "Caesar's," he turned the sentiment of their question back on them, saying: "Render, therefore, to Caesar those things which are Caesar's and to God those things which are God's,"[112] as if the coin in itself were the reason that tributes should be payed.

---

108. Reate was an ancient Sabine town, afterward called Rieti. Rome's empire depended on its excellent roads that connected the city with other regions. Appius Claudius Caecus (the Blind), a censor, consul, praetor, and dictator, started the Appian Way between Rome and Capua in the late fourth century B.C.E.; later it was extended all the way to Tarentum (Tarento) on the opposite coast, allowing easier trade with Greece. The censor Aurelius Cotta began the Aurelian Way from Rome through Pisa and Genoa to Antibes in southern France in 241 B.C.E. Gaius Flaminius (d.217 B.C.E.), a general, tribune, consul, and censor, built the Flaminian Way from Rome to Ariminum (Rimini) in 220 B.C.E. The Aemelian Way, built in 187 B.C.E. by Lucius Aemilius Paulus Macedonicus, a general, praetor, censor, and consul, connected Ariminum (Rimini) and Placentia (Piacenza).

109. Valerius Maximus, *Memorable Deeds and Sayings*, 1.1, but Valerius does not specifically mention the role of roads.

110. 1 Esdras (Ezra) 4.4.

111. John 2.20.

112. Matthew 22.20–21.

[2] I have already sufficiently treated the matter of coins and how it is necessary for a king to have them in abundance. Now we may consider coinage insofar as it is a certain measure which allows an excessive abundance or deficit of things to be restored to the mean, as Aristotle says.[113] Coinage was invented to do this, to resolve quarrels in commerce and be a measure for exchange.

[3] Although there are many kinds of exchange, as Aristotle maintains,[114] that for which coinage is said to have been invented is the most expedient of all. For this reason, as is apparent from what I have already said, Aristotle criticized the polity of Lycurgus, who first handed down laws to the Spartans and Lydians, forbade coinage, and permitted only the mutual exchange of goods.[115] Aristotle concludes that coinage was constituted because of the necessity for exchange,[116] since through it commerce could be accomplished more expeditiously and the occasion for strife in exchange could be removed. Indeed, we have received this doctrine from our father Abraham, who lived long before Lycurgus or any other philosopher, for in Genesis it is written that he bought a field for his burial at a price of 400 shekels of common and approved money.[117]

[4] Although coinage is necessary in itself, there are two reasons why it is proper in every government, but especially in that of a king. One comes from considering the king, the other from considering the people subject to him.

[5] With regard to the first, proper coinage or money distinguishes the king and kingdom and any other government, because the image of law is represented on it, such as the image of Caesar, as I said above.[118] Nothing else preserves his memory so brightly, since human hands use nothing else as often as the coins of the king or other lordship.

[6] Moreover, it demonstrates his excellence, in that money regulates and is the measure of things for sale, and his image on the coin regulates persons in

---

113. Aristotle, *Ethics*, 5.5.1133a.
114. Aristotle, *Politics*, 1.9–12.
115. Aristotle, *Politics*, 2.9.1271b.11–15. Aristotle says only that there was no money in the treasury. Lycurgus was the traditional ninth-century B.C.E. lawgiver of the Spartans. There is little or no reliable historical evidence about him. Most accounts start with the fifth-century Herodotus. Aristotle (*Politics*, 2.10.1271b.20–30) and Ptolemy (4.18) report that the Spartan and Cretan constitutions derive from Lycurgus, but do not mention Lydia. Lydia here is probably a mistake, since Aristotle does state that the Lyctians were a Spartan colony, who went to Crete and adopted the constitution they found there.
116. Aristotle, *Ethics*, 5.5.1133b.20–29.
117. Genesis 23.7–16. Here the word used is "*moneta*," the actual root of our "money."
118. Matthew 22.20–21.

their commerce. Money gets its name "because it warns the mind and prevents fraud among persons."[119] Since it is a measure of worth, it should be trusted, so that the image of Caesar should be, as it were, a divine image to human beings, as Augustine explains in treating this matter,[120] and coinage gets its name because "the names of rulers and their likenesses designate it," as Isidore tells us.[121] From all this it is manifest that the majesty of lords shines forth from coinage, and this is why, for their own glory, cities and towns, rulers and prelates, individually procure their own special coinage from the emperors.

[7] Another argument is that proper coinage serves the ruler's advantage, as I said above, because it measures tributes and other exactions made from the people, as divine law mandated in the case of oblations and redemptions in the place of sacrifice.

[8] Its manufacture by authority of the ruler is also convenient for the king, since no others may stamp the same image and inscription, as the laws[122] of nations mandate. Although by right it is licit for a ruler to make demands about how the coinage is stamped, any ruler or king ought to be moderate in changing or in decreasing the weight or the metal. This would work to the people's detriment, since money should be the measure of things, as I said above, but the more the money or the coinage is changed the more the value or the weight changes. In Proverbs it is written that this displeases God: "Both differing weights and values are abominable before God."[123] Pope Innocent criticized the king of Aragon quite severely for this because he had changed the coinage by diminishing it to the detriment of his people, so since the son had obliged himself by an oath to preserve the said money, Innocent absolved him from the oath and mandated that he restore the money to its former state.[124]

---

119. Isidore of Seville, *Etymologies*, 16.18. "To warn" in Latin is "*monere*," and "money" is "*moneta*."

120. Augustine, Sermon 90.10. Augustine explains that Caesar's image on his coin is analogous to God's image stamped on human beings, and that just as Caesar wants back what is his (the coin), God wants us back. He also refers to God as "our Caesar." See also Sermon 113A.8 and *On the Gospel of John* 40.9.

121. Isidore of Seville, *Etymologies*, 16.18. "Coinage" in Latin is "*numisma*," and "name" is "*nomen*."

122. *Iura*.

123. Proverbs 20.10.

124. Innocent III, *Register*, 2.28, Letter to Pedro II, April 1199; also found in *The Body of Canon Law: Extra Book* 2.24.18. As written, this is rather confusing. What happened was that King Pedro II (r.1196–1213) had sworn to uphold the coinage of his father (thus the reference to "the son") Alfonso II (r.1162–1196), but it turned out that this coinage was debased and so Pedro asked Innocent to be absolved of his oath. Innocent in effect said that he did not need this

[9] The laws[125] that concern coinage also protect loans and contracts, for it is mandated that loans be discharged and contracts preserved in the coinage of the particular time in full measure of quality and quantity.

[10] Therefore, I conclude that coinage is proper and necessary for any king whatsoever.

[11] With regard to the people, what I have already said also makes it apparent that the king's coinage is proper and necessary.

[12] First, because it is expedient as a measure in exchanges. The common people also accept it more than other measures because there are many who are ignorant of other monies, and this makes it easy for simple people to be defrauded, which is contrary to the form of regal government. The Roman rulers took care of this. The histories tell us that in the time of our Lord Jesus Christ, as a sign of subjection to the Romans, there was only one coin in the whole world, which bore Caesar's image, and when the Lord Jesus Christ questioned the Pharisees in order to expose their fraud, they immediately recognized the coin.[126] That coin was worth ten ordinary denarii, and anyone could use it to pay the rulers' toll-collectors or those who acted in their place in the provinces, cities, or towns.

[13] Second, one's own coinage is more fruitful. When foreign money is involved in exchanges, it is necessary to have recourse to the art of money-changing, since coinages may not be as valuable in other regions as in their own. This cannot help but be harmful, and this situation comes up especially in parts of Teutonia and regions thereabouts, which is why those who travel from place to place are compelled to carry a mass of gold or silver to sell as needed to make exchanges for things for sale.

[14] Hence, Aristotle, in distinguishing the species of money making in the pecuniary art and in coinage—that is, money changing, *obolistatica*, and *tocos*—

---

absolution, since either he took the oath in good faith, in which case he was bound to uphold its spirit—to preserve the integrity of the coinage—or he took it knowing that the coinage was debased, in which case it was not a valid oath to begin with. See Thomas N. Bisson, "'Quanto personam tuam' (X 2.24.18): Its Original Significance," *Proceedings of the Fourth International Congress of Medieval Canon Law* (Vatican: Biblioteca Apostolica Vaticana, 1976), 229–49.

125. *Iura.*

126. Matthew 22.19–21; Mark 12.15–17; Luke 20.24–25. All these report that they showed him a denarius with the portrait of Caesar. In different times this coin was worth from ten to sixteen asses. See Peter Comestor, *Scholastic History*, On the Gospels, 4.

says that money changing alone is natural since it is ordained for the exchange of natural things, resulting solely in the provision of the proper coinage, as is apparent from the things I have said. On account of this he commends it alone after scorning the other two. I will speak about these below.[127]

[15] Therefore, we must conclude that for the preservation of lordship and especially of regal lordship every government must have its own coinage, and this is the case whether we consider the people, or the king, or the kind of government.

Chapter 14

Weights and measures are necessary for the good of a kingdom or other lordship. Examples and reasons to show this.

[1] Now that I have treated these matters I must turn to weights and measures, which are as necessary as the coinage for preserving the government of any lordship, since they are used in the payment of tributes, since their use decreases quarrels and protects fidelity in purchases and sales, and, finally, since they, like coins, are instruments of human life and, even more than coinage, imitate natural action. As is written in the book of Wisdom, God disposed all things "in number, weight, and measure."[128] If such limits bound all creatures, it seems that weights and measures take their origin from nature more than coinage does, and therefore they are even more necessary in a republic or a kingdom.

[2] Further, weights and measures are nothing in themselves; they are always ordained for measuring and weighing, but a coin, although it is a measure and an instrument in exchanges, can be something in itself. If it is melted it still will be something, namely gold or silver, and, therefore, it is not always ordained for exchanges.

---

127. Aristotle, *Politics*, 1.10.1258a38–b8. Note that Ptolemy, following William of Moerbeke, uses forms of the Greek words "ὀβολοστάτης, τόκος," "usury, interest," although perfectly good Latin words were available. I have chosen to retain the Greek forms, since, partially because of William's translation, partially because of a literal interpretation of "money making," Ptolemy completely misconstrues the passage. He interprets Aristotle's reference to the honorable making of money in household management as referring to money changing to obtain goods. And when Aristotle condemns usury, using two words, Ptolemy understands him to be referring to two ways of making money. See below 2.14.3.

128. Wisdom 11.21

[3] This is true even for other species of monies; indeed, it is more true, for example in money changing, which is not properly ordained to be a measure of things for sale, but rather for the exchange of coins. Likewise, in *obolistatica*, which depends on coins of excessive weight, and when these are found to be overweight they are melted down into metals, to be weighed in balances and with other weights.¹²⁹ Likewise in *tocos*, that is, the usurious art,¹³⁰ which is ordained to coins as an end in themselves and excludes other exchanges. Aristotle takes up these species; I touched on them above and will discuss them again below.¹³¹

[4] Moreover, those acts are especially necessary in a republic or a kingdom which proceed from natural right, since the laws that rulers institute are not just unless they originate in it. Such laws come from natural right because they achieve natural justice. Thus, measures and weights are necessary for the true government of a kingdom or polity.

[5] Hence, as Isidore described,¹³² at the same time that Moses, the first leader of the Israelite people, handed down the first divine laws, he also established weights and measures, such as the ephi and gomor,¹³³ or the modius and sextarius for food and drink, or cubits for the measurement of land and cloth, or statera and other weights for gold, silver, and coins. When in Leviticus Moses exhorted the people to do justice, he immediately added the rules of natural justice, as Origin explains when he comments on this passage: "Do not do anything unfair . . . in weighing and measuring. Let the statera be just and the weights equitable; let there be a just modius and an equitable sextius."¹³⁴

---

129. See above note to 2.13.14. Aristotle says that in this way, money is made from money itself. He means usury, but since Ptolemy did not read the passage correctly, he is forced to come up with a way literally to make money from money. Even understanding this, the translation is problematic, and to make sense of it I have had to distort the words, rendering "weighers" as "weighed." The Latin is *"Item in obolostatica quae consistit circa pondera excessum in numismatibus, quibus inventis supra pondus in metalla resolvuntur, ut sunt ponderatores in trabuchetis et aliis ponderibus."*

130. The usual Latin term, *ars faeneraria*.

131. Ptolemy says Aristotle takes this up in *Politics* 4, but the correct reference is 1.10.1258a.38–b9. See above 2.13.14. Ptolemy does not discuss these "species" below.

132. Isidore of Seville, *Etymologies*, 16.25.

133. Exodus 16.32–36. Grain measures. Moses orders Aaron to measure out a gomor of Manna; the narrator comments that 10 gomor = 1 ephi. There is no indication there that Moses established these measures.

134. Leviticus 19.35–36. 1 modius = sixteen sextarii; both are biblical and Roman grain measures. A stater is a weight or a silver coin equal to four drachma; among the Jews it was synonomous with shekel. The cubit, probably around nineteen inches, was used in passages of the Bible before Moses appears, for example, in the myth of Noah (e.g., Genesis 6.15).

[6] Isidore reports that Pheidon of Argos gave measures to the Greeks, when the kingdom of the Argives flourished about the time of the leader Moses.[135] The histories relate that Ceres gave the measures for agriculture and grain to the Sicyonians, for which reason she was called the grain and measure goddess.[136] These things make it clear that kings and other lords must naturally give measures and weights to the people subject to them for their good government, for the reasons that I have already given and by the example of the rulers that I have cited.

Chapter 15

To preserve his state, a king or other lord must take care that the public treasury provides for paupers. Examples and reasons to prove this.

[1] There is another thing that pertains to the good government of a kingdom, province, city, or any other rule, and that is that the ruler, who is in charge of the needs of paupers, minors, and widows and of assistance to foreigners and pilgrims, should provide for them from the common treasury. If nature does not fail in necessities, as Aristotle says,[137] still less should art, which imitates nature, and among all arts none is more superior or complete than the art of living and governing, as Cicero tells us in his *Tusculan Disputations*.[138] Therefore, kings and rulers ought not to lack for what is necessary for the indigent; on the contrary, they ought to give them assistance.

[2] Kings and rulers stand in the place of God on earth, and it is through them, as secondary causes, that God exercises governance over the world.

135. Isidore of Seville, *Etymologies*, 16.25. Isidore speaks of the Argive "Phidon" and Ptolemy of "Sidon." The city of Argos was founded in the early second millennium B.C.E., but the tyrant Pheidon, who must be who Isidore had in mind, lived in the seventh century B.C.E., when Argos became the dominant Peloponnesian city, so Pheidon lived long after Moses (assuming Moses is a historical figure).

136. Isidore of Seville, *Etymologies*, 17.3 relates this myth but does not use the words "demetrian" or "Sicyonian." The word "*demetria*," which I have translated "measure," is ambiguous in the Latin. The goddess Demeter is the Greek equivalent of Ceres, and the Greek adjective "*demetria*" would be most properly translated "grain" or "bread." In context, and since it suggests an etymology from words for measure (especially from the verb *metior*), it seems more likely to me here that Ptolemy intends it to mean "measure." Sicyon is an ancient Peloponnesian city near Corinth, the chief town of Sicyonia.

137. Aristotle, *On the Heavens*, 3.2.301a.11.

138. Cicero, *Tusculan Disputations*, 4.3.5. Although Cicero is here talking of scholars being called into public life as ambassadors, he says that *philosophy* is the most fruitful of all arts since it teaches the way of right living.

Hence, when the Israelite people spurned the prophet Samuel's lordship and he laid his complaint before God, he received the response that they had not spurned him but God, in whose place he stood.[139] As is said in Proverbs: "Through me kings reign and those who institute laws decree what is just."[140]

[3] The care of paupers comes especially from God, to supplement the defect of their nature. For this reason divine providence acts toward the indigent as a father toward weak children, whose greater needs make greater solicitude incumbent. God himself reckons that what is done to a pauper is done to him, and this is attested to by him who says: "What you have done to one of my least, you have done to me."[141] Therefore, rulers and prelates, who stand in the place of God on earth, are like debtors and fathers for supplementing the defect of paupers. As Aristotle says, duty compels them to be helpers of their subjects,[142] and they should take special care to benefit them.

[4] Vegetius writes that Philip, king of Macedon, had such solicitude for Pythias, who had previously committed an offense, that when he heard that that noble and his three daughters were oppressed by poverty, he reprimanded those responsible and asked whether it is better to cut off a sick part of the body than to cure it. Then Philip summoned Pythias and spoke with him familiarly. When he understood Pythias's difficulty with domestic necessities, he provided him with money and thereby made him more faithful.[143]

[5] Moreover, since kings and rulers act for the whole and have universal diligence for their subjects, and since no one person suffices for proper actions, they must lack for many things, since such action or actions in guiding the people, such as judging and providing for their subjects according to each one's merit, transcends natural virtue. For this reason it is said that the government of souls is the art of arts, and it is extremely arduous, in that those who do not even know how to hold the rudder of their own lives become judges of others' lives.[144] So, after the Prophet Samuel had elevated Saul and anointed him as king, Saul was ordered to go up to a group of prophets, so that, through elevating his mind and prophesying with them about the guidance of

---

139. 1 Kings (1 Samuel) 8.4–7.
140. Proverbs 8.15. The personification of Wisdom, which is God, is speaking.
141. Matthew 25.40.
142. Aristotle, *Ethics*, 8.11.1161a.11–15.
143. Not actually Vegetius, but Frontinus, *Strategematicon*, 4.7.37. Ptolemy calls him "Phisia." Philip II of Macedon (r.359–336 B.C.E.) conquered Greece and was the father of Alexander the Great.
144. At 4.20.6 Ptolemy attributes this to Gregory.

the people, he might receive fame from doing things under divine influence. He did this, as 1 Kings makes clear.[145] Thus, for the reason I have given, it is impossible for kings and rulers not to err unless they turn themselves to him who guides all things and is the founder of all. This is why Ecclesiasticus says of the kings of the Israelite people: "except for David, Hezekiah, and Josiah," who were spiritual men illuminated by God, "all sinned against God." [146]

[6] That defect is relieved through the good deed of alms, which sustains the poor. This is what was said through the prophet Daniel to that heathen ruler Nebuchadnezzar, king of Babylon, supreme monarch of all the east: "Redeem your sins with alms, and your iniquity with acts of mercy toward the poor." [147] Therefore, the alms that rulers give to the needy are, as it were, a certain surety to God on their behalf for paying the debts of their sins, which is similar to what Aristotle says about the relationship of coins to things for sale.[148] As coinage is a measure for exchanges in the corporal life, so alms are in the spiritual life, which is why it is said in Ecclesiasticus: "The alms of a man are like a purse for him, and they will preserve a person's grace like the apple of his eye." [149]

[7] It should now be sufficiently clear that it is suitable for kings and other lords to provide for the poor in their government from the common treasury of the republic or from the regal treasury. For this ministry, individual provinces, cities, and towns should have hostels,[150] which the kings or citizens should institute to alleviate the paupers' want, and not only faithful rulers but infidels as well should do this. The latter instituted homes of hospitality to assist the poor, which, as 2 Maccabees makes clear,[151] were called "hostels of Jupiter" because astrologers attributed the effect of benevolence and piety to that planet. The histories tell us that even Aristotle directed letters to Alexan-

---

145. 1 Kings (1 Samuel) 10.5–13.

146. Ecclesiasticus (Sirach) 49.5.

147. Daniel 4.24.

148. Aristotle, *Ethics*, 5.5.1133b12. Aristotle says that money is, as it were, a surety for a future exchange.

149. Ecclesiasticus (Sirach) 17.18. The New American Bible translates more clearly, if less appropriately in context: "A man's goodness God cherishes like a signet ring, a man's virtue, like the apple of his eye." Some Vulgate manuscripts, and apparently this coincides with the Hebrew, have "*signaculum*," "signet ring," instead of "*sacculum*," "purse."

150. The word is "*hospitalia*," which gradually took on the meaning of "hospital."

151. 2 Machabees (Maccabees) 6.2. This is not what the passage says. Rather it speaks of an emissary sent by Antiochus to force the Jews to defile their temples, in particular by calling the temple in Gazarim the temple of Jupiter Hospitalis, one of Jupiter's many manifestations.

der, exhorting him to be mindful of the needs of the poor in order to increase his government's prosperity.[152]

Chapter 16

A king and anyone exercising lordship must attend to the divine cult. What fruits there are of this.

[1] Now that I have considered these things, I must take up the divine cult, for which kings and rulers ought to be zealous with all their effort and solicitude, since it is the end that binds them. Therefore in this final book,[153] I will discuss that about which the magnificent king Solomon wrote in Ecclesiastes: "Let us all hear together the end of what is being said. Fear God and observe his mandates, for this is everything to a person."[154] Although that end, namely the divine cult and reverence for the observance of mandates, is, as I already said, necessary for everyone; nevertheless, it pertains more to a king and he is a particular debtor in this regard because of three of his aspects—namely, because he is a person, because he is a lord, and because he is a king.

[2] He is a debtor as a person because the human species was a unique creation of God. God made other creatures by speaking, but when he created the human species he said: "Let us make the human species in our image and likeness,"[155] as if to imply that we participate in the divine nature. Paul in the Acts of the Apostles reports the words of the poet Aratus saying that we are of the stock of God.[156] From this perspective we are all debtors to God, required in general to show reverence to the divine, and this is the first precept of the first tablet.[157] This is why in Deuteronomy it is said through Moses to the Israelite people and consequently to us: "Hear, Israel, the Lord God your

---

152. The probable source of this letter is § e of the pseudo-Aristotelian *Secreta Secretorum* (*Secret of Secrets*) (London, 1528; reprinted New York: Da Capo Press, 1970), which contains the supposed advice sent to Alexander by his teacher Aristotle. Other medieval legends of Alexander the Great included an apocraphal correspondence between Alexander and Aristotle, though most of it goes the other way: Alexander writes to Aristotle about the wonders of the east.

153. Presumably Ptolemy means the final chapter of book 2. The other alternative is that Mohr is right (see introduction) and Ptolemy wrote neither Book 1 or 2.

154. Ecclesiastes 12.13.

155. Genesis 1.26.

156. Acts 17.28. Paul does not identify the poet he is quoting, but it is Aratus of Soli (c.315–c.245 B.C.E.). The quote is from the invocation to Zeus in *Phainomena* 5.

157. That is, the first of the Ten Commandments (Deuteronomy 5.7) given on the two Tablets of the Law: "You shall have no other gods before me."

God is one,"[158] as if he alone were the one to whom reverence and honor are owed, in so much as we were created by him alone and brought forth with a unique prerogative. On account of this, and considering this great benefit, Moses adds immediately in the same passage: "Love the Lord your God with all your heart and with all your spirit and with all your strength,"[159] wanting to show by this that we owe all that we are to God. In recognition of this the precept of tithes was instituted,[160] to which everyone is obliged since it derives from divine right, and it is not restricted to coins but applies to anything at all,[161] for the reason I already mentioned.

[3] Although everyone is obligated to this, rulers as private personages are even more obligated, since they participate more in the nobility of human nature by reason of the stock from which they come and their nobility, as Aristotle tells us.[162] Moved by this consideration Caesar Augustus, who also was called Octavian, as the histories tell us, did not accept the divine honors which the Roman people bestowed on him because of the beauty of his body and the probity of his spirit, but he asked the Tiburtine Sibyl about his creator and maker, whom he learned about and adored, and by a public edict he prohibited any of the people to adore him any longer or call him "God" or "Lord."[163]

[4] He is a debtor as a lord, since, "There is no power except from God," as Paul said in the book of Romans.[164] Thus, he stands in the place of God on

---

158. Deuteronomy 6.4.

159. Deuteronomy 6.5.

160. Leviticus 27.30, Numbers 18.26.

161. What Ptolemy actually says is that tithes are required "not in the quantity of number but of anything at all." This could mean that it is not 10 per cent per se that is required (although this would contradict his texts), but it seems more likely that the word "*numeri,*" "of number," is a mistake for "*nummi*" or "*numi,*" "of coin."

162. Aristotle, *Rhetoric,* 2.14.1390b15–30. Aristotle is talking about the effects on character of being wellborn. In general he feels that after a time the wellborn will increasingly lack nobility of character.

163. Actually, Augustus was concerned to be seen as the preserver of the Republic, and so was unwilling to be regarded as other than "first citizen." The "Tiburtine Sibyl" was written in the mid or late fourth century C.E., possibly to explain the disastrous defeat of the emperor Valens by the Goths at Adrianople in 378 or the murder of the orthodox emperor Constans I in 350. The Christian author, prophesying ex post facto, tied together the Christian Roman empire with a new eschatology, and his work became an influential source for Christian apocalyptic movements, especially via several medieval reworkings, and it may be connected to the influential seventh-century pseudo-Methodius. It introduced the figure of the good Last World Emperor, who would reign in the Last Days. Since this sibyl purportedly prophesied several generations before Christ, Augustus could "ask" the sibyl something only in the sense of consulting the written prophesies. For some texts in translation, see Bernard McGinn, *Visions of the End: Apocalyptic Traditions in the Middle Ages* (New York: Columbia University Press, 1979), 43–50. For the Last World Emperor, see Norman Cohn, *Pursuit of the Millennium* (New York: Oxford University Press, 1970).

164. Romans 13.1.

earth, as I said above,[165] so that his whole virtue as God's minister depends on God. Where there is dependence in lordship, it is necessary to show reverence to the superior, since the ministers of those who have regal responsibilities do nothing on their own account. Whenever Apocalypse treats the ministry of the heavenly spirits, those it designates as elders and animals (the elders are more mature in their actions and the animals, rather than moving, are put into motion in their ministry by the intense divine irradiation), it always adds that they fell on their faces and adored God,[166] which certainly are two acts of worship and the divine cult. As is written in Daniel, Nebuchadnezzar, the monarch of the east, was transformed into a beast in his own imagination because he did not recognize that his lordship was from God. It was said to him: "Seven times will pass over you until you know that the Most High exercises lordship over the kingdom of human beings, and gives it to whomever he wishes."[167]

[5] As the histories tell us, even Alexander was warned about this. As he was rushing into Judea and approaching Jerusalem, intending to destroy the region, Jaddus, the High Priest of the Jews, in his white robes and accompanied by the ministers of the temple, came to meet him. Alexander became gentle, descended from his horse, and showed reverence to him who stood in the place of God. After entering the temple he honored it with great gifts and presented the whole people with liberty because of his reverence for the divine.[168]

[6] Kings are obligated to the divine cult, not only as persons and as lords, but also as kings, because they are anointed with consecrated oil. This is clear in the case of the kings of the Israelite people, whom the hands of the prophets anointed with holy oil. For this reason lords are called "christs" on account of the excellence of the virtue and grace in their joining to God, with which they ought to be well-furnished. Through their unction they acquired a certain reverence and transference of honor, which is why, as is written in 1 Kings, even David struck his breast in sign of repentance for having cut King Saul's tunic.[169] King David, when he was mourning the death of Saul and Jonathan with great lamentations, became angry about the irreverence of the foreigners, who had killed King Saul "as if he had not been anointed with oil," as is written at the end of 2 Kings.[170] We may also take an argument for

---

165. 2.15.2, 3.
166. Apocalypse (Revelation) 4.4–11, 5.8–9, 5.14, 11.16–17, 19.4.
167. Daniel 4.22.
168. Flavius Josephus, *Antiquities of the Jews*, 11.8.5.
169. 1 Kings (1 Samuel) 24.5–6.
170. Actually 2 Kings (2 Samuel) 1.21. David is angry with only one foreigner, an Amalecite, whose people David had recently massacred. This man said that he had come on Saul, who

their sanctity from the *Deeds of the Franks* and the Blessed Remegius, in the case of Clovis, the first Christian king among the kings of the Franks, who was anointed through the dove's transference of oil from above. His descendents were afterward anointed with signs and portents and with various cures coming from them on account of this unction.[171]

[7] Moreover, as Augustine says, the true king and priest was prefigured in this unction.[172] According to the prophet Daniel: "When the Holy of Holies comes, your unction will cease."[173] Therefore, in so far as kings in their unction stand as a figure of the one who, as is said in the Apocalypse, is "King of Kings and Lord of those exercising lordship,"[174] who is Christ our Lord, kings are debtors who should imitate him, so that there is a proper proportion of the figure to the one figured, of the shadow to the body, in which the true and perfect divine cult is contained.

[8] Therefore, it is clear how any lord must be devoted and reverent to God, but especially a king for the preservation of his government. We take an example of this from Romulus, the first king of Rome, as the histories tell us. In the beginning of his regal government in the Roman City he built a place of asylum, which he called the "temple of peace," glorifying it through many favors, and, because of its divinity and his reverence, he gave immunity to any wicked person of any status who fled there. Valerius Maximus writes in his first book about how his descendents fared, both those who were negligent toward the divine cult and those were fervent for it.[175]

[9] What can I say about the God-cultivating kings in the Old and New Testament? All who were solicitous for divine reverence ended their lives happily,

---

had fallen on his sword but had not died and, at Saul's request, finished him off. David had him killed (2 Kings [2 Samuel] 1.13–16).

171. Aimoinus Floriac, *History of the Franks*, 1.16. Also called Remi (c.437–c.533) and known as "the Apostle of the Franks," Remegius was Archbishop of Reims from 459 and baptized Clovis. The motif of someone "anointed" by a dove, the symbol of the Holy Spirit, occurs sporadically in medieval literature. The account of the baptism in Gregory of Tours, *History of the Franks*, 2.31, omits this legend.

172. Augustine, *The City of God*, 17.6, 17.17. In 17.6 Augustine also talks about the incident of Saul's tunic.

173. Daniel 9.24 says that the after seventy weeks the current dispensation will come to an end, sin will end, justice will come, and a Holy of Holies will be anointed, but Ptolemy's words are not a quotation.

174. Apocalypse (Revelation) 19.16.

175. Valerius Maximus, *Memorable Deeds and Sayings*, 1.1.1–15 (those who were fervent), 1.1.16–21 (those who were negligent).

but those who did the opposite, had an unhappy end. The histories tell us that in every monarchy from the beginning of the age three things come along in order, one after the other: the divine cult, scholastic wisdom, and secular power.[176] These three things followed in order, one after the other, in King Solomon and they were consummated through his merits. When he went down into the place of speech in Hebron, he was elevated as king through his divine reverence; he followed wisdom and through both of these his regal virtue excelled that of the other kings of his time. But when he fell away from the true cult of God, he had an unhappy end, as is clear in 3 Kings.[177]

[10] In this book I have written about what pertains to the good government of lordship, especially regal lordship.

176. *Potentia.*
177. 3 Kings (1 Kings) 11.

Book 3

Chapter 1

In this first chapter I consider and prove that all dominion is from God by considering the nature of being.

[1] "The heart of a king is in the hand of God, and it will go wherever he has willed," as is written in Proverbs.[1] Cyrus, king of the Persians, that great monarch of the east, announced this in a public edict after his victory over Babylon, which he razed to its foundation, and after the slaying of its king, Belshazzar, as the histories tell us: "Cyrus the Persian says these things: The Lord God of heaven has given all the kingdoms of the world to me."[2] It is apparent that all lordship comes from God, as from that First One who exercises lordship. We can show this in the three ways touched on by Aristotle, that is, with regard to being, to motion, and to ends.

[2] With regard to being, since all being must be reduced to the First Being, which is the origin of all being, as all heat is reduced to the heat of fire, as Aristotle makes clear.[3] For this reason, all being derives from the First Being, as does lordship, since it is founded on being. To the extent that it is founded on a more noble being, it comes before the others to exercise lordship over persons who are equal by nature, so that there is no cause for pride, but rather

1. Proverbs 21.1.
2. 1 Esdras (Ezra) 1.2; 2 Paralipomenon (2 Chronicles) 36.23. Belshazzar is mentioned only in a confused account in Daniel 5.1–30, where Darius the Mede, not Cyrus the Persian, is given as conqueror of Babylon. In actuality the last king of Babylon was Nabodinus (r.556–539 B.C.E.). Belshazzar was his son and heir and apparently commander of part of the Babylonian armies. Cyrus the Great (r.550–529 B.C.E.), king of the Medes and Persians, conquered the Median, Lydian, and the Babylon Empires, establishing the vast Persian Achaemenian Empire. The Bible celebrates him for ending the "Babylonian Captivity" and allowing the Jewish elite to return to Judah.
3. Aristotle, *Metaphysics*, 2.2.994a–994b.30. Aristotle discusses the First Cause here, but does not specifically mention being as such or heat.

a cause for humanely exercising governance over the people, as Seneca says in his letter to Lucilius.[4] On this account it is said in Ecclesiasticus: "Did they make you rector? Don't exalt yourself, but be among them as if you were one of them."[5] Thus, all being derives from that being which is the First Cause, and all lordship that a creature exercises derives from God as from that one who first exercises lordship and as from the First Being.

[3] Further, every multitude proceeds from one and is measured by one, as Aristotle makes clear.[6] Therefore, the multitude of those who exercise lordship takes its origin in the same way, from the one who exercises governance, which is God. We see the same thing in regal courts, in which there are many who exercise governance in various offices, yet all derive from one, namely the king. On that account Aristotle says that God or the Prime Cause stands in the same relationship to the whole universe as a leader, from whom the whole multitude of a camp derives, stands in relationship to the whole army.[7] In Exodus, Moses himself calls God the leader of the people: "In your mercy," he says, "You have been a leader to your people that you have redeemed."[8] All lordship, therefore, takes its origin from God.

[4] There is another argument with regard to being. A virtue is proportionate to the being of which it is a virtue and is made equal to it, because virtue flows from the essence of a thing, as Aristotle makes clear.[9] Therefore, the virtue of any being whatever stands in the same relationship to that uncreated virtue

---

4. Seneca, *Letters to Lucilius*. This is a series of many letters that deal with philosophy, but also journeys, visits, and personal material. Letter 47 says that slaves are equal by nature and that you should treat inferiors as you would wish your superiors to treat you, in particular, you should treat slaves with courtesy and compassion. Letter 90 says the first mortals were uncorrupted in their obedience to nature and reports that Posidonus said that the wise ruled then and that to govern was to serve, not to reign, but that vice transformed monarchies into tyrannies, which made law necessary. The fact that Ptolemy does not cite Letter 90 elsewhere, when it so clearly bears on his concerns and ideas, suggests to me that he did not have this letter available to him. Ptolemy misspells "Lucilius" as "Lucillus," as did Dante and Nicholas Trevet in his *Commentary on Boethius's "The Consolation of Philosophy."* See Davis, "Ptolemy of Lucca," 38–39.

5. Ecclesiasticus (Sirach) 32.1.

6. Aristotle, *Metaphysics*, 10.1.1052b.32–1053a.2.

7. Aristotle, *Metaphysics*, 12.9.1075a.13–15.

8. Exodus 15.13.

9. Ptolemy refers to Books 1 and 2 of *On the Heavens*, which deal with the heavenly bodies. Integral to Aristotle's theory is the idea (see, e.g., 1.2.268b.10–269b.18) that each simple body has a principle of motion natural to it (fire goes straight up, the heavenly spheres move in a circular motion, etc.), which is one application of the idea Ptolemy cites. As I mentioned in the introduction under "The Translation," and in a note to 1.9.4, Aristotle defines virtue as action in accordance with true ends or functions, that is, any excellence at all, and, given teleological causation with its belief in a natural motion and desire of any created thing to its end, virtue obviously flows from the essence of a thing.

which is God as created being stands to the uncreated being that is God, because whatever is in God is God. But all created being takes its origin from uncreated being, and, therefore, created virtue takes its origin from uncreated virtue. Moreover, lordship presupposes virtue, since there is no lordship where there is no might or virtue. Therefore, all lordship comes from uncreated virtue, and this is God, as I said above. This is just what I previously showed. As Paul says to the Hebrews, God supports "all things by the word of his virtue." [10] And in Ecclesiasticus it is written: "There is one, highest, omnipotent creator of all, a potent king, one to be feared exceedingly, who sits on his throne and who is God exercising lordship." [11] These words make it quite clear what it is from which every creature, and even more so a king, receives its essence, virtue, function, and consequently its lordship, as I showed above.

Chapter 2

I prove the same thing by considering the movement of any created nature.

[1] We can prove that lordship comes from God not only by reason of being, but also by reason of movement. First, we must take up Aristotle's argument that since everything that moves is moved by something, and it is impossible to regress infinitely through a series of moving things and things moved, it is necessary to come to some immovable Prime Mover, which is God, or the First Cause. [12] But kings, rulers, and all who have precedence are among those persons who possess reason for movement to a greater degree than others, whether they exercise governance, judge, defend, or engage in other acts pertaining to the responsibility of government. As Seneca says of Caesar in his little book *On the Shortness of Life, to Paulinus*, when he exhorts Paulinus to have contempt for the world:

> When you want to forget everything else, think of Caesar. . . . All things are permitted to the one who is Caesar, but for this reason many things are not permissible for him. Caesar's vigilance defends the homes of all, his labor defends the repose of all, and his activity defends the leisure of all. For this, Caesar has dedicated himself to the world, has robbed him-

---

10. Hebrews 1.3.
11. Ecclesiasticus (Sirach) 1.8.
12. Aristotle, *Physics*, 8.6.258b.10–259a20. Aristotle does not mention God, although he does say that the first mover will be one. Thomas used the idea of the impossibility of infinite regress to prove the existence of God as a first mover, *Summa Theologiae*, 1.2.3.

self from himself, and acts by the custom of the stars, which, unresting, always follow their courses.[13]

[2] Therefore, if kings and other lords have so much reason for movement, they cannot perfect this movement other than through the influence and virtue of the Prime Mover, which is God, as I proved above. On this account, when the author of the Book of Wisdom (in which the effects of divine virtue acting through divine wisdom are enumerated) wants to show how all things participate in the influence of divine movement, he adds immediately: "Wisdom is more active than all other active things, for it reaches everywhere on account of its purity,"[14] identifying as "purity" the absolute, surpassing, and unmixed divine virtue directed toward moving all things toward a likeness of corporal light, which in this regard imitates the divine nature.

[3] There is another argument with regard to movement. Every primary cause has more influence over what it causes than a secondary cause does. Since the Primary Cause is God, and since all things are moved by virtue of the Prime Cause, all things receive the influence of its movement, and, therefore, the movement of lords derives from the virtue of God and from his moving.

[4] Further, if there is an order among corporal movements, so much more will there be an order among spiritual ones. If we consider bodies, we see that inferior ones are moved by superior ones and that all movements are ultimately reduced to the movement of the supreme body, which is the ninth sphere, according to Ptolemy in *Almagest*, but the eighth according to Aristotle.[15] If, therefore, all corporal movements are regulated by the first movement and receive their capacity to influence movement from it, it is true of spiritual substances to a much greater degree since they are more similar to the first movement. Because of this, they are more fit to receive the influence of the first and supreme mover or motion, which is God. The Blessed Dionysius himself tells us about this movement in his books *On the Divine Names* and *On the Celestial Hierarchy*, where he distinguishes the same kinds of motion among spiritual substances as among corporal bodies: circular, right, and oblique.[16] These spiritual movements consist of certain illuminations that

13. Seneca, *On the Shortness of Life, to Paulinus*, 7.1–2.
14. Wisdom 7.24.
15. Ptolemy, *Almagest*, 1.8. Ptolemy gives a description and does not assign a cause for motion. Aristotle, *On the Heavens*, 2.7.12. Although Aristotle does not explicitly mention the number of spheres here, it can be determined by counting the spheres he lists.
16. Pseudo-Dionysius the Areopagite, *On the Divine Names*, 4.8–9. "Divine minds are moved in a circular direction by being united to the illuminations of the Beautiful and Good, without beginning or end; in a direct line whenever they advance to help a subordinate by accom-

they receive from superior ones for the purpose of acting, as the same doctor explains, but in order to receive such illuminations it is necessary to have a disposition of mind suited to the influence of that movement.

[5] Kings, rulers, and others exercising lordship in the world are among those who ought to be more prepared for this, both because they have been trained to perform the universal actions of government (for which reason their minds are more elevated to the divine) and also because it is incumbent on them to dispose themselves to provide the care imposed on them in exercising governance over their flocks and in doing other things necessary for the acts of government (these things are above rulers and beyond their particular natures). Through such movement they should be sufficiently led to the divine influence.

[6] King David disposed himself in this way, and through the movement of prophetic illumination he earned the spirit of prophetic understanding in his psalms beyond that of all other kings, even above that of the prophets, as the doctors of Sacred Scripture tell us. But, for acting in a contrary manner, the heathen rulers, whom the prophet David mentions, such as Nebuchadnezzar and his son Belshazzar,[17] deserved to be overshadowed. The influence of divine illumination affected their fantasy with imaginary visions, as the book of Daniel shows clearly,[18] to let them know what they should do in their regal government, but because their minds were embroiled in the darkness of sin and not properly disposed, their minds could not apprehend the meaning of these visions. They lacked the light of the prophet Daniel, to whom was given the spirit of understanding those things to be interpreted, in order to verify what Solomon said in the book of Proverbs: "Counsel and impartiality are mine, prudence is mine, and fortitude is mine. Through me kings reign and those who institute laws decree what is just. Through me rulers command and the mighty decree justice."[19]

[7] These things make it clear how we can show that all lordship is from God by considering movement.

---

plishing everything directly; in a spiral direction since, even in providing for the more indigent, they remain fixedly, in identity, around the Good and the Beautiful because of their identity." The soul is also moved circularly in uniting, spirally in illumination, and straightly led to simple contemplations.

    17. See 3.1.1 and Daniel 5 for Belshazzar. Confusingly, in Daniel 4, Daniel himself is called Belteshazzar and in the Vulgate both are called Balthasar. The confused account in Daniel calls Belshazzar Nebuchadnezzar's son, although at most he was his grandson.

    18. Daniel 2.1 ff., 4.1 ff., 5.5 ff.

    19. Proverbs 8.14–16. The personification of Wisdom, which is God, is speaking.

Chapter 3

I argue the same thing by considering the end.

[1] The same thing is also apparent by reason of ends. If it is a human characteristic to act to achieve an end through the reason of the intellect, which
appoints an end for any of its actions in advance, then, to the degree that any
particular nature acts in an intellective manner, it acts to achieve an end. Since
God *is* his intelligence and the pure act of intelligence, he even more includes
an end in his action. Therefore, one must say of necessity that an act of divine
intellect, which we also call divine providence, may be discerned in advance
in any particular end, which we may take as the ultimate end of any particular created thing, and that through this act God disposes the whole and leads
it to its destined end, as Boethius puts it in *The Consolation of Philosophy*.[20] By
this reasoning the book of Wisdom says: "divine wisdom reaches boldly from
end to end and disposes all things sweetly."[21]

[2] We can conclude from this that something participates in divine action to
the degree that it is ordained to an excellent end. This describes a kingdom
of any community or an association, whether it is regal, a polity, or of some
other condition, since when one intends a exceptionally noble end, as Aristotle notes,[22] we understand that divine action is in it from the start, and that
the government of lords is subjected to its virtue. Perhaps Aristotle states that
the common good is especially divine[23] because government takes its origin
from the truth.

[3] Further, in government the legislator should always intend that the citizens be directed to live according to virtue. Indeed, this is the end of the
legislator, as Aristotle says,[24] and for this reason Paul says in Timothy: "the
end of the precept is charity."[25] We cannot come to this end without divine
motion, just as heat cannot make something hot without the virtue of the
heat of fire, nor can lucidity make something shine without the virtue of light.
And the divine virtue surpasses and transcends created virtue and every type
of work to the extent that the motion of the Prime Mover is higher and more

20. Boethius, *The Consolation of Philosophy*, 4.6.
21. Wisdom 8.1.
22. Aristotle, *Ethics*, 8.13.1161a11–15. Aristotle mentions the exceptional end, but then
simply concludes that a good being will benefit its subjects if it acts as a pastor to sheep.
23. Aristotle, *Ethics*, 1.2.1094b.10. Ptolemy also refers to the *Politics*, but although Aristotle
does constantly mention and praise the common good, he does not call it divine there.
24. Aristotle, *Ethics*, 2.1.1103b.3–6. See also *Politics*, 3.9.1280b.5–11.
25. 1 Timothy 1.5.

excellent. It also influences things strongly, to such an extent that the Prophet Isaiah says: "You have worked all our works, Lord,"[26] and the Evangelical Voice says: "Without me you could do nothing."[27]

[4] There is another argument with regard to ends. An end sets the efficient cause in motion, and we find that it is a more noble and better end to the degree that it is more effective, as the good of a nation is with respect to the good of a city or household, as Aristotle says.[28] The end which a king should principally intend for himself and his subjects is eternal beatitude, which consists of the vision of God. Because that vision is the most perfect good, it ought to set the king and any lordship in motion, so that the subjects should follow that end, since one governs best by intending such an end. Moreover, the King and Priest was governing and exercising governance over his subjects in this manner when he said in the book of John: "I give them eternal life," and again: "I came so that they might love life and that they might have it more abundantly."[29]

[5] A king does this especially when he watches over his flock like a good shepherd, because then the divine light shines on him and inspires him to govern well, as the light shone on the shepherds at the birth of our king and savior.[30] We see that in the shinings that I have mentioned which inspire good government in the ruler and subjects, there is circular, right, and oblique motion. I distinguished these earlier in this chapter, and the Blessed Dionysius speaks about them in *On the Divine Names*.[31] Motion is called "right" when it comes about through the divine illumination of rulers for governing well or from the illumination of the people through the ruler's merits. It is called "oblique" when rulers govern their subjects through divine illumination in such a way that their subjects live virtuously, with the praise of God and the action of grace rising up in them. As an analogy to the action of these two motions consider the bowlike figure made from a straight[32] string and an oblique bow. Finally, we say that the divine illuminations act with a circular motion of the divine rays when they shine on rulers or subjects and elevate them to contem-

---

26. Isaias (Isaiah) 26.12.
27. John 15.5.
28. Aristotle, *Politics*, 1.1–2.1252a.10–1253a.40, especially 1252b.35–1253a.1 and 1252a.1–6. Aristotle does not make this distinction between the city and the nation; rather he mentions the family, neighborhood or village, and polity.
29. John 10.28, 10.10.
30. Luke 2.9.
31. Pseudo-Dionysius the Areopagite, *On the Divine Names*, 4.8–9.
32. "Straight" is *"rectus,"* i.e., "right" in Latin.

plate and love God. This motion is called "circular" because it is continuous and leads back to the same point,[33] which is a property of circular motion.

[6] Aristotle posits this motion when he writes that the Prime Mover or First Cause, which is God, moves things "as something desired," that is, by reason of the end, which is himself.[34] The Prophet David also speaks about this in the Psalms, although according to the sacred doctors what he says ought to be interpreted with reference to Christ our king: "God, give your judgment to the king and your justice to the king's son, that they might judge your people with justice and your paupers with judgment; that the mountains may preserve peace and the hills justice for the people."[35] A king and all other lords ought to entreat God for these things for the good government of their people, for which they ought principally to strive, as I said above.[36] And because their minds are disposed to receive the divine influence for the health of their subjects, David immediately adds: "He will descend like the rain on sheep, like raindrops dropping on the earth. Justice and an abundance of peace will arise in his days."[37]

[7] All these things make it quite clear that lordship comes from God for pursuing an end, whether remote, which is beatitude itself, or near, which is to act according to virtue.

Chapter 4

God provided for the lordship of the Romans because of their zeal for their fatherland.

[1] Because the kings and rulers of the Roman world were more solicitous than any others for these things, God inspired them to govern well, and for this they deserved an empire. In proving this, Augustine gives many reasons and causes, but we can reduce them all to three.[38] At the moment I am only

---

33. Aristotle, *Metaphysics*, 12.6.1071b.8–12. Aristotle says that the only continuous motion is motion in a place, and of this only circular motion is continuous.

34. Aristotle, *Metaphysics*, 12.7.1072b.1–4. Aristotle, of course, does not mention God. The assumption of teleological causation is that anything naturally desires its end.

35. Psalms 71.2–3 (72.2–3).

36. 2.4.8.

37. Psalms 71.6–7 (72.6–7).

38. Augustine discusses the Romans' qualities throughout *The City of God*. Here 5.12–22 seems most appropriate. As mentioned in the introduction, Ptolemy converts Augustine's ambivalent recognition of Roman virtue into the highest praise. While recognizing Roman civic

touching on the subject, and if I eliminate the others I can be more concise. A consideration of these reasons shows that they deserved lordship. One reason comes from love of their fatherland, another from their zeal for justice, and a third from the virtue of benevolence.

[2] The first of these virtues is in itself sufficiently deserving of lordship, because it participates in the divine nature by directing its affection to the community. It is oriented to universal actions of the people, just as God is the universal cause of things. Thus Aristotle says that the good of a nation is a divine good.[39] Since regal government, or any other kind of lordship, brings about community, one who loves the community deserves the community of lordship, so that the reward might go along with the quality of merit. For the condition of divine justice requires everyone to pay wages in accord with the workings of virtue, so that the words written in Apocalypse are fulfilled in them: "Their works follow them."[40] Again, in Matthew it is written: "the Lord gave to each one according to their virtue."[41]

[3] In addition, the root of love of fatherland is that love which "prefers the common things to one's own, not one's own things to common ones," as the Blessed Augustine says in explaining Paul's position on love.[42] Moreover, the virtue of love precedes every virtue in merit, because the merit of any other virtue derives from the virtue of love. This means that the love of fatherland, more than all other virtues, deserves to be rewarded with an honorable rank—and this is lordship. Therefore, one deserves rule by reason of one's love of the fatherland. Cicero writes about this love of the fatherland in his book *On Duties*:[43]

> Of all societies none is more pleasing, none dearer than that which abides in the republic. Our parents are dear to each of us, our children are dear,

---

virtue, Augustine traces them to the vice of love of praise and glory; yet it was for these limited virtues—those that were good according to the standards of the earthly city—that he granted empire to them (5.13, 5.19). If he had not given them an empire, they would not have received a reward for their good qualities, since they could not hope for an eternal reward (5.15). God's other purpose was to provide an example to the members of the City of God—to show them what love they should have for their city, if the earthly city had received such devotion from its citizens, and what reward was to be theirs if the Romans should receive such great reward for merely civic virtue (5.16). However, Augustine also stresses that God gave power to the tyrants as well as to the good emperors, for just, if inscrutable, reasons (5.21.).

39. Aristotle, *Ethics*, 1.2.1094b.8–10.
40. Apocalypse (Revelation) 14.13.
41. Matthew 25.15.
42. Augustine, *Regulation for the Servants of God*.
43. Cicero, *On Duties*, 1.17.

our neighbors and household staff are dear, but one's fatherland encompasses all these loves. What good person would hesitate to seek death on its behalf if they could be helpful to it?

Sallust relates the great extent of the love that the ancient Romans had for their fatherland in *The War with Catiline*. He gives Cato's opinion, who includes this love in an enumeration of some of their virtues:

> You should not judge that our ancestors made our small republic great by arms—in fact, arms and horses are more abundant with us than with them—but because they displayed industry at home, just command abroad, a free spirit in counseling, and were addicted neither to lust nor transgressions. But instead of these things we now have luxury and avarice, poverty in public but opulence in private; we praise wealth, we seek idleness, we make no distinction between the good and the evil, and ambition reaps all the rewards of virtue.[44]

[4] Love of fatherland also seems to include first and foremost the mandate that the Evangelist Luke mentions.[45] Those who are zealous for common affairs become similar in their love to the divine nature, in so far as they, like God, show loving care toward the multitude. Likewise, they carry out love of their neighbor when, from paternal affection, they bear solicitude for the whole people committed to them and thus fulfil the previously mentioned mandate, about which Deuteronomy says: "Love the Lord your God with all your heart and with all your mind and with all your strength, and love your neighbor as yourself."[46] Since there can be no dispensations from that divine precept, Cicero says in *On the Republic*: "there is no cause for which one's own fatherland should be denied."

[5] We may mention the noble soldier Marcus Curtius as an example of this love of fatherland. As the histories and the Blessed Augustine tell us, fully armed and sitting on his horse, he jumped headlong into a precipitous cleft in the earth in order to rid the City of pestilence.[47] As another example, Marcus

---

44. Sallust, *The War with Cataline*, 52.21. See above and below 2.8.3, 3.20.5, 4.23.5.

45. Luke 10.27, referring to the injunction of Deuteronomy mentioned a few sentences later. Luke 10.28–37 explains this in terms of helping others and gives as an example the the story of the good Samaritan.

46. Deuteronomy 6.5. Earlier, 2.16.2, Ptolemy, used the usual word "spirit" instead of "mind."

47. Augustine, *The City of God*, 5.18. Marcus Curtius, who lived in the fourth century B.C.E., according to legend leaped into an earthquake fissure when a soothsayer said it could only be closed by the sacrifice of Rome's greatest treasure, and Curtius interpreted this to be a brave man.

Regulus preferred the health of the Republic to his own. He was a mediator of peace between the Roman people and the Carthaginians, and after the former consulted him, he returned to Africa, where the Carthaginians killed him.[48] The cleanhanded manner in which their rulers conducted their offices for the preservation of the Republic is clear from the example of Marcus Curius, about whom Valerius Maximus wrote in his fourth book:[49] "he had contempt for the wealth of the Samnites." When their legates were admitted to his presence after his victory over them, they found him sitting on a bench by the fire and eating from a wooden bowl. They brought out a large amount of gold and ingratiatingly asked him to take it, but he immediately broke out laughing and said: "You are ministers of a superfluous, or, I might even say, an inept, delegation. Tell the Samnites that Marcus Curius prefers to command the rich than to become rich. And remember that I can neither be conquered by an army nor be corrupted by money."[50] In the same book Valerius Maximus also tells us about Fabricius, who despite the fact that he had more honors and authority than any others of his age, "was no more prosperous than the poorest." When the Samnites, who were his dependents, sought him out, he showed contempt for the money and servants they brought him and sent them back disappointed. His moderation and zeal for his fatherland benefited him: he was very rich without money and had many attendants without a household, since he was made rich through not possessing many things but desiring few.[51]

[6] Writing about these things, Augustine concludes that the power of exercising lordship is given to humans only by the providence of the Most High God, when he judges human affairs to be worthy of such gifts.[52] He says many similar things in this passage and seems to determine that the Romans' lordship was legitimate and conferred on them by God.

[7] As another example, Mattathias and his sons, although they were of priestly stock, deserved lordship among the Israelite people because of their zeal for the law and their fatherland, as 1 and 2 Maccabees make clear. When

---

48. Augustine, *The City of God*, 5.18. The point is that he returned voluntarily, knowing his fate, because he had given his word to the enemy. Marcus Atilius Regulus (d.250 B.C.E.) was a consul and general who defeated the Carthaginians in 256, but was himself defeated and captured in 255. He was sent on his mission to Rome in 250.

49. Valerius Maximus, *Memorable Deeds and Sayings*, 4.3.5.

50. Manius (not Marcus) Curius Dentatus was an early third-century B.C.E. general and consul who defeated the Bruttians, Lucanians, Sabines, and the Greek leader Pyrrhus, as well as the Samnites.

51. Valerius Maximus, *Memorable Deeds and Sayings*, 4.3.6. This is very close paraphrase. Gaius Fabricius Luscinus was a third-century B.C.E. Roman general and consul. See above 2.8.3.

52. Augustine, *The City of God*, 5.19.

Mattathias was near death, he spoke to his sons as follows: "Strive mightily for the law and give your spirits for the testament of your fathers," which we take to mean the Republic of the Israelites. Afterward, he added: "And you will receive great glory and an eternal name," which we understand to mean the rule of his sons, who ruled successively: first Judas, then Jonathan, and finally Simon, and whichever of them was priest and leader flourished among the Israelites.[53]

Chapter 5

The Romans deserved lordship because of the very holy laws that
they passed down.

[1] There is another reason why the Romans were worthy of lordship—their zeal for justice. Through it they acquired rule by natural right, from which all just lordship originates. First, because, as Augustine writes, "They freely consulted about the fatherland," banishing avarice and foul gain from their exercise of lordship, "and they were guilty neither of lust nor any crime,"[54] through which lordship is destroyed. Instead, they inspired human beings to love them, so that, because of their exceptionally just laws, others spontaneously subjected themselves to their lordship. As the Acts of the Apostles relates, when the Jews inflicted vexatious injuries on the Apostle Paul, he appealed to Caesar and subjected himself to Roman laws in the presence of Festus, ruler of the part of Palestine that includes Caesaria.[55] This book also describes the kind of laws the Romans had and how holy they were. When Festus was in Jerusalem, the ruling priests visited him and demanded that Paul be condemned to death. Festus answered that according to the way that individuals are subject to the Romans' laws, "it is not the custom of the Romans to condemn them," or to pardon them, "unless their accusers are present and they have the chance to defend themselves and clear themselves of the accusation."[56] For this reason Augustine says: "It pleased God that the Romans

---

53. 1 Machabees (Maccabees) 2.50–51. Jewish priests were not traditionally chosen for political office. These men are the important members of the first two generations of the Maccabean or Hasmonaean family, which dominated Israelite politics in the second and first centuries B.C.E. Mattathias (d.c.166) revolted against the Hellenizing Antiochus IV Epiphanes. His son Judas (r.166–160) seized Jerusalem. He was succeeded by his brothers Jonathan (r.160–143) and Simon (r.143–134), who established an independent Judea.

54. Augustine, *The City of God*, 5.15.

55. Acts 25.11. Porcius Festus was the Roman procurator of Judea from about 58 to 62 C.E.

56. Acts 25.16.

should conquer the world, so that it might be pacified by being brought far and wide into the single society of the Republic and its laws."[57]

[2] There is further argument to the same point. Someone having care of another should take a wage by natural right, because, as is written in Proverbs: "God gave mandates to all about their neighbors."[58] For this reason, if the goods of another are misappropriated by robbers or plunderers, by rights someone else can recover these things, deduct expenses incurred in the recovery, and receive a reward according to the merits of the action. Given this, granting lordship for the purpose of preserving peace and justice in various regions and for stopping disagreements is appropriate and seems to be harmonious with both nature and reason.

[3] Likewise, it seems that evil ought to be punished and good promoted. This is the office that lords fulfill, acting in this like those who take charge of their neighbors, and on that account they may take their wage—the taxes and tributes they receive for this office. The Apostle to the Romans showed that all lordship comes from God in the following words, and in other statements about lordship in the same passage: "There is no power except from God." Afterward, he concluded: "Therefore also you offer tributes; for they are ministers of God serving him in this."[59] To the extent, therefore, that for their probity virtuous persons are placed ahead of others to guide a multitude of people that lacks a king and has no rector, and to the extent that they assume the care of and direct the people under the laws, to that extent it seems that God's instigation motivates them and that they seem to act in place of God in their lands, because they preserve the multitude of persons in civil society, which, according to Aristotle, is a necessity for them as naturally social animals.[60] Thus, in this case also, lordship seems to be legitimate.

[4] In proving this, Augustine writes: "Take away justice, and what are kingdoms but certain kinds of robberies?"[61] Under that assumption, he seems to concede the legitimacy of kingdoms and all other kinds of lordship. To show what he means, he introduced the example of the pirate Dionites, whose captor, Alexander, asked him why he had infested the sea. He answered with

---

57. Augustine, *The City of God*, 18.22.
58. Actually Ecclesiasticus (Sirach) 17.12.
59. Romans 13.1–6.
60. Aristotle, *Politics*, 1.2.1253a.2–3. Actually, Aristotle says "political animals." See the introduction under "Political Thought of the First Contributor."
61. Augustine, *The City of God*, 4.4.

unrestrained obstinacy: "I do the same as you do to the whole world. But because I do it in a small ship, I am called a robber. And because you do it with a great fleet, you are called emperor."[62] For that reason God conferred lordship on the Romans. Augustine also writes that because of their most holy laws, they strove as it were by a righteous "path to honors and empire and glory, and they do not have any reason to complain of the justice of the Most High and true God, for they have received their wage,"[63] namely by exercising lordship justly and exercising governance legitimately.

[5] Moreover, the extent to which the ancient Roman consuls were zealous against evildoers is manifest in many examples. Augustine wrote that Brutus killed his own sons because they were stirring up wars among the people and deserved death by the vigor of justice.[64] "He conquered," as Vergil said, for he possessed "love of the fatherland and an immense desire for praise."[65] He relates that Torquatus also killed his son, who, under provocation, attacked the enemy with youthful ardor against his father's edict. Although he emerged victorious, Torquatus sentenced him to death according to military laws because he exposed his nation's camp to danger. Augustine says that Torquatus did this, "So that the evil resulting from this example of contempt for command would not be greater than the good from the glory of crushing the enemy."[66] Valerius Maximus says that he preferred to be without his son than to indulge in transgressing military discipline.[67] From these things it is clear why the Romans merited lordship because of their zeal for legal justice.

---

62. Augustine, *The City of God*, 4.4. Augustine does not give the name of the pirate; Ptolemy gets this from John of Salisbury, *Policraticus*, 3.14, where the pirate is called Dionides. George Cary, *The Medieval Alexander* (Cambridge: Cambridge University Press, 1956), 96–97, points out that there are two medieval traditions of this story, one coming from John, the other from Augustine. Although Ptolemy takes some details from John, he is in the other tradition, in that he focuses on the application of the pirate's words to Alexander—going beyond others to say that God effectively transferred empire to the Romans at this point because of the lack of justice in Alexander's empire. Those in the other tradition focus on the self-restraint that Alexander showed in the face of the pirate's arrogance.

63. Augustine, *The City of God*, 5.15.

64. Augustine, *The City of God*, 5.18. Lucius Junius Brutus was the first consul of the Roman Republic (509 B.C.E.). Brutus sentenced his sons to death for their part in a conspiracy to restore King Tarquin.

65. Vergil, *Aeneid*, 6.23.

66. Augustine, *The City of God*, 5.18. For Torquatus, see above 1.8.5.

67. Valerius Maximus, *Memorable Deeds and Sayings*, 2.7.6.

Chapter 6

God conceded lordship to the Romans because of their civil benevolence.

[1] The third virtue through which the Romans subjugated the world and merited lordship was a singular piety and civil benevolence. As Valerius Maximus tells us in his fifth book: "The sweetness of humanity penetrates the character of barbarians,"[68] and experience validates this. It is said in Proverbs: "a sweet word multiplies friends and makes enemies mild,"[69] and also: "A soft response subdues wrath, but hard speech stirs up furor."[70] The reason for this is generosity of spirit which, as Seneca says, "is led more than it is dragged along. For the mind has a sublime and elevated quality making it unable to endure a superior, but it is subjected by delight in a certain reverence or gentleness, through which it feels that it can ascend to equality and not descend to its own rank." On account of this Aristotle says that benevolence is the beginning of friendship.[71] Some examples of the ancient Romans' behavior will show the extent to which they excelled in this virtue, by which they drew foreign nations to love them and willingly subject themselves to them.

[2] As a first example, consider Scipio, who at twenty-four was leader of the Roman army in Spain, fighting against the nation of Hannibal and Carthage.[72] As Valerius Maximus reports, as he was driving back the power that the Carthaginians brought against him, he captured an exceptionally lovely virgin from that region, whom he knew to be betrothed and noble. He restored her to her parents inviolate and even added the gold paid to ransom her to her dowry. Because of this deed the enemy came to love the Romans.[73] Such pure, moderate temperance on the part of this ruler was astonishing because, while Valerius Maximus says he was rather free-living in his youth, he preserved himself steadfast in great liberty and power, immune from all trans-

---

68. Valerius Maximus, *Memorable Deeds and Sayings*, 5.1, ext. 6. Valerius says, "even penetrates."

69. Actually, Ecclesiastes 6.5.

70. Proverbs 15.1.

71. Aristotle, *Ethics*, 9.5.1167a.3.

72. Hannibal (247–183 B.C.E.) was a Carthaginian general and political leader during the Second Punic War between Carthage and Rome. He campaigned successfully in Italy for fifteen years (218–203). In his forced return to Africa, he was defeated, but continued the fight against Rome.

73. Valerius Maximus, *Memorable Deeds and Sayings*, 4.3.1. Publius Cornelius Scipio the Elder (237–183 B.C.E.) was a general, proconsul, and consul who also invaded Africa, forcing Hannibal to return from Italy and defeating him at Zama (202).

gression.[74] Livy relates in *On the Punic War* that when Scipio addressed the man betrothed to this virgin,[75] he displayed a modesty fit for rulers to imitate and worthy of lordship. Livy also writes about the benevolence that he showed in the course of his victory. Before he sent hostages to the Romans, he exhorted them to be of good spirit: "for they had come under the power of the Roman people, who preferred to bind humans through good deeds than through fear and preferred to have foreign nations joined to them by trust and society than subjected by harsh servitude."[76]

[3] Augustine also writes in this regard that it was characteristic of the Romans "to spare their subjects and vanquish the proud, and they preferred to forgive injuries than to avenge them."[77] The same Doctor also refers to Marcus Marcellus who, after his capture of the city of Syracuse, wept at the prospect of its ruin, and who had such great modesty and such a temperate spirit and generous mind that before he ordered the attack on the town he issued a public edict that no one should violate the body of a free person.[78] We may cite many other examples, such as the Maccabees—Judas, Jonathan, and Simon—who established friendship with the Romans in consideration of their benevolence, as is written in 1 Maccabees.[79] They did this although they were of the Jewish nation, which characteristically spurns the society of other countries because of the prohibitions of their laws and because this is how those born under Saturn behave, as Macrobius says in commenting on Scipio's dream.[80] 1-Maccabees adds briefly, among the other commendable qualities by which the Romans drew peoples and various nationalities to love them and to be subjected politically or despotically to them, that among the Roman chiefs:

> no one wore a diadem or assumed the purple so as to be glorified by those things, and they took care to consult daily with the 320, always taking

74. Valerius Maximus, *Memorable Deeds and Sayings*, 6.9.2.

75. Livy, *History of Rome*, 26.50.

76. Livy, *History of Rome*, 26.49.

77. Augustine, *The City of God*, 1.6. Augustine is quoting Virgil, *Aeneid*, 6.853 in the first clause and Sallust, *The War with Cataline*, 9.5 in the second.

78. Augustine, *The City of God*, 1.6. The word translated as town is not the word usually translated as town, "*castrum*," but rather "*oppidum*." Marcus Claudius Marcellus (c.268–208 B.C.E.) was a general and consul who, in addition to capturing Syracuse (212) defeated the Gauls (222) and defeated Hannibal at Nola (216).

79. 1 Machabees (Maccabees) 8.17–32.

80. Perhaps Ptolemy is referring to Macrobius, *Commentary on Scipio's Dream*, 1.19.19, but there Macrobius refers only to a general deleterious effect of Saturn on people. Or 1.19.26, where he says that Saturn and Mars are unfavorable to human life since they are not in numerical harmony with the sun and moon, on which we principally depend.

council about matters concerning the multitude so that they might do those things that were worthy. They committed their magistracy to one person to exercise lordship over all the lands for a single year, and all obeyed that one, and there was neither ill-will nor jealousy among them.[81]

It is important to note how a political government was ordained in Rome at that time, because it was their especial motive to desire lordship over every country and province and to subject them to the Roman yolk.

[4] They had another trait that encouraged subjection: because of their desire to exercise lordship, they did not call themselves lords but allies and friends. Suetonius writes that Julius Caesar's knights were were not subject to him and that he called them allies and comrades.[82] The ancient consuls acted in a similar way toward the Jews, who, although they had only a modest lordship in the east, were confederated with the Romans in a treaty of friendship. As the book of Maccabees makes clear, even when the Romans obtained full monarchy in the east, the west, and other regions of the world they did not disdain to enter into an alliance with the Jews, and in a public edict they attested to the equality of of the two parties.[83]

[5] The things that I have written make it clear that the merit of virtue among the ancient Romans made them deserving of lordship. Other nations were attracted to their lordship because they were impressed by the Romans' love of their fatherland, on behalf of which they despised all other things; they were impressed by their vigor in pursuit of justice, on account of which they set themselves against every evildoer and disturber of the peace; and they were impressed by their civil benevolence by which they drew other nations to love them. Considering all these things and all the causes and reasons that I have detailed above, and considering the merit of the virtues among the Romans, divine goodness itself seems to concur in their rule. For it is for such qualities that persons deserve lordship, as Aristotle tells us, when he says that we do not allow those who simply possess human nature to rule, but those who are perfect in reason, as I said above.[84]

---

81. 1 Machabees (Maccabees) 8.14–16. The quotation is off by a few insignificant words.

82. Suetonius, *The Twelve Caesars*, "Julius Caesar," 67, where he calls them "comrades," and 70, "citizens." It is probably this last reference that Ptolemy has in mind when he says they were not subject to him, since by definition a citizen participates in government and so can be considered not to be a subject.

83. 1 Machabees (Maccabees) 8.2–11, 23–28.

84. Aristotle, *Ethics*, 5.10.1134a35; above 1.14.2, but also possibly 3.3.1. See also below 4.8.2.

Chapter 7

*God permits lordship for the punishment of the evil, and such
lordship is an instrument of divine justice against sinners.*

[1] In Sacred Scripture we also find another reason for which God permitted
lordship, that is, on account of the merit of the peoples, and this is not contrary to the opinions of the philosophers and wise ones of this world. The
blessed Augustine gives this reason, when he proves that servitude was introduced on account of sin.[85] Sacred Scripture makes the same point in Job: "He
makes a hypocrite reign because of the sins of the people."[86] This is obvious
since, as the histories tell us, those who first exercised lordship in the world
were iniquitous persons, such as Cain, Nimrod, Belus, Ninus, and his wife
Semiramis, who had lordship in the first and second age of the world.[87] We
can show the reason that they had that lordship either with regard to the subjects or to those exercising lordship.

[2] With regard to the subjects, they had lordship because tyrants are instruments of divine justice for punishing human transgression, as was the king of
the Assyrians over the Israelite people,[88] and Totila, king of the Goths, the
Scourge of God, over Italy, as the histories relate.[89] Another example is Dionysius in Sicily, under whom the people were captive, until at last he gave them
their liberty, as Valerius Maximus writes.[90] And the Prophet Isaiah showed

85. Augustine, *The City of God,* 19.15.
86. Job 34.30.
87. That is, before and after the flood. Traditionally, Nimrod, whom Ptolemy and Isidore
call Nembroth, established an empire in Shinar (Babylonia) (Genesis 10.8–10), Belus was the
founder of Babylon and Ninus, his son, the first king of Assyria, who built Nineveh. According to Augustine, *The City of God,* 16.17, Ninus was an older contemporary of Abraham. Isidore
of Seville, *Etymologies,* discusses Belus and Ninus (8.11) and Nembroth and Semiramis (7.6.22;
15.1.4). At 5.39 Isidore divides the generations as follows: first, Adam to Noah; second, Shem
to Abraham; third, from Isaac to Saul; fourth, David to the destruction of the temple; fifth,
Babylonian Captivity to Julius Caesar; sixth, Jesus Christ to the end of the world. See also Peter
Comestor, *Scholastic History,* On the Book of Daniel, 2.
88. The kingdom of Israel (which had been split from the kingdom of Judah and the capitol
of Jerusalem since Solomon's death in 925 B.C.E.) fell to the Assyrians in 722 B.C.E. Hosea 1–8 attributes this to the many sins of the Israelites, failing to follow God above all. See also Isaiah 9–10.
89. Aimoinus Floriac, *History of the Franks,* 2.33. Totila (r.541–52 C.E.) was the last king of
the Ostrogoths in Italy. He led the final resistance of the Goths against the Byzantine reconquest,
and although he was initially rather successful, he was eventually defeated. The Byzantine invasion
and the subsequent wars led to the destruction of the Italian economy and cities, population decline, and, ultimately to the victory of the Lombards. The phrase "scourge of God" suggests that
Ptolemy may be confusing Totila with Attila (c.406–453), leader of the Huns, who invaded Italy
in 452 and was only stopped from capturing Rome by a pestilence that swept his forces.
90. Valerius Maximus, *Memorable Deeds and Sayings,* 4.7, ext. 1. Valerius Maximus here tells
the story of Damon and Pythias under the category of "friendship." Dionysius freed them, but

how the king of the Assyrians was destined to punish the transgressions of God's own people: "Asshur is the rod and the very staff of my wrath; in his hand is my indignation; I will send him to the deceitful people, and I will give him a mandate against the people of my wrath: to take away the spoils, to divide the booty, and to tread that people underfoot as if they were the mud of the streets."[91] All these things came to pass when the Chaldeans besieged Jerusalem, when Nebuchadnezzar, king of the Assyrians, captured and burned it, and when, after capturing its rulers and king, Zedekiah, he put out the king's eyes and killed his sons, as the book of Kings relates.[92] This example demonstrates sufficiently how God punishes the sinner through the hand of a tyrant.

[3] We can conclude, therefore, that tyrants are instruments of God, as are demons, whose power the Sacred Doctors hold to be just, even though their will is always iniquitous. A tyrannical government itself shows this to us, because it is not ordained except as a burden and annoyance to its subjects. It is characteristic of tyrants to seek their own, and only their own, utility and convenience, as I said above,[93] and as Aristotle relates, when he maintains that tyrants act in the same way toward their subjects as lords toward servants and craftspersons toward their implements and instruments.[94] This is punitive to the subjects and against the nature of lordship, as I proved above.

[4] With regard to those exercising lordship, God seems to have conceded the legitimacy of this lordship. First, in the opposite case or when God makes a disposition on behalf of the subjects to bring about a better result when a ruler, although a sinner, strives to please God.[95] Isaiah writes this about Cyrus, king of the Persians: "I, the Lord, say these things to my Christ, Cyrus, whose right hand I have grasped, so that I might subject the nations to him

---

Valerius says nothing about him freeing the people as a whole. Ptolemy is probably just muddling this story here, but if the freedom of the people is the result, the reference must be to the overthrow of Dionysius II by Timoleon in 345. See above and below 1.11.3, 4.22.2. For Dionysius, see note at 1.11.3.

91. Isaias (Isaiah) 10.5–6. The Bible uses "Asshur," Shem's son, to stand for Assyria, to which in myth he gave his name, although in reality the biblical authors undoubtedly assigned him this name to provide an ancestor of the Assyrians.

92. 4 Kings (2 Kings) 25.1–7. Nebuchadnezzar (r.605–562 B.C.E.) was actually king of the (Neo)-Babylonian Empire, as Ptolemy sometimes acknowledges. He captured Jerusalem and brought down the kingdom of Judah in 586 B.C.E. Ptolemy conflates the two empires here in order to make Isaiah's account of the fall of Israel do double duty as a prophecy of the fall of Judah, which Isaiah 3 predicted.

93. 1.2.2, 1.4.5.

94. Aristotle, *Ethics*, 8.11.1161a34–35.

95. "Opposite case" probably refers to the fact that the rulers discussed here are not tyrants. This case still fits under the topic being discussed because it concerns rule as a result of the people's merits.

and turn the backs of kings. I will open the doors before him, and the gates will not be closed."[96] This was fulfilled, as the histories tell us. When the beds of the Tigris and Euphrates Rivers, which ran through the center of Babylon, suddenly dried up, Cyrus entered the city and killed the Babylonian king, Belshazzar, together with his nation and destroyed the city. He then transferred their monarchy to the land of the Medes, where Darius, a kinsman of Cyrus, then reigned, as Josephus writes.[97] God disposed things in this way because Cyrus showed humanity toward his faithful Jews who were being held as captives in Assyria. Afterward he sent them back as free persons to Judea with the vessels of the Temple and ordered that the Temple be rebuilt. As a result of these good and virtuous works in favor of the divine cult and the people of God he obtained the monarchy of the whole east, as I showed above.[98]

[5] But King Belshazzar was killed, as Daniel argues, because he was ungrateful to God and because he abused the vessels of the Temple of God during a feast. Daniel said to him:

> Because you did not humble your heart, but raised it up against the Dominator of heaven, because the vessels of his house were brought into your presence and you, your optimates, and your wives drank wine from them, and because you have not glorified God, who holds your status and all your ways in his hands; for these reasons, he has sent the finger of his hand against you.[99]

We take this to be a divine sentence against him, as future events proved. The history of Daniel relates that when Belshazzar, king of the Babylonians, persisted in his outrages against God, he saw, on the far side of the table at which he was feasting, the fingers of a hand writing on the wall. This act of writing completely terrified him, as if it were the messenger of his death.[100] The Scripture of Daniel also reports that from the appearance of the writing (and he did not actually see the writing, but only the image of the fingers of a hand):

96. Isaias (Isaiah) 45.1. The Hebrew word used is "messiah," which originally meant simply "anointed," and came to mean anyone anointed by God to help the Jewish people, and then a Jewish king who would vanquish the Jew's enemies and establish Jewish hegemony. It sometimes became something more, especially in the apocayptic ferment of the first centuries on either side of the beginning of the Common Era, in both Jewish and Christian writings.

97. These items are not part of Josephus's account of Cyrus in *Antiquities of the Jews*, 11.6.1–2. Making a Darius ruler of the Medes at this time is Ptolemy's attempt to make Daniel's confused historical account, which does not mention Cyrus or the Persians at all, make sense.

98. 3.1.1.

99. Daniel 5.22–24. The Vulgate and the Matthis edition of *On the Government of Rulers* have "*flatum*," "breath" instead of "*statum*," "status." In Gothic script these two words are practically indistinguishable and it is not clear what Ptolemy understood it to be.

100. Daniel 5.5.

"his face was completely changed and his thoughts disturbed him, the valves
of his kidneys opened, and his knees knocked against each other,"[101] all of
which things signify immense fear and a future judgment over him. Since the
king could not make out the writing, he summoned Daniel, who interpreted
it as three words, namely: Mene, Tekel, Peres, which Scripture expounds as
follows: "Mene: God has numbered your kingdom and has completed it,"
that is, he has placed bounds on it, like a numbered coin which is taken up
and separated from a heap of money; "Tekel: You were weighed in the balance and found wanting," for which reason you are worthy of death; "Peres:
Your kingdom is divided and given to the Medes and Persians," as I showed
above.[102] All these things make it sufficiently clear that those clauses do not
receive their significance merely from some linguistic idiom but rather from a
divine disposition, as does also the particular deed in which the Prophet ap-
prehends the divine will around us. We conclude that in the book of Daniel
God brought his sentence against the ruler of Babylon because his sin rendered him worthy of death and to have regal rule taken away from him, according to that verse of Scripture: "A kingdom is transferred from nation to
nation on account of injustices and deceits."[103]

Chapter 8

*Sometimes the result of such lordship is the evil of those who exercise
lordship, since they become puffed up with pride and fall violently
because of their ingratitude.*

[1] Now it is time to take up the question of the role of divine providence
in lordship. Sometimes a virtuous person assumes rule and continues stead-
fastly in this rule for some time. But it often happens otherwise, that those
who experience human favor and the prosperity of regal affairs become puffed
up with pride and become ungrateful to God for the benefices[104] that God
gathers for them. Aristotle says: "rule shows the man,"[105] and this is exactly

---

101. Daniel 5.6.
102. Daniel 5.25–28.
103. Ecclesiasticus (Sirach) 10.8.
104. The word *"beneficiis"* could also simply mean "benefits." In fact, a dispute over these
two meanings was the basis for the "Incident at Besançon," (1157) in which the emperor, Frederick Barbarossa (r.1152–1190), accused Pope Adrian IV (1154–59), of saying that the Empire was
a papal fief. See Tierney, *Crisis of Church and State*, 105–9.
105. Aristotle, *Ethics*, 5.1.1130a.2. At 1.10.5 this is called a "proverb of Bias," but Ptolemy
got it from Aristotle. See also 4.7.5.

what happened with Saul. 1 Kings says: "in the whole tribe of Benjamin there was no man better than him,"[106] but after two years his government made him disobedient to God. For this reason God said to the Prophet Samuel: "How long will you mourn for Saul, since I have cast him out that he may not reign over Israel?"[107] as if he should be driven out by virtue of the irresistible divine sentence. On that account this ruler and his sons were eventually killed, and the Lord totally removed his lineage. The book of Paralipomenon concludes that Saul died because of his iniquities.[108]

[2] The same thing is true of Solomon, who was magnified over all kings who came before him, as is written in Ecclesiastes: "All the earth wanted to hear the wisdom of Solomon."[109] But, as Augustine says,[110] what happened afterward harmed the king, since he fell into luxury and then rushed into idolatry, becoming abominable to the people, so much so that his servants rebelled against him, plundered the spoils of his region, and devastated the land without any resistance, whereas before all obeyed his nod, as the queen of Sheba testifies in 3 Kings.[111] Therefore, although he began his government by doing great things because of the divine reverence that he showed, at the end he fell into vile acts because of the transgressions that he committed, since "sin makes peoples wretched."[112] Nevertheless, the Hebrews tell us, as Jerome reports in his commentary on Ecclesiastes, that at the end of his life, plagued on all sides, he recognized his error, disposed himself for penitence for his offenses, and composed the book of Ecclesiastes.[113] Speaking as an expert in this book, he said that all things were subject to vanity, and he submitted himself through divine fear to observe God's commands. Thus, at the end of the book he concludes: "Let us all hear equally what the end of this discourse is. Fear God and observe his mandates: for this is the entire human duty."[114]

[3] Putting aside for the moment those kings who followed the divine cult, what about the heathen rulers? So long as they were in God's grace and cultivated virtues, they flourished in their lordship. But when they became exalted in their lordship and turned onto the opposite path, they died badly,

---

106. 1 Kings (1 Samuel) 9.2.
107. 1 Kings (1 Samuel) 16.1.
108. 1 Paralipomenon (1 Chronicles) 10.13.
109. Actually 3 Kings (1 Kings) 10.24.
110. Augustine, *The City of God*, 17.8, 20.
111. 3 Kings (1 Kings) 10.6–9.
112. Proverbs 14.34.
113. Jerome, *Commentary on Ecclesiastes*, on Ecclesiastes 1.12.
114. Ecclesiastes 12.13.

as happened with the aforementioned monarch Cyrus, king of the Persians. The histories tell us that after he subjugated all Asia and Parthia he eventually took his long struggle to the Scythians and vanquished Scythia with his sword. Tomyris, queen of the nation called the Massagetae, was then exercising lordship there. At first Cyrus struggled against her young son and, when he was victorious, killed him and annihilated a huge multitude, sparing none on account of their age. Because he showed cruelty in Babylonia and the kingdom of Lydia, because he butchered the kings and rulers of both, bringing them to a bad end, and because he did the same thing in the kingdom of the Massagetae, God punished him with the same kind of judgment. The history narrates that Queen Tomyris gathered an army of Massagetae and Parthians against him and made a series of well-prepared ambushes against his camps in the mountains. The assault of her soldiers devoured them: 200,000 of Cyrus's army were killed and Cyrus himself was captured. The queen ordered his decapitated head to be enclosed in a wine skin full of blood and shouted to him invectively: "You thirst for blood; drink blood," as if to signify that the disgraceful death he suffered was proof of his barbarity.[115]

[4] The same is true for all the monarchs who followed him. In Greece, for example, Alexander the Great succeeded and prospered in his monarchy, so long as he treated his Macedonians with reverence, calling his knights "fathers," as if they were elders. But he grew ungrateful to them and was poisoned by his own sister. A chief cause of this was that, after his victory over Darius and his marriage to Darius's daughter, he began to postpone military affairs and turned instead to the luxurious life. Becoming unmindful of his own affairs, his life ended with a painful death.[116]

[5] I could add many examples of other heathen rulers, such as Julius Caesar and Hannibal, who were slain and ended horribly when they abused their

---

115. Valerius Maximus, *Memorable Deeds and Sayings*, 9.10, ext. 1, although he does not cite figures, the peoples involved, or give this quote. Herodotus, *Persian Wars*, 1.205–214, tells a slightly different story. The Massagetae were a tribe living east of the Caspian Sea.

116. There were many medieval legends of Alexander the Great, and I have not identified the exact source of this incident. One of the main sources for these legends was the *Greek Alexander Romance* (New York: Penguin, 1991), a Greek work of the third to second centuries B.C.E., translated into Latin in the third century C.E. This and other versions report that Alexander was poisoned. However, it attributes the poisoning to a usurper, Antipater, in Macedonia acting through Alexander's cupbearer Iolaus. Cary, *Medieval Alexander*, 284, can find no precedent for Alexander's sister's involvement and cites Ptolemy's comments on Alexander's decline as a rare attack before that of Petrarch in the mid-fourteenth century. Darius III Codomanus (r.336–330 B.C.E.) was defeated by Alexander and assassinated by his own satrap Bessus. Alexander married Darius's daughter, Statira, in 324, on the same day as he married the daughter of Artaxerxes III, from another branch of Persian royalty. Although he probably died of natural causes, Alexander displeased his Macedonian soldiers and officials by adopting what they considered to be a decadent oriental lifestyle.

lordship.[117] This is fitting for them according to what is written in Ecclesiastes: "Sometimes a person dominates another to the first person's own harm,"[118] nor does what the prophet Isaiah says, that tyranny has a proper place, obviate this. For, after Isaiah had shown that tyrants were executors of divine justice against sinners, executioners, as it were, of lords, as is clear in the passage I discussed above ("Asshur is the rod and the very staff of my wrath, etc."[119]), he immediately added: "But he will not judge it to be thus, and his heart will not reckon it to be so." That is, he acts as the instrument of God, "but his heart will be set to the destruction and to the killing of more than a few peoples; for he said: 'Are not my rulers also kings?' "[120] that is, tyrants will attribute their actions to their own virtue and not to that of God who moves them to punish those who transgress divine mandates. The Lord quickly convicts and severely punishes tyrants for such ingratitude and presumption, as is clear in the case of the rulers I have mentioned. The prophet adds: "Will the ax glorify itself at the expense of the one who cuts with it? Or will the saw be exalted at the expense of the one who wields it? How could a rod be raised against the one who raises it or a staff, which is merely wood, be exalted?"[121]

[6] I must point out an appropriate analogy here. The virtue of someone exercising lordship stands in the same relationship to God as the virtue of a staff does to the one striking and as the virtue of a saw does to the artisan.[122] Moreover, it is evident that the virtue of a saw or ax is of no account in a craft unless the artisan moves and directs it; this is also true for the virtue of one who exercises lordship, for it is nothing unless it happens through God moving and exercising governance. Therefore, it is foolish and most presumptuous to glory in one's own virtue.

[7] The reason for this is quite clear and can be derived from the words of Aristotle that I cited above,[123] because the virtue of any moveable thing depends on the virtue of a first mover and is its instrument. Thus it is that such glorying displeases God because it detracts from divine might. It is written in

117. Caesar was assassinated by a group of senators (44 B.C.E.) who accused him of abuse of power, but Hannibal killed himself in exile (183 B.C.E.) in Bithynia, when it appeared that he could no longer escape the Romans. His death was not because of abuse of power, but defeat by a foreign enemy.

118. Ecclesiastes 8.9.

119. Isaias (Isaiah) 10.5.

120. Isaias (Isaiah) 10.7–9.

121. Isaias (Isaiah) 10.15.

122. As I wrote in the introduction under "The Translation" and in a note to 1.9.4, Aristotle defines virtue as action in accordance with true ends or functions, and so it can apply to inanimate objects.

123. 3.2.21.

the book of Judith: "God humbles those who glory in their own virtue,"[124] and the prophet Isaiah adds to the words I have already cited:[125] "On this account, the Dominator, the Lord of Armies, will send leanness among his fat ones and will kindle a conflagration under their glory as if in the burning of a fire."[126] This signifies the sensible[127] punishment that will be inflicted on such tyrants and the annihilation of their rule, as is clear from the things that I have already said.

[8] It remains that all lordship, legitimate or tyrannical, is from God and is given for various reasons known only to his inscrutable providence.

Chapter 9

Human beings naturally exercise lordship over the animals of the forest and other irrational things. Many reasons prove this.

[1] Now I must attend to the diverse species of exercising lordship, classified according to the various modes and ranks of lordship and rule among human beings. First, there is a certain general species that pertains to all, which belongs to humans by nature, as Augustine and Aristotle tell us.[128] Scripture confirms this, when in creating the nature appointed for humans, God said: "Exercise lordship over the fish of the sea and the flying things of the heavens and all animals which move over the earth."[129] These words show that he gave this power to human nature as he instituted it. He said, "Let the earth put forth the green herb,"[130] which implies that he gave the power of germinating to trees. Similarly, he then said: "Exercise lordship over the fish of the sea, etc." Thus, from all the things that I have said, it is clear that the lordship of human beings over other, inferior creatures is natural. By the same reasoning Aristotle proves that hunting and fowling come from nature.[131] Augustine proves the same thing by citing the lordship that the ancient Fathers were accustomed to have as herders of cattle,[132] which I defined above as natural wealth.[133]

124. Judith 6.15.
125. 3.8.5.
126. Isaias (Isaiah) 10.16.
127. That is, pertaining to the senses, not the usual modern meaning.
128. Augustine, *The City of God*, 19.5; Aristotle, *Politics*, 1.2.
129. Genesis 1.28.
130. Genesis 1.11.
131. Aristotle, *Politics*, 1.8.1256a.30–b.23.
132. Augustine, *The City of God*, 19.15.
133. 2.6.1, 3.

[2] Although such lordship may have been diminished on account of sin, so that now even vile animals exercise lordship among us and have become harmful to us, which would not happen were the human species without sin; nevertheless, to the extent that we participate in this lordship we approach the State of Innocence. The Evangelical Voice promises us this if we imitate Christ in our justice and sanctity. When the Lord exhorted his disciples to preach the word of God for the health of their spirits, he declared the virtue of these things by saying: "They will cast out devils in my name, they will speak in new languages, they will pick up serpents, and if they should drink anything deadly it will not harm them." [134] The experience of virtuous and exceptionally perfect men has taught us that such things have happened, as has been written in accounts of the deeds of the holy Fathers. For example, the Acts of the Apostles tells us that the viper did not injure the Blessed Paul, [135] nor venom the Blessed John the Evangelist. Similar things are written about many other exceptionally holy Fathers who waded through the Nile over the horrible beasts called crocodiles or walked over the most venomous reptiles, so that it is fulfilled in them that which the Lord said in Luke: "Behold, I have given you the power to tread on serpents and scorpions, and on all the force of the enemy." [136]

[3] I can give three reasons why that lordship was suitably conferred when humans were first instituted. First, it follows from a consideration of the process of nature itself. Just as in the generation of things, in which we understand there to be a certain order of advancement from the imperfect to the perfect, since matter exists on account of form and the more imperfect form exists on account of the more perfect, so also in the use of natural things such an order is present, since more imperfect things exist for the use of those that are more perfect. Plants use the land for their own nutrition, but animals use plants, and humans use both plants and animals. Therefore, I conclude that humans naturally exercise lordship over animals. It is with this reason, as I mentioned above, that Aristotle proves that the hunting of animals of the forest is naturally just, because by it humans lay a legal claim for themselves to that which naturally is theirs. [137]

[4] Second, it follows from a consideration of the order of divine providence which always governs inferior things through superior ones. Humans are

---

134. Mark 16.17–18.
135. Acts 28.3–6.
136. Luke 10.19.
137. 3.9.1; Aristotle, *Politics*, 1.8.1256a.30–b.23.

above other animals, since they are made in the image of God, and so human governance suitably subjects other animals.

[5] Third, it follows from a consideration of the peculiar nature of humans and other animals. In other animals we may discover a certain participation in prudence toward particular acts according to a natural faculty of judgment, but in humans we find a useful prudence which comes from the rational ability of doing things. But all that exists only through participation is subjected by that which exists essentially and universally. Thus, it is clear that other animals are naturally subject to humans.

[6] The truth of whether the lordship of human being over human being is natural or whether it is merely permitted or foreseen by God can be deduced from what I have already said. If we speak of lordship involving the mode of servile subjection, this was introduced only on account of sin, as I said above,[138] but if we speak of lordship as it pertains to the office of counseling and directing, this mode can be called natural, because it existed even in the State of Innocence. This is also Augustine's opinion.[139] Therefore, the second kind of lordship pertains to human beings, as naturally social or political animals, as I said above.[140]

[7] Moreover, it is necessary that a society be mutually ordained, and in all cases involving things that are mutually ordained, one thing must always be the principal and first directing thing, as Aristotle tells us.[141] This follows from the very raison d'être of order or nature. As Augustine writes: "Order is the disposition of equal and unequal things giving to each its due."[142] It is therefore manifest that the word "order" itself implies inequality, and this is so by the raison d'être of lordship. By this argument the lordship of human over human is natural, lordship exists even among the Angels, it existed in the First State, and it exists even now. We must now consider sequentially the various kinds of lordship according to their own dignities and ranks.

138. 2.9.4–5.
139. Augustine, *The City of God*, 19.14–15.
140. 1.1.3, 3.5.3.
141. Aristotle, *Politics*, 1.5.1254a.20–25.
142. Augustine, *The City of God*, 19.13.

Chapter 10

Distinctions of human lordship according to rank and dignity.
How the pope's lordship is preferred to all other lordship.

[1] We can subdivide lordship into four types by the same criterion. One type is sacerdotal and regal at the same time, another is regal alone, under which we include imperial, a third is political, and the fourth has to do with household management.

[2] I mention sacerdotal and regal first for a number of reasons, but especially since it exists by the divine institution of Christ. Since all power was conferred on him by virtue of his humanity, he communicated all this power to his vicar when he said, as we read in Matthew: "I say to you: 'you are Peter, and on this rock I will build my Church, and the gates of Hell will not prevail against it. And I will give you the keys to the kingdom of heaven, and whatever you bind on earth will be bound in heaven, and whatever you loose on earth will be loosed in heaven.'"[143] All four clauses of this statement signify the lordship of Peter and his successors over all the faithful, and because of this the Supreme Pontiff, the Roman Bishop, can deservedly be called king and priest. If our Lord Jesus Christ is called king and priest, as Augustine proves,[144] it does not seem unsuitable to apply the same titles to his successor. This is clear enough from what I have said, but in order to adduce more reasons we must go back to the four clauses that I just mentioned, of which the first refers to the magnitude of the title given, the second to the fortitude of lordship, the third to the amplitude of lordship, and the fourth to the fullness of lordship.

[3] We begin with the first clause, when the Lord says: "I say to you: 'you are Peter and on this rock I will build my Church.'" As the Sacred Doctors Hilary and Augustine explain,[145] the Lord made known the might of Peter by using this name. Peter was called "rock," which, as Paul says, signifies Christ, whom Peter was the first to acknowledge,[146] so that by participating in this name, since a name may acquire power, he would deserve to hear: "And on this rock I will build my church," as if lordship among the faithful depends completely on Peter and his successors.

143. Matthew 16.18–19.
144. Augustine, *The City of God*, 17.6, 17.17.
145. Hilary, *Commentary on Matthew*, 16.7, on Matthew 16.18–19; Augustine, Sermon 295.3.
146. 1 Corinthians 10.4. Paul says Moses and the Jews drank of the spiritual rock that followed them, which rock was Christ. *"Petra"* is the word used for rock.

[4] The second clause introduces the fortitude of lordship, signified by the next words: "And the gates of hell will not prevail against it." As those same Sacred Doctors tell us, these gates are in the care of tyrants and persecutors of the Church, and they are called "the gates of hell" because they are the cause of all sinners within the Church Militant. For all are polluted by contact with such rulers, as happened in the courts of Frederick, Conradin, and Manfred.[147] Yet these men did not prevail against the Roman Church; rather, they all died badly because, as is said in the book of Wisdom: "Dire are the ends of an iniquitous nation."[148]

[5] The amplitude of lordship is shown when the Lord adds: "And I will give you the keys to the kingdom of heaven." For by these words he makes known to us the power of Peter and his successors, which extends to the entire Church, namely the Church Militant and the Church Triumphant, which are designated by the words "the kingdom of heaven," both of which are locked by Peter's keys.

[6] The fullness of lordship is shown when he says at the end: "And whatever you bind on earth will be bound in heaven, and whatever you loose on earth will be loosed in heaven."

[7] In the mystical body the Supreme Pontiff is head of all the faithful of Christ, and since in a real body the head is the source of all motion and sensation, the same will be true in the mystical body. For this reason it is necessary to say that the fullness of grace is found in the Supreme Pontiff, because he alone confers a full indulgence for all sins, so that what we say about the first and principal Lord pertains to him: "We have all received from his fullness."[149] It cannot be that this refers to spiritual power alone, since the corporal and temporal always depend on the spiritual, just as the mode of operation of a body depends on the virtue of the spirit. Therefore, just as a body receives its being, virtue, and mode of operation from the spirit, as Aristotle and Augustine[150] make clear, so also the temporal jurisdiction of rulers receives these things through the spiritual power of Peter and his successors.

---

147. These were three Hohenstaufen kings involved in a fierce struggle with the papacy in the first part of the thirteenth century. Frederick II (1194–1250), as King of Sicily and Roman Emperor, tried to unite Italy and Germany in a great empire crushing the papal states in between. He apparently died of dysentery. Manfred (1232?–66) was a son of Frederick II who became King of Naples and Sicily. He died in the battle of Beneventum fighting Charles of Anjou, who had been given the kingship of Sicily by the pope. Conradin (1252–68) was the grandson of Frederick II, who took up Manfred's struggle against Charles, but he was captured and publicly beheaded.

148. Wisdom 3.19.

149. John 1.16.

150. Aristotle, *Politics*, 1.5; Augustine, *On the Immortality of the Spirit*, 1.

[8] We can support this argument from accounts of the acts and deeds of the Supreme Pontiffs and the Emperors, since they yielded to spiritual jurisdiction. Constantine clearly did this when he yielded his empire to Pope Sylvester.[151] Likewise, Charlemagne, whom Pope Adrian constituted as emperor.[152] Likewise Otto I, whom Pope Leo created and constituted as emperor, as the histories relate.[153] And the power of popes is apparent when we consider the deposition of rulers by apostolic authority. Pope Zacharias exercised this power over the king of the Franks, when he deposed him from his kingdom and absolved all barons from their oath of fidelity to him,[154] as did Innocent III, who took away the empire from Otto IV.[155] And Honorius, the immediate successor of Innocent, did the same thing to Frederick II.[156] In none of these matters did the Supreme Pontiffs extend their hand except by reason of transgression.[157] Their power, and that of any other lordship, is ordained to the end of profiting their flocks, so that those whom vigilance inclines toward the utility of their subjects are deservedly called shepherds. Otherwise they are not legitimately lords but tyrants, as Aristotle proves[158]

151. A reference to the eighth-century forgery called the Donation of Constantine, accepted throughout most of the Middle Ages, by which Constantine I (r.306–37), on leaving for the east to found his new capitol at Constantinople yielded his power in the west (or by some interpretations the entire imperial power) to the pope. See below 4.16.3.

152. Charlemagne (742–814), king of the Franks, was crowned Roman Emperor by Pope Leo III (795–816) (not Pope Adrian I [772–795]; Ptolemy makes the same mistake at 3.18.3) on Christmas Day, 800 c.e. One of the reasons Charlemagne may have been unhappy with this event was that it provided a precedent for popes to claim the right to appoint, or at least crown, emperors.

153. Otto I "The Great" (r.936–973) was crowned Roman Emperor by the notorious John XII in 962. Subsequently Otto deposed John, which makes this incident perhaps not the best example for Ptolemy to use. Ptolemy has in mind Leo VII (r.936–939), who was pope when Otto came to power, as is shown by his explicit reference at 3.19.1.

154. Responding to a query from the nobles of Germany, Zacharias (r.741–53) responded that it was better for the person who effectively exercised the office of king (Pepin) to be king than the one who had only the name of king (Childeric). Pepin was crowned in 751.

155. Innocent III (1198–1216) excommunicated him 1210 as one act in the long struggle of the papacy to limit the empire. Innocent at first supported the Welf Otto and crowned him emperor, but was disillusioned by his independence and attempt to unite Sicily with Germany. Innocent's favor next went to Frederick II, who would become the papacy's greatest enemy.

156. Honorius III (r.1216–1227). Actually, it was Honorius's successor, Gregory IX (1227–1241) who excommunicated Frederick in 1227. Innocent IV repeated the excommunication in 1245. Honorius made the great error of crowning Frederick emperor without making him give up Sicily, but in his last years Honorius was beginning to turn against him.

157. Popes sometimes claimed that they could only act in secular affairs in cases of sin. Of course this gave them very wide latitude, since almost anything could be interpreted as sin. Even the powerful pope Innocent III (1198–1216) wrote to King Philip Augustus of France in the decretal "Novit," which Ptolemy could well have known from The Body of Canon Law: Decretals, 2.1.13: "Let no one suppose that we wish to diminish or disturb the jurisdiction and power of the king . . . we do not intend to judge concerning a fief, judgment on which belongs to him— except when some special privilege or contrary custom detracts from the common law—but to decide concerning a sin, of which the judgment undoubtedly belongs to us." See Tierney, Crisis of Church and State, 134–135, for a translation of the decretal.

158. Aristotle, Politics, 3.7.1279b.6–8.

and as I wrote above.[159] As the book of John reports, the Lord harshly questioned his successor, the blessed Peter, and told him three times that if he loved him, he should feed his flock. "Peter," he asked, "Do you love me? Feed my sheep,"[160] as if the whole of pastoral care consists in the profit of the flock.

[9] Therefore, supposing that he acts for the utility of the flock, as Christ intends, it is apparent from what I have said that his lordship is elevated above all other. This is manifest from the first vision of Nebuchadnezzar of the statue whose head was gold, whose breast and arms were silver, whose belly and thighs were brass, but whose legs were iron and whose feet were partially iron and partially clay. While the king was contemplating the statue in this vision, a stone was cut off without hands from the mountain and caused all the parts of the statue to crumble, then this stone became a great mountain and filled up all the earth.[161] As Jerome and Augustine explain,[162] the prophet Daniel relates this statue to the four monarchies: that of the Assyrians because of the gold head, that of the Medes and the Persians because of the silver arms and breast, that of the Greeks because of the brass belly and thighs, and finally, that of the Romans because of the iron legs and the feet partially iron and partially clay. "But after these," says the prophet, "the God of heaven will raise up a kingdom that will not scatter throughout eternity, and his kingdom will not be handed over to another people, and it will crush all kingdoms and will itself stand for eternity."[163] We say that all of this refers to Christ, and to the Roman Church in his place, if it directs itself to feeding the flock.

[10] I must note that this divine institution cannot be abandoned, since Christ elevated his vicars solely as dispensers and ministers, as Paul said in 1 Corinthians: "Let one so judge us, as ministers of Christ and dispensers of the mysteries of God."[164] For Christ alone founded the Church whose ministry

159. 1.2.2, 1.4.5, 3.7.3.
160. John 21.15–17.
161. Daniel 2.31–34.
162. Jerome, *Commentary on Daniel*, on Daniel 2.31–40. Jerome lists the empires as those of the Babylonians, Medes, Macedonians, and Romans. Peter Comestor, *Scholastic History*, On the Book of Daniel, 2 gives the same list (with Medes and Persians instead of simply Medes). Augustine does not adopt the four empire theory. He tends to see two great empires in world history — the Assyrian-Babylonian and the Roman *(The City of God*, 18.2). But he does not connect these with Daniel. He does say that the Assyrian Empire was transferred to the Medes, but only to show how the Assyrian Empire fell at the same time as Rome's rise began (18.21–22). His follower, Orosius, who wrote *Seven Books of History Against the Pagans* at Augustine's request, to complement *The City of God*, although it departs from its ideas in several regards, does follow a four-empire schema (7.2), listing the four as the Assyrian, Macedonian, African (Carthaginian), and Roman.
163. Daniel 2.44. Daniel (2.37–45) interprets the dream somewhat in this manner, but does not specify what particular empires are signified.
164. 1 Corinthians 4.1.

he committed to Peter: "For no one can lay another foundation except the one that was laid, which is Christ Jesus."[165] For this reason the Sacred Doctors attribute a certain power to Christ, which they call "excellent," which neither Peter nor his successors had. Thus the power of Peter and his successors is not equal to that of Christ; on the contrary, Christ's power totally transcends Peter's. For example, Christ could save someone without baptism, for which reason Jerome says in commenting on Matthew: "He healed no one in body whom he did not heal in mind, yet he did this without baptism, which Peter could not do."[166] For Peter baptized Cornelius the Centurion and his whole household, as we read in Acts, even after the Advent of the Holy Spirit.[167] Christ could change the form and matter of the sacraments, which neither Peter nor his successors could do.

[11] This suffices for the present, and I will leave for the wise the other and more subtle things that could be said. Nevertheless, the conclusion of this chapter, that the Vicar of Christ ought to be preferred to all other lords, should stand for the reasons I have given.

Chapter 11

What regal lordship consists of, how it differs from political lord-ship, and how it is distinguished in different ways in different regions.

[1] Now we must go on to regal lordship, and we must distinguish it with re-spect to various regions and with respect to the ways it is described in various sources. First, in Sacred Scripture, Moses tells us the laws of regal lordship in one way in Deuteronomy, and the Prophet Samuel in another way in 1 Kings, but both do this in the persona of God. In Deuteronomy, God ordains the king for the utility of his subjects, which, as Aristotle tells us,[168] is character-istic of kings. "When a king has been constituted," Moses says, "he will not

---

165. 1 Corinthians 3.11.

166. I cannot find this quotation in Jerome, *Commentary on Matthew*. Jesus did cure many people without baptizing them, but I can find no evidence that it was standard dogma that such physical cures had a spiritual effect like that of baptism. A clearer case would be Luke 23.43, where Jesus, from the cross, promises one of the thieves being crucified with him that he would be saved, though Jesus clearly could not baptize him then. Jerome does comment on the fact that the other gospels seem to depict both thieves negatively, to say that there is no contradiction since the thief repented at the end. Jerome, *Commentary on Matthew*, On Matthew 27.44.

167. Acts 10.44–48.

168. Aristotle, *Ethics*, 8.10.1160b.1–3. The same point is made in the *Politics*, 3.7.1279a.32.

multiply horses for himself, nor, being puffed up by the size of his cavalry, lead the people back into Egypt. He will not have many wives who will attract his spirit, nor an immense amount of silver or gold." [169] This book also tells us how he wanted the king to understand this: "he will copy this law of Deuteronomy for himself . . . and he will keep it with him and read it all the days of his life, so that he might learn to fear the Lord his God and guard his words and ceremonies," [170] so that he can direct the people according to divine law. So also King Solomon at the beginning of his government asked God for wisdom to direct his lordship for the utility of his subjects, as is written in 3 Kings. [171] Moses added in Deuteronomy: "Let his heart not be lifted overflowingly over his brothers, nor incline to the right or the left, so that he and his son may reign for a long time over Israel." [172] But in 1 Kings the laws of a kingdom are handed down more for the utility of the king, as I made clear above, [173] where I quoted those words as clearly pertaining to a servile condition. Nevertheless, Samuel says that the laws that he hands down are regal, even though they are completely despotic.

[2] In the *Ethics* Aristotle is more in accord with the first set of laws. He posits three things about a legitimate king: first, he principally intends the good of his subjects; second, he is found to be sufficient in himself and to excel superabundantly in all good qualities, not burdening his subjects; and third, he undertakes the care of his subjects so that they may function well, just as shepherds act toward their sheep. [174]

[3] From this it is clear that in this mode despotic is much different from regal, as Aristotle seems to say. [175] Likewise, it is clear that the kingdom does not exist on account of the king but rather the king on account of the kingdom, because it is for this that God provided for kings to govern and exercise governance over their kingdoms and preserve everyone according to their own right, and this is the end of government. If they do otherwise and turn things to their own advantage, they are not kings but tyrants. The Lord speaks against such tyrants in Ezekiel: [176]

169. Deuteronomy 17.16–17
170. Deuteronomy 17.18–19.
171. 3 Kings (1 Kings) 3.9.
172. Deuteronomy 17.20.
173. 2.9.2.
174. Aristotle, *Ethics*, 8.10.1160b.1–7, 11.1161a.11–15.
175. Aristotle, *Politics*, 1.1.
176. Ezechiel (Ezekiel) 34.2–4.

Woe to the shepherds of Israel who feed themselves. Are not the flocks fed by the shepherds? You continually drank the milk and covered yourselves with the wool and killed that which was fat, but you did not feed my flock. What was weak you did not fortify, what was sick you did not heal; what was broken you did not bind together; what was cast off you did not bring back, and what had perished you did not seek, but you commanded them with harshness and might.

In these words God tells us about the form of government he favored by criticizing the contrary form.

[4] Moreover, human beings constitute a kingdom just as walls a home and members the human body, as Aristotle says.[177] Therefore, it is necessary for the king to keep them safe if the government is to be prosperous. Hence, the common good of any kind of rule includes the participation of divinity; as Aristotle says, the common good is a divine good.[178] Just as God, who is "King of Kings and Lord of those exercising lordship,"[179] by whose virtue rulers command, as I proved above,[180] governs us and exercises governance over us not for himself but for our salvation, so too should kings and others exercising lordship in the world. But since no one ever provides their own pay for being in the military, and because by natural right all should receive a wage for their labor, as Paul proves in 1 Corinthians,[181] we hold that it is permissible for rulers to collect tributes and annual poll taxes from their subjects. After Paul proved to the Romans that God provided for all lordship, he finally persuaded them to return payment according to their labor: "Therefore, you are responsible for tributes, for they are ministers of God serving him in this."[182] Augustine proves this same thing, commenting on these same words of Paul in *On the Words of the Lord*.[183] Therefore, we must conclude that legitimate kings ought to govern and exercise governance according to the form described in Deuteronomy.

177. Aristotle, *Politics*, 3.1.1274b.39.
178. Aristotle, *Ethics*, 1.1.1094b.10.
179. 1 Timothy 6.15, Apocalypse (Revelation) 19.16.
180. 3.1–3.
181. 1 Corinthians 9.7.
182. Romans 13.6.
183. Augustine, Sermon 90.10, mentions paying tribute to Caesar. *On the Words of the Lord* is a name earlier collections of Augustine's letters gave to some of the Epistles on the New Testament (now Sermons 51–147A). Neither here nor in *Exposition of Certain Propositions from the Epistle to the Romans*, 72–75 does he quote Romans 13.6, but in commenting on Romans 13.1, 3–5, in the latter work he refers to the necessity of paying taxes and tributes.

[5] Examples warn us that they should do this, since all who do the contrary
meet a bad end. For instance, as the histories tell us, the Roman kings, such as
Tarquin the Proud and his son, were ejected from the kingdom for their pride
and violence.[184] Likewise, as is written in 4 Kings, Ahab and his wife Jezebel
met a bad end, perishing as a consequence of the violence that they inflicted
on Naboth to get his vineyard.[185] We are also told that the dogs licked the
blood of their corpses in that vineyard, as a rebuke for the evil deed they committed against Naboth. But nothing of the kind happened to King David. As
is written in 2 Kings,[186] he bought a threshing floor from Araunah the Jebusite when he wanted to build an altar to appease God, who was exceedingly
offended because King David had haughtily counted the people. When Araunah offered it for free the king refused, and as is written in 1 Paralipomenon,[187]
David gave 600 shekels of gold of just weight for that threshing floor.

[6] From this example we conclude that rulers ought to be content with their
pay and may not burden their subjects by taking their goods and possessions.
The only exceptions are in the following two cases: by reason of transgression
or on behalf of the common good of their government. In the first mode, one
deprives one's vassals of a fief for their ingratitude, and others of their goods
and possessions by reason of justice, for which lordship is granted, as I said
above.[188] In Proverbs it is said: "the throne of a king is made firm through
justice."[189] For this reason, divine law mandates that transgressors of divine
precepts be stoned and tormented with various penalties. This seems quite
appropriate if we consider any created thing, but especially the human body,
because we cast off a more vile part in order to preserve a part that is more
noble. We amputate a hand so that the heart and brain, in which a human
being principally consists, might be preserved. Evangelical law approves this:
"If your eye tempts you to evil, or your hand or your foot," which Augustine interprets to be the rank of human beings,[190] "rip it out and hurl it from

184. Lucius Tarquinius the Proud (r.534–510 B.C.E.) was, according to Roman legend, the
last of the seven kings of early Roman history. Tarquin's son, Tarquinius Sextus, raped Lucretia,
wife of another relative of the king, Lucius Tarquinius Collatinus. Tarquin was expelled for this
and for his cruelty. See note at 4.26.1.
185. 3 Kings (1 Kings) 21; 4 Kings (2 Kings) 9.36. When Naboth would not sell his vineyard to King Ahab, Ahab had him falsely accused of blasphemy against God and the king, and
he was stoned to death.
186. 2 Kings (2 Samuel) 24.
187. 1 Paralipomenon (1 Chronicles) 21.25. The accounts in 2 Kings and Paralipomenon
contradict each other. 1 Kings says David payed 50 silver shekels to Araunah the Jebusite, Paralipomenon that he payed 600 gold shekels to Ornan the Jebusite. The first is only about $20, the
second about $10,000.
188. 1.13.3, 3.5.1, 3.7.2, and passim.
189. Proverbs 25.5.
190. Augustine, *The City of God*, 21.9. Augustine explains that Jesus uses body parts to stand

you, because it is better go through life crippled or lame, than to be sent to Gehenna with two eyes or two hands."[191]

[7] Likewise, the reason is at hand to show what one could demand for the good of the republic, for the defense of the kingdom, or for any other cause that rationally pertains to the common good of one's lordship. Since we have supposed that human society is natural, as I proved above,[192] all things necessary for the preservation of this society are done by natural right. But this is contained in the proposition. Therefore, if we assume that a regal lordship is legitimate, the king can demand from his subjects that which is required for their good.

[8] Furthermore, as Aristotle tells us, art imitates nature in so far as it can,[193] so, since nature does not fail to provide necessities, neither does art. The art of living is better and greater than all other arts, as I mentioned before,[194] and as Cicero proves in his *Tusculan Disputations*,[195] because the other arts are ordained for it. Therefore, the king, who is the artisan-architect of the society we were discussing, ought not to fail to provide the necessities of his kingdom that pertain to the preservation of human social life; rather, he ought to make good any defect within society itself. We must conclude that in that case legitimate exactions, tallages, and poll taxes or tributes can be imposed, but they should not exceed the limits of necessity. Augustine, in expounding the passage of Matthew: "Render to Caesar those things which are Caesar's,"[196] says: "Therefore, you must bear Caesar's precepts, you must tolerate his commands, but it becomes intolerable when tax collectors accumulate plunder." Afterward, expounding the words of John the Baptist to the knights: "You should neither extort money by threats nor commit calumny, but be content with your pay,"[197] he says: "This opinion applies as well to military praetors and to all rectors."

[9] In John's opinion, those who seek more for themselves than the pay publicly decreed are to be condemned as calumniators and violent extortionists.

---

for those people whom we love like ourselves, and that if necessary we need to cut ourselves off from them rather than be dragged down to hell by them.

191. Not an exact quotation. Matthew 5.29–30 mentions an eye and a right hand, 18.8–9 mentions all three but not in this order; Mark 9.42, 44, 46 mentions all three but separately.

192. 1.1.3–6, 3.5.3, 3.9.6.

193. Aristotle, *Physics*, 2.2.194a.21–22.

194. 2.15.1.

195. Cicero, *Tusculan Disputations*, 4.3.5.

196. Matthew 22.21.

197. Luke 3.14.

From this, despotic rule is reduced to regal rule in two ways, but especially by reason of transgression, on account of which servitude was introduced, as Augustine says.[198] Although there had been lordship even in the First State, it existed only in the offices of counseling and directing, and not out of lust for exercising lordship or with the intention of subjecting anyone servilely, as I said above.[199] But the laws of regal lordship that the Prophet Samuel passed on to the Israelite people were given with the following consideration: that this people, on account of its ingratitude and because it was stiff-necked, deserved to have such laws. For sometimes when a people does not know the benefit of a good government it is expedient to exercise tyranny over it, because even tyrannies are the instruments of divine justice. For this reason, certain islands and provinces, according to what the histories relate, always had tyrants on account of the evil of the people, because they could not be governed otherwise than with an iron rod. In such ill-tempered regions, despotic rule is necessary for kings, not according to the nature of regal lordship, but according to the merits and pertinacity of the subjects, and this is the reason Augustine gives.[200] When Aristotle distinguishes the types of kingdoms, he also shows that among certain barbarous nations regal lordship is altogether despotic, because otherwise they could not be governed, and that this kind of lordship flourishes especially in Greece and among the Persians, at least with regard to popular government.[201]

[10] This is all I have to say at this point about regal lordship, and how despotic rule is reduced to it, and for what reason it is opposed to political rule, but I will show this still more clearly in a later chapter on political lordship.

Chapter 12

Where the name "imperial lordship" and certain other names come from. How they are distinguished incidentally from monarchy and how long they lasted.

[1] Now that I have written about political and regal lordship, I must say something about imperial lordship, since it holds the middle ground between

198. Augustine, *The City of God*, 19.15.
199. 3.9.6.
200. Augustine, *The City of God*, 19.15.
201. Aristotle, *Politics*, 3.14.1285a.16–29. Aristotle says that the barbarians are more servile than Greeks or Europeans, and so they do not rebel against a despot. He does not mention this form in Greece or Persia, nor does he mention popular government.

political and regal lordship. Since it is more universal, it ought to come before regal lordship, but there is a reason why it comes afterward, which I omit for now.

[2] We must attend to three things about imperial lordship. One has to do with its name, because that name takes its origin haughtily and proudly from the Supreme Lordship, as if it refers to the Lord of all. When the Jews asked the proud Nicanor to show deference for the day of sanctification, that is, for the Sabbath, he asked them arrogantly if there were a Mighty One in heaven who commanded [*imperavit*] that they observe this day. When they responded that there was such a one in heaven, the Lord God, he said with immoderate disdain: "And I am the mighty one on the earth who commands [*impero*] you to take up arms."[202] Because of this Judas Maccabeus later defeated him in a way that dishonored him. When Judas captured him in battle he amputated his head and the right hand that he had raised against the temple, and so his life ended with a bad death.[203]

[3] Certain excellent men used other names to refer to imperial lordship because they had some prerogative that pertained to this rule, such as Julius who used "Caesar," as the histories tell us. Isidore writes that he was called this because "he was born by being cut [*caeso*] from the womb of his dead mother, or because he was born with a full head of hair [*caesarie*], and the emperors who followed him were also called this because they had long hair."[204] And Octavian was called "Augustus," as Isidore also wrote, because he augmented the republic.[205]

[4] The second thing we must attend to has to do with the progress of that empire. Previously we touched on the fourfold monarchy;[206] but now we can add a fifth, which I will talk about below. The first was that of the Assyrians, whose head, Ninus, lived in the time of the patriarch Abraham. This empire lasted 1240 years, as Augustine writes,[207] up to the time of Sardanapalus

---

202. 2 Machabees (Maccabees) 15.2–5.

203. 2 Machabees (Maccabees) 15.28–33. Judas displayed publicly Nicanor's head and arm and hanged the latter in the temple. He also gave Nicanor's tongue to the birds.

204. Isidore of Seville, *Etymologies*, 9.3. The quote is not exact.

205. Isidore of Seville, *Etymologies*, 9.3.

206. 3.10.9.

207. Augustine, *The City of God*, 4.6. For Sardanapalus see *The City of God*, 2.20. Sardanapalus is actually the great Assyrian ruler Assurbanipal (668–626 B.C.E.), whom classical historians made into a libertine through confusion with another ruler of Assyria (c.822 B.C.E.). The Medes and Babylonians defeated the Assyrian Empire in 612 B.C.E. Augustine is following Eusebius for the 1240 figure, but he says elsewhere (18.21) that if you count the rule of Belus, the father of

who lost his rule because of his womanly qualities. Arbaces transferred the empire to the Medes and Persians, in the time that Procas reigned as duke of the Romans, as Augustine also says.[208] The monarchy of the Medes and Persians lasted for 233 years, up to the time of Alexander, until this ruler defeated Darius, as Augustine also writes.[209] But the monarchy of the Greeks began and ended with Alexander, about whom 1 Maccabees says: "Alexander reigned for twelve years and died."[210] Although the Greeks may not have held universal lordship, they held the kingdom of Macedonia for 485 years, up to the death of Alexander, which Augustine also mentions, and it was in this kingdom, as the histories tell us, that the ruler Alexander began his lordship by succeeding his father, Philip.[211]

[5] After this monarchy Roman rule began to be strong. The book of 1 Maccabees tells us many things about the Romans in the time of Judas Maccabeus,[212] who flourished almost immediately after the death of Alexander, at the same time as Ptolemy of Lagus.[213] The might of the Romans seemed to be diffused through all the regions of the world under the consuls, but they were still vexed by kings who survived in adjoining regions, and up to that time they demonstrated moderation and virtue.[214] This consulate, or rather

---

Ninus, the figure is 1305 years, which accords with the figure of 1300 years he gives in 12.11 as according to the "Greek records."

208. Augustine, *The City of God*, 18.21. See also M. Junianus Justinus, *Philippian Histories of T. Pompeius Trogus*, 1.prologue, 1.3. Augustine cites Vergil, *Aeneid*, 6.767, for Procas as one of the distant successors to Aeneas as king of Latium. His successor was Aemulius, whose neice Rhea was the legendary mother of Romulus. It is M. Junianus Justinus, *Philippian Histories of T. Pompeius Trogus*, who says that Arbaces, praefect of the Medes, killed Sardanapolus and transferred the empire from the Assyrians to the Medes. In the prologue to Book 1, he deals with Assyria from Ninus to Sardanapolus.

209. Augustine, *The City of God*, 12.11. Alexander defeated Darius III Codomanus (r.336–330 B.C.E.) several times, decisively at Arbela in 331, but adding this date to 233 gives only 564 instead of 622 as the beginning of the Medean-Persian power. The 233 figure is from Augustine, who refers to what he calls the "Greek records," although both Curtius and Jerome give 230 years. While not exact, these figures accord fairly well with the establishment of the Persian Empire by Cyrus the Great (r.550–529 B.C.E.).

210. 1 Machabees (Maccabees) 1.8.

211. Augustine, *The City of God*, 12.11. Augustine's figure accords with that of Velleius Paterculus, *Roman History*, 1.6, but differs with Justinus, *Philippian Histories of T. Pompeius Trogus*, 33.2, who gives 924 years.

212. 1 Machabees (Maccabees) 8.

213. Ptolemy I Soter (r.323–285 B.C.E.), son of Lagos, was the first king of the Macedonian thirty-first dynasty of Egypt founded by Alexander. But Judas ruled in the 160s, long after. Ruling Egypt at the same time was Ptolemy VII Philometor (r.181–145), which is who Ptolemy of Lucca probably had in mind, especially since he was allied with Rome, which restored him to the throne twice when he was overthrown.

214. Ptolemy actually says they were "of moderate virtue," but this has another connotation in idiomatic English.

this monarchy,[215] lasted up to the time of Julius Caesar who first usurped command [*imperium*]. After this, he survived only a short time; indeed, the senators killed him for his abuse of lordship. Afterward, Octavius, the son of Julius's sister,[216] succeeded and took the monarchy for himself alone, after he exacted vengeance against the killers of Julius and slew Antony who held the monarchy in the east.[217] As a result of his modesty Octavius maintained his rule for a long time, and in the forty-second year of his government, when the seventy-ninth period of seven days foretold by Daniel was completed,[218] when the kingdom and priesthood had come to an end in Judea, Christ, who was true king, priest, and monarch, was born. When he appeared to his disciples after his resurrection, he said: "All power in heaven and earth was given to me."[219] According to Augustine and Jerome we must take this to apply to his humanity, since no one doubts that he always had it with respect to his divinity.[220]

Chapter 13

How Christ's monarchy excels in three ways, and how Octavian
Caesar stood in the place of Christ.

[1] This fifth monarchy, which according to the Truth succeeded that of the Romans, surpasses all the others in three ways. First, from the number of its years, because it lasted longer, lasts up to the present time, and will last until the renovation of the world, as is clear from the vision of Daniel that I mentioned above[221] and about which I will now say more.

[2] Second, its excellence is apparent from the universality of its lordship, because: "their sound went out to all the earth and their words to the ends of the

---

215. Ptolemy is not calling the Roman Republic a monarchy in the sense of a governmental form, but rather commenting on its role as the Fourth Universal Monarchy, in the sense of exercising singular control over many lands.
216. Augustus was actually the grand-nephew of Caesar, since he was the son of Atia, the daughter of Julia, Caesar's youngest sister, and Octavius.
217. Marcus Antonius (Marc Antony) (c.83–30 B.C.E.) was an associate of Caesar who became Octavian's chief rival after Caesar's death. Both he and Octavian were instrumental in punishing Caesar's assassins. From 40 to 36 he was given power over the eastern part of the empire, including Egypt, where he came under the influence of Cleopatra, but he was defeated decisively by Octavian at Actium (31), after which he committed suicide.
218. Daniel 9.24–25.
219. Matthew 28.18.
220. Jerome, *Commentary on the Gospel of Matthew*, 4, on Matthew 28.18.
221. 3.10.9.

globe."[222] There is no corner of the world and no region in which the name of Christ is not adored. As Paul maintains: "He subjected all things beneath his feet."[223] The prophet Malachi also points to that lordship when he says: "The Lord of Armies says: 'From the rising to the setting of the sun, my name is great among the nations, and in every place a clean oblation is sacrificed and offered to my name, because my name is great among the nations.' "[224]

[3] These words make it sufficiently clear that Christ's lordship is ordained to the salvation of the spirit and to spiritual goods, as we will soon see, although it is not excluded from temporal matters in so far as they are ordained to spiritual things. Thus it is that although Christ was adored by the Magi[225] and glorified by the Angels as a sign of his universal lordship, he nevertheless lay in a humble place wrapped in ordinary swaddling clothes. Persons are drawn to virtue better in this way than by force of arms. He intended this, although more often he used his might as the true Lord.

[4] Therefore, he lived in humility and sustained the lordship of Augustus so that the whole globe might be counted at the time of the birth of the Lord, as the Evangelist Luke testifies.[226] A poll tax or tribute was levied based on this count, as the histories tell us, in recognition of the servitude that was owed.[227] There is a mystery in this, since he who was born was true Lord and Monarch of the world, and Augustus stood in his place, although he did this not through his understanding but through the motion of God, in the same way as Caiaphas prophesied.[228] Feeling this instinctively, Caesar Augustus issued a mandate, as the histories relate, that none of the Roman people should call

222. Psalms 18.5 (19.5).
223. 1 Corinthians 15.26
224. Malachias (Malachi) 1.11.
225. Matthew 2.11. Magi, members of the Persian priest class, and called "Wise Men" in the Bible gradually became identified as kings especially after the late tenth century. This seems to be the underlying assumption here, for otherwise how do they attest to Christ's "universal dominion"? For the transformation see Alexander Murray, *Reason and Society in the Middle Ages*, corrected edition (Oxford: Oxford University Press, 1985), 118.
226. Luke 2.1.
227. Peter Comestor, *Scholastic History*, On the Gospels, 4.
228. Caiaphas was high priest of the Jews 18–36 C.E. Jesus was brought before him and the Sanhedrin before he was taken to Pilate. Some Jews were worried that if Jesus were left alone, and many came to believe in him, the Romans would act against the Jews as a whole. Caiaphas advocated killing Jesus, replying to those opposed: "you do not consider that it is better that one person should die for the people and so that the nation should not perish." A high priest was believed to have the power of prophecy, and John 11.49–52 interprets this as a prophecy that Jesus would die for the nation and to gather together the dispersed children of God. This obviously is not what Caiaphas thought he was saying, just as Augustus was not conscious that he was standing in for Jesus, and so he was acting as an unconscious prophet of Christianity.

him "Lord."[229] Augustus, who subjugated the whole earthly globe, held the position of monarchy for fourteen years after the nativity of Christ, the True Lord, and he ruled for a total of fifty-six years and six months as described in accounts of the acts of the Roman rulers. Tiberius, who succeeded Augustus, as the histories relate, wanted to translate Christ, as True Lord, to a place among the gods, but he was impeded in this by a proud and haughty senate impatient of any lordship.[230]

[5] Third, the greater excellence of Christ's monarchy over the other four that preceded it is apparent from the dignity of the one who exercises lordship, since that one is both God and human. By this consideration the human nature in Christ participates in infinite virtue, which means that it is a greater and higher fortitude and virtue than human fortitude and virtue. The prophet Isaiah describes this in speaking of the temporal virtue of Christ, for which virtue we call him "Monarch": "A little one was born to us, and a son was given to us, and rule was put on his shoulders; and his name will be called Admirable, Counselor, Strong God, Father of the Future Age, Ruler of Peace. His empire will be multiplied, and there will be no end of peace."[231] In these words Isaiah touches on all the things that are required for a true ruler; though, to be sure, he transcends the limits of all other lords, as I will declare in the following chapter, and as is clear to anyone who looks.

[6] Therefore, this rule or monarchy brings to naught and destroys all other lordship, because all kingdoms are subjected to the same one, as the same prophet foretold: "'I am alive,' says the Lord, 'because every knee will be bowed to me.'"[232] And the Apostle Paul writes in Philippians: "In the name of Jesus every knee should be bent, all those that are celestial, earthly, or infernal."[233] After he has explained the vision in Nebuchadnezzar's dream, Daniel concludes about this monarchy: "In those days," that is, after the four monarchies of the Assyrians, the Persians and the Medes, the Greeks, and the Romans, "God will raise up the kingdom of heaven, which will not dissipate

---

229. Actually, Augustus was concerned to be seen as the preserver of the Republic, and so was unwilling to be regarded as other than "first citizen."

230. Orosius, *Seven Books of History Against the Pagans*, 7.4, reports the apocryphal story that after Pilate told Tiberius (r.14–37 C.E.) about Jesus's death, Tiberius wanted to deify him. Gregory of Tours, *History of the Franks*, 1.24 , also repeats this story and says that the Senate did not go along because it was angry that Pilate's report had not come to it first.

231. Isaias (Isaiah) 9.6–7.

232. Isaias (Isaiah) 45.23. The Vulgate actually says, "The word of justice will go out of my mouth and it will not return, because every knee will be bowed to me and every tongue will swear."

233. Philippians 2.10.

in eternity, and his kingdom will not be handed over to another, and it will crush all these kingdoms and itself stand through eternity."[234] Indeed, the reason it will last through eternity is at hand, because that one is joined to eternal rule, since he is both Lord God and human.

[7] We have now come full circle, because I proved above that all lordship takes its origin from God. Rule is bounded by this true rule, to mention human motions, as by something immovable beyond which there is no motion. We must conclude from these things that this Lordship can not fail.

Chapter 14

Questions about Christ's monarchy: when did it begin? how and why did it spread? Two causes for its concealment and a exposition of the first.

[1] Then the question arises when the Lord's rule began, since it is evident that many afterward have commanded. He chose an abject life, which is why it is said in Matthew: "Foxes have pits and the birds of heaven nests, but the Son of Humanity has no place to lay his head."[235] Likewise, we read in John that when he had fed the multitude he hid himself, because the people wanted to carry him off and make him king.[236] Likewise, in the same book he says: "My kingdom is not of this world."[237]

[2] One could respond to this question by saying that the rule of Christ began at the very time of his nativity, by using as arguments the ministration and declaration of the Angels on that day. For it is written in Luke: "The Angel said to the shepherds: 'I announce a great joy to you, because there was born to you today the Savior of the world.'"[238] Another argument is the adoration of the Magi. In Matthew it is said: "When Jesus was born in Bethlehem of Judah in the days of King Herod, behold Magi from the east came to Jerusalem, saying: 'Where is he who was born king of the Jews? For we saw his star in the east, and we come to adore him.'"[239] These acts sufficiently designate his rule and the time when it began, which was prophesied and foretold

---

234. Daniel 2.44.
235. Matthew 8.20.
236. John 6.15.
237. John 18.36.
238. Luke 2.10–11.
239. Matthew 2.1–2. See note on Magi at 3.13.3.

by Isaiah in the words cited above. We must note that in order to show the excellence of his lordship, more of his virtue and might were evident during his infancy than when he was an adult, so as to suggest that his weakness was voluntary, not necessary. He assumed this weakness and used his lordship publicly only for two reasons. These answers suffice for the present.

[3] One reason he assumed weakness was to teach rulers humility, which makes them gracious in their government, since humility deserves grace according to the Proverb: "Glory will raise up the humble in spirit."[240] And again: "Carry out your works in mildness, and you will be loved with greater than human glory."[241] And in the first letter of the Blessed Peter: "God resists the proud, but gives grace to the humble."[242] But just as humility is more necessary for a ruler, so too do the teeth of unyielding envy lacerate him more because of the superior eminence of his station. Realizing this, King David, as 2 Kings tells us, responded to Michal, the haughty daughter of the former king, after she had insulted him by saying that he had uncovered himself in his handmaids' presence to praise God and give reverence to the divine Ark, which then was being kept for the divinity: "I will play before the Lord, and I will become lower than I was made, and I will be humble in my eyes before the Lord who chose me rather than your father."[243] Christ wanted to follow this regulation himself, according to the will of God the Father, as foretold by the prophet Zechariah, which the Evangelist Matthew declared to have been fulfilled in Christ: "Behold, your king comes to you meek, sitting on an ass and a foal, which was born of one subjected to the yoke."[244]

[4] If the rulers of the world are commended for humility and poverty, through which they become gracious to their subjects and their lordship becomes prosperous, why will we not commend more the perfect humility of Christ? Valerius Maximus and Augustine write that when the Peloponnesians were fighting against the Athenians, Codrus, king of the Athenians, consulted Apollo, who informed him that that army would prevail whose leader was consecrated to death. King Codrus then dressed himself as a pauper so that he would be killed by the enemy and thereby save his nation. When he was killed the enemy was put to flight, and the Athenians claimed that Codrus had been

---

240. Proverbs 29.23.
241. Ecclesiasticus (Sirach) 3.19.
242. 1 Peter 5.5.
243. 2 Kings (2 Samuel) 6.21–22. Michal was the daughter of Saul, and she remained childless because of her remark. David had just brought the Ark back to Jerusalem and had celebrated by leaping and dancing in public.
244. Matthew 21.5 with reference to Zacharias (Zechariah) 9.9.

translated to a place among the gods.[245] Augustine and Valerius Maximus also tell us about certain Roman consuls, such as Lucius Valerius, who died in such great indigence that his friends needed to take up a collection of coins for his burial.[246] Valerius Maximus (Vegetius also says the same thing, as I related above)[247] commends the consul Fabricius for this very thing. He writes that although Fabricius was as poor as any pauper, when the legates of the Epirotes offered him a huge amount of gold, he refused: "Tell the Epirotes that I prefer to command those having these things than to possess them."[248]

[5] What more can we urge? All great rulers and monarchs have subjugated the world with humility, but lost their lordship through the haughtiness of self-exaltation, as I showed above.[249] For this reason, it is written in Ecclesiasticus: "The greater you are, the more you should humble yourself in all things, and then you will find grace in the presence of God."[250] But if we commend the virtue of humility and benevolence in any ruler, how much more ought we to praise it in our ruler Christ, as one constituted in the supreme rank of virtue.

[6] Therefore, for the reasons I have already given, I conclude that, although he was the legitimate Lord, Christ's humility and poverty are consonant with reason.

Chapter 15

The second reason why the Lord assumed an abject and concealed
life, although he was the true Lord of the world, and an exposition
of the words of Isaiah on this subject.

[1] There is also another reason why our Lord assumed a humble state, even though he is Lord of the world, and that is to make known the difference be-

245. Augustine, *The City of God*, 18.19. Valerius Maximus, *Memorable Deeds and Sayings*, 5.6, ext. 1. Valerius Maximus says that the oracle predicted that his army would prevail when he fell to the enemy. For Codrus, see note at 2.9.6.
246. Augustine, *The City of God*, 5.18. Valerius Maximus, *Memorable Deeds and Sayings*, 4.4.1. Valerius Maximus and Livy, *History of Rome*, 2.16, report this story of Publius Valerius Publicola, one of the founders of the Republic, and, with Brutus, one of its first consuls (509 B.C.E.).
247. 3.4.
248. Valerius Maximus, *Memorable Deeds and Sayings*, 4.3.6. Ptolemy refers to *On the Military*, Book 4, but Vegetius does not mention Fabricius there or elsewhere. Gaius Fabricius Luscinus was a third-century B.C.E. Roman general and consul. For more on Fabricius, see above 2.8.3, 3.4.5, and below 4.15.5.
249. 3.9.
250. Ecclesiasticus (Sirach) 3.20.

tween other rulers' lordship and his own. Although he was Lord of the globe temporally, he directly ordained his rule to the spiritual life, for as John writes: "I came that they might have life and have it more abundantly."[251] This verifies his words that I cited above: "My kingdom is not of this world."[252] Thus, he lived humbly so that by his example he might encourage his faithful to act according to virtue.

[2] In order to follow this path it is more suitable to have humility and show contempt for the world—a view the Stoics and Cynics put forward, as Augustine and Valerius Maximus report.[253] Seneca himself, who was the perfect Stoic, exhibits these qualities in his little book *On the Providence of God* and in *On the Shortness of Life, to Paulinus*.[254] It is through them that one is made worthy of the eternal kingdom, and their pursuit is the principle intention of lordship. The Lord himself said to his disciples and followers in Luke: "You are the ones who have persevered with me in my temptations, and I have arranged that you should eat and drink at my table in my kingdom."[255] Therefore, for the reason already mentioned, the Lord wanted his adherents to live humbly by his example, as Matthew writes: "Learn from me because I am mild and humble in heart."[256] He also wanted them to ordain their temporal lordship to this. This is why the spiritual life of the faithful is called the kingdom of heaven, because it differs in its manner of living from the worldly kingdom and because it is ordained to the true eternal kingdom, not to temporal lordship.

[3] Therefore, so that there would be no suspicion in human hearts that he has taken up rule in order to exercise lordship in the world and that this is his end, as it is the end of other lords, he chose an abject life. Nevertheless, he was true Lord and Monarch, since "Rule was put on his shoulders," as the Prophet said in the passage cited above.[257] This was best foretold in the further words of Isaiah, also cited earlier, in the first place because he is represented as humble and abject: "A little one," he says, "was born to us." In the second clause of

251. John 10.10.

252. John 18.36.

253. Augustine, *The City of God*, 19.1; Valerius Maximus, *Memorable Deeds and Sayings*, 4.3, ext. 3 and 4.

254. Seneca, *On the Providence of God*, 4; *On the Shortness of Life, to Paulinus*,14. See also *Letters to Lucilius*, 18.

255. Luke 22.28–30.

256. Matthew 11.29.

257. Isaias (Isaiah) 9.6: "A little one was born to us, and a son was given to us, and rule was put on his shoulders; and his name will be called Admirable, Counselor, Strong God, Father of the Future Age, Ruler of Peace. His empire will be multiplied, and there will be no end of peace." In the Latin *"fortis,"* "strong," follows "God," which explains Ptolemy's comment in 3.15.4.

that sentence the virtue and excellence of his lordship are joined to that little-ness: "and a son," he says, "was given to us." Because the humanity of Christ was joined to the divinity of the Son, his lordship is, as it were, his instrument of omnipotent virtue, and therefore in the same passage the Prophet shows that his lordship is ineffable by using a circumlocution in many clauses show-ing his singular might. All these clauses have to be understood distinctly as Jerome explains them, as the order of the clauses makes clear.[258]

[4] First, with regard to the security and solidity of his lordship, he says, "rule was put on his shoulders." Things which are borne on the shoulders are more firm, and burdens are carried more securely in that way. Second, with regard to the newness of his lordship, he adds: "And his name will be called Admi-rable," for he is worthy of admiration because he is humble and a pauper, yet Lord of the world. Third, with regard to the clarity of his wisdom (and this is especially necessary for rulers, because, as is said in Ecclesiastes:[259] "Woe to the land whose king is a boy," which happens when a ruler can do nothing by himself, but acts or, to put it better, is caused to act, only with the support of others' counsel), he adds: "counselor." Fourth, with regard to the dignity of his lordship, he adds: "God." Since we may suppose that he is one in him-self, that is, one divine persona in which are united his divine and human nature, we may idiomatically interchange the qualities of these natures, as John Damascene says,[260] so that the "little one" is called "God." For the same reason, the rule of Christ in virtue follows once we have supposed the divine nature, and therefore the word "Strong" follows, which is the fifth clause. For the divine virtue which was personally in him influences the rule of Christ, and Christ used this might at the time of his passion when the Jews looked for him because they wanted to kill him. For when he said: "I am he," they im-mediately fell to the earth, as John writes.[261] This certainly exceeds the limits of his successors. It is apparent that the Vicar of Christ is not God, and in this Christ's power transcends the might of his successors. Thus, Christ can do many things that concern the ordination of his faithful and his rule which neither the blessed Peter nor his successors can do, as I showed above.[262] From the same perspective, namely of him as a little one, a sixth condition of his singular rule is added—that his governing is benign, because he is "Father of the Future Age." We can refer this to the fullness of grace, by which those

---

258. Jerome, *Commentary on the Prophet Isaias*, on Isaias 9.6.
259. Ecclesiastes 10.16.
260. John Damascene, *Exposition of the Orthodox Faith*, 3.15. John does not mention the "Little One." John Damascene (John of Damascus) was an eighth-century doctor of the Eastern Church, but he was canonized also in the west.
261. John 18.5–6.
262. 3.10.10.

who are full of grace bear the yoke of the law lightly. As Paul said to the Galatians: "If you are led by the spirit, you are not under the law,"[263] which makes the iron rod unnecessary for governing such ones, and this applies only to Christ's rule. The same reason leads to the seventh and last clause concerning the tranquility of his governing, when it is added: "Ruler of peace," although this refers to the heart, not the body. Christ, our king and ruler, offers this to his faithful by living, and in dying he left it behind as a fief: "In the world," he said, "you will have affliction, but in me peace,"[264] and this also applies to his rule alone.

[5] Thus, he founded his lordship in humility and poverty. Sallust and Valerius Maximus relate the opinion of Cato that prove the same thing—that the Roman Republic increased, not through haughtiness or public displays of pride, but in adversities, labors, and hardships.[265]

Chapter 16

Examples of the ancient Romans show that the Republic grew in that way. Also, something about Constantine.

[1] Hence it is that our king Jesus Christ, ruler of the age, both by living and by dying, allowed others to exercise lordship until the time when his kingdom is completed and prepared in his faithful through their virtuous works and it is crowned with laurel by their blood. For if the Carthaginians killed Regulus, who is also called Marcus because of his zeal for his fatherland, if Marcus Curtius threw himself into a steep cleft in the earth for the liberation of his fatherland, if Brutus and Torquatus killed their sons for justice and to preserve military discipline, as the histories tell us (and it was by such zeal that the Republic, from small beginnings, was made great); likewise, if Zaleucus, who exercised lordship among the Locri, as Valerius Maximus reports, deprived his son of one eye and himself of another for his son's adultery, so that he might serve justice with regard to his son's transgression and yet by an admirable and equitable temperament show himself to be both a merciful father and a just legislator,[266] why should Christians not be even more praiseworthy if they ex-

---

263. Galatians 5.18.
264. John 16.33.
265. Sallust, *The War with Cataline*, 52.21; Valerius Maximus, *Memorable Deeds and Sayings*, 4.4.11.
266. Valerius Maximus, *Memorable Deeds and Sayings*, 1.1.14 (Regulus); 5.6.2 (Marcus Curtius); 5.8.1 (Brutus); 2.7.6 (Torquatus); 6.5, ext. 3 (Zaleucus). For Curtius, see above 3.4.5; for Brutus 3.5.5; for Torquatus, see above 1.8.5, 3.5.5, where Ptolemy cites Augustine, *The City*

pose themselves to suffering and torment out of zeal for faith and love of God and undertake to make virtues flourish so as to pursue the eternal kingdom and to ensure that the rule of Christ might grow through their merits?

[2] Augustine treats these things very subtly and copiously throughout nearly the whole of *The City of God*. He wrote it for this reason and to relate what happened in the intermediate time from the passion of the Lord to the time of the blessed Sylvester and Constantine. During this period of the age an infinite multitude of people were dedicated and united to Christ their Lord through their death and followed his leadership and rule.[267] The first leaders were the Apostles and other disciples of Christ and all the successors of Peter, the vicar of Christ, for a period of 350 years. It was through their blood, bodies, and merits that the Church was founded, as from living and precious stones,[268] on an infallible foundation, against which neither the winds, nor the rains, nor any tempestuous passions, nor any kind of perturbations can prevail.

[3] When the appropriate time came for the kingdom of Christ, which was built in this manner, to manifest itself to the world, the force of our ruler Jesus Christ caused distress to Constantine, the ruler of the world, by striking him with leprosy and then curing him, which is beyond the capability of human force. When he had proof of this, Constantine yielded his lordship to the blessed Sylvester, the vicar of Christ, to whom this lordship belonged by right, for the causes and reasons I assigned above.[269] By this cession a temporal kingdom was appended to the spiritual kingdom of Christ, while the

---

of God, 5.18. Zaleucus was a seventh-century B.C.E. Greek of Locri in Magna Graecia. According to legend, he was born a slave and commissioned by the Locrians to write a code of laws to end their anarchy. When he realized that he had inadvertently violated this code, he killed himself.

267. Literally, "his leader ("*ducem*") and ruler ("*principem*")."

268. Augustine, *The City of God*, 18.48, says that the church of the New Testament is more glorious than that of the Old, since the living stones of which it is constructed are better. In 18.49–50 Augustine discusses the Apostles and martyrs, who were especially important in this.

269. See above 3.10.8. This is a reference to the eighth-century forgery known as the Donation of Constantine, according to which Constantine moved his capital to Constantinople, leaving the government of Rome to Pope Sylvester I (314–335) and his successors. This document was widely believed to be authentic throughout the Middle Ages. The Donation incorporated the legend of Constantine's leprosy and his subsequent baptism at the hands of Sylvester himself, was known by the end of the fourth century in the *Acts of Liberius* (Duchesne, ed., *Liber Pontificalis*, 1.94ff.), and was transmitted through the Middle Ages by the fifth-century *Life of St. Sylvester* (Duchesne, ed., *Liber Pontificalis*, 1.107 ff.). The portion of the Donation included as an addition to the *Decretum*, D.96, c. 14, omits this story. Lorenzo Valla, in his "The Falsely-Believed and Forged Donation of Constantine," suggests that it was based on the biblical story of Naaman and Elisha (4 Kings [2 Kings] 5.1–27), and in Gregory of Tours, *History of the Franks*, 2.31. the comparison of Clovis and Remegius to Constantine and Sylvester could be interpreted to mean that both were cured of leprosy by the pope, although the clearest meaning is simply that Clovis's sin was washed away by baptism like Constantine's leprosy.

spiritual retained its vigor. The faithful of Christ ought to seek the spiritual in itself, and the temporal only in a secondary way, to assist the spiritual. Otherwise they act against Christ's intention.

[4] Then was fulfilled what comes after those clauses of Isaiah: "His empire will be multiplied and there will be no end of peace."[270] For the churches practiced openly by this time, and Christ began to be preached publicly, which could not be done before without danger of death. In the same year in which Constantine was cured of leprosy and converted to the faith more than 100,000 persons were baptized in the Roman territories as a consequence of the virtues shown by the vicar of Christ.

[5] We must now attend to what the prophet says: "And there will be no end of peace." It is well known that after Constantine's death his son was infected by the Arian heresy and threw the church into disorder. Under him, established doctors of the Church—bishops Hilary of Gaul, Athanasius of Alexandria, Eusebius of Vercelli, and many other doctors and clerics of the Church—suffered exile. As the histories tell us, even the head of the Church, the Supreme Pontiff Liberius, wavered in the true faith under the many persecutions of Constantius.[271] After him came Julian the Apostate, the brother of Gallus and cousin of Constantius,[272] who inflicted a second persecution on the faithful, under which the brothers John and Paul suffered.[273] How then were the words of the Lord (those that I cited above and the prophet proclaimed) verified?

[6] One must relate these things to the peace of the heart, not to the peace of the body. The Lord himself, when he offers peace to his disciples in the book of John, speaks of such a peace: "I leave peace with you. I give my peace

270. Isaias (Isaiah) 9.7.

271. Constantius II (337–40) reversed his father's policy and favored the Arians, who taught that God the Father and Christ were of different substance. Hilary (c.315–67) was bishop of Poitiers (c.353) and strongly opposed Arianism. Constantius exiled him to Phrygia. Athanasius (295–373) was the leader of the anti-Arian party whom Constantius exiled three times. Eusebius of Vercelli (283–371), though a staunch opponent of Arianism, strove to bring peace to the factions. Liberius (352–66) was forced into exile for supporting Athanasius, but was at last induced to accept a compromise semi-Arian definition of the nature of God.

272. Julian the Apostate (r.361–63) was the son of Constantine's half brother Julius Constantius, and so cousin of Constantius II. His half-brother Gallus (325–354) was appointed Caesar (junior colleague and chosen successor of an emperor) in 351, but his cruel reign and unpopularity led to his execution by Constantius. Julian, like Gallus, was raised as a Christian, but converted to paganism as a result of his philosophical studies in Athens. As emperor he tried to reestablish paganism in the form of the cult of sol invictus (the Unconquered Sun).

273. The story of Saints John and Paul, officers in the service of Constantine's daughter Constantia, is found, among other places in Jacob de Voragine, The Golden Legend, part 1, June 26. Julian executed them in 364 according to this version (though Julian died in 363) for refusing to serve him and sacrifice to the gods and for distributing Constantia's money to help Christians.

to you, but I do not give you the sort of peace that the world gives."[274] It is obvious that those words were said to the disciples when his passion was imminent, and it is well known that those same disciples endured persecution; for this reason the Lord said to them at the same time: "If they have persecuted me, they will also persecute you."[275] Therefore, the chosen faithful of Christ cannot lose this peace unless they wish to. But if the Stoics could say that the human goods that they call virtues always stay with a person and cannot be taken away from the virtuous against their will, as Aulus Gellius in *Attic Nights* and Augustine report,[276] why can we not say even more about the minds of the faithful that "there will be no end of their peace," since they cleave to an end that lives without end?

Chapter 17

The emperors at Constantinople following Constantine were obedient and reverent to the Roman Church, as is shown through the four councils to which these rulers subjected themselves.

[1] After these events, when Julian had been killed in the war against the Persians, his brother Jovian, a Catholic man whose reign was too short, restored the peace of the Church.[277] It is notable that from then on until the time of Charlemagne, we find that all the emperors were obedient and reverent to the Roman Church just as if it had rule, both with regard to spiritual lordship, as defined by the sacred Nicene synod, and to temporal lordship. As Pope Gelasius wrote to the Emperor Anastasius and as the histories tell us, the emperor depends on the judgment of the pope and not the contrary.[278] According to ecclesiastical history, Valentinian, who was Jovian's immediate successor,[279] was reported to have said when the election of the Milanese archbishop was approaching: "We, who exercise governance over an empire, may sincerely

274. John 14.27.

275. John 15.20.

276. Aulus Gellius, *Attic Nights*, 1.2; Augustine, *The City of God*, 5.10. Aulus Gellius, however, is making fun of a pompous would-be Stoic who claims this, among other things.

277. Jovian (r.363–64) restored all privileges to the Christians and supported the orthodox against the Arians. He was one of Julian's generals, but not his brother; he was raised to the imperial office by the soldiers after Julian's death in Persia.

278. Gelasius I (492–496) was used by advocates of both the dualist and hierocratic position. He wrote to Anastasius that there were two powers in the world—priestly and royal—but that the "responsibility of priests is more weighty in so far as they will answer for the kings of humans themselves at the divine judgment." See Tierney, *Crisis of Church and State*, 13–15 for a translation.

279. Valentinian I (r.364–375) was banished by Julian and brought back by Jovian.

submit our heads to such a one constituted for us in the pontifical seat and accept his admonitions when we have committed a fault, as humans do, just as we necessarily accept healing remedies."[280]

[2] I must treat the emperors up to the time of Charles here, because that material is fruitful for showing the reverence of rulers to the vicar of Christ. After this, between the times of Charles and Otto I, three changes were made: first with regard to the mode of electing the emperor, second with regard to the mode of his succession, and third with regard to the mode of providing an emperor. In order to make this clear, I must tell you something about the sequence of emperors from the time of Constantine and how they, other than the tyrants that I have already mentioned, were subject to the Church.

[3] As the histories relate,[281] after Constantine ceded the empire to the vicar of Christ, he transferred himself with his satraps and rulers to the province of Thrace, where Asia Major begins and Europe ends. There he seized on one city, called Byzantium, and, as the histories tell us, made it equal to Rome and called it by his own name.[282] This city was the imperial seat until the time of Charles, when Pope Adrian called a council in Rome and transferred the empire from the Greeks to the Germans in the persona of Charles. Other histories say Stephen did it, but the first report is better. From this, it appears that the emperors in Constantinople depended on the vicar of Christ, the supreme Pontiff, as Pope Gelasius wrote to the emperor Anastasius.[283] Thus, their empire is ordained to execute the government of the faithful according to the mandate of the Supreme Pontiffs, so that the emperors could deservedly be said to be their executors and coadjutors and cooperators with God for the purpose of exercising governance over the Christian people. I will show this first for four emperors who reigned in the intermediate period, who also were present at four solemn and universal councils, approved their statutes, and subjected themselves humbly to them.

[4] The first, in the time of Constantine, was the Nicene Council, which consisted of 318 bishops. As the histories tell us, Arius, an Alexandrian priest who asserted that the Son was less than the Father, was condemned there. It is said that this ruler bore all the expenses of the council, as if recognizing the

---

280. Paul the Deacon, *Roman* (or *Mixed*) *History*, 12, under Valentinian.
281. Paul the Deacon, *Roman* (or *Mixed*) *History*, 11, under Alexander.
282. That is, Constantinople, the new capital of the empire after 323, and also called "New Rome."
283. See above 3.10.8.

vicar of Christ as his lord. The whole council stood in the place of the blessed Sylvester since he was absent for a particular reason.[284]

[5] As the histories tell us, the second council was celebrated at Constantinople under Pope Cyriacus (though some say it was under Damasus), with the senior Theodosius present; it consisted of 150 bishops.[285] Many heresies were condemned there, but especially that of Bishop Macedonius of Constantinople, who denied that the Holy Spirit was God consubstantial with the Father and Son. Moreover, Theodosius had such great reverence for the Church that, as Gelasius wrote to the Emperor Anastasius, when the blessed Ambrose prohibited him from entering his church, he did not dare enter, and when Ambrose excommunicated him, because he had consented to the slaughter of a multitude in Thessalonica who had killed an imperial judge, as the *Tripartite History* narrates,[286] this Catholic ruler bore it patiently. At last, since Ambrose sternly criticized him, Theodosius did public penance before he could gain entrance to the church.

[6] The third council was celebrated under the younger Theodosius, son of Arcadius, in Ephesus, and consisted of 200 bishops, in the time of Celestine I, who was not present, but Bishop Cyril of Alexandria, who had Theodosius's confidence, took his place. As the histories tell us, Theodosius was so honorable and gave such mature council and reverence to the divine cult that from a tender age he was permitted to command. This synod gathered against Nestorius, bishop of Constantinople, who posited two personae in Christ and through this supposition of two natures eliminated the true unity of each.[287]

284. The Nicene Council (325), the first ecumenical council of the church was called by Constantine to deal with the Arian problem, not by Sylvester I (314–35). Although legates represented Sylvester, they did not chair the council, nor was their approval considered especially necessary. Constantine himself was the dominant force at the council and forced through the Nicene creed. Sylvester did confirm the decree, but in later years Constantine began to favor the Arian party.

285. Actually it was during the reign of Damascus I (366–84), not Cyriacus (or Siricius) (384–99) that the Council of Constantinople met (381). However, it was Theodosius I (r.379–395) who called it, the 150 bishops were all from the east, and the council neither asked for nor received the help or approval of the pope. The flap with Ambrose occurred in 390 after a mob killed the imperial governor, Botheric, who had jailed a popular charioteer. It was Theodosius who declared Christianity the only legal religion in the Roman Empire.

286. Cassiodorus, *Tripartite History*, 9.30. See also Paul the Deacon, *Roman* (or *Mixed*) *History*, 13, under Theodosius.

287. Again, the emperor called the Council of Ephesus (431) at the urging of both Nestorius (d.c.451) and Cyril (376–444). Cyril's demands to Nestorius, and indeed the actual condemnation of Nestorius, exceeded the authority Celestine (422–32) gave him, but there really was nothing he could do about it, and Theodosius II (r.408–50) exiled Nestorius. Nestorianism became widespread in the east, in Persia, India, and China, and there are pockets of it that remain

[7] The fourth council was celebrated in Chalcedon and consisted of 630 bishops under Leo I, with the ruler Marcian present.[288] It is said that out of reverence for the Roman Church, Marcian declared in the seventh session of this synod: "We wish to attend this council in order to confirm the faith, not to show our might, and to follow the example of that most religious man, Constantine, so that when the truth has been found the multitude will not cause further discord under the attraction of perverse doctrines." Given these examples, I maintain that it was the whole intention of the rulers in antiquity to show favor toward the faith and reverence and honor to the Roman Church. In this council Eutyches was condemned with Dioscoros, an Alexandrian bishop who, in the manner of Nestorius, posited distinct natures and personae in Christ and thus asserted confused and mixed-up ideas.[289]

Chapter 18

The two councils following those four, which were celebrated in the time of Justinian and Constantine the Younger, and the reason why the empire was transferred from the Greeks to the Germans.

[1] There were also many other councils, although these were the principal ones that met from the time of Constantine up to that of Charles. In the other councils rulers also showed themselves subject and faithful to the Church, but this is especially the case with Justinian 120 years after the fourth synod, in a council with Pope Julius presiding.[290] This is obvious from Justinian's laws,

---

today, mostly in Iran, Iraq, and Syria. "Tender age" refers to the fact that Theodosius became emperor at the age of seven.

288. Leo I (440–51) called this council in 451. It confirmed the united nature of Christ and the doctrine that this unity was of the divine and human natures of Christ. Marcian (r.450–57) was the Eastern Roman Emperor and a strong supporter of orthodoxy as represented by the council.

289. Eutyches (c.375–c.454) taught that Christ had two natures before the Incarnation, but one afterward. Dioscoros represented the extreme wing of Cyril's party that took over after his death and insisted on restoring the language of the "one nature" of Christ, which had been modified in a compromise of 433.

290. There is only one medieval Pope Julius, Julius I (337–52). This cannot be who Ptolemy has in mind, especially since he refers to the four previous major councils. Justinian I (527–65) called the Second Council of Constantinople in 553, 102 (not 120) years after the Council of Chalcedon or 122 years after Ephesus. Although this was later accepted as the Fifth Ecumenical Council, it is hardly a good example of an emperor showing reverence toward the pope. In fact, the council excommunicated the pope, Vigilius (537–55), who then was coerced into accepting its decrees. That this is the council Ptolemy had in mind, however, is shown by his later reference to Theodore. This is Theodore of Mopsuestia (c.350–c.429), a monk and bishop of Mopsuestia in Cilicia, who was condemned by the Council of Constantinople for his Christological views (basically Nestorian) and his opposition to Mary's title of *Theotokos*, mother of God, which had been confirmed at Chalcedon.

which he established in favor of the ecclesiastical state; likewise, from the letter which he sent throughout the globe after the council had been celebrated in Constantinople. In this letter Justinian subjected himself to the Church and mandated that his people should obey it in all things, and he repeated the statutes of the four councils mentioned above and confirmed in this same letter the holy sanctions or laws subjecting the people to ecclesiastical institutions, especially in matters of usury and matrimony, on which things civil life turns. This synod was celebrated in Constantinople against Theodore and his followers who said that the Word of God is one thing and Christ another, and who denied that the Blessed Mary was the Mother of God.

[2] The sixth synod was celebrated in this same royal city, with the Emperor Constantine the Younger attending to matters at the request of Pope Agatho. It consisted of 150 bishops, and was called against Macharius, a bishop of Antioch, and his allies, who asserted according to the perfidious teaching of Eutyches that there was one mode of operation and one will in Christ. In this synod, Constantine, who was a ruler 150 years after Justinian, showed much favor to the faith by destroying the Monothelite heretics, whom his father and grandfather had patronized, and he restored churches that they had destroyed.[291]

[3] I have mentioned these things to show that the emperors in Constantinople were protectors and defenders of the Roman Church until the time of Charlemagne. Then, since the Church was burdened by the Lombards at a time when the empire of Constantinople did not bring aid because its might had been reduced to the point that it could not do so effectively, the Roman Pontiff summoned the king of the Franks to his defense against those barbarians. First, Pope Stephen and his successor Zacharias summoned Pepin against King Aistulf of the Lombards; then Adrian and Leo summoned Charlemagne against Desiderius, the son of Aistulf. When Charlemagne had defeated and annihilated Desiderius and his nation, Adrian celebrated a council in Rome of 155 bishops and venerable abbots, and on account of Charlemagne's great deed transferred the empire from the Greeks to the Germans in the persona of the magnificent ruler Charles. This deed demonstrates sufficiently how the power of empire depends on the pope's judgment. For so long as the rulers

---

291. Constantine IV Pogonatus called a council recognized as the Sixth Ecumenical Council in 680 in Constantinople after discussions with Pope Agatho (678–81). The intent of both was to condemn the Monotheletist heresy. The Monothelites accepted the doctrine of Chalcedon and the subsequent councils that there were two persons in Christ, but emphasised the unity of Christ through one will and one operation. This also went too far for the orthodox.

of Constantinople defended the Roman Church, as Justinian did by sending Belisarius against the Goths and as Maurice did against the Lombards, the Church favored these rulers, but after they failed, as they did in the time of Michael, the contemporary of Charles, it provided another ruler for its protection.[292]

Chapter 19

How the mode of empire changed from Charlemagne to Otto III,
and the source of Highest Pontiff's fullness of power.

[1] Then the mode of empire changed. Up to the time of Charles the ancient mode was preserved through election in Constantinople—sometimes emperors were elevated from the same stock as the previous emperor, sometimes from another; sometimes the ruler elected his successor, sometimes the army did it. But when Charles was instituted election ceased, and emperors were elevated by succession, which meant that the emperor's firstborn always become emperor. This lasted up to the seventh generation after Charles, when

292. Belisarius (c.505–565) was sent by Justinian I (r.527–65) to recapture the western parts of the Empire. He defeated the Vandals in Africa (533–34) and the Goths in parts of Italy (535–40). The Empire was unable to hold on to most of these conquests, in part because of an outbreak of plague. Maurice (Mauricius) (r.582–602) conducted a struggle against the Lombard invaders of Italy and created the exarchate of Ravenna. Although he made gains in the 590s, the Lombards reduced Byzantine holdings in Italy to a few areas within a short time after Maurice was deposed. Afterward, the Byzantine emperors were unable to help the pope against the Lombards, which is why they increasingly turned to the Franks. After Aistulf (r.749–56) recaptured Ravenna and what remained of the Byzantine central Italian holdings and invaded the Roman region, Popes Zacharias (741–52) and Stephen II (752–57) appealed to Charlemagne's father Pepin (r.751–68). Pepin invaded twice in the mid-750s and restored the lost territories to the pope (the so-called "Donation of Pepin," on which later defenses of the Papal States were partially based). His successor, Desiderius (r.756–74) invaded this region again in 772, and this time Pope Adrian I (772–95) called on Charlemagne for help. He led two campaigns against the Lombards, in 773 and 774, when after a long siege he took Pavia, the Lombard capital, and took the title "king of the Lombards" himself. The emperor at the time Charlemagne assumed the title of emperor in 800 was actually Irene (in power for most of the years 780–802, officially sole ruler 797–802). Adrian was no longer pope at this time, but Ptolemy makes the same error at 3.10.8. It was Pope Leo III (795–816) who refused to recognize a woman emperor (she deliberately used the male title) and used this as one excuse to crown Charlemagne. The council to which Ptolemy refers was neither voluntarily called by the pope nor connected directly with the coronation. Leo had been attacked and mutilated in 799 (so badly, however, that his subsequent recovery could be touted as a miracle), and Charlemagne sent an army to restore him. When Charlemagne arrived in Rome in November, he was to preside over a council to try Leo for fornication and perjury, but his mind was already made up. The council declared itself to have no jurisdiction to try the pope; instead Leo swore publicly to his innocence two days before Charlemagne's coronation. Michael I Rangabe (r.811–13) was a contemporary of Charlemagne; his significance was that he officially recognized Charlemagne's title.

the succession failed in the time of Louis. At this time the Church was being vexed by the iniquitous Romans, and it summoned Otto I, duke of the Saxons, to assist it. After he liberated the Church from the vexation of the Lombards, the impious Romans, and the tyrant Berengar, he was crowned emperor by Leo VII,[293] and his Alemanni stock held the empire through three generations, and each of these three emperors was called Otto. Afterward, as the histories tell us, Gregory V similarly provided for election from Teutonic stock, which continued through seven rulers of Alemannia, and this continues today after a period of 270 years or thereabouts.[294] As long as it lasts, so long will last the Roman Church, which has the supreme rank in rule and has judged what is expedient for the faithful of Christ.

293. The imperial title remained in Charlemagne's family until Louis III the Child (r.899–911), who claimed it but was never crowned, but it did not consistently go from father to son. Louis was the last Carolingian king of Germany to claim the imperial title, but Berengar I, grandson of Louis the Pious, ruled in Italy and was crowned emperor (r.915–24). Leo VII (936–39) did not crown Otto I the Great (king 936–73), but he was pope at the beginning of his reign. Ptolemy probably mentions him here because he is intent on ascribing Otto's power to a papal decision, which was never the case even later. The tenth-century papacy was often the pawn of powerful Roman families, to which Ptolemy alludes. Otto replaced the "iniquitous Romans" with his own popes. The Lombard kingdom had come to an end as such with Charlemagne's conquest, but whoever ruled Lombardy, again beginning with Charlemagne, often styled themselves "king of the Lombards." A series of "Lombards" "vexed" popes during Otto's reign. Hugh of Arles (king of the Lombards 926–47), formerly count of Provence, had been invited to Italy by Pope John X (914–28) for help against the powerful Roman noblewoman Marouzia, who ended up marrying Hugh during the reign of her son, Pope John XI (931–36). Another son, Alberic, deprived by this marriage of his political ambitions, stirred up the Romans against John and his mother, imprisoned her, drove Hugh from Rome, and after John's death appointed Leo VII pope. Hugh attacked, but eventually the war was ended with a truce. Otto came to Italy in 951, invited not by the pope but by Adelaide, the dispossessed widow of Lothar, Hugh's son and successor (r.947–50). Otto defeated Berengar II (king of the Lombards 950–61), grandson of Berengar I, and it is this Berengar to whom Ptolemy refers. Otto had himself crowned king of the Lombards, married Adelaide, and demanded the imperial crown, but Alberic would not let his third pope, Agepetus, comply. He was crowned, under duress, in 962 by Alberic's son and successor Octavian, who became Pope John XII (955–64), the pope who began the custom of choosing a new name on election to the papacy. Otto deposed him in 963 in favor of his ally Leo VIII (963–65), whose short rule was interrupted by the restoration of John XII, who immediately died.

294. In the usual classification of imperial dynasties there were four emperors of the Saxon dynasty: Otto I, Otto II, Otto III (r.983–1002), and Henry II (1002–24). Henry, however, was not a descendent of the Ottos, but of Otto I's brother. These were followed by five Salian (or Franconian) emperors beginning with Conrad II (1024–39), a descendent of Otto II's sister. These were followed by seven Hohenstaufen emperors (only four of whom were crowned) and three uncrowned emperors of various houses up to the time Ptolemy was writing (he mentions these three below 3.20.2), during the rule of Albert I of Austria (1298–1308). The 270 year figure must refer to Conrad II, who was crowned by John XIX (1024–32) (not Gregory V, who was pope from 996–99 during the reign of Otto III) in 1027. But in *A Short Determination*, c. 13, 31, Ptolemy gives the date as 1030. Adding 270 to this gives 1300, which is close to the time Ptolemy is writing. It is not clear to me where he gets seven emperors, since even if we begin with Conrad and count only those actually crowned we get nine. And when he discusses the contemporary uncrowned emperors below, he does call them emperors.

[2] It seems that the vicar of Christ has a fullness of power in this case, that is, on behalf of the good state of the Universal Church. This is manifest in the words of the Lord cited above, and this power has been given to him by a threefold right: first by divine right, because the words cited above indicate that Christ wanted this to be so (and I will show this below); second, by natural right, because once we suppose that he holds the first place in rule, it follows necessarily that he should be affirmed to be the head from which all motion and sensation in the mystical body derive, and for this reason we maintain that all the influence of government depends on him. Further, it is necessary to attend to the conservation of any community, because human nature, which can not thrive outside of society, requires this. Among any rank of persons this conservation can only occur through a first directing principle. With regard to human acts this is the First Hierarch, which is Christ, so that he is the first directing, the first counseling, and the first moving principle, and the Supreme Pontiff stands in his place.[295]

[3] I said above that the ruler's position in the kingdom is the same as God's in the world and the spirit's in the body.[296] But it is certain that the entire operation of nature depends on God, as on that which exercises governance, moves, and conserves, because, according to the Acts of the Apostles: "through him we are moved and exist,"[297] and as the prophet Isaiah says: "you work all our works in us, Lord."[298] We can say the same thing about the spirit, because every act of nature in a body depends on the spirit for three kinds of reasons.

[4] We see that God, in exercising governance over and directing the world, permits the corruption of a particular being for the conservation of the whole. Nature does the same thing in the life of the human body through the virtue of the spirit. The same thing happens with rulers, because in order to conserve their whole government over their subjects and their kingdom their power is amplified to impose tallages and destroy cities and towns. Therefore, the same thing will be even more true for the highest and supreme ruler, that is the pope, for the good of the whole of Christianity.

[5] For this reason, the First Synod, the Council of Nicaea, with Constantine present, attributed primacy to the pope in the first canons that it instituted.

---

295. As Ptolemy indicates below, standing in the place of God is the third right by which the pope exercises plenitude of power.
    296. 1.13.3.
    297. Acts 17.28.
    298. Isaias (Isaiah) 26.12.

The rights that were formulated after this council raise up this ruler singularly in these matters, to the extent that his sentence ought be held in the same repute as if it had emerged from the mouth of God, and Charlemagne himself acknowledged this.[299] Likewise, it is not licit to appeal his sentence. Likewise, he has no superior.

[6] Likewise, he is the one who takes the place of God on earth, and this is the third way or reason through which I can show and conclude that the Supreme Pontiff has fullness of power in the said case. There are two cases in which his power is amplified, as I have made clear above: either by reason of transgression or for the good of the whole faith.[300] The prophet Jeremiah shows this to us elegantly, for it was said to him in the persona of the vicar of Christ: "Behold, I have set you over nations and kingdoms so that you may pluck out and destroy and bring to ruin and scatter."[301] I interpret this to refer to the reason of transgression and those four designations to apply to various kinds of penalties that can be inflicted on any one of the faithful or on a subject (when he says, "over nations") or over a lord (when he adds, "and over kingdoms"). But Jeremiah also demonstrates the second case of the amplified power of the Supreme Pontiff, when it was said to him afterwards: "And you will build and plant," which pertains to the providence of the vicar of Christ for the good of the Universal Church.

Chapter 20

A comparison of imperial lordship to regal and political lordship,
and how it accords with both.

[1] Now that I have covered these things I must compare imperial lordship to political and regal lordship because it overlaps with both, as is apparent from

---

299. While Charlemagne was personally pious (see Einhard, *Life of Charlemagne*, 26) and a partisan and ally of the Roman pope, he certainly never accepted papal hegemony in either secular or religious affairs. This may be one of the reasons that he was, according to Einhard, 28, so angry over the pope crowning him as emperor on Christmas Day 800 that, "he asserted that he would never have entered the church, although it was a high holy day, if he had known the pope's plans." See the introduction for more on the "special relationship" of pope and emperor.

300. At 3.11.6 Ptolemy gives these reasons (with common good substituted for good of the faith) for a secular ruler to take the subjects' possessions beyond that allowed by customary taxation. Innocent III (1196–1216) sometimes diplomatically claimed that interventions in secular matters were only to "decide concerning a sin." See above note to 3.10.8 and Tierney, *Crisis of Church and State*, 134–35 for a translation.

301. Jeremias (Jeremiah) 1.10. In his coronation address Innocent III applied this quote to himself; he was probably the first pope to do so. See Tierney, *Crisis of Church and State*, 131–3,2 for a translation.

what I have said. It accords with political lordship in three ways. The first
is election. Just as Roman consuls and dictators, who governed the people
politically, were elevated through election by the people or senators, so also
were the emperors, by the Roman army or senators. As the histories tell us,
Vespasian was elevated by the army in Palestine, and similarly Phocas through
a military sedition in the east against the Emperor Maurice, whom he afterward killed. Sometimes they were elected by the senators, as were Trajan and
Diocletian, although one was from Spain and the other from Dalmatia, and
similarly Aelius Pertinax was elevated from the senate. The second similarity
is that the emperor did not always come from noble stock, but sometimes
from obscure stock, as is evident in the case of the previously named Caesars
Vespasian and Diocletian, as the histories tell us.³⁰² This also happened with
the Roman consuls and dictators, as is clear in the accounts above of Lucius
Valerius ³⁰³ and Fabricius.³⁰⁴ And Augustine mentions that Quintus Cincinnatus had only four jugers to cultivate when he was made dictator, a greater
office than consul.³⁰⁵ The third comparison or similarity of imperial to political lordship is that the emperors' lordship did not pass on to their descendents
but ended at their death.

[2] With respect to those two examples, emperors were elected even in modern times, namely Rudolf the Simple, count of Hapsburg, on whose death
Count Adolf of Nassau was elevated as emperor. And after Albert, the son
of Rudolf, killed Adolf, Albert himself was elevated in the same way.³⁰⁶ Elec-

302. Vespasian (r.699–79), founder of the Flavian dynasty of emperors was of low birth.
After several military commands, his soldiers chose him as emperor at Alexandria. He left his
son Titus in Palestine to continue the Jewish war. Phocas (r.602–10) was chosen by his troops to
oppose Emperor Mauricius (or Maurice, r.582–602), whom he killed. The Spaniard Trajan (r.98–
117) was adopted by Nerva (r.96–98) as his successor and given the nominal approval of the
Senate. Diocletian (r.284–305), a low-born Dalmatian and founder of the tetrarchy, was actually
elevated by the army after the murder of Emperor Numerianus (r.283–84). Publius Helvius Pertinax (r.193) was a distinguished senator, former consul, and governor who was made emperor
unwillingly after the murder of Commodus in a palace coup. The senate happily confirmed the
election; the Praetorian Guard, which had prospered under Commodus, was more reluctant. In
this sense it can be seen as a senatorial election, though the senate did not nominate him. Despite
his virtues the Guard killed him within months.

303. 3.14.4.

304. 2.8.3, 3.4.5, 3.14.4.

305. One juger equals 28,800 square feet or about .66 of an English acre. Augustine, *The
City of God*, 5.18, says he cultivated it with his own hands. The untranslated word "*boum*" occurs
after "*jugera*." in this sentence. Possibly this was either added after misreading "*jugera*" as "*juga*,"
which would make the expression mean "only four teams of oxen," or it should be "*a mano*," "by
hand." The Matthis edition does not include "*boum*" at all. Lucius Quintus Cincinnatus, a sixth-
and fifth-century general, consul, and dictator, was a supporter of the patricians against the plebeians. The Senate informed him of his appointment as dictator while he was working on his
small farm; he raised and army, defeated the Aequians, and resigned his office within sixteen days.

306. Rudolf I (r.1273–91) was the first of the Hapsburg emperors. He got papal approval
by agreeing to give up his claims to the papal lands and Sicily and to organize a crusade. Adolf

tion was the general method, except perhaps when emperors were elevated through their own probity or by the grace of their fathers, as happened with Arcadius and Honorius, the sons of Theodosius the Elder, and similarly with Theodosius the Younger, son of Honorius.[307] Since they governed the republic and the imperial court well, they deserved to have lordship remain in their stock for some time.

[3] A similar thing happened with the Roman consuls. Although consuls were chosen only for a single year, at least in terms of their magistracy, as 1 Maccabees makes clear,[308] it nevertheless often happened that, on account of the probity of the personage or stock, the consulship was passed on to his descendents. This happened to Fabius Maximus, about whom Valerius Maximus wrote: "Since he looked unfavorably at the fact that he and his ancestors had so often held the consulate—he himself five times, and his father, grandfather, and great-grandfather—he pleaded firmly with the people that it exempt the Fabian stock from this honor, so that this highest command should not continue so long in one family."[309] There also was no election when the empire was usurped through violence, not granted for the merit of virtue. This was the case with the most wicked Gaius Caligula, nephew of the Tiberius under whom Christ suffered, and similarly this occurred with Nero.[310] The same thing also happened with consuls of the City, such as Sulla and Marius, who stirred up the City and the world and who impiously usurped lordship, as the

---

of Nassau (r.1291–98) was elected emperor after Rudolf's death. Albert I of Hapsburg (r.1298–1308), son of Rudolf I, deposed and killed him. None of these were actually crowned emperor.

307. After the death of Theodosius I the Great (r.379–95), the Empire was divided, not for the first time, into eastern and western parts, ruled by Theodosius's two sons—Arcadius (r.395–408) in the east and Honorius (395–423) in the west. Theodosius II (r.408–50) was actually the son of Arcadius, as Ptolemy correctly says at 3.17.6.

308. 1 Machabees (Maccabees) 8.16.

309. Valerius Maximus, *Memorable Deeds and Sayings*, 4.1.5. Fabius Maximus (d.203 B.C.E.) was also censor, dictator, and army commander. He is famous for avoiding defeat by Hannibal in the Second Punic War by the "Fabian" strategy of quick strikes against the enemy and backing away from major battles. His grandfather, also called Fabius Maximus (d.c.290 B.C.E.), was consul six times, dictator, and commander in the Third Samnite War. Many other members of his family also were consuls or other high Roman officials. I have translated *"familia"* as "family" here, instead of the more usual and generally more accurate "household."

310. Eutropius, *A Brief History of Rome*, 7.11, 7.14–15. Tiberius (r.14–37 C.E.) appointed Caligula (r.37–41) as his successor and this was rubber-stamped by the Senate, the common practice at the time, so that although Caligula's reign was marked by unusual cruelty and violence, he did not come into power by violence. Claudius I (41–54) also nominated Nero (r.54–68), and although Claudius's son Britannicus was a rival, the praetorian guard elevated Nero on Claudius's death, and again the Senate acquiesced. Nero was reviled for, among other things, instituting the first major persecution of Christians.

histories tell us.[311] All this makes clear the way imperial lordship accords with political lordship.

[4] Now I will show how imperial and regal lordship accord in three ways.

[5] The first is in the mode of governing. Those who hold such lordship have jurisdiction as kings, and they act by natural right, whereby no one can transgress the tributes and taxes that kings institute without sinning except by a superior regal right. But neither consuls nor any other rectors of Italian cities who govern in a political government can do this, as I have already said.[312] For tributes and taxes come to the public treasury, and Sallust reports that in his oration Cato criticized the Roman consuls of his time for this. After he commended those who "displayed industry at home, just command abroad, a free spirit in counseling, and were addicted neither to lust nor transgressions," he added: "Instead of these things we now have luxury and avarice, poverty in public but opulence in private."[313]

[6] The second way emperors are like kings is their crown, since they are crowned as kings. Those elected as emperor receive a double crown, one near Milan in a village called Monza, where the kings of the Lombards were buried.[314] This iron crown is said to be given to symbolize the subjugation of the Lombard kings and their nation by Charlemagne, the first German emperor. He receives the second crown, which is made of gold, from the Supreme Pontiff, who presents it to him with his foot to signify the emperor's subjection and fidelity to the Roman Church. Neither the consuls nor the dictators of Rome had the dignity of this exalted rank because, as is written in 1 Maccabees, among the Roman chiefs "no one wore a diadem or assumed the purple,"[315] but emperors and kings do both.

---

311. Eutropius, *A Brief History of Rome*, 5. Sulla (138–78 B.C.E.) waged a civil war against his rival Marius (c.155–86) and later his son Marius (109–c.82) and established one-person rule, serving as dictator (82–79). All three were consuls, the older Marius seven times.

312. Since Ptolemy says in many places that all rectors can collect taxes and tributes, his meaning here must be that they cannot do it on their own authority, but only according to statutes (see 2.8.1). Nor can they appropriate for themselves more than a just wage. See also 2.13.7, 2.14.1, 3.5.3, 3.11.4, 3.11.8.

313. Sallust, *The War with Catiline*, 52.21. See above and below 2.8.3, 3.4.3, 4.23.5.

314. The sixth-century cathedral in Monza is the current and traditional home for the iron crown of the Lombards, allegedly made from a nail of Christ's cross. The Lombard capital, however, was Pavia, where the kings were often crowned. The crown was also used as one of the imperial crowns by many emperors, including Charlemagne (who took the title of "king of the Lombards" after his conquests of 774), Charles V, and Napoleon I.

315. 1 Machabees (Maccabees) 8.14.

[7] The third way emperors are like kings and differ from consuls or political rectors is in the institution of laws and the arbitrary power that they have over their subjects in the kind of cases I have mentioned. Because of this their lordship is called "majesty," namely imperial and regal majesty. This is not appropriate for political rectors, because it is not licit for them to act except according to the form of laws handed down to them or from the will of the people. Beyond this they cannot judge.

[8] This makes clear the qualities of imperial government in different times and how it compares to political and regal government.

Chapter 21

The lordship of rulers who are under emperors and kings, and what their different titles mean.

[1] Now that I have determined what pertains to regal and imperial government, I must speak of the lordships that are annexed to them, such as princes,[316] counts, dukes, marquises, barons, castelans, and various other titles that refer to such dignities according to diverse regional customs. There are also other titles of dignities under kings that Sacred Scripture mentions, such as satrap. As Daniel writes: "The satraps, magistrates, and judges of the king of Babylon were gathered together."[317] In the same passage Daniel mentions the "optimates" of the king.[318] 1 Maccabees cites four titles of dignities: "Judas constituted leaders for the people—tribunes and centurions, pentacontarchs, and decurions—against Nicanor."[319] And we read in accounts of the deeds of the Romans that they referred to their rectors by certain particular names after the kings were driven out, namely consuls, dictators, magistrates, tribunes, senators, patricians, and prefects; also scipios,[320] censors, and censorinos.

[2] We must deal with all this under two headings. First, I will consider the kind of government of those whose titles are properly annexed to the status

316. Here and in the following sections I have chosen to translate *"princeps"* as "prince" instead of "ruler," because Ptolemy seems to be referring more to what we would call a prince than a generalized ruler. Elsewhere, however, Ptolemy does use this word in a general sense.

317. Daniel 3.94.

318. Daniel 3.91.

319. 1 Machabees (Maccabees) 3.55. In the Roman army a centurion was over 100 soldiers, a pentacontarch over 50, a decurion over 10. The words "against Nicanor" do not appear in the Vulgate. Nicanor was the Syrian general defeated by the Maccabees.

320. A *scipio* is a staff carried by high ranking people.

of emperors and kings, from whom they take their origin. Second, I will take up those who properly pertain to political rule.

[3] The proper name for someone holding a dignity subject to emperors and kings is "prince," that is, a lord of a province, who as it were holds the first place under regal or imperial lordship, and who thus sometimes exercises lordship over barons and counts, as happens in Teutonia and the Kingdom of Sicily. However, even Scripture often extends this name to every kind of lordship and especially to noble lordship—by analogy, one order of Angels is called Princes because they exercise lordship over a whole provence. Thus, it is written in Daniel: "The prince of the Persians resisted me for twenty-one days."[321] Joseph himself, who was second to the king in Egypt, calls himself "prince," as is written in Genesis.[322]

[4] The second title is "count," which is a title first used by the Roman people after they expelled the kings. As Isidore tells us in his *Etymologies*, they chose two consuls for each year, one of whom administered military affairs and the other civil affairs. Those two consuls were at first called counts, from a word that means "coming together in true concord,"[323] and the republic was increased under them, as Sallust tells us in *The Jugurthine War*.[324] In the course of time that title was abolished in the Roman government and was transferred to a certain status of dignity commissioned under kings and emperors. So they are now called counts from the word for "accompanying," since it is especially their duty to follow kings and emperors in matters pertaining to war or any military affair and to do whatever else is necessary for the utility of the whole kingdom.[325]

[5] Dukes are so-called from the fact that they lead the people,[326] especially in camps. Their duty is to direct the army and to go before it in battle. The

---

321. Daniel 10.13.
322. Genesis 45.8.
323. Isidore of Seville, *Etymologies*, 9.3. "Count" is "*comites*"; "coming together" is "*commeando*." The title actually comes from "*comes*," "companion," as Ptolemy himself suggests a little later in the same paragraph.
324. Perhaps Sallust, *The Jugurthine War*, 85.36–37?
325. "*Comitando*" means "accompanying"; but it seems rather odd for there to be two etymologies. Probably what Ptolemy means, and this throws some light on how medieval writers viewed "etymologies," is that the titles could be appropriately used since they could be understood as referring to their function. He may well not mean that the titles were literally derived in our sense from the words.
326. Isidore of Seville, *Etymologies*, 3.22. "Leader" is "*dux*" (plural "*duces*"); "leadership" is "*ducatus*." Isidore says a count is called this as the leader of the army.

children of Israel, under attack by the Canaanites, sought mutually among themselves, as is written in the book of Judges: "Who will go up before us against the Canaanite, and who will be duke of war?"[327] This title properly suits such rectors on account of the difficulty of governing in a battle; so, from the excellence of their government they are suitably called dukes. For this reason, Joshua, or Jesus, was called this because he fought the wars of the Lord. That distinguished ruler Mattathias testifies to this in 1 Maccabees: "Joshua was made duke in Israel since he fulfilled the word."[328] And those who were zealots for the Jewish law said to Jonathan on the death of Judas Maccabeus: "We choose you as ruler and duke to fight our war."[329]

[6] Still another title of a dignity subject to emperors and kings is "marquis," which is equivalent to "*comitatus*," and this title is assigned from the severity of justice involved. A marquis is so-called from a "mark," which is a particular quantity of wealth,[330] through which is signified the right and rigid justice of the ruler. This appears to be quite suitable for these rulers because, as we commonly find in the regions known to us, all rulers who are called by that name rule either in harsh provinces (which is why some call these mountainous and rocky regions "marches"), or in licentious provinces, both kinds of which are preserved through rigorous justice.

[7] There is also another title, that of "barons," who are so-called either from their labor or because they are strong in their labors, as Isidore tells us, for "*bara*" in Greek is what in Latin is called "heavy" or "strong."[331] This is characteristic of rulers, for they are continually in gymnasia, as is customary in parts of Gaul and Germany, or in hunting, fowling, or tournaments. This was also their practice in antiquity, as Aimoinus, the distinguished writer of histories, writes.[332] Vegetius, in *On the Military*, explains the reason for this—that it is necessary that they be the first to make war on behalf of their subjects and that they be made bold by habit. He adds that no one hesitates to strive after what they believe they have learned well.[333] And because the exercise of labor

---

327. Judges 1.1. This is one of the many cases when "*dux*" clearly means simply "leader," but I translate "duke" for consistency.

328. 1 Machabees (Maccabees) 2.55. This is another place one should read "leader" instead of "duke."

329. 1 Machabees (Maccabees) 9.30.

330. That is, the monetary unit known as the "mark."

331. Isidore of Seville, *Etymologies*, 9.4. In classical Latin "*baro*," the same spelling used for baron, means simpleton. But the word for baron actually is Germanic in origin. "βάρος" in Greek does mean "burden" or "weight."

332. Aimoinus Floriac, *History of the Franks*, preface, chapter 2. Ptolemy calls him "Ammonius."

333. Vegetius, *On the Military*, 1.1, 1.7.

pertains to all rulers, that title is common to all, whether they are princes or counts; and the same holds for others who exist under regal lordship.

Chapter 22

Certain individual regional titles of dignities and their kind of government.

[1] There are also other titles which come about in consequence of regal or imperial lordship in certain regions or provinces and mean something, such as the title of satrap and optimate among the Persians and Philistines. The former may signify "promptitude of serving," since satraps are said, as it were, to be sufficiently prepared.[334] This is a duty of rulers that arises from the fidelity that they swear to their superior. Alternately, it may signify "sufficiently rapacious,"[335] which that title seems to mean because of its haughtiness, as is apparent in Sacred Scripture. The title of optimate seems to signify its supreme rank under the ruler, since it comes from the word for "best."[336] Magistrates are so-called from the preeminent position counsel and teaching have in government.[337] The great ones of the court of the king of France are styled thus, as if they were great ones in status, that is, "steron" in Greek or "station" in Latin.[338] Judges, who, as it were, dictate to the people on questions of right, are properly called "assessors," and even "praetors," and they hold a place before others in court. "Provincial governor" is a title found in Sacred Scripture,[339] so-called, as Isidore tells us,[340] because such a one has the respon-

334. "Sufficiently prepared" is "**sat**is par**at**i." Satraps were provincial governors under the Persian Cyrus the Great (559–530 B.C.E.) and his Achaemenian Empire. Later, Alexander the Great and his successors preserved the satraps as administrators in their empire. Ptolemy cites a biblical mention of them at 3.21.1 and calls some of Constantine's officials satraps at 3.17.3. "Satrap" is actually a Greek version of the Median word "khshathrapavan," which means "protector of the kingdom."

335. "Sufficiently rapacious" is "**sat**is **rap**ientes."

336. "Best" is "*optimus*" in Latin. "Optimate" was a common term for the powerful in the northern Italian city-states of Ptolemy's day and used as a general term for the powerful everywhere. Elsewhere, at 3.7.5 and 3.21.1, Ptolemy cites biblical use of the term, but always with reference to the Babylonians, not the Philistines. The Philistines were remnants of the mysterious Sea Peoples who brought down the Egyptian and Hittite Empires. In the Bible they were competitors with the Israelites for control of Palestine and consequently vilified.

337. Isidore of Seville, *Etymologies*, 9.4. Presumably from "*magister*," which means "master." The master's degree, to which the name "master" often refers specifically, is equivalent to a modern doctorate, and gave the recipient the right to teach. Professors in medieval universities were called either "*magister*" or "*doctor*."

338. Isidore of Seville, *Etymologies*, 15.4.5, 15.6.1.

339. 1 Esdras (Ezra) 7.25; Ecclesiasticus (Sirach) 39.4; Matthew 10.18, 27.2, 11, 14, 15, 21, 23, 24, 28.14; Mark 13.9; Luke 2.2, 20.20, 21.12; Acts 23.24, 26, 33, 24.1, 10, 26.30.

340. Isidore of Seville, *Etymologies*, 9.4.

sibility for protecting a place in the manner of one presiding.[341] There are also two titles that pertain to a dignity in a king's court, which were mentioned as being among the officials of Solomon's court in 3 Kings, the "Recorder" and the "Scribe."[342] These were distinguished in their duties since the latter had precedence over the legion of those whom the ruler established to do writing (the Scribe seems to be that magistrate), and the former was put in charge to make responses on behalf of the kingdom (we call this office "Chancellor").

[2] Besides these there are also two other titles that are common in parts of Gaul. Perhaps these come from the idiom proper to some particular nation, which we can use to derive an etymology. These are "marshall" and "seneschal," who properly are rectors entrusted with the universal business of a region. Both of these titles mean "marshall," that is, "lord of labor." "Maris" is the equivalent in the Syrian language of "female lord" or "male lord" in Latin, and *"callus"* implies labor.[343] "Seneschal" comes from the word for "old person," because of the maturity which is necessary for government, and from the word for "callous" because of its toughness.[344] For only persons of great experience and those assiduous in their labors ought to be entrusted with such an office.

[3] Among the Spanish all rulers under the king are called "wealthy persons" and this is especially true in Castile. The reason for this is that the king provides money to individual barons according to their merits, or, according to his pleasure, he demotes one group and exalts another. As in many other matters, they have no fortifications or jurisdictions other than by the king's will, and so they are called "wealthy persons," because that one is the greater ruler to whom the king provides a greater sum and who can therefore provide more knights. The Roman military also followed this method, since they lived on pay.

[4] There are others in Spain who are called "Infants," and others "Infantios." The first, as sons or nephews of the king, are of royal stock. In their inno-

---

341. *"Praeses"* means "provincial governor"; *"praesidialiter,"* "in the manner of a provincial governor," but both stem from the verb *"praesedere,"* "to preside," and it seemed better to use a form of this for *"praesidialiter"*; otherwise, the etymology would seem to be redundant.

342. 3 Kings (1 Kings) 4.3.

343. *"Dominus"* and *"domina"* are the words translated "male lord" and "female lord." *"Callus"* means "hard skin" or "a callous" in Latin. Marshall is *"mariscallus"* in Latin, which by Ptolemy's etymology equals *maris* plus *callus*.

344. Seneschal is *"senescallus"* in Latin, which by Ptolemy's etymology equals *"senex"* ("old person") plus *callus*.

cence the people call them "Infants" because they ought to injure nothing, but preserve and cherish everything in justice and obey the king in all things as infants do, but today in Spain they follow these precepts badly. The second are called "Infantios" because they ought to follow the Infants as ones greater than themselves. They are nobles who have more virtue than simple knights and are lords of castles and villas, such as are called "castellans" elsewhere. But they are called "Infantios" because they can cause little injury among the other rulers since they lack might, as do boys who are just emerging from infancy. If they injure their subjects, those who adhere to the greater rulers rebel, and they lose their lordship. Likewise, they do not have the greater rulers' might, just as boys do not have a man's might.

[5] I have now said enough about rulers who are subject and subordinate to kings and about what their titles signify and mean.

[6] In some of the following sections I will speak about dignities other than those that I have presented already, since in many ways they pertain more to a polity, although some are common to both. Now I must ask what kind of government is characteristic of the rulers that I have discussed, and to this question I must reply according to the opinion of Sacred Scripture, since according to Ecclesiasticus: "As is a judge of the people, so also are the judge's ministers, and as is the rector of a city, so also are its inhabitants."[345] Such rulers commonly govern by the regal or imperial mode, unless by chance a different practice arises in some place from usurpation, from tyranny, or from the evil of the nation, which could not be subdued except through a tyrannical government, as I said above.[346] This happened on the islands of Sardinia and Corsica, on certain Greek islands, and on Cyprus, where nobles exercise their lordship through a despotic or tyrannical rule. The histories also tell us that the island of Sicily was always the wet nurse of tyrants. In parts of Italy the necessary custom has arisen that even counts and other rulers govern their subjects politically and civilly, perhaps so that they do not tyrannize through their use of violence.

[7] In these parts of Italy we find certain titles of dignities that depend on the right of the empire and transcend the simple military titles mentioned above, titles such as "Valvasals" and "Captains," who are also called "Procers." They have jurisdiction over subjects, although today, through the might of the

345. Ecclesiasticus (Sirach) 10.2.
346. 3.12.9.

cities, their jurisdiction has been diminished or even totally eliminated. Valvasals are so-called from the word for "leaves of a door,"[347] because they were deputed to guard the gates of the regal or imperial palace, like those whom we call "Door Keepers." Captains are so-called from the universality of their works in the courts of rulers (for we signify the whole by the Greek word "*catha*") and the fact that they are more active than other simple knights.[348] They are also called "Procers," since they "proceed," as it were, before others.

[8] There are many other titles used in various regions and languages and instituted for the pleasure of rulers. But these suffice for the present, and I will reserve the rest until I treat the government of a polity, which I must take up separately because of the diffusion of the material. I will then take up the titles of dignities which depend on what the nature of this government allows according to the various customs of provinces, as the philosophers and historical writers tell us.

347. *"Valva"* means "leaves of a door" or "a folding door."
348. "Captains" is *"Catani"* in Latin. The Greek refers to "καθολικός," "universal," which derives from "κατὰ ὅλου," "according to the whole."

Book 4

Chapter 1

The difference between the rule of a kingdom and political rule, and two kinds of political rule.

[1] "You will constitute them as rulers over all the earth; they will be mindful of your name, Lord."[1] Although God instituted all lordship or rule, as I said above,[2] Aristotle and Sacred Scripture tell us about different modes of lordship. Since I have already treated the monarchy of one—namely the lordship of the Highest Pontiff, regal lordship, and imperial lordship—and their nature and the things that go along with them,[3] I think that it is now time to treat the lordship of many, which we call by the common name "political." I described this earlier in two ways: with respect to the mode of elevating those who rule and with respect to the mode of life under political rule.[4] The mode of elevation to this rank is elective, and someone from any stock at all is eligible, not just one selected by birth, as is the case with kings. This is what the words of constitution mean: "You will constitute them as rulers," and it adds, "over all the earth," showing the general regulation in political rule, which extends to any human stock. Not just any person should be chosen, but one who is virtuous. This refers to the mode of living, for which reason the Psalm adds: "they will be mindful of your name, Lord," in consideration of the divine and of his precepts, which serve as right reason to those who govern for what must be done. Proverbs says that "the mandate of the Lord

---

1. A paraphrase of Psalm 44.17–18 (45.17–18): "You will place them as princes in the whole earth; I [some versions have 'they'] will think of your name in all generations to come."
2. 3.1.1.
3. Ptolemy treats the various kinds of monarchy in Book 3: papal, 3.10; regal, 3.11; imperial, 3.12–3.22.
4. 3.20 (election); 2.8–10 (way of life).

is a lamp, and his law a light,"[5] and Valerius Maximus writes that Caesar fostered virtues and punished vices by celestial providence.[6]

[2] Therefore, in the present book I will treat this rule, which Aristotle and I distinguished as follows:[7] if a few virtuous ones guide a government it is called "aristocracy" (as was the case in the city of Rome under the two consuls and the dictator just after the expulsion of the kings), but if many guide it (which the histories relate happened in the course of time in the same city under the consuls, dictators, and tribunes, and afterward under the senators) they call such a government a polity from the word "*polis*." This word means "plurality" or "city," because this government is characteristic of cities, as we see especially in parts of Italy. Such a government also once thrived in Athens after the death of Codrus, as Augustine reports,[8] for at that time the Athenians abandoned regal lordship and elevated magistrates of the republic, just as in Rome. In either of these two modes, political rule is distinguished from kingdom or monarchy, and the opposite of each of these is also distinguished from the opposite of kingdom or monarchy, because the opposites of two opposite propositions are still opposite.[9] As Aristotle mentions, both these are kinds of political rule, as distinguished from regal or despotic rule, because both include plurality.[10]

[3] I must now consider all the ways in which political rule differs from regal, imperial, or monarchical rule, which to some extent can be seen from what I have said above in Books 1 and 3.[11] One difference is that political rectors are bound by laws and cannot proceed beyond them in seeking justice, but this is not the case with kings and other monarchical rulers, because laws are hid-

5. Proverbs 6.23. The word "*domini*," "of the Lord," does not appear in the Vulgate, and the translation "his" in the second clause is only a reflection of "Lord" in the first.

6. Valerius Maximus, *Memorable Deeds and Sayings*, preface.

7. Above, in 1.2, the first author repeated Aristotle's six-fold classification of polities from *Politics*, 3.7.1279a.

8. Augustine, *The City of God*, 18.20. For Codrus, see note at 2.9.6.

9. That is, the opposite forms of rule of aristocracy and polity, namely, oligarchy and democracy are also distinct from the opposite of monarchy, namely, tyranny.

10. From his references to Books 1 and 3 of Aristotle's *Politics*, Ptolemy must have 1.1.1252a.15–17 and 3.7 in mind, but Aristotle does not say exactly what is attributed to him. In the first passage Aristotle does not mention aristocracy or polity at all, but he does imply (ambiguously, especially in the Latin) that plurality is a characteristic of political as opposed to regal rule. In the second passage, where Aristotle first defines the six simple forms of government that Ptolemy discusses here, he does not contrast these two modes but does define aristocracy and polity as involving plurality (although he does not use this word or say the two forms share a characteristic missing in monarchy), since they represent the rule of the few or the many.

11. The Book 3 references are those just cited (3.10–3.22), especially 3.20, but the first author does not make the distinction between political and non-political rule in Book 1, so the reference must either be to the general description of monarchy or to the sixfold classification of rule in 1.2.

den in their hearts and applied in each individual case, and what pleases the ruler is held to be law.[12] This is what the laws[13] of nations tell us, but we do not find the same thing said about political rectors, because they do not dare to do anything new beyond the written laws.

[4] In 1 Maccabees it is written that the Romans "took care to consult daily with the 320, always taking counsel about matters concerning the multitude so that they might do those things that were worthy."[14] Considering this, I hold that in the Roman government, lordship was political from the expulsion of the kings up to the usurpation of empire. This happened when Julius Caesar, after he had prostrated his enemies, after Pompey and his sons had been killed, and after he had subjugated the globe, took up sole lordship for himself in the form of monarchy and converted a polity into a despotic or tyrannical rule. As the histories tell us, after these events Caesar seemed inclined to be contemptuous of the senators; thus provoked, the great ones of the city, instigated by Brutus and Cassius and most of the senate, ran him through with twenty-four daggers in the Capitol.[15]

[5] I should add that although the book of Maccabees says that one person exercised lordship in a given year,[16] as happens in the cities of Italy even now, government depended on the many, and therefore it was not called regal but political. This is also true of the judges of the Israelite people since they did not govern regally but politically, as I said above.[17] Cities live politically in all regions, whether in Germany, Scythia, or Gaul, although they may be circumscribed by the might of the king or emperor, to whom they are bound by established laws.

[6] Still another difference is that rectors more often are examined to see if they have judged well or governed according to the laws handed down

12. *The Body of Civil Law: Institutes* 1.2.6; *Digest* 1.4.1.
13. *Iura*.
14. 1 Machabees (Maccabees) 8.15.
15. Eutropius, *A Brief History of Rome*, 6.25. Eutropius says Caesar received 23 wounds. Gnaius Pompeius (106–48 B.C.E.), a general and consul, was a member of the First Triumvirate with Caesar and Crassus (60), but later opposed Caesar and was defeated by him (48), after which Ptolemy of Egypt killed him. His son of the same name (c.75–45 B.C.E.) was captured and executed by Caesar. His other son Sextus Pompeius (75–35 B.C.E.) was captured and executed by Antony in 35, long after Caesar's death in 44. Marcus Junius Brutus (c.85–42 B.C.E.) and Gaius Cassius Longinus (?–42 B.C.E.) were the two main conspirators against Caesar, and both killed themselves after their defeat by Octavian and Antony at Philippi. Both became Republican heroes.
16. 1 Machabees (Maccabees) 8.16.
17. 2.8.2, 2.9.2.

to them, and if not they are subjected to penalties. It is written in 1 Kings that Samuel himself, because he had judged the Israelite people in a political mode, exposed himself to such a sentence after Saul had been elevated as king: "Behold," he said, "I am here; speak of me before the Lord and his Christ," namely Saul, "whether I have taken anyone's ox, whether I have slandered anyone, whether I have oppressed anyone, whether I have accepted a gift from anyone's hands."[18] The histories also tell us this about the Roman consuls, which is why Scipio Africanus left Rome when his impious rivals accused him of being corrupted by money, and eventually such false accusations led to civil wars.[19] Such examinations have no place among kings or emperors, except that regions now and then rebel against them if they overstep the rights of the kingdom, as happens frequently in parts of Spain and Hungary.[20] In the east also they fairly often plot the death of their lord, as Egyptians do against the sultan,[21] and the Persians and Assyrians against the Tartar rulers.[22]

18. 1 Kings (1 Samuel) 12.2–3.

19. The Scipios came under attack by their rivals in the 180s B.C.E. Scipio Africanus the Elder was possibly accused of something in 184, and although he was not condemned, he left Rome and died shortly afterward. His brother Lucius had been accused of financial misconduct in 187. Ptolemy does not mean that there is a direct connection between this incident and the much later civil wars, only that accusations of this kind led eventually to civil wars.

20. Hungary had had much political instability and many uprisings of the nobility from the tenth century on, but Ptolemy is probably thinking especially of the imposition of the Golden Bull on King Andrew II by the Hungarian nobles in 1222, which was a charter of rights. Engelbert of Admont, writing about the same time, *On the Government of Rulers*, 1.8.22–24, characterized the period after this as a mixture of kingdom, democracy, and oligarchy. Again, there is much to choose from in the various kingdoms that made up the Christian portions of the Spanish peninsula, but one controversy from Ptolemy's time might be significant—the violent struggles between the king and magnates in Castile that began in the 1270s over the future succession to Alfonso X (1252–84) and continued for many years over the respective constitutional rights of king and nobles.

21. Islamic Egypt had been the scene of many dynastic upheavals and violent deaths of rulers in the few centuries before 1300. The atypically intolerant Fatimid caliph al-Hakim (r.996–1021) was murdered, Saladin (sultan 1174–93) deposed al-'Adid, the last Fatimid caliph in 1171 and established the Ayubbid dynasty, and the sultan, Turanshah (r.1249–50) was overthrown and killed by the Mamelukes. The man chosen to succeed him, 'Izz al-Din Aybak (r.1250–57), was murdered by the order of his wife Shajar al-Durr, who wanted power for herself. She, however, was herself bludgeoned to death with the shoes of the slave women of Aybak's first wife. The new regent, al-Muzaffar Sayf al-Din Qutuz (r.1257–60), deposed Aybak's son and took power himself, but he was killed and replaced by the Mameluke Baybars (r.1257–77).

22. Usually Persis (the word used here) is the country of Persis, now Farsistan, which was the place of origin of the Persians and part of the empire, and "Persia" is Persia. The word "Tartar" or "Tatar" was used imprecisely in the Middle Ages for a variety of Turkic and Mongolian peoples, and not just for the Tatars proper of Russia. At the time Ptolemy was writing the Mongols were in control of both Persia and Mesopotamia, which is probably what he has in mind when he refers to the Assyrians, and even today there are people calling themselves Assyrians, who live in parts of Iran and Iraq and speak the ancient Semitic language Aramaic. Baghdad fell to the Mongols in 1258. But before this there had been two centuries of Turkish rule that was marked by violent struggles between competing groups and rulers, as well as the increasing power of the terrorist Shi'ite Assassins. Though the Mongols further devastated the economy

[7] As Aristotle reports, since rulers often turn into tyrants, certain regions judge it to be unworthy for kings to have perpetual rule through their sons in their provinces, that is, for the kings' sons to succeed to the kingdom. When the king dies the people choose the one they think is most distinguished according to their customs. This happens with emperors, as I made clear above,[23] and it also happens in Egypt up to the present time. The Egyptians seek eligible boys in various regions, especially in parts of Aquilonia, where they are tall and suitable for military discipline; they feed these boys from the public treasury, and exercise them in gymnasia and in scholastic disciplines. We are told that they then assist the sultan in his ministry in civil acts and matters of war, and after his death those who have proved themselves are elevated as rulers. In this way Egypt is protected from violence, tyranny, and haughty ambition.[24]

[8] Aristotle mentions some other differences of government having to do with the length of rule and other characteristics, but what I have said above in Books 2 and 3 will suffice.[25]

Chapter 2

Because community is a necessity of human life, it is also necessary
to constitute cities, where we most often find political rule.

[1] I must now take up the constitution of political government, since it is found most often in cities, as is apparent from what I said above.[26] Provinces

---

and culture of the region at first, their Il-Khan dynasty (1256–1335) eventually provided greater stability, prosperity, and culture. There are some political upheavals of this period as well, which Ptolemy may have had in mind. The Il-Khan Ahmed Takudar was dethroned (1282), but by his Mongol superiors, and there was widespread anti-government disorder under his successor, the Il-Khan Arghun. Finally, Arghun's son Ghazan (r.1295–1304) brought peace and reform.

23. 3.20.1–2.

24. This describes the general practice, similar to that of the Ottoman Empire a few centuries later, of the Mameluke, or slave, sultans of Egypt, who ruled from 1250 until their defeat by the Ottoman sultan in 1517. They had themselves been brought into the Ayyubid caliphate as slaves by Saladin (sultan 1174–93) and his successors. After they seized power they continued the practice of recruiting new soldiers and administrators from foreign slaves, so as to avoid the problems of hereditary succession. But Aquilonia is a town in southern Italy, which does not seem appropriate. The usual source of new slave was from Caucasians, Russians, and Eurasian nomads captured by Mongols and sold to Venetians, who brought them to Egypt.

25. Ptolemy refers to *Politics* 4, which considers many varieties of all the forms of government, but does not specifically deal with the differences between political and nonpolitical governments.

26. 4.1.2, 4.1.5.

seem to favor regal government, which is found in most of them, with the exception that Rome exercised governance over the globe through consuls, tribunes, and senators, as the book of Maccabees shows,[27] and also with the exception of certain Italian cities, which are governed politically, even though they exercise lordship over provinces. First of all, I must demonstrate that it is necessary to establish a city[28] and determine what its community consists of; second, I will discuss how many parts there are in a city and what kinds of persons comprise it.

[2] The necessity of establishing a city comes first from a consideration of human need, which compels a person to live in society, as is written in Job: "A person born of a woman lives for a brief time filled with many miseries,"[29] that is, with the necessities of life that make misery apparent. For this reason human beings are social and political animals by nature, as Aristotle proves.[30] Thus, I conclude that the community of a city is necessary to obtain the necessities of human life.

[3] Nature provides hereditary ornaments and defenses for other animals. They avoid harmful things and love suitable ones by using their natural virtue of estimating, without having to resort to any previous direction, since the work of nature is a work of intelligence in them, as Aristotle tells us.[31] This is not true for human beings, who, on the contrary, lack an instructor for choosing that which is proportionate to their nature, and on that account they have nurses to teach them those things.

[4] Another argument to the same end is that animals and plants are born with the attire and coverings that adorn them, but human beings lack these things. This signifies that they have needs which make it necessary to resort to the multitude of persons, and it is for this that the city is constituted. The Lord shows that the lilies of the field, the birds of the heaven, and other similar species are in a better condition than the human species by comparing their condition to the needs of that magnificent king Solomon, who had great abundance: "Look at the birds of heaven—they neither sow nor reap nor gather into barns. . . . Consider the lilies of the field—they neither labor

27. 1 Machabees (Maccabees) 8.

28. Although this seems to repeat Book 1, and perhaps give support to Mohr's argument (see introduction), Ptolemy explains why he takes this question up again in 4.2.9.

29. Job 14.1.

30. Aristotle, *Politics*, 1.2.1253a.2f. Aristotle refers to "political animals." See the introduction under "Political Thought of the First Contributor."

31. Aristotle, *Physics*, 2.8.199a.20–23.

nor spin." Afterward, he adds: "I say to you that Solomon in all his glory was not covered as one of them,"[32] as if Solomon had a greater need of provisions, vestments, and coverings than the plants and animals.

[5] We come to the same conclusion when we consider the ferocity of animals, which became harmful to humans after the Fall of Adam. A community of human beings is a necessary to provide security to every person in a fear-provoking situation, and from this consideration a city is constituted to make human beings secure. For that reason Cain was motivated to construct a city, according to Genesis,[33] and it is also said in Ecclesiasticus: "The building of a city will confirm a name."[34]

[6] We prove the same thing when we consider human health. Necessities beyond the necessities of a healthy body arise when the body is diseased, and human beings are often subject to disease. But they cannot tend alone to their own repair when they are suffering. Animals can do this; nature has provided cures for them without the intervention of the human medical art, since they know through the judgment given to them which herbs are healthful for them and other things that were ordained for their well-being. Since human beings are ignorant of those things, they need physicians, the medical art, and the ministry of other persons, and all these things require the multitude of persons which makes up the city.

[7] Finally, there are many cases in which unexpected events bring down persons, from which society lifts them up. As is written in Ecclesiastes: "Woe to one who is alone, since there will be nobody to lift that one up. But if there are two, they will sustain each other."[35]

[8] For all these reasons I conclude that the city is a necessity for human beings, and that it is constituted on behalf of the community of the multitude, without which humans can not live decently. To the extent that a city is greater than a town or village, there will be more arts and artisans present there to assure the sufficiency of human life, and it is from these that the city is constituted. Augustine defined it in this way, that the city "is a multitude of human beings bound together by one chain of society."[36]

32. Matthew 6.26, 28–29.
33. Genesis 4.17.
34. Ecclesiasticus (Sirach) 40.19.
35. Ecclesiastes 4.10–11.
36. Augustine, *The City of God*, 15.8.

[9] You should notice that I also proved at the beginning of Book 1[37] what I proved here—that human society is necessary, but I have done this in two different ways. There I showed how society is ordained to a ruler, here that the various parts of the multitude are mutually necessary for each other. For this reason, cities and towns are instituted of necessity just as they are ordained to political government.

Chapter 3

The necessity of constituting the city can also be proven from a consideration of the spirit, whether one considers the intellect or the will.

[1] This argument, that constructing a city is necessary according to nature, is persuasive and true not only from consideration of the body, that is, of the sensitive virtue, but is also apparent from consideration of the rational spirit. The more one is human, the more one needs society, as we can see by considering the intellect.

[2] We distinguish two parts of the rational spirit, namely intellect and will. There are two kinds of actions with regard to the intellective part, namely speculative and practical, and political government depends on these. The moral virtues are included under practical action and refer more to works than to knowing, as Aristotle says.[38] They include virtues such as temperance, fortitude, prudence, and justice.[39] All of these actions are ordained to another person and therefore require the multitude of persons from which a city is constituted, as I said above.[40] Although these virtues do not all have the intellect as their subject—for fortitude is part of the irascible appetite and temperance of the concupiscible, which pertain to the sensitive part—nevertheless they participate in reason in so far as they are regulated by it. Prudence directs them, since prudence is the application of right reason to things that it is possible to do, as Aristotle says.[41]

[3] Sacred Scripture itself also ordains these virtues to the same purpose, for, speaking of God, the book of Wisdom says this about them: "She teaches so-

---

37. 1.1.
38. Aristotle, *Ethics*, 5.6.1106a.17–18.
39. These are the four classical and medieval "cardinal virtues."
40. 4.2.4, 6, 8.
41. Aristotle, *Ethics*, 6.5.1140b.4–5.

briety and wisdom, justice and virtue, and nothing is more useful to humans in their life than this."[42] Then, in reference to the merit of those virtues, it adds: "On that account," namely the knowledge or experience of those virtues, "I will have fame, accolades, and honor among the elders,"[43] and it goes on to add many other things which pertain to the multitude of persons.

[4] The same thing is clear about speculative action, because, as Aristotle shows: "It is generated and grows especially through teaching, and it needs experience and time,"[44] all of which things presuppose the multitude of persons from which the city is constituted, as I said above.[45]

[5] Another proof of the same thing is that there are two educable senses, as Aristotle tells us,[46] namely vision and hearing; but hearing presupposes a multitude.

[6] Aristotle also says: "it is wisdom's nature to order";[47] but order, which Augustine says is "the disposition of equal and unequal things, giving to each its due,"[48] cannot exist without a multitude.

[7] Even speech itself, which brings into the open what is in the heart, pertains to the intellect, as Aristotle says, and is ordained to be heard by someone else. As Ecclesiasticus says, "What use is there in hidden wisdom or an unseen treasury?"[49] The same thing could also be said about writing, since it presupposes a multitude, without which it could not be effectively done or explained.

[8] The same conclusion follows from a consideration of the second part of the rational spirit, the will. Aristotle speaks of this rational potency. There are two virtues of the will that are ordained to someone else and require a multitude. One is justice, which the law[50] of nations defines in terms of will—it is "the unchangeable and universal will giving to each what is theirs by right."[51] This is so whether we speak of legal justice, which Aristotle calls "just domi-

---

42. Wisdom 8.7. "She" refers to a personification of wisdom, that is, "*sapientia*," which is feminine in Latin.

43. Wisdom 8.10. The adjective translated "that" is feminine and refers to Wisdom, but Ptolemy interprets it as agreeing with the feminine nouns "knowledge" and "experience."

44. Aristotle, *Ethics*, 2.1.1103a.15–17.

45. 4.2.4, 6, 8; 4.3.2.

46. Aristotle, *On Sense*, 1.437a.11–18.

47. Aristotle, *Metaphysics*, 1.2.982a.15–19.

48. Augustine, *The City of God*, 19.13.

49. Ecclesiasticus (Sirach) 20.32.

50. *Ius.*

51. *The Body of Civil Law: Institutes* 1.1.1, *Digest* 1.1.10.

nation," or distributive or commutative justice. All these parts of justice are political. In cities they are all especially necessary; indeed, as Aristotle tells us, without cities there can be no exercise of justice, nor can cities be preserved without justice. For these reasons, I conclude that the construction of the city is necessary according to nature for the virtue of justice.

[9] The second virtue of the will that refers to the multitude is friendship, which principally requires a community and does not exist without it. Aristotle says that friendship is especially necessary for human life, in that no one chooses to live without it.[52] In the same passage Aristotle enumerates the utilities of that virtue so as to show its necessity, but he always puts it in the context of the multitude. Its first utility comes when misfortune strikes, because at such times one has recourse to friends. Likewise, when one has good fortune, because this is preserved through friends, so that it is especially necessary for those who have riches and hold ruling positions to have friends, as Aristotle says in the same passage. Even the young need friends so that they may be held back from concupiscence, to keep them from sinning, and the old need friends to wait on them. For similar reasons all the different kinds of persons need friends.

[10] Thus, I conclude that by nature the community of a multitude is necessary for human beings, and consequently so too is the construction of a city. If friendship thrives and concord is nurtured there, the city displays a certain harmony and pleasantness of spirit, as Augustine says, "from the highest orders, from the lowest, and from those in the middle,"[53] through which it is moderated. As the prophet says: "Behold how good and pleasing it is that brothers live in unity!"[54] Likewise, Augustine constitutes his Two Cities according to the two loves that characterize the inhabitants of each.[55]

[11] There is a further reason that shows that the community of a multitude of persons is necessary, and that is the human appetite for sharing one's works with the multitude. It would be difficult for someone do a virtuous act in the absence of human society, for which reason Cicero says in his book, *On Friendship*: "nature loves nothing that is solitary."[56] What I heard from our elders that Archytas of Tarentum used to say is true: "If someone ascended into heaven and beheld the nature of the world and stars, it would not be

---

52. Aristotle, *Ethics*, 8.1.1155a.2–10.
53. Augustine, *The City of God*, 2.21. Augustine is quoting Cicero, *On the Republic*, 2.42.
54. Psalms 132.1 (133.1).
55. Augustine, *The City of God*, 14.28 and passim.
56. Cicero, *On Friendship*, 23.

pleasant for them to admire that beauty if there were no friend or companion there."[57] As Boethius says, even riches themselves do not become bright unless they are spread out among the multitude.

[12] Therefore, it is clear that humans must of necessity live in a multitude, whether we consider their bodies, their sensitive parts, or their rational natures, and this implies that the construction of the city is necessary by nature. For this reason Aristotle says that all naturally incline to such a community as exists in the community of a city.[58] And although Scripture represents those who first instituted cities as evil persons, such as the fratricide Cain,[59] Nimrod, an oppressor of persons and builder of Babylon,[60] or Asshur who, according to Genesis, built Nineveh after fleeing from Nimrod;[61] nevertheless, they were motivated to construct cities by the conveniences such communities bring to human beings, as I have already mentioned. Although they acted to maintain their own lordship, the preservation of necessities resulted in the gathering of a multitude into one community.

Chapter 4

What the community of the city consists of. An explanation of the opinion of Socrates and Plato, which was reported by Aristotle.

[1] Now that I have shown the necessity of constructing the city on behalf of the community of human beings, it seems to me that I should now ask what this community consists of. As Aristotle reports, various philosophers and wise ones have constituted their polities according to their differing views of community. In his *Politics* he first relates Socrates' and Plato's opinion. In their polity community involves everything; in other words, all things are to be held in common, not only riches, but also wives and children.[62] In proposing this they were motivated by the good of union in a community, for which a republic is commended and through which it grows.

---

57. Archytas of Tarentum (fl.400–365 B.C.E.), a Pythagorean friend of Plato who wrote on a wide variety of topics, including philosophy, moral philosophy, and science. He was also a general and famous for a collection of sayings about morals, ethics, and especially happiness.

58. Aristotle, *Politics*, 1.2.1252b.30f.

59. Genesis 4.17. Cain killed his brother Abel out of jealousy since God preferred Abel's animal sacrifice to that of Cain's laboriously produced agricultural goods.

60. Genesis 10.9–10. For Nimrod see note at 3.7.1 above.

61. Genesis 10.11. For Asshur see note at 3.7.2 above.

62. Aristotle, *Politics*, 2.1.1261a.4–6. Ptolemy would also have known about the community of property in Plato from *The Body of Canon Law*. Gratian's *Decretum*, D.8, where Gratian shows that although all things are common by natural right, by customary law this is not true. Gratian

[2] Furthermore, since that which is good spreads itself out and shares itself, the more something is common to all, the closer it seems to come to the quality of goodness. Therefore, sharing all things comes closer to the raison d'être of virtue and goodness.

[3] Besides, love is a virtue that unites, as Dionysius tells us.[63] So, wherever love is a major reason for union, the virtue of love (which constitutes and preserves the city, as Augustine says, and as I said above)[64] will be stronger. Therefore, it would make a better polity to have all things in common, including wives and children, as well as riches.

[4] Aristotle reports these reasons and many others that reflect Socrates and Plato's opinion, if not in the same words, at least in a way that does not conflict with their sentiment. But if we take into consideration the qualities of these philosophers, persons who, above all other philosophers, emphasized the virtues, because they associated the good of human beings solely with virtue, it does not seem credible that they could advocate such a community as the one Aristotle seemingly imputes to them, because it seems more bestial than human for women to be in common with regard to the mingling of the flesh. In its first precept for human beings, Sacred Scripture separates the mother from the son and the daughter from the father, joins a man to his wife, and distinguishes the two of them alone in marriage. Genesis says: "Wherefore a person will leave their father and mother and adhere to their spouse, and they will be two in one flesh."[65] It does not say "many in one flesh."

[5] Children also make this impossible, since in the act of generation two seeds do not come together, but one alone, from the man.[66] For this reason even animals know their own offspring for as long as is necessary to nourish their

---

comments that "with Plato, that city is held to be most just in which no one knows their own attachments." Gratian is quoting from the Latin version of Plato's *Timaeus*, and the word *"affectus"* translated here as "attachments" originally referred to children, but the sense was lost in the translation and could be applied to property, which is the subject of the distinction. See Stephan Kuttner, "Gratian and Plato," in *Church and Government in the Middle Ages*, ed. C.N.L. Brooke et al. (Cambridge: Cambridge University Press, 1976), 93–118. There is no problem explaining away the change from the natural law, since sin was held to have introduced property as well as government. But to say that by natural law wives and children were in common was something else. In the light of Aristotle's explanation of Plato's polity, Ptolemy may have guessed the true sense of this passage and felt even more the necessity of refuting Plato's ideas.

63. Pseudo-Dionysius the Areopagite, *On the Divine Names*, 4.15.
64. Augustine, *The City of God*, 14.28 and passim. Ptolemy quotes this at 4.3.10.
65. Genesis 2.24, quoted also in Matthew 19.5.
66. According to Aristotelian biological principles, the father provides the form of the baby, the mother merely the matter. See Aristotle, *On the Generation of Animals*, 1.20.727b–729a.

children, especially young birds before they can fly. The reasonable conclusion, that Plato and Socrates are less fit than animals, seems absurd, for they are ones who directed their entire philosophy to putting morality in order and correcting it. This is what Augustine reports about Socrates,[67] and his disciple, Plato, used his teaching most fertilely, as Valerius Maximus writes. The wisest of his time, Plato was eagerly sought by zealous youths in Athens; he went down into Egypt, where the Egyptian priests taught him the multiplex numbers of geometry through observation of the celestial movements, and, then, he wandered into Italy, where Archytas and Arion instructed him in Pythagorean precepts.[68]

[6] It is astonishing to attribute such a polity, in which the order of nature is destroyed, to such great men. But even Aristotle's commentators say that he did not fully report the opinions of others and especially those of Socrates and Plato. Eustratius, for example, says this in commenting on the idea of goodness in his commentary on the *Ethics* and Simplicius on the generation of the world in his commentary on *On the Heavens*.[69] Augustine reports the same thing—that some attributed an opinion about the passions of the spirit to the Stoics (whose prince Socrates was) that was not in accord with wisdom.[70] Aristotle also imputed this to Socrates, and yet Augustine says that the attribution is false, according to Aulus Gellius's opinion in his book *Attic Nights*.[71]

[7] We must understand all these things as referring to the effect of love. Plato and Socrates were well endowed with virtues and bent their efforts to virtue. Moreover, the virtue of love orders us to be equal to our neighbor: "Love your neighbor as yourself."[72] Since the philosophers were accustomed to speak in metaphors and wanted to persuade their fellow citizens to practice that love through which the city profits, they posited a community having mutual love with regard to wives and children, and sharing the possession of necessities: "If someone sees a brother to be in need, yet shuts up their heart

---

67. Augustine, *The City of God*, 8.3.

68. Valerius Maximus, *Memorable Deeds and Sayings*, 8.7, ext. 3. This is a close paraphrase of Valerius Maximus, but there is probably a transcription error. Valerius says "the numbers *and* the reason of their celestial observation" and mentions Archytas, Timaeus, Arion, and Caetus of Locri. The word I have translated "movements" is actually "*rationes*." Archytas of Tarentum (fl. 400–365 B.C.E.) was a Greek Italian Pythagorian, scientist, and general. In addition to his moral teachings, he is known for his work on music, geometry, and alleged invention of the pulley.

69. Eustratius, *On "The Ethics," 1*, on Aristotle, *Ethics*, 1.6.1096a23ff.; Simplicius, *On "On the Heavens,"* on Aristotle's *On the Heavens*, 1.

70. Augustine, *The City of God*, 9.4. Augustine does not mention Socrates.

71. Augustine, *The City of God*, 9.4; Aulus Gellius, *Attic Nights*, 19.1.

72. Matthew 19.19, 22.39.

from him, how does the love of God remain in them?"⁷³ This was particularly characteristic of the Stoics, for they were contemptuous of external things and riches, as Jerome reports of Socrates.⁷⁴

[8] This observation makes it clear how to respond to the objection that there is a gradation of union and love among inferior beings, since union is more perfect in an animate body if the virtue of the spirit is diffused to the various organs having various functions united in the one substance of the spirit, as is apparent in animate bodies that have the sense of touch alone, such as worms and certain other animals that Aristotle calls "imperfect animals."⁷⁵ For this same reason Paul compares the mystical body, that is, the Church, to a true and natural body having various members with various potencies and virtues, but all having their roots in the one principle of the spirit. Similarly, Paul reproves the alleged union of 1 Corinthians: "If all the body were an eye, where would be the hearing? And if all the body were hearing, where would be the smelling?"⁷⁶

[9] It is necessary in any congregation (and, above all, this is what a city is) for there to be distinct ranks among the citizens with regard to homes and households and with regard to arts and offices; nevertheless, all are united by the chain of society, which is the love shared by its citizens, as I said above.⁷⁷ Paul wrote about this to the Colossians, when just after he listed various virtuous works to which citizens are mutually obliged, he added: "Value charity above all these, for it is the chain of perfection. And let the peace of Christ, through which you are called to one body, exult in your hearts."⁷⁸ Here he distinguishes among the members according to the state of the citizens. Therefore, the greater the diversity of arts and offices in a city, the more celebrated it is, because in it the sufficiency of human life can be found to a greater degree, and it is for this reason that constructing a city is necessary.

[10] To forestall those who might mention that among the disciples of Christ all things were held in common, let me say that this should not be taken as a statement of common law, since the disciples' state transcended all other modes of life. For their polity was not ordained for wives or children, but

73. 1 John 3.17.

74. Jerome, *Against Jovinian*, 2.14. Jerome actually makes an implicit comparison of Socrates to Christ, having him tell prospective students to sell their possessions and distribute them publicly.

75. Aristotle, *On the Spirit*, 3.1.425a.9–10, 3.11.1.434a.1.

76. 1 Corinthians 12.17.

77. 4.3.10, 4.4.3.

78. Colossians 3.14–15.

to the celestial city, in which "They will neither marry nor be married, but they will be as the angels of God."[79] With regard to riches, goods were held in common, but this is characteristic of the perfect alone. As the Lord says: "If you want to be perfect, go and sell all your things, give to the poor, and follow me."[80]

[11] The Socratics and Platonists did this also, since they had contempt for temporal things, as Mercury Trismegistos wrote about Plotinus[81] and as Macrobius wrote in the "Dream of Scipio."[82] But in other cities, the common state makes it expedient to have distinct possessions to avoid quarrels, as is written in Genesis about Abraham and Lot. When their shepherds argued about pasture for their flocks, Abraham said to Lot: "Let there be no dispute, I beseech you, between me and you, and my shepherds and yours. Behold, all the earth is before you. For we are brothers. If you will go to the left, I will keep to the right; if you should choose the right, I will proceed to the left."[83] From this I conclude that it is expedient for riches to be distinct within cities to preserve the society. I think that this clarifies my response to what was said before.

Chapter 5

Socrates and Plato's opinion that women should be exposed to matters of war.

[1] Now let us return to the polity of Plato and Socrates. Among other things Aristotle attributes to them the desire to have women instructed in matters of war.[84] He advances as one of their arguments that in the case of rapacious

79. Matthew 22.30.
80. Matthew 19.21.
81. Ptolemy and other Latin writers call the "author" usually known as "Hermes Trismegistos," "Mercury Trismegistos," which is actually a collective name for the authors of the seventeen treatises of the *Corpus Hermeticum*, neoplatonic works of the first three centuries C.E. and numerous other works of popular occult and mystical subjects produced from the Hellenistic period through the early centuries C.E. The name reflects the identification of the Greek god Hermes with the Egyptian god Thoth, both of whom were associated with writing and the arts, particularly the magical arts. Hermes was often assumed to have written long before any of the famous philosophers and to have influenced them, but Ptolemy appears to understand the real chronology. Plotinus (205–70) was the major founder of Neoplatonism. It was in this form that Platonism became a great religious philosophy and went on to influence the development of Christian thought, especially by way of Augustine and pseudo-Dionysius.
82. Macrobius, *Commentary on Scipio's Dream*, 1.8.9.
83. Genesis 13.8–9.
84. Aristotle, *Politics*, 2.6.1264b.37–38.

birds we observe the females to be more ferocious and to fight more effectively than the males. The same thing is true for beasts, as is especially manifest among ferocious animals.

[2] Furthermore, when females engage in physical exercise, they increase the
virtue of their bodies and their fortitude, as the examples of female maidser-
vants and rustic women, who are stronger and healthier than other women,
make clear. It is characteristic of a virtue that it makes the one having it
good and that its operation restores the good. If, therefore, feminine virtue is
greatly strengthened in gymnasia and in warlike activities, it would seem to
be appropriate for the practice of war to pertain to them.

[3] Furthermore, a consideration of the proportion of first qualities, such as
warm and damp, cold and dry, leads to the same conclusion, since it is best
that excesses be moderated, and that which is mixed be fortified in its own
virtue.[85] For example, we see that if the moisture in green wood is consumed
and reduced to a moderate amount, it burns more strongly. Thus, by reason
of their motion, female rapacious birds have a stronger nature and greater cor-
pulence than the males. Therefore, moisture, which abounds in women, and
also in boys, is consumed by motion and is reduced to a temperate amount,
which imparts vigor.

[4] As further evidence they say that the histories tell us that the Amazonian
kingdom was the strongest in the east, and that it subjugated all of Asia, the
third part of the globe, as it were.[86] The Amazons originated among the eastern Scythians, and among the Scythians, from whom the Tartars descended,
women are exposed to matters of war and perform military service with
their men.

[5] It was for all these reasons, perhaps, that Plato and Socrates were motivated to constitute a polity in which women would be exposed to the practice
of war.

85. This refers to Aristotelian ideas about qualities of physical objects—that is, the categories of moist and dry, cold and warm. These qualities are the components of the four elements;
it is their proportion that determines physical properties and their change that explains physical change. They are combined in an organism in the form of the four bodily fluids, or humors.
There is also an optimal balance of the humors and qualities in any organism, which to some extent can be modified by behavior. Women and boys, for example, deviate from the optimal by an
excess of moisture. For boys it is a developmental problem they outgrow, but it is permanent for
women; menstruation is one way the body tries to get rid of its excess moisture. Another way of
getting rid of it is through motion, such as exercise. It is amusing to note that Heloise used the
same belief about women's greater moisture to argue that women become drunk less easily and
so nuns should be permitted to drink more wine than what Benedict prescribed for men.
86. Jordanes, *History of the Goths*, § 7–9.

[6] There are also strong reasons against this polity, to which it is difficult to respond. Aristotle points out one of these—the same reasoning does not apply to animals and human beings, since animals are not subject to the lordship of household management.[87] Humans alone attend to the governance of the household, and this could not happen if women were exposed to arms. Just as offices are distinct in political affairs, so also in matters of household management, so that the paterfamilias attends to outside affairs and women to the internal acts of the household. Here we can make an analogy to the Roman Republic, which, as the histories tell us, had two consuls: one attended to matters of war, the other exercised governance over the Republic. The same thing is also written about the Amazons—there were two queens or monarchs in their kingdom or monarchy, whose offices were distinguished in the same way as those of the Roman consuls.

[7] A second reason derives from the ineptitude of women's members for fighting. Aristotle distinguishes between males and females in this way[88] since a male has stronger members, arms, hands, nerves, and veins (which results in the production of a rougher voice), buttocks, belly, and other more subtle attributes. Women are just the reverse, so they are more suited for the act of generation, and their breasts for nourishing their offspring—but all of these things impede fighting. It is written that, for this reason, Amazon girls cut off their right breasts and press down their left, so as not to be impeded in shooting arrows.

[8] A third reason derives from the disposition of their spirit. Aristotle tells us that "a woman is a stunted male,"[89] so that just as women are deficient in their physical constitution, so also are they deficient in reason. Thus it is that, because of their deficient heat and physical constitution, women are timid and fearful of death. But this is especially to be avoided in wars. Since their reason is defective, women lack astuteness for war, a quality by which fighters often become victors, as Vegetius tells us.[90] The histories tell us that Alexan-

---

87. Aristotle, *Politics*, 2.5.1264b.4–7. Aristotle brought this up to discredit Plato's desire to have all things in common, including wives and children, in the perfect polity, an argument that Ptolemy himself has just taken up in the previous section. Plato, *Republic*, 5.451, had used an analogy with wild animals to make his case.

88. Aristotle, *On the Generation of Animals*, 1.19.727a.18–20. Aristotle comments on the greater strength of men; he does not mention fighting or specific body parts here.

89. Aristotle, *On the Generation of Animals*, 2.3.737a.27–28. Ptolemy's word "*occasionatus*," or "stunted," is not the word that appears in William of Moerbeke's translation, which is "*orbatus*," or "deprived."

90. Vegetius, *On the Military*, 1.1, 3.19–20. Vegetius actually says here that thorough training is most important. He admits, for example, that the Greeks were more prudent than the Romans. Much of the book, however, is on astuteness in fighting.

der conquered the Amazons through his astuteness and blandishments more than by his fortitude in making war, although at the time their kingdom was the strongest and mightiest in Asia.[91]

[9] A fourth reason derives from the dangers of commerce with women, since the venereal act corrupts prudent judgment, as Aristotle tells us.[92] It is impossible to understand anything during it, and the result is enervation of the manly spirit. The histories relate that after Julius Caesar decreased the extent of war, he decreed that all delights should be kept away from the camps, especially women. Cyrus, king of the Persians, could not subjugate the Lydians because they were extremely strong and accustomed to labor, and he finally succeeded in taming them, even though they were disposed to virtue and fortitude, only after games and venereal activities enervated them. Vegetius wrote about the ancient Romans: "Therefore, they were always perfect in war, because they were not broken by delights or desires for pleasure."[93] What more is there to say, since even the strongest horses, who otherwise are the boldest fighters and smell war from afar, are distracted from fighting by the presence of a mare. For this reason, as the histories relate, the Amazons accepted no men in their own battle lines.

[10] What I have said should make it clear that women ought to be excluded from matters of war.

Chapter 6

The other side: that it is unsuitable for a woman to be exposed to
matters of war. A response to the arguments made to the contrary.

[1] Because the arguments that Plato and Socrates advance make their conclusion seem probable, I must respond, treating them with reverence.

[2] They give the example of rapacious birds and certain beasts, which they say are bolder and stronger in fighting and seizing prey; they conclude that the situation is similar with women. To this I respond that birds and beasts are

---

91. See note at 3.8.4. The *Greek Alexander Romance*, like many medieval versions, reports a version of Alexander and the Amazons.

92. Aristotle, *Ethics*, 7.10.1152a.6–9.

93. Vegetius, *On the Military*, 1.3. This is not an exact quote. At 1.28 he says that in some periods the Romans were weakened by soft living.

not similar to women. As I said above, human beings are naturally civil and household-management animals, and in the governance of their own household the characteristic act is the woman's, whether it be nourishing children, honorably preserving the things of the home, or providing food. None of these things could happen if women became intent on matters of war. For this reason, nature disposed women so as to remove the occasion of fighting from them, because, as Aristotle says, women have more feeble bodies than men and have less heat, and the only members they have that are thicker than men's are those ordained to the act of generation and bearing, such as the belly, buttocks, and breasts for nourishment. All their other members are more slender and more feeble than men's, and they are less vigorous in those members in which fortitude consists, such as the feet and legs, hands and upper arms, and all other individual members which are the foundation of fortitude, as I said above.[94]

[3] They also say that the fortitude of women increases through exercise, which is true, and they conclude that it is therefore expedient for them to fight. To this I can respond that, as Vegetius proves, fortitude alone does not suffice for victory in a fight but rather astuteness in making war, which women lack: "For the rough and ignorant multitude is always exposed to slaughter."[95] As Vegetius says in the same passage, the short-bodied Romans prevailed against the tall Germans. Therefore, women should not to be exposed to acts from which they would otherwise be excluded by their qualities.[96] This would happen if they were assigned to matters of war, since inciting lust is inherent in them and also comes from their consorting with a man. For this reason, nature provides many bridles for a woman: shame, which is particularly her chain, as Jerome wrote to the virgin Celantia,[97] clothes reaching to her ankles, a ring on her finger, and servitude to her husband, for Sacred Scripture testifies that a woman will be under her husband's power.[98] But attending to matters of war in a republic merits liberty, which is why the laws[99] of nations concede special high privileges to knights.

[4] What they say above about fortitude for making war: "a consideration of the proportion of first qualities, such as warm and damp, cold and dry, leads

94. 4.5.7.
95. Vegetius, *On the Military*, 1.1.
96. *Virtibus.*
97. Jerome, Letter 148, which is now usually considered to be unauthentic.
98. Genesis 3.16.
99. *Iura.*

to the same conclusion, since it is best that excesses be moderated, and that which is mixed be fortified in its own virtue," might be true if fortitude alone were the cause of victory and female members had the same aptitude for fighting as those of the male. But I have already proven the contrary. Besides, it is a woman's nature to acquiesce to a man and not to act, but as an act of fortitude, fighting is the highest action, which in itself, if it is done laudably, deserves a crown.

[5] Therefore, I must say simply that a woman ought not to be exposed to matters of war, but ought to live in the home and take care of household matters, as I said above. Solomon commends a woman's fortitude in a song that he composed using each of the letters of the Hebrew alphabet, in which he attributes all of her fortitude to domestic action: "Who will find a strong woman? Her price is far beyond any limits,"[100] He implies that she should be highly revered if she is skilled in the things he mentions. The first is the art of spinning: "She sought wool and flax, and labored with the counsel of her hands,"[101] thus showing that this was a proper part of her offices. As is recorded among his deeds, Charlemagne also mandated that his dearly beloved daughters take up the distaff and spindle and be industrious with them.[102] Further on, Solomon added other womanly acts referring to the domestic home, such as taking care of children, running the household, providing for her home, honoring the friends of her husband, and making up for his defects. These are proper things for a wife to do, and they pertain to the good of marriage, as is clear from what is written about Abigail, wife of Nabal of Carmel.[103] Since such solicitude involves many disturbances, as the Lord says in Luke: "Martha, Martha, you are solicitous and disturbed about many things,"[104] and since such things should be the object of virtue and fortitude, the Wise One quoted above calls such a woman strong, not because she shows fortitude toward works of war, but because she patiently guides her household, as I showed above.

100. Proverbs 31.10. Each of verses 10–31 begins with a different Hebrew letter in alphabetical order.

101. Proverbs 31.13.

102. Einhard, *Life of Charlemagne*, 19. More unusually, he also educated his daughters (and sons) in the liberal arts. Even more unusually, he was so fond of them that he did not let any of them marry.

103. 1 Kings (1 Samuel) 25. When Abigail learned that Nabal had spurned David's messengers she went to David with an offering to apologize for her husband's folly and bad temper and successfully begged for forgiveness.

104. Luke 10.41.

Chapter 7

Another opinion of these philosophers with regard to rule, which they wanted to be for life. A disputation from both sides as to which is better.

[1] Another condition that Aristotle attributes to Socrates and Plato's polity is having governmental magistrates according to the custom of the Attic region, which Athens headed after the death of King Codrus.[105] In the Roman Republic these magistrates were called senators. Socrates and Plato wanted them, and all other officials in their polity, to be established for life; their motive, as Aristotle puts it, was to imitate nature.[106] We see that the parts of the earth always maintain themselves in the same manner: in the same part of the earth gold mines always produce gold and silver mines silver. As is written in Job: "Veins of silver have a beginning, and there is a place where gold is melted down."[107] From this principle they conclude that if the place where gold or silver is found never changes, then neither does the place of lead or iron, and if the place where lead or iron is found never changes, then neither does the place of gold or silver. The same thing should happen in rule, that neither rulers nor their officials ought to change so as sometimes to become subjects, or for subjects to become rulers, because art imitates nature in so far as it can.[108]

[2] An argument leading to the same conclusion comes from what Aristotle says: "Experience makes art, and inexperience chance,"[109] and likewise Vegetius: "Knowledge of military affairs nourishes boldness. For no one fears to do that which they are confident that they have learned well."[110] Given this, we argue that if a change of rectors, rulers, or magistrates occurs, an inexpert one is sometimes elevated, which leads to many mistakes in the polity.

[3] What I said in Book 2 leads to the same conclusion.[111] Such changes detract from the government, because subjects have an incentive not to obey in hopes

---

105. For Codrus, see note at 2.9.6.
106. Aristotle, *Politics*, 2.5.1264b.7–16. Aristotle does not actually speak about mines and uses the metals metaphor differently, saying that rulers must be the same according to Socrates because the gold, silver, brass, and iron that God gives to any human being (that is, that person's qualities) never changes, but is always the same from birth.
107. Job 28.1.
108. Aristotle, *Physics*, 2.2.194a.21–22.
109. Aristotle, *Metaphysics*, 1.1.981a.3–5.
110. Vegetius, *On the Military*, 1.1.
111. 2.8.1–5, especially 2.8.2, 2.9.5.

of evading the hand of the temporary ruler or of coming into rule themselves.
So what motivated Socrates and Plato seems to be consonant with reason.

[4] On the other hand, what motivated the wise ones of Rome or of the Roman Republic was quite different, because after the expulsion of the kings they
established consuls with an annual term. Thus, in 1 Maccabees it is written,
among other commendable things about the Romans: "they annually commit their magistracy to one person, who exercises lordship over all their land,
and all obey that one."[112] The histories give as a cause for this that such a one
would not long remain insolent but would be more moderate and quicker
to give assistance.[113] Aristotle also touches on this, saying that sometimes to
change rule and dignities and to distribute the magistracy to suitable personages is a cause of greater peace in a city and, in fact, in any polity at all.[114]

[5] Another cause comes from one of Aristotle's principles: "rule shows the
man."[115] For it sometimes happens that personages elevated to a dignity were
virtuous persons in their own rank, but after they achieve the state of a ruler
they become puffed up by pride and turn into tyrants. This happened to Saul,
about whom 1 Kings says that when he was elevated as king, there was no
better man among the children of Israel,[116] but that he remained in his innocence for only two years. Afterward, when he had turned into a tyrant and
had become disobedient, it was said to him through Samuel: "Because you
have cast off the word of the Lord and have not obeyed his voice, the Lord
has cast you off, so that you should not be king."[117]

[6] There is also a certain gradation in human nature with regard to virtues
and graces. Certain people are disposed to subjection, but are less suited to
take part in government, and for others the reverse is true. Thus, because a
good subject might be elevated but govern badly, it would be a cause of division in the city for such a one should to have rule for life.

[7] There is an inherent appetite for honor among human beings, which is
why Valerius Maximus says: "there is no humility so great that it may not be

---

112. 1 Machabees (Maccabees) 8.16.
113. Eutropius, *A Brief History of Rome*, 1.9.
114. Aristotle never says this exactly, but it is implicit in many sections of the *Politics*, including 2.2, 2.11, 3.6, 3.12. He also stresses the right of free men to take part and their dissatisfaction
if they are prevented.
115. Aristotle, *Ethics*, 5.1.1130a.1–2. At 1.10.5 this is called a "proverb of Bias," but Ptolemy
got it from Aristotle. See also 3.8.1.
116. 1 Kings (1 Samuel) 9.2.
117. 1 Kings (1 Samuel) 15.23.

touched by that sweetness."[118] Hence, humans are impatient of superiors, and to give rule to one alone is a cause of sedition among the multitude. This why Aristotle says that by always making the same ones rulers, Socrates creates a cause of sedition among those having no such dignity. Seeing that they were utterly without status, those who were virile and full of spirit would exert themselves, causing discord among the citizens.[119] Valerius Maximus says that since Fabius, a Roman leader about whom I spoke above, had often had the consulate, and since that dignity had come to his lineage for a long time through succession, the Roman people acted to exempt the Fabian stock from this honor.[120] Therefore, the more laudable polity is that in which honors are distributed in turn according to the merits of each individual citizen, as the ancient Romans did, and Aristotle also finds this to be more commendable.

Chapter 8

It is better not to have perpetual rectors in a polity. A response to the opposite position.

[1] What Socrates and Plato say about mines neither compels assent, nor is it a proper analogy, because mines, whether of gold, or silver, or of any other metal, are imprinted by the celestial bodies, which determine them to be only one thing. So, just as figs, and not other fruit, always grow on fig trees, because they all have the same internal principles mediated by celestial influence, so also the same part of the earth is so disposed that gold mines always produce gold. This is not true of the human will, which is not subject to the stars, as Ptolemy proves in *Centiloquium*,[121] because it is mutable, which is why Aristotle identifies human acts as contingent.[122] Will can change from good to evil and back again, and so perpetuation is dangerous.

[2] As for the argument that follows concerning experience, it presupposes that a capable expert would be chosen who knows how to govern and direct the citizens toward virtue, for if one of insufficient worth or love were chosen, the polity would be corrupted. Jethro, Moses's relative, tells us in Exodus the form of choosing the rulers and assessors of the people: "Provide mighty men from all the plebeians, in whom there is truth and who hate avarice, and con-

118. Valerius Maximus, *Memorable Deeds and Sayings*, 8.14.5.
119. Aristotle, *Politics*, 2.5.1264b.7–10.
120. Valerius Maximus, *Memorable Deeds and Sayings*, 4.1.5. See above, 3.20.3.
121. Ptolemy, *Centiloquium*, 1.8.
122. Aristotle, *Ethics*, 3.1.1110a.15.

stitute from them tribunes and centurions and ones set over fifty and ten who may judge the people."[123] Aristotle says that we do not allow a person to rule in whom human nature alone is present, but rather one who is perfect according to reason.[124] If it were otherwise those elevated to rule would give more goods to themselves and thereby turn into tyrants.

[3] As for the final argument, that the changing of rule detracts from government, I must emphasize what I touched on in Book 2,[125] which is that regions differ in their human inhabitants, who, like other living things, have diverse physical constitutions and ways of living according to the configuration of the heavens, as Ptolemy tells us in *Quadripartus*.[126] Plants, for example, adapt to the nature of the region to which they are transplanted, as do fish and animals. As it is with other living things, so it is with humans. The nature of Gauls who move to Sicily becomes like that of the Sicilians. This is apparent since, as the histories relate, the Gauls populated this island three times — first in the time of Charlemagne, second three hundred years later in the time of Robert Guiscard, and now in our own times by king Charles, and they have already soaked up the Sicilian nature.[127] Assuming this, it follows that government and lordship ought to be ordained according to the disposition of the particular nation, as Aristotle himself tells us.[128]

[4] Certain provinces are servile by nature, and despotic rule should guide these, counting regal rule as despotic. Certain others have a virile spirit, a bold heart, and a confidence in their intelligence, and these cannot be ruled other than by political rule, using the common name here to extend also to aristocratic rule. Such lordship is especially strong in Italy, where, for the reason mentioned, the inhabitants were always less able to be subjected than others, so that if you should want to bring them under despotic rule, this could not

---

123. Exodus 18.21–22. The quote is not exact.
124. Aristotle, *Ethics*, 5.6.1134a.35–36.
125. 2.8.4, 2.9.5.
126. Ptolemy, *Quadripartus*, 2.3–4.
127. Robert Guiscard, a Norman and son of Tancred, was appointed duke of Sicily by Pope Nicholas II in 1059, and he proceeded to conquer the island. Charles of Anjou, brother of St. Louis of France, was brought in by Pope Urban IV in 1263 to oppose the Hohenstaufen Manfred, whom he killed in battle in 1266; afterward he occupied the island. During the reign of Charlemagne (r.768–814) Sicily was under Byzantine rule. Although he defeated the Lombards and had himself crowned king of the Lombards, the Duchy of Benevento, later part of the Norman Kingdom of Sicily remained independent and had few Frankish immigrants. Sicily did, however, have close ties to the Roman Church until the mid-eighth century, and Gregory of Tours, *History of the Franks*, 3.32, reports (mistakenly) the Frankish conquest and occupation of Sicily in the time of king Theudebert (d.548).
128. Aristotle, *Politics*, 4.1.1288b.20–34.

be done unless the lords tyrannized. This is why the islands in the region, which always had kings and princes, such as Sicily, Sardinia, and Corsica, always had tyrants. And in parts of Liguria, Aemilia, and Flaminia, which today is called Lombardy, no one could have rule for life except by the path of tyranny. The exception is the duke[129] of Venice, but he has a temperate government. Therefore, up to the present time rule is better sustained in the regions mentioned above.

[5] What was said about political rule detracting from the polity is not true if suitable ones are chosen; if not, as I said, the polity is corrupted. Aristotle tells us that suitable ones come from the middle ranks of the city, that is, ones neither exceptionally mighty, who would easily tyrannize, nor ones of exceedingly low condition, who would immediately democratize.[130] For when they consider themselves to be on top, unmindful of themselves and inexperienced in government, they are submerged in the pit of error, either through improvident care for their subjects, or through presumptuous boldness toward the troubles of others, by means of which the polity is also corrupted and made unquiet. Therefore rectors ought to be elevated in turn in a polity, so long as suitable ones can be found, whether they be called consuls, magistrates, or any other title.

[6] There is no danger in this, because rectors judge according to laws handed down to them to which they are bound by oaths. Since the multitude itself instituted these laws, the rectors can not give rise to scandal in punishing. It does not detract from their lordship if the law prescribes light punishments according to the nature of the subject nation, because sometimes in such regions the polity is better preserved by overlooking guilt or dispensing with the penalty. In doing this, the virtue of equity, about which Aristotle speaks[131] and which has the effect of decreasing legal justice, seems to be relevant. In this government, it is important to heed the regulations set down by that Highest Shepherd, the blessed Gregory in his *Register* and *Pastoral Regulation*, who tells us that the mode of correction should vary according to the state and quality of the personages involved.[132]

---

129. Usually this official is called the "doge," but I have translated "duke" for consistency.
130. Aristotle, *Politics*, 4.11.1295b.25–35.
131. Aristotle, *Ethics*, 5.10.1137a.31ff.
132. Gregory I, Letters, 11.46, *Pastoral Regulation*, 3, especially the prologue.

Chapter 9

A dispute about the community of goods with regard to possessions, which a certain philosopher by the name of Phaleas said ought to be equalized among all. That which the philosopher Lycurgus believed is false.

[1] Since Socrates and Plato's opinion centered on the community of possessions, it is fitting to mention others here who constituted their own polities in ways related to possessions. Two philosophers who thought that disputes in cities arose when one had a surplus of what another was lacking wanted their own polities to equalize possessions within their cities. One was Phaleas of Chalcedon, whom Aristotle discusses,[133] and the other was Lycurgus, the son of the king of the Spartans, who established laws[134] for the Lacedaemonians, as Justin tells us, "so that the fact of equal possessions would ensure that no one was more mighty than another."[135]

[2] Aristotle relates the mode of equalizing possessions that Phaleas favored — that it should be incorporated into the constitution of the city itself, taking into consideration the multitude of the citizens and fields. He judged that if this were not done it would be difficult to achieve success. So that this equality would last, he ordained the contracting of matrimony between those of greater and lesser position in order to eliminate strife and injury and remove the occasion for arrogance or pride. To back up his position he gave the example of other polities in which disturbances often occurred where there was inequality of temporal goods. Inequality provides a stimulus for envy, which leads to cupidity, and this, according to Paul, "is the root of all evils."[136] This is why Lycurgus, in the laws that he handed down to the Lacedaemonians for preserving their polity, forbade artificial riches or coins to be used in the exchange of things for sale, allowing interchanges for natural riches alone.

[3] Aristotle rejects this position, and shows such equalization to be utterly impossible and, consequently, against reason.[137] First he approaches the pro-

---

133. Aristotle, *Politics*, 2.7.1266a.39ff. Phaleas is known only from Aristotle's account, which says he is from Chalcedon and the first to propose communal property.

134. *Iura*. Lycurgus was the traditional ninth-century B.C.E. lawgiver of the Spartans. There is little or no reliable historical evidence about him. Most accounts start with the fifth-century Herodotus.

135. M. Junianus Justinus, *Philippian Histories of T. Pompeius Trogus*, 3.2–3.

136. 1 Timothy 6.10.

137. Aristotle, *Politics*, 2.7.

posal from the perspective of human nature, which does not increase equally in all families,[138] since it could happen that the paterfamilias of one home has many children, while that of another has none. It would be an impossible situation if these two had equal possessions, since one family would lack for food while the other would have an excess. This would be against the provision of nature, because the family that had more offspring would sink to the bottom of the polity on account of its increase in size, as compared to the family that failed to generate as many offspring. On the contrary, by right of nature, the first family deserves to have the republic or polity provide more for it.

[4] Further, nature does not fail in necessities, as I said above,[139] and therefore neither does the art of civil government, but this would happen if possessions were equalized among families, because citizens would die of penury, which would lead to the corruption of the polity.

[5] It also follows that the equalization of possessions is unsuitable from a consideration of the gradation of personages as well as from human nature. There is a difference between citizens, just as there is between members of a body, to which I compared a polity above;[140] moreover, the virtue and function of different members is different. It is well known that someone who is noble must make greater expenditures than one who is not noble—it is for this reason, for example, that the virtue of liberality is called magnificence in a ruler on account of the great cost involved. This could not happen where possessions were equal, and this is why the voice of the Evangelist itself testifies that the paterfamilias or king who set out for foreign parts distributed goods to his servants, but not equally: "to one he gave five talents, to another two, and to another one, to each one according to their particular virtue."[141]

[6] Nor does the very order of nature allow equality, for divine providence constituted created things with a certain inequality, both by their nature and their merit. So, to enforce equality in temporal goods such as possessions is to destroy the order inherent in things, which Augustine defines in terms of inequality. For order is "the disposition of equal and unequal things giving to each its due."[142] This is why Origen was criticized for what he said in his *Peri-*

---

138. I have translated "*familia*" as "family" in this passage, instead of the more usual and generally more accurate "household."
139. 2.15.1, 3.11.8.
140. 2.7.7, 3.11.4, also 1.14.2.
141. Matthew 25.15. There is no mention of a king there.
142. Augustine, *The City of God*, 19.13.

archon—that all things are equal by their nature but were made unequal on account of their defect, that is, on account of sin.[143] Therefore, equalization of possessions does not avoid disputes; on the contrary, it increases them, and doing it destroys or infringes on natural right when possessions are taken away from one who is needy and more deserving.

[7] Likewise, it is against reason that all things should be equal in a polity, since God instituted all things "in number, weight, and measure," as is said in the Book of Wisdom,[144] which quantities implant a gradation of inequality in beings, and, consequently, in cities or polities.

Chapter 10

Another look at the polity of Plato and Socrates, with regard to the five kinds of persons required in it. Much dispute about the number of warriors.

[1] Now I must return to the polity of Socrates and Plato, because there are several things that they constituted in it that I did not mention above. For example, they distinguished five kinds of persons in their city, namely rulers, counselors, warriors, artisans, and farmers. This division seems sufficient for the perfection of the city, because it includes all the kinds of persons that have to do with political government. But Aristotle seems to criticize them in this matter, because the number of warriors that they propose, namely between one thousand and five thousand, is out of proportion to the size of the city. The second thing that is reprehensible to Aristotle is that the warriors were so distinguished from the others that the other citizens would never involve themselves in the warlike activities of the warriors.[145]

[2] As to the first point, it does not seem that a definite number of warriors should be proposed, since not all cities are of equal might and virtue. One must consider the size of the multitude of people in the city and constitute

---

143. Origen's Περὶ Ἀρχῶν, *On First Principles*, 1.6. This is also known as *On Rulers* or *On Rules*. Augustine criticized it in *On the City of God*, 11.23. Origen's point as interpreted by Augustine was actually that matter was created to imprison sinning, originally equal souls and that the worst sinners got the lower and heavier bodies. Origen (c.185–c.250) was one of the leading Greek Fathers of the Church, but many of his doctrines came under attack and were condemned at the Second Council of Constantinople in 543.

144. Wisdom 11.21.

145. Aristotle, *Politics*, 2.6.1165a.9–18.

the warriors accordingly. Likewise, one must consider the size of the region to ensure that there is a sufficiency of pastures and provisions. Aristotle says that to have such a multitude of warriors as they propose in the city it would be necessary for it to be the equal of Babylon,[146] a city with an exceedingly great national multitude and with extensive fields.

[3] If we consider the name given to warriors, that is "knights," Plato's and Socrates' polity concords, according to one explanation in the histories, with the civic entity of Romulus, who first constructed Rome and who also originated the name of "knight." For it is said that the knights chosen for war took their name from the number "one thousand,"[147] because there were then one thousand armed knights whom Romulus chose to fight against the adversaries of Rome: the Sabines at first and later the Samnites. Romulus is thus in accord in this matter with Socrates and Plato, although the founder of Rome lived long before these frequently mentioned philosophers.

[4] According to another way of thinking a knight is called this because he is, as it were, one in a thousand[148] (in this way, Scripture says in commending a saint for constancy and fortitude: "My beloved is white and ruddy and chosen out of thousands."[149]), in order to signify the excellence in fighting of those whom Sacred Scripture in Genesis calls "armed domestic servants."[150] There, it is written that after the capture of his nephew Lot and all his household Abraham proceeded against four kings with 318 armed domestic servants who then vanquished five kings. It seems likely that Abraham had a greater multitude than this for fighting, but those particular ones are named because of their probity in attacking. Thus also Gideon chose 300 of the people of Israel for fighting against the camps of the Midianites, as the Book of Judges tells us. He proved by divine mandate that these were more apt for fighting, from the fact that when the people crossed a body of water and all the people drank from it, everyone else bent their knees, but those ones alone lapped like dogs without bending their knees.[151] Therefore, it does not seem possible that there could be a thousand chosen in this way from the city, still less five thousand, so Aristotle's criticism of Socrates and Plato, if this was their intention, is valid.

146. Aristotle, *Politics*, 2.6.1165a.14.
147. Isidore of Seville, *Etymologies*, 9.3.32. "One thousand" is *"mille"* in Latin; *"miles"* is "knight."
148. Isidore of Seville, *Etymologies*, 9.3.32.
149. Canticle of Canticles (Song of Songs) 5.10.
150. Genesis 14.14.
151. Judges 7.5–7.

[5] The second thing that Aristotle proves has to do with the way Socrates and Plato distinguish the warriors, as if the other citizens, such as counselors, artisans, and farmers, were immune from war. This is not true when a multitude of enemies attacks the citizens. Although warriors are more apt for fighting because they have experience and have learned the art of fighting (as Vegetius says, "No one fears to do that which they are confident that they have learned well") [152]; nevertheless, they could not sustain the attack of a multitude other than with an opposing multitude. Judas Maccabeus, for example, failed when the multitude of his nation withdrew from him and he fought with a only few against the multitude of Bacchides, prince of king Demetrius, as 1 Maccabees makes clear.[153] Hence it is that although King Saul chose three thousand men to defend his government (for there were two thousand with him where he held court in Michmash and in Bethel and one thousand with Jonathan in his own home in Gibeah of Benjamin),[154] he nevertheless made use of the multitude against the multitude of enemies. When Nahash the Ammonite, king of his region, besieged Jabesh-gilead with a multitude, he gathered 300,000 of the children of Israel in camps and 30,000 from the tribe of Judah to expel these Ammonites, as is written in 1 Kings.[155]

[6] I must note that the military teaching of Vegetius, which accords with the opinion of the Spartans and Athenians, restricted the number who exercise arms to 10,000 foot soldiers and 2,000 on horse.[156] He demonstrates that a great multitude is injurious: first, because it is more difficult to govern it; then, because it is more laborious to provide it with food. In this passage he even includes in the enumeration of the army not only the recruits but also the auxiliaries, which we count as citizens not deputed to military service. In teaching how to choose recruits, Vegetius also depends more on farmers and artisans, because they were accustomed to labor.[157]

[7] Therefore, it should not only be warriors who are called up for fighting but also citizens of every kind, whether they are counselors, artisans, or agriculturalists, provided that they do not have the kind of body that is an impediment to fighting, as do fat and heavy people, who have difficulty walking, or citizens given over exceedingly to delights, or people of advanced age, whom the ancient Romans held to be unfit for service. It also seems proper to exclude from fighting people whom divine law prohibits from fighting, as is clear in

152. Vegetius, *On the Military*, 1.1.
153. 1 Machabees (Maccabees) 9.1–21.
154. 1 Kings (1 Samuel) 13.2.
155. 1 Kings (1 Samuel) 11.1–8.
156. Vegetius, *On the Military*, 3.1.
157. Vegetius, *On the Military*, 1.3.

Deuteronomy when the praetor called out the prohibitions of the law in the presence of the army.[158] In that passage, four kinds of persons are mentioned who are excused from fighting. The first three are those who had built a new house and had not used it, those who had planted a new vineyard, and those who had been about to marry a wife; and, indeed, these three things distract one's intention from fighting, and thereby make one less bold. The fourth kind are those with an excessive fear of death, those who are called "fearful ones" by Sacred Scripture. Vegetius says that among the artisans five kinds of persons ought to be excluded from the camps, namely fishers, fowlers, confectioners (that is, those who attend to delights), linen weavers (that is, those who are soft and flexible), and those who attend to the women's quarters (that is, to women's work, such as weaving or sexual work).[159]

[8] It does not pertain to the present business to say more about the order of camps or the army and its rectors or movers, because it is not suitable for me to teach about how to fight or to go on about the gymnasia necessary for this fighting, but only to tell about the true polity. Through this, if we attain it, we are disposed to live according to virtue[160] and, as it were, participate in the celestial polity, which is the City of God, about which glorious things are said.[161]

Chapter 11

The polity of Hippodamus, who is criticized because he posits only three kinds of person and because of the number of the people.

[1] In Book 2 of the *Politics*, Aristotle treats many polities and those who treat polities extensively; among these is Hippodamus the philosopher, the son of Euryphon whose fatherland was Milesius, the birth place of Thales, one of the Seven Wise Ones.[162] He constituted his polity from many elements and ordained it for many purposes, and the first thing he did was to determine that

---

158. Deuteronomy 20.5–8.

159. Vegetius, *On the Military*, 1.7. It is Ptolemy who interprets these occupations symbolically. In the period in which Vegetius was writing, "*gynacea*," which originally meant "women's quarters," had come to refer to government weaving shops. Ptolemy must know something of this, but also thinks that it refers to the prostitutes who accompanied armies.

160. See Aristotle, *Ethics*, 2.1.1103b.3–6, *Politics*, 3.9.1280b.5–11.

161. Psalms 86.3 (87.3), but, of course, a reference to Augustine's *The City of God* as well.

162. Aristotle, *Politics*, 2.8.1267b.22–1269a.29. Hippodamus was a fifth century architect. His political ideas are known through Aristotle. Thales (c.640–546 B.C.E.) was a philosopher and scientist credited for beginning study of astronomy and geometry. He believed that all matter was composed of water. For the Seven Wise Men, see note at 1.10.6.

the number of the multitude of the city should be about 10,000 men, which he thought was sufficient for any city. Perhaps what I said above about the camps [163] was his motive, because a city is guided better and can be provided with food more suitably through rectors. He reduced this multitude to three kinds of persons: warriors, artisans, and farmers. In this division, he made each kind distinct, because he thought that the warrior should not cross over to become a cultivator of the land or a businessperson, nor should a farmer take up arms. He said that there should be a sufficiency of these three kinds of persons, because they are ordained to the preservation of human life: farmers to nourishing, artisans to clothing, and warriors to the preserving or guarding of goods.

[2] If we take heed of what I said above [164] and what I will say below, we can more easily perceive the error of this philosopher, since we can not determine in advance a specific number of personages that should live in a polity. Rather, a people grows larger because the place is pleasant, the region famous, or the nation fertile. We also see that cities are of greater might and are judged to be more famous the more numerous their nation, nor is their government impeded on that account so long as they are well disposed through rectors or officials, since the penalties that persons institute through laws avert evil and act as medicine in the polity, as Aristotle tells us.[165]

[3] On the other hand, the kinds of persons ought not to be so sharply distinguished that, when the situation requires, they might not be mixed together. Artisans and farmers sometimes become warriors, since recruits are chosen from those two kinds of persons especially, about which I quoted Vegetius above.[166] Conversely we say that warriors often become artisans and farmers, since warriors often originate as that kind of person.

[4] Nor is his division into only three kinds of persons sufficient, because he does not include counselors and wise ones, who are a principal part of the polity, without whom the polity can not suitably be governed. As the histories tell us, Demosthenes of Athens described these experienced men and any other expert old ones by saying that they are to the polity as dogs to the flock, whose guardianship keeps off the wolves.[167] Wise ones and advocates in cities

---

163. 4.10.6–7?
164. 4.10.1.
165. Aristotle, *Ethics*, 2.3.1104b.17.
166. 4.10.6.
167. Demosthenes (c.385–322 B.C.E.) was a great Athenian orator and political figure especially known for his opposition to Philip of Macedon and his son Alexander the Great.

are like this, because they are the dogs of the people. For this reason Cicero wrote in his book *On Duties* that Solon was of greater profit to the republic of the city of Athens, because he was learned in their laws and institutions, than was Themistocles through his victory, because the war was waged with the counsel of the magistrates and the senate instituted by Solon, who was one of the Seven Wise Men.[168] It is written in Ecclesiastes: "Wisdom is better than the arms of war."[169] Vegetius and Valerius Maximus say about Aristotle that although he was "scarcely preserving the remnants of the last stages of life in his old and wrinkled members and pursing the exalted leisure of letters, he so valiantly watched over the well-being of his fatherland, which had almost been leveled to the ground, that, lying on his Athenian bed, he snatched it out of the grasp of hostile arms."[170] Ecclesiastes makes a similar point about the wise: "There was a small city with few men in it, and a great king came against it and surrounded it with a rampart and palisades and raised bulwarks in a circle, and the siege was perfect," just as Philip, king of the Macedonians, did to the Athenians, as the histories tell us. "And there was discovered in that city a poor and wise man," someone like the said philosophers, a mark of whom was to spurn their own world and choose, as it were, a religious life, as Jerome wrote. Afterward Ecclesiastes adds: "he freed the city through his own wisdom."[171]

[5] Therefore, I conclude from this that counselors should not be excluded from the polity. Likewise, rectors ought not to be excluded, since they are the head of the civil corporation on which the whole body depends.

Chapter 12

Hippodamus's opinion of possessions, which he divides into three parts, and how his position can be defended.

[1] Hippodamus also proposed other things for his polity, such as a distinction of possessions, for he divided the possessions of the whole region of the city into three parts. Certain things were deputed to sacred affairs, namely those which were dedicated to the divine cult, as ecclesiastical goods are today.

---

168. Cicero, *On Duties*, 1.30. Solon (c.638–c.559 B.C.E.), another of the Seven Wise Men of Greece, reorganized the government and social structure of Athens as archon (c.594). Many aristocrats opposed his reforms, and he left the city and traveled for ten years. Pisistratus became tyrant of Athens not long after Solon's return. Themistocles (c.527–c.460 B.C.E.) built up the Athenian navy and was commander of the fleet in the victory over the Persians at Salamis in 480.
169. Ecclesiastes 9.18.
170. Valerius Maximus, *Memorable Deeds and Sayings*, 5.6, ext. 5.
171. Ecclesiastes 9.14–15.

He assigned certain other things as common possessions to be dispensed to the warriors and still other things as individual possessions, which were owed to the farmers. He assigned nothing at all to the artisans, since they could live sufficiently well through their art.

[2] Although this division seems to be insufficient in many ways, it is laudable to some degree because it apportioned something for showing reverence to the divine, which, indeed, we ought to do by natural and divine law.[172] The ancient Romans followed this custom during the time that they maintained strong discipline. And it is written in Exodus that in the time of Joseph all the land of Egypt, which was menaced by famine, was reduced into servitude to the king, except for the land of the priests,[173] namely that which was dedicated to God and could not be alienated. The same thing is true today of the possessions of the Church, which cannot be alienated except occasionally in legitimate cases. Aristotle reports that the Egyptians were among the first to have leisure for philosophy and that this was especially true in the mathematical arts. He gives as a reason for this that the priestly nation was permitted more leisure, since they enjoyed such abundance from the possessions allotted to them that they were relieved from the care of seeking nourishment.[174] Although the Mosaic law prohibits priests from having possessions in their brothers' lands, it nevertheless concedes more to them, in that they enjoyed the tenth part of the possessions of all the citizens.[175] As is written in Malachias, "Bring all the tithe, so that there may be food in my house."[176] And in Luke the Pharisee praises himself in this regard, as if he were doing a work of perfect justice: "I give a tithe," namely to the priests and Levites, "of all that I possess."[177]

[3] Since they serve the community zealously, it was reasonable for Hippodamus to ordain that the warriors or knights should receive pay from the community's goods. The Roman Republic also established that they should live from the public treasury, and it is for this reason that John the Baptist says to the knights, as is written in Luke: "Be content with your pay,"[178] and Paul asks in 1 Corinthians: "Who ever performs military service yet provides their own pay?"[179]

172. *Ius* in both cases.
173. Actually Genesis 47.20–22.
174. Aristotle, *Metaphysics*, 1.1.981b.20–25.
175. Numbers 18.20–21.
176. Malachias (Malachi) 3.10.
177. Luke 18.12.
178. Luke 3.14.
179. 1 Corinthians 9.7.

[4] When Hippodamus assigned personal possessions to farmers alone, he was departing from his own polity, unless perhaps he was referring to agricultural produce, which is the characteristic product of farmers' acts, so that farmers are said to have personal possession of the results of cultivation, but other citizens have these only with regard to use; otherwise the polity would be imperfect and defective. It is certainly true, as I said above,[180] that possessions are reckoned among natural riches, which are called this because human beings naturally need them for the necessities of human life, and on account of their pleasantness for reviving the spirit. Hence, the first person used them by divine mandate, because he was placed in Paradise, which the Lord had planted with various kinds of trees, so that he might work and guard it, and indeed the work itself was delectable and without fatigue, as Augustine explains.[181] And Genesis relates that the first art that Cain and Abel, the first children of Adam, learned was exercising governance over natural riches, for Cain became a farmer and Abel a keeper of sheep.[182] Genesis wants to show by this that those things were instituted for the needs of life and, therefore, that possessions should not be assigned to farmers alone, as Hippodamus says.

[5] Therefore, perfecting the polity requires that not only farmers, but all citizens, should have personal possessions, except for the way that I just described, and to the degree that they possess things more abundantly they should have a more elevated position, as I said above about kings.[183] Perhaps, however, it may be more expedient for warriors or knights to have common possessions, as the Roman Republic established and I already made clear,[184] so that they would not be distracted from the things of war through an excessive care for temporal things or be softened by their exceeding pleasantness, which would contribute not a little to the detriment of the polity. For this reason Hippodamus also took away personal possessions from them, so that they would attend only to arms.

---

180. 2.5.2.
181. Augustine, *On the Literal Meaning of Genesis*. 8.8–10.
182. Genesis 4.2.
183. In 2.5–7 Ptolemy discusses the necessity for kings to have an abundance of riches, but he doesn't say position should be directly proportional to wealth.
184. 4.12.3.

Chapter 13

Hippodamus's opinion of judges and assessors. He gives a multiple
and notable classification of what judges must do.

[1] Since Aristotle has a long discussion about Hippodamus and says a lot about his polity, I need to summarize what remains of his teaching. It would be laborious to write and tiresome to hear a report of every polity, when every city may have a different one.

[2] Hippodamus's institutions are frequently concerned with judgments, as Aristotle reports.[185] First, judgments in their own right, since he reduced all judgments to three types of human litigation: those concerning harm to things and two types of those concerning injury to a personage—either an offense in word or gesture or an injury by striking or wounding. Following Hippodamus, Aristotle calls the first of these injuries to a personage a "dishonor," and the second a "death," because it is ordained to death, and he has a long discussion of civil right with respect to these things. He says that they are unjustified, because they are exercised against justice.

[3] Hippodamus also distinguished judgments with regard to those who judge. He refers to two kinds of these: the first, the ordinary praetorium, and the second, which he calls the principal praetorium, exists for challenges, to provide the refuge of an appeal. As Aristotle tells it, Hippodamus wanted the principal praetorium to be constituted from chosen elders of the city, who might revoke a matter that had been badly judged. The Tuscans call such elders *Anziani* or priors,[186] who were designed for this purpose as well. Sometimes a syndic is constituted for the same purpose, so-named for taking care of the polity, so that it is not harmed through injustice.[187] This is what the stewards of associations do also.

[4] In his polity Hippodamus established that the wise ones of the ordinary and principal praetorium should not gather together to make judgments, but that each should individually write their counsel on tablets with regard to the

---

185. Aristotle, *Politics*, 2.8.1267b.35ff.

186. During the period of the *popolo*, that is, of widespread guild government, in northern Italian cities, elders (*Anziani*), or priors (*Priori*), as they were called in Florence, were often at the center of government. The office originated in Bologna in 1231 and spread rapidly.

187. "Syndic" derives from the Greek for "with justice," although Isidore does not give this etymology.

sentence to be handed down and present them in secret to the ordinary or appellate judge. Aristotle asserts that it was to be done this way so that they do not perjure themselves and turn aside from the truth out of fear of the citizens. The Tuscans follow this method today in their polity. They place beans or small coins in containers corresponding either to an affirmative or negative choice for proposed actions on behalf of the republic, or for condemning or absolving a citizen.

[5] Hippodamus also established pious laws that were consistent with natural right about certain kinds of persons in his polity. First, with regard to the wise, if one of them should ordain something that is expedient for the city or town, that one should receive honor according to the merit of the work, just as the Pharaoh honored Joseph, according to Genesis[188] and Ahasuerus honored Mordecai.[189] They honored them for the benefits that each had conferred, the former to the region, the latter to the ruler himself. Hippodamus ordered the same thing for the warriors, so that the offspring of any who died in war for the defense of the fatherland and the good of the city would receive food from the public stores. As the histories tell us, the Roman Republic above all made an effort to honor victorious knights, both in death and in life, but especially in their sons, for their memory is sufficiently perpetuated in the sons as likenesses of their fathers. It is true what is written in Ecclesiasticus: "For he is dead, and it is as if he is not dead, for he has left a likeness after himself," that is, in the benefit acquired through the father as cause.[190]

[6] Hippodamus also established that the whole people—warriors, artisans, and even farmers—should choose the ruler, for they were unwilling to choose a ruler through hereditary succession. For the most part, the cities of Italy follow this method.

[7] He also established that the ruler should take especial care for three things—the common goods, pilgrims, and orphans—calling all those who were without might and who could not procure their own rights "orphans." Divine law also especially orders this, because others can easily harm those who are impotent to resist.

---

188. Genesis 41.41–45. Pharaoh placed Joseph in command as vizier over all Egypt.

189. Esther 6.11. Ahasuerius clothed Mordecai with his own robe and had him publicly ride on his horse as a reward for foiling an assassination plot.

190. Ecclesiasticus (Sirach) 30.4. Ptolemy refers to the belief that the father is, in Aristotelian language, the formal cause of the child, while the mother is merely the material cause.

[8] These are the things that Aristotle tells us about this polity. Aristotle criticizes it for many things that, as human acts, can be disputed for and against, since they come from contingent matter; nevertheless, Hippodamus wrote many laudable things which concord with the Roman polity, as I will show below. This is enough about Hippodamus for the present.

Chapter 14

A criticism of the polity of the Spartans with regard to its government of servants and women and with regard to its warriors.

[1] Now I must go on to the other polities about which Aristotle reports, such as those of the Cretans and the Spartans,[191] which seem to be renowned because of the fame of their regions, their antiquity, and their founders.

[2] Aristotle commends the Spartan polity for many things; nevertheless, in the same passages he has much to say critical of it. First, he criticizes the Spartans for slackness with regard to their servants, who, treated as friends, not subjects, became wanton and puffed up and stirred up strife among the Spartans' neighbors against the tyrants, so that it would be suitable to say of them what is said in Proverbs: "One who nourishes servants delicately from childhood, in the end will find them to be obstinate."[192] In the same place it also says: "Servants can not be corrected by words, because they understand what you say but disdain to answer."[193]

[3] Perhaps this is not without reason in times when there is a threat of fights with enemies, because when servants are emancipated they are bolder in attacking. In 3 Kings it is written that by God's mandate King Ahab smote Syria and put it to flight using the footmen of the city.[194] It was for this reason, the Roman histories tell us, that after their conflict at Cannae, so great was the slaughter that they were compelled to recall those who had been banished and outlawed, give the servants their freedom, and use them to form a battle line for the defense of the City.[195] Therefore, since the Spartans had unsafe borders, they treated their servants rather gently. For the Spartans bordered,

191. Aristotle, *Politics*, 2.9–12.1269a.29–1274b.30.
192. Proverbs 29.21.
193. Proverbs 29.19.
194. 3 Kings (1 Kings) 20.13–20.
195. Hannibal delivered a devastating defeat to the Romans at Cannae in 216 B.C.E. Livy, *History of Rome*, 22.57 reports that the Romans were forced, among other things, to free 8000 slaves to fight.

as Aristotle himself says, on two regions, namely Arcadia and Messinia (there was a similar situation in Thessalonica), and there was a threat from another part of Achaea from the Thebians, who were quite virile in antiquity.[196]

[4] Therefore, for the reason mentioned above, the Spartans are reprehensible if they treat those whom they call servants as compatriots and do not bridle their stupidity. But this can be tolerated if their borders were exceedingly unsafe, as I said above, because the servants are made bold to attack and bridle the evil of the enemies.

[5] For the same reason they gave liberty to women, who, as a result, became wanton. In this matter, Aristotle criticized them for not restricting their women from running about, because this is a snare of lust to a woman. This happened to Dinah, the daughter of Jacob, according to Genesis, who was raped by Shechem, the son of King Hamor, because she was going about through the region without being watched.[197] As we read in Ecclesiasticus: "Set a strict watch on a daughter who does not herself turn away, to prevent her from abusing herself when she finds the occasion."[198] So also with the Spartans, they lived voluptuously as a result of excessive liberty. But Aristotle excused them since the Spartans were constantly involved with the exercise of wars, so that their wives were compelled to go about for the governance of their household. If compulsion had not existed, but men had put up with this situation, the polity would have been bad.

[6] The third thing about the Spartans that Aristotle disputes is whether the knights ought to have wives or be otherwise linked with women, which distracts them from fighting. The act of carnal pleasure softens the spirit and makes it less virile, as I said above,[199] and it is Plato's opinion, as Theophrastus reports, that it is not expedient for those who attend to military things to marry.[200] Aristotle disagrees with that argument on the grounds that warriors are naturally prone to be lascivious. A certain book, *On Problems*, which the Emperor Frederick translated from the Greek into Latin,[201] explains the rea-

---

196. "Thessalonica" is a mistake; it should be "Thessaly." This is somewhat muddled, but Aristotle says that all the neighbors of the Spartans were enemies, including the Messianians and Arcadians, and that the same situation existed in Thessaly (2.9.1269b.2–7). Later, he adds that Spartan women were useless during the Theban invasion (2.9.1269b.36–40).

197. Genesis 34.1–2.

198. Ecclesiasticus (Sirach) 26.13.

199. 4.5.9.

200. Theophrastus (d.c.287 B.C.E.) was a disciple of Aristotle and the next head of the Peripatetic school; he was especially noted for his biological writings.

201. A reference to the pseudo-Aristotelian *Problems*, dedicated to Frederick II by its first Latin translator. Although not authentically by Aristotle, it is believed to incorporate some of

son for this, and in the passage that I just cited Aristotle mentions one of the poet Hesiod's fables, which joined Mars to Venus.[202] If they were to abstain from women, they would approach males sexually, and for this reason Aristotle disagrees with Plato's opinion, since it is less evil to have carnal relations with women than to fall into vile and shameful acts. Thus, Augustine says that a whore acts in the world as the bilge in a ship or the sewer in a palace: "Remove the sewer, and you will fill the palace with a stench." Similarly, concerning the bilge, he says: "Take away whores from the world, and you will fill it with sodomy."[203] For this reason Augustine says that the earthly city made the use of harlots a licit foulness.[204] Aristotle himself says that the vice of sodomy exists because of depraved nature and perverse usage,[205] and with respect to such things one should not even speak in terms of continence or incontinence since they are not in themselves things delectable to human nature, so that one cannot refer to moderate virtue in this case. This agrees with Paul, who in the book of Romans calls such acts "passions of ignominy."[206]

[7] The fourth thing that Aristotle criticizes in the Spartans' polity has to do with their unequal division of possessions, because one citizen took possession of almost the whole region through a pecuniary transaction, as often happens with money lenders. Other citizens are plundered and flee, and in this way the polity remains destitute.

[8] There is a similar problem with wives, who by reason of their doweries take possession of two parts of their dead husbands' goods, as happens in France with half of the goods, with the residual amount being distributed to heirs and fulfilling other bequests. However much the Spartans tolerate the diminution of possessions for other citizens, they should not put up with it for the warriors, because it is through them that the city is preserved in its virtue. Aristotle says that this had happened to the Lacedaemonians, that is to the Spartans,[207] who as a result were reduced to nothing, when they were

---

the material from a lost book Aristotle wrote with the same title. *Problems* 4.7 asks the question why men who continually ride are more inclined to sexual intercourse, but does not specifically mention warriors. The answer ascribes this to the effects of heat and motion stimulating the genitals and motion causing the body to develop large pores, which are conducive to sexual desire. In ancient Greece, soldiers were not generally cavalry, but the medieval knights were.

    202. Aristotle, *Politics*, 2.9.1269b.28–29. Hesiod was an eighth-century B.C.E. poet, whose *Theogony* tells of the origins of the world and the gods.

    203. Augustine, *On Order*, 2.4.12, writes about the necessity of prostitutes to avoid worse behaviour, but he does not use these words.

    204. Augustine, *The City of God*, 14.18. Ptolemy locates it in Book 13.

    205. Aristotle, *Ethics*, 7.5.1148b.28–30.

    206. Romans 1.26.

    207. I have actually reversed things. Aristotle generally refers to the people under discussion as "Lacadaemonians," which it makes sense to translate in the more familiar form as "Spar-

still accustomed to having ten thousand warriors, which was not a moderate number among the ancients. These are those Spartans treated in 1 Maccabees, who, because of their virile spirits, had a special friendship with the Jews and the Romans.[208]

Chapter 15

Further criticism of the Spartan polity with regard to laws about children and with regard to judges, the question of whether paupers should be elevated to the government of the polity.

[1] There is also another thing that Aristotle criticizes in this polity, in the matter of generating children. In order to stimulate the citizens to be zealous in producing many offspring, they established in their polity that anyone who had three sons would be elevated to a dignified position in public affairs and anyone who had four would be free from taxes.[209] The effect was to impoverish the citizens, from which they lost the might to resist invading enemies, and it was also a cause of dissension among them, through which the region's virtue diminished. Their policy is repugnant to reason, because one who produces many children does not thereby show a virtue that merits preeminence: fighting for the republic, which shows fortitude, counseling the city, which involves prudence, governing the citizens, which involves justice, or having honorable intercourse with the citizens, which involves temperance. Why should someone deserve a reward in a republic for producing a child, which has nothing to do with virtue, since even a vile person can have a strong generative force? What is honored in this policy is not worthy of it, because there should be no honor given other than for virtue, as Aristotle says.[210]

[2] Therefore, with the exceptions already mentioned, a polity ought to give equal consideration to burden and honor among its citizens in all its acts, so that it would be true what David said in 1 Kings, when the spoils of Ziklag had been recovered from the Amalekites: "There will be an equal portion for those going to war and those remaining with the baggage."[211] Although the Mosaic law may curse the barren, as is spelled out in Exodus[212] and Deu-

---

tans." Here, however, Aristotle uses "Spartans" and feels called on to explain that he means the "Lacadaemonians."

208. 1 Machabees (Maccabees) 12.2–21, 14.16–23, 15.23.
209. Aristotle, *Politics*, 2.9.1270b.1–4.
210. Aristotle, *Ethics*, 4.3.1123b.34–35.
211. 1 Kings (1 Samuel) 30.24.
212. Exodus 23.26.

teronomy,²¹³ and although many wives may have been allowed in order to increase the population, this was conceded only out of regard for virtue, so as to increase the divine cult, as Augustine tells us.²¹⁴

[3] Another thing that Aristotle criticizes about the Spartans, which corrupted their polity, has to do with the election of judges. They chose paupers who, compelled by need, were corrupted by money from the great, and through this justice is overthrown and tyrannies arise.²¹⁵ Therefore, in comparison Aristotle commends democracy more than that polity, because, if the city lacks virtuous persons for the government, from whom the rule called "aristocracy" is constituted, rich and evil ones rule it better, from whom is constituted the rule called "democracy."²¹⁶ Therefore it is not expedient for the polity to elevate paupers and the greedy to the judiciary. The histories relate that the Roman consuls chose two men to exercise governance over Spain, of whom one was exceedingly poor and the other exceedingly avaricious. When an accusation had been made in the Capitol against them, because they were quarreling, Scipio Africanus did not consult to find out about either one; instead, he identified both as corruptors of the polity or of any government, because their position in the city was just like that of leeches on the human body. This is why it is written in Proverbs: "There are two daughters of the leech, saying: 'Bring, bring,'"²¹⁷ as if their principal intention were to extort money.

[4] But what will we say about the consul Fabricius who was very poor, as Valerius Maximus wrote?²¹⁸ Or about Lucius Valerius, who, as I said above, died in extreme poverty?²¹⁹

[5] To answer this I must distinguish between two kinds of indigence: voluntary and necessary.²²⁰ Christ and his disciples had voluntary indigence, and

---

213. Deuteronomy 7.14.
214. Augustine, *The City of God*, 16.38.
215. Aristotle, *Politics*, 2.9.1270b.6–34.
216. Something is clearly wrong here, and it is likely the text is corrupt. The rule of rich and evil rulers is normally called "oligarchy," and the rule of the common people, including paupers, "democracy."
217. Proverbs 30.15.
218. Valerius Maximus, *Memorable Deeds and Sayings*, 4.36.
219. Valerius Maximus, *Memorable Deeds and Sayings*, 4.4.1. The text refers to Valerius Publicola. For both Lucius and Fabricius, see above 2.8.3, 3.14.4 and also 3.4.5, 3.20.1.
220. Such a distinction was always necessary in the Middle Ages since all monks took a vow of individual poverty, and yet most of the clergy and nobility usually showed contempt for the truly poor. It was even more necessary at this time because of the controversy over Apostolic

so did Fabricius, as well as the other Roman consuls who showed contempt for riches so as faithfully to exercise governance over the Republic. Fabricius preferred to command riches than to become rich, as was said above about him.[221] Therefore those who are voluntarily indigent should not be driven out of government, but only those who are indigent by necessity, because such ones hardly ever govern or counsel well unless they are given enough to satisfy their appetites.

[6] The reason for and difference of the two kinds of poverty can be derived from their different ends. The end of voluntary poverty is an honorable good or the good of virtue, but the end of necessary want is a useful good to which the appetite is prone; this is an end for the sake of which something is done, as Aristotle says. Whatever those who have such indigence do, they do to the end of filling their stomachs and their purses, but those who are voluntarily indigent ordain all things to virtue, since they are contemptuous of riches. Therefore, when they exercise governance or govern citizens they always attend to the good of virtue in them, which is human good, as Aristotle also says.[222]

[7] Further, nature does nothing in vain, as Aristotle says.[223] But the appetite of one whose lack of riches comes from necessity, not from will, always tends to having riches. If this does not happen, the appetite will be in vain, and therefore nature impels it to this, just as a vacuum flees that which it cannot sustain. Therefore, it is difficult for such a one to avoid striving in every way to have riches. For this reason it is dangerous for the polity or the republic to elevate a pauper to the consulate or the judiciary, as Aristotle says, except when one is content with poverty, because then cupidity, which "is the root of all evils,"[224] as Paul wrote, is cut off. Just such an indigent one is best for the government of the polity, which is why it is said in Ecclesiastes that "there was found a poor and wise one who liberated the city through wisdom,"[225] since that one was not impeded by cupidity.

---

poverty in the Franciscan Order, whose members vowed both individual and collective poverty. As explained in the introduction, in the 1320s John XXII declared this very idea to be heretical.

221. 3.4.5, 3.14.4.
222. Aristotle, *Ethics*, 1.2.1094b.5–7.
223. Aristotle, *On the Heavens*, 1.4.271a.33.
224. 1 Timothy 6.10.
225. Ecclesiastes 9.15.

Chapter 16

*A criticism of the Spartan polity with regard to their king, and
the inconveniences that follow from this.*

[1] Now I must consider the government of the Spartans. The histories, such
as that of Justin the Spaniard, a great writer of deeds, maintain that this city
had a king, but Aristotle affirms that a king is suited for a region or province,
as happened in Rome.[226] We see that many parts of western and northern
Europe, namely Spain, Gaul, and Germany, have a king, but that each individual city has its own laws and polity. So, the Lacedaemonians, who are
called Spartiates or Spartans,[227] had a king, and among them Charillus reigned,
whom Lycurgus, as Justin tells us, tutored in his student days, as I will make
clear when I write about the Cretans' polity.[228]

[2] Aristotle proceeded to criticize the government of the king of the Spartiates or Lacedaemonians in many respects. First, in the provisions they made
for the king, because they did not allow for his government to be perpetual,
or even for life, since they wanted to preserve the mode of political rectors.
As a precedent this does not seem to be a moderate kind of government, since
in it the kings' power was enervated and subjects were given the opportunity
to recoil from obeying the laws; thus, their kings could not make them into
perfect and virtuous men. For this reason, as the histories tell us, although
Aristotle does not mention it, the Spartans were an untamable nation, except
when Lycurgus regulated Sparta with the perfection of his morality and his
splendid laws, which I speak about below.[229] As Aristotle says, it was unbe-
fitting that the city sent as legates to a city, province, or region some who
fought for the king and others who were his enemies, because their dissension
would become known, with the result that they would be less esteemed and
would rarely be able to fulfill their delegation's intention.

---

226. M. Junianus Justinus, *Philippian Histories of T. Pompeius Trogus*, 3.2. Aristotle, *Politics*,
2.9.1271a.18–21. Presumably Ptolemy's reference to Rome is to the rise of monarchical emperors
and the end of the Republic after Roman expansion. Aristotle says a king should be chosen because of his life, but Ptolemy and others always say "region."
227. Here I have kept Ptolemy's terms for Spartans.
228. M. Junianus Justinus, *Philippian Histories of T. Pompeius Trogus*, 3.2. Aristotle mentions Lycurgus's guardianship of King Charillus at 2.10.1271a.25, when he is discussing the Cretan polity since he says that Lycurgus then went abroad and lived in Crete, and that this explains
the similarity of the governments. For Crete, see below 4.18.
229. 4.18.5.
230. 2.8.1, 3.6.6, 3.20.3, 3.21.4, 4.7.4.

[3] You should notice that although the consuls in Rome were annual, as I said above [230] (and there explained the reason for this), as was the magistracy in Athens, this should not be the case with a king. On the contrary, if he is not for life there is an exceedingly great danger to the citizens. As I said above, the difference between kings and political rectors is that political rectors judge the people of the city by the laws alone, but regal rulers judge beyond both the laws that came down to them and those which they themselves have established previously.[231] They use laws that fit the times, and these they carry in their hearts for the well-being of their people and for better results in their government.[232]

[4] If such rulers should govern only for a time, they would be precipitous in making judgments either against citizens who they were concerned were going to judge them, or to gain the possession of something out of cupidity, or to show favor to their friends, none of which they would be so ready to do if they reigned permanently. With regard to the first there is the example of the one who said in Luke, in explaining the literal meaning: "Bring those enemies who are unwilling for me to reign over them here and kill them in my presence."[233] The histories tell us that Herod killed many of the nobles of the Jews in this same way, because they attempted to take the kingdom away from him. With regard to the second, I can cite an example from the same Gospel of the iniquitous overseer, which can be extended to every grade of government, because overseers stand in the place of earthly lords, just as rulers of the globe do with respect to God. Since he feared to be removed from the office of his lordship in the public treasury, he acted to gain friends.[234] From all these things it is manifest that there is the greatest danger in conferring the decision of governing in matters of making justice to temporary rectors. But if lordship is for life, rectors will care for their subjects as if they were attending to their own affairs, for which they are daily and continually solicitous, they will be as solicitous as for their own natural riches and for an unfailing treasury. On that account they govern them as shepherds their flocks and gardeners their plants, who treat any harm to them as a cause of offense.

231. 2.8.1, 2.8.6, 3.21.7, 4.1.3.
232. Based on *The Body of Civil Law: Codex* 6.23.19.1.
233. Luke 19.27. This is the conclusion of the parable of the talents in Luke, which awkwardly incorporates another parable about a lord going to a distant country to obtain a kingship.
234. Luke 16.1–8.

Chapter 17

Certain reprehensible things in the Spartan polity that arose from
the same cause, namely that matter for dissention existed among
the people.

[1] Perhaps the practice of lords in the Spartans' polity comes from this same
reason. These rulers did not care for the republic, so they made exactions
against the people for their festivals and for the rulers' public displays, which
stirred up the oppressed paupers to sedition and enervated the polity. Aristotle, as he had in the matter of the public treasury,[235] more highly commends
the custom or constituted law that he says prevailed in Crete, since the multi-
plication of exactions or taxes among the people, other than for an urgent
cause or for the preservation of the city or region, stirs it up and is a cause of
dissension and quarrel.

[2] Another unsuitable consequence came about for this same reason: there
was a separate naval ruler, which resulted in a division of spirits and dissention in the polity. This would not have happened if the ruler had been for
life, because any other leader of the city would then have been subject to that
ruler. Aristotle mentions naval warfare because the Spartans often exercised
lordship on the sea. He concludes that this people's polity was evil since it did
not elevate brave military men, those having the virtue of fortitude, one of
the four principal virtues.[236] It is through this that citizens expose themselves
to death on behalf of the republic, as Regulus did among the Carthaginians,[237]
but the Spartan knights or rulers only had one part of this virtue, and this is
why Aristotle inveighs against them.

[3] Aristotle distinguishes two kinds of fortitude.[238] One kind, which he calls
"military fortitude," rests on bodily strength alone. Aristotle calls this a part
of virtue or fortitude, since it is sometimes required for true fortitude. The
other is that which shows itself on behalf of the public good and does not
yield or flee when dangers arise. About this Seneca writes in his book *On the*
Providence of God: "Fortune seeks the bravest ones equal to itself."[239] Through
this Mucius experienced fire, Fabricius poverty, Rutilius exile, Regulus tor-

---

235. Aristotle, *Politics*, 2.9.1271b.11–16.
236. The four classical and medieval "cardinal virtues" are prudence, justice, temperance,
and fortitude.
237. Valerius Maximus, *Memorable Deeds and Sayings*, 1.1.14. See above 3.4.5, 3.16.1.
238. Aristotle, *Ethics*, 3.8.1116a.18–b.22.
239. Seneca, *On the Providence of God*, 4.4.

ments, Socrates poison, and Cato death.[240] It is about this that Mattathias speaks in 1 Maccabees in regard to his son: "Let Judas, who is brave and has shown strength from his youth, be your ruler, and he will conduct the wars of his people."[241] Through this virtue and for the sake of the republic, he did not yield to the enemies but died for its sake, dissolute in heart after being overwhelmed in the slaughter.

[4] The first kind of fortitude is an imperfect virtue, but the second is a most perfect one. Therefore, it is not characteristic of a good polity to elevate a ruler or any knight to make war who is not brave according to the second kind of fortitude, because often such ones become tyrants or yield to dangers, as I said above. For the same reason, that is, because the ruler was not perpetual or for life, it happened that the common expenses for warriors in the Spartan polity were not provided. Since pay, which the republic could not provide, was lacking, it followed that experienced knights did not wage the people's wars. Idiots rather, that is, the unexperienced, namely plebs and lovers of money, were being sent to war. Aristotle criticizes this because such ones often were the ruin of the people.

[5] What I have said about the Spartan polity will suffice for now.

Chapter 18

The Cretan polity and its differences from the Spartan. The founders of this polity and Lycurgus's laws.

[1] In the same book Aristotle thoroughly treats the polity of the Cretans,[242] which he says was passed down from Lycurgus, brother of Polydecta, king of

---

240. C. Mucius Scaevola was captured after his attempt to assassinate the Etruscan king Porsena, who was besieging Rome in 509 B.C.E., and when threatened with being burned alive thrust his own right hand into the fire. Impressed with his courage Porsena spared his life. See Livy, *History of Rome*, 2.12. For Fabricius, see above 2.8.3, 3.4.5, 3.14.4, 4.15.5. Rutilius Rufus (c.150–afer 100 B.C.E.) was a consul, jurist, and general who was falsely accused of corruption by the equestrian order, after which he went into exile at Smyrna and wrote his memoirs. For Regulus, see above 3.4.5, 3.16.1, 4.17.3. Socrates (c.470–399 B.C.E.) killed himself by drinking poison hemlock after he had been condemned to death by an Athenian court for corrupting the youth and dishonoring the city's gods, although the court expected him to go into exile. Marcus Porcius Cato the Younger (95–46 B.C.E.) also committed suicide on word that his enemy Julius Caesar was victorious.

241. 1 Machabees (Maccabees) 2.66.

242. Aristotle, *Politics*, 2.10.1271b.20–1272b.22.

the Spartans, whose father was Charillus, as Justin reports,[243] and also passed down from Minos, king of this island.[244] Aristotle mentions these two, who were the first founders of laws in Greece. Pythagoras traveled to learn these laws and taught them to the inhabitants of Crotona, as Justin tells us.[245] Although various stories of Lycurgus have been told, I follow Justin's version for the most part, since he was the most famous writer of histories in antiquity. Perhaps this was the reason that the Spartans and the Cretans had the same polity. Aristotle says that the Spartans imitated the Cretans and took their laws from them.

[2] Although they agree in many ways, they differ with regard to common meals and festivities, for which the Cretans provided from the common treasury funded by the inhabitants from the fruits and cattle offered in sacrifices as tithes to the gods. Another difference has to do with women, since the Cretans were not as zealous for having many offspring as were the Spartans. A third difference has to do with agriculture, for the inhabitants, who made the oblations that I have just mentioned, cultivated the Cretan lands themselves, instead of using servants, as in the Spartan lands. A fourth difference occurred because the Cretans chose their consuls or wise ones, whom they called Kosmoi, that is, "distinguished old ones," not from among all but only from among the greater, and they chose more of them. In contrast, the Spartans chose the Ephors, that is, procurators of the republic, from among all, but they chose fewer of them. Aristotle commends this more, because it was less likely to incite the crowd.

[3] The reason for dissension among the Cretans is that they once had a king, as I mentioned above, but by the time of Aristotle they had only a leader chosen by the wise ones, and, since the people never had a choice, jealousy, and consequently hatred, were fomented. Although the Spartans only kept a king for so long as it pleased them, they chose him from the wise ones, who were elevated from all the ranks of citizens. It seems to be consonant with reason that they were elevated to the government of the people with the consent of all counsel, as today is common in Italian cities. The name "city" implies this,[246] which, according to Augustine, is, "a multitude of human beings bound together by some chain of society,"[247] so that a city is, as it were, a

---

243. M. Junianus Justinus, *Philippian Histories of T. Pompeius Trogus*, 3.2.
244. Minos was a legendary king and lawgiver of Crete and founder of the Cretan Empire. He was the son of Zeus and Europa; his wife gave birth to the Minotaur.
245. M. Junianus Justinus, *Philippian Histories of T. Pompeius Trogus*, 20.4.
246. "*Civitas*," "city," comes from "*cives*," "citizen."
247. Augustine, *The City of God*, 15.8.

unity of citizens. Therefore, since the name "city" includes all citizens, it indeed seems reasonable that it ought to search for its government from the separate kinds of citizens, since the merits of individuals are necessary for the state of civil government. For this reason, the Spartan polity seems to be better in this regard than that of the Cretans.

[4] So, although these two regions agree in many things, as Aristotle tells us, they differ in others in the ways described above. This will be enough about the Cretan polity according to Aristotle's opinion.

[5] But since he mentions Lycurgus, I think it is fitting here to insert what the histories say about his laws. Justin, whom I cited already,[248] tells us that he wrote those canons for the Spartans and for the Cretans, and that he bound the Spartans by an oath to observe them until he returned from the pilgrimage that he pretended to be making to the temple of Apollo to consult about their well-being. Then, this legislator traveled to Crete, and there, after he had imparted his laws to them and was dying, ordered that his bones be thrown into the sea so that he might make the laws,[249] which he had been the first to implement, eternal. Justin gives a summary of the laws that he imparted:

> He stabilized gold and silver. He allowed the people the power to bring the senate together and to create those magistrates that it wanted. He divided the farms of all equally among everyone, so that, since inheritances were equalized, no one would be more mighty than another. He decreed that all should eat together publicly, lest they have riches or luxury in secret. He allowed youths to dress in not more than one set of clothes for the whole year, and said that no one should go out dressed more elegantly than another or feast more opulently. He decreed that items should not be bought with money, but that compensation be made with goods. He mandated that pubescent boys should not be taken into the forum but into the field, so that they might not conduct their early years in luxury, but rather in work and labor. He decreed that they should not use a support during sleep,[250] that they should live without sauces, and that they should not return to the city before they become men. He wanted virgins to marry without a dowry, so that wives should not be chosen for monetary reasons and that men should not restrict their wed-

---

248. 4.18.1.
249. *Iuribus.*
250. Justin has "*substernere*," "cover" instead of "*sustinere*," "support," which suggests no blanket instead of no mattress.

dings so severely, since they would not be reined in by the dowry. He established that the greatest honor should be not of riches nor of might but of old age, and he established that no place in their land should be more honored than an aged person.[251]

These are the laws of Lycurgus's polity that Aristotle does not mention. Disputing these would require a long discussion, so I will omit it for the time being, but these laws do not contradict the things that Aristotle said about him.

Chapter 19

The fame of the Chalcedonian polity and how it is similar to and differs from the polities of the Spartans and Cretans.

[1] Now I must take up the polity of the Chalcedonians, which Aristotle commends greatly,[252] saying that the three polities of the Spartans, Cretans, and Chalcedonians were the most famous among the Greeks, because, more than others, they were ordained according to virtue. Chalcedon is the city in Thrace where the Fourth Church Council of 630 bishops under Leo I was celebrated, in the presence of the ruler Marcian.[253] It could not have taken place there if the region had not had such abundance as to have been able to provide for this great multitude of prelates. Aristotle prefers this polity to the others, although he lived much closer to the other two, and he gives three signs of its perfection and goodness. One is that the officials of this polity lived ordinately and pursued their offices calmly and with stabile morality. The second is that there seemed to be sufficient concord among them in the ministry of the republic, and there was never a sedition worth mentioning, either in writing or in any other way. Aristotle takes the third argument for its goodness from its calm lordship; for no lord, noble, or any mighty one ever arose among them to exercise tyranny.

[2] Aristotle describes the similarities between the Spartans and the Chalcedonians, but the Chalcedonian way was more excellent. First, both paid

---

251. M. Junianus Justinus, *Philippian Histories of T. Pompeius Trogus*, 3.2–3.

252. Aristotle, *Politics*, 2.11.1172b.24–1273b.26. Aristotle writes here about Carthage in north Africa, not Chalcedon or Calcedonia in Thrace. The mistake was William of Moerbeke's, and most medieval writers followed him in this.

253. See above 3.17.7.

for the common meals and feasts made to designate honorable personages through contributions, but the Chalcedonians did it in a more honorable way, without oppressing the paupers. The second thing in which they agreed was the election of elders and the king, but they differed in that the Spartans elevated those few elders whom they called Ephors from the people, and to them alone pertained the election of the king. In contrast, the Chalcedonians chose many elders but from those who were better. There were 104 of them in Chalcedonia, and Aristotle calls them "rulers," on account of the virtue of their government in which no one rules better. Aristotle also calls them "Gerousia," that is "honored ones," and their office was both to choose and assist the king.

[3] Likewise, they differed from the Spartans in that they did not choose from every stock nor from those who lacked distinction, but only from those with qualities that were more desirable according to virtue. Aristotle gives as a reason for this that when ones from a vile place are elevated to rule they frequently injure the polity and sometimes injured Chalcedon. According to the poet: "Nothing is more harsh than a humble one who has risen to the heights."[254] So also it is written in Ecclesiastes, as if this should be a great detriment to a government: "There is some evil that I have seen under the sun and as it were through an error coming forth from the face of the ruler: a fool placed in a lofty dignity, and the rich sitting beneath. I saw servants on horses, and rulers walking on the earth as if they were servants."[255]

[4] Likewise, the Chalcedonians did not always choose from the same stock, because nature often fails in the succession of offspring; rather, they elevated those that were better, wherever they could find them, either as ruler or to the Gerousia, that is, honored elders. In this they imitated an aristocratic polity, which is rule by a few virtuous ones. This certainly was true among the Chalcedonians because the king together with some honored and virtuous ones treated those matters necessary for the city, and in so doing they sought the consent of the people, as was written about the Romans in 1 Maccabees—that they took council of the 320 "concerning the multitude so that they might do worthy things."[256] Although the king could act together with the honored ones, at times and for certain matters he required the people, and

---

254. Claudianus, *On Eutropius*, 1.5.181. Claudius Claudianus (c.370–c.404) was the last important classical Latin poet. *On Eutropius* is a diatribe against one of the Emperor Arcadius's ministers.

255. Ecclesiastes 10.5–7.

256. 1 Machabees (Maccabees) 8.15.

it was licit for the people to consent or not, so that nothing would happen unless the people accepted the proposal. In these cases the state of the polity was reduced to democratic rule because these things were done in favor of the plebeian nation. Sometimes something was committed to the few, and then it could be called oligarchic rule, for five, whom Aristotle calls Penta-contarchs, were chosen from the wealthy, and it pertained to them to elevate those 104 honored ones called the Gerousia. This is characteristic of the Chalcedonian polity, and today the cities of Italy and especially of Tuscany observe this mode.

[5] This procedure was also observed in Rome for the whole time that the consulate lasted. First the two consuls were created, then, as the histories tell us, the Dictator and the Master of Equites,[257] to whom belonged the whole civil government, and so Rome was governed by an aristocratic rule. Later, tribunes were set up to favor the plebeians and the people, so that the consuls and the others I mentioned could not exercise government without them, and in this way democratic rule was appended. In the course of time the senators took over the power of governing. Romulus first established the senators when he divided the whole city into three parts: senators, knights, and plebeians. Then, when there were kings in Rome, the senators held the place of the elders called Ephors in Sparta, Kosmoi in Crete, or Gerousia in Chalcedon, as I made clear above. And because the senators were principally from the multitude, the rule of the Romans was called political. But when the polity was corrupted through the might of some, in the time when the civil wars arose, it was governed by an oligarchic rule.

[6] I have mentioned these things to show that the government of the Greeks in the time of Aristotle was quite similar to our own.

Chapter 20

Aristotle tells us more about election in the Chalcedonian polity—whether they should choose a wealthy person or a pauper, how a pauper should be kept virtuous, and whether one ruler should have many lordships.

[1] One thing that Aristotle tells us about the Chalcedonian polity with regard to election is that they choose not by art or by chance but instead choose

257. The order of knights, who in Rome ranked between the patricians and the plebeians.

only the virtuous, since if they chose by lot paupers would sometimes be chosen. Their rule would be dangerous, because, as he says, and as I showed above,[258] it is impossible for the needy to rule well and to apply themselves legitimately to public affairs. Driven by necessity, they gape at wealth and recoil from virtue, nor can they have the leisure for themselves so that their spirits might rest, or so that, as Sallust says of the ancient Romans: "their spirits might be free in counseling."[259] Another thing that Aristotle tells us was also established in the Chalcedonian polity is that if they did find virtuous paupers, the republic provided them with their necessities to remove the occasion for immersion in illicit wealth.

[2] So it is that every government institutes pay, either from the public treasury (as Augustine says in *On the Words of the Lord*,[260] to prevent those who are seeking to provide for their expenses from becoming thieves), or from any kind of goods that the government establishes for this, such as tributes and taxes owed to a lord by natural right. Paul proves this in Romans: "Therefore, you are responsible for tributes, for they are ministers of God, serving him in this,"[261] and likewise in 1 Corinthians: "Who ever performs military service yet provides their own pay? Who feeds a flock and does not eat from its milk?"[262]

[3] Then a question comes up, which Aristotle touches on in discussing this polity: should the rich always be chosen to rule? In any mode this would give the material for persons to be lovers of money, since human nature is always desirous of honor, as Valerius Maximus writes.[263] Aristotle has a lot to say about this, comparing oligarchy to aristocracy, since in the first rule the rich are chosen, but in the second the virtuous are always elevated. Therefore, in a true polity those who live according to virtue are elevated, whether they are paupers or rich. But there is less danger with the rich, since they have the instruments of human life necessary to pursue their office honorably and preserve justice for their subjects.

[4] Aristotle wrote many other things about the Chalcedonian polity, comparing the various rules to each other, and he comes to two conclusions criti-

---

258. 4.15.3, 5.

259. Sallust, *The War with Cataline*, 52.21.

260. *On the Words of the Lord* is a name earlier collections of Augustine's letters gave to some of the Epistles on the New Testament (now Sermons 51–147A).

261. Romans 13.6.

262. 1 Corinthians 9.7.

263. Valerius Maximus, *Memorable Deeds and Sayings*, 8.14. Valerius does not use the word "nature," but it is implied in 8.15: "There is no humility so great that it is not touched by a desire for glory."

cal of them. One is that they allow a single ruler to have many rules, which Aristotle criticizes by showing that it is much better or more worthy for there to be many rulers or that many should come together for one rule than that one ruler should have many rules.[264] Aristotle gives as his reason that in diverse rules one person's act impedes another's, from which derives the principle central to this argument that one person can best complete one work.

[5] He gives two examples of this. One has to do with pipers (or cithara players) and tanners, since these occupations are contrary with regard to their work and instruments. A pipe or a cithara requires a person who understands melodies and has agile and subtle hands, but for tanning none of these are required, because even a rustic person with gnarled hands suffices. So also diverse lords are mutually contrary, just as a piper and a tanner. He gives another example of naval and field wars. It is unsuitable for there to be one rector for both, since the actions are not similar, for there is one mode of fighting on a field and another in the water, and field and naval wars require different instruments, and, consequently, different actions. The conclusions are that it is not suitable for one lord to have many lordships, and that it would be difficult to guide them both well, because of their contrary actions and instruments.

[6] This would also weaken virtue, since individual persons scarcely suffice for their own personal government. It is harsh that those who do not know how to hold the rudder of their own life should be judges of another's, as Gregory says.[265] So, for the reasons cited, how much more difficult would it be for one person to control many governments?

Chapter 21

Pythagoras's polity, which he based on the teachings of the philosophers Minos and Lycurgus, and how he devoted all his efforts to accustoming human beings to virtue.

[1] There is one more philosopher's polity that Aristotle does not mention in his *Politics*, namely that of Pythagoras, who lived two centuries earlier,[266] and from whom the name "philosophy" derived, as Valerius Maximus writes.[267]

264. Aristotle, *Politics*, 2.11.1173b.7–16.
265. Ptolemy gives this same quote without attribution at 2.15.5.
266. Ptolemy actually says that Pythagoras (who lived in the sixth century B.C.E. preceded Aristotle (fourth century) by "two human ages."
267. Valerius Maximus, *Memorable Deeds and Sayings*, 8.7, ext. 2.

He did not dare to call himself wise nor count himself in the number of the Seven Wise Ones who had preceded him, but he called himself a philosopher, that is, a lover of wisdom.[268] As Justin the Spaniard tells us, after Pythagoras had travelled throughout Egypt to learn about the motion of the stars and the origin of the world, he came back to Crete and then proceeded to Sparta to investigate the laws of Minos and Lycurgus that I discussed above,[269] and he based his polity on these. Beyond the laws that I have already mentioned, Justin writes about him that, coming to Crotona:[270]

> By his authority he recalled to the practice of frugality the people who had fallen into indulgence; daily he praised virtue and restrained vices and enumerated the cities that had fallen to this pestilence. He was so successful in persuading the multitude to zeal for thoroughly learning frugality, that it seemed incredible that some of them had once been guilty of indulgence.

[2] Cicero tells us that he extinguished the vice of indulgence in persons with certain musical harmonies. He says that when Pythagoras heard that a certain youth from Tauromenium was burning with lust and raving at the door of the whore who was his lover, he decreed that a psaltery should play a spondee, and in this way he called him back to mental health.[271] Also he frequently used a different method for teaching matrons than he did for men, and for children than for parents, just as the fiery sermon of a preacher and the virtuous working and excellent life of a scholar differently effect religious conversion. At one time he taught the men propriety and zeal for letters, at another time he taught the matrons modesty, asserting that modesty was the true ornaments of matrons, so that they would put away their gold-trimmed clothes and the other ornaments of their dignity as so many instruments of indulgence and take them all away to the temple of Juno to consecrate them to that goddess. After he had lived in Crotona for twenty years, he moved to Metapontum and died there. He was so greatly admired that they made a temple of his home and worshiped him as a god. Jerome writes about him in *Against Jovinian* that he had a daughter of such great modesty that she pre-

268. Augustine, *The City of God*, 8.2. For the Seven Wise Men, see note at 1.10.6.
269. 4.18.
270. M. Junianus Justinus, *Philippian Histories of T. Pompeius Trogus*, 20.4.
271. I have not located the Cicero reference, but it is reported in Iamblicus, *Life of Pythagoras*, who says that he had originally been aroused by a Phrygian song, but Pythagoras got the musician to change to the slower spondaic rhythm.

served her own virginity, had precedence over a chorus of similar virgins, and instructed them in the doctrine of chastity.[272]

[3] All this makes it apparent that in his polity Pythagoras focused his whole intention and effort to drawing persons to live according to virtue. Aristotle also teaches this, and that every true polity is corrupted if it falls away from this end.[273]

Chapter 22

Pythagorean lessons handed down figuratively and as enigmas.
Two exceptionally faithful Pythagorean friends.

[1] Jerome also tells us that, according to the custom of the ancients, some of the Pythagorian laws for the preservation of his polity were handed down in the form of paradigms and parables. He says: "'Shun languor in all ways and cut it off from the spirit, indulgence from the belly, sedition from the city, discord from the home, and intemperance from everything in the commune.' These things also are part of the Pythagorian laws: 'All things should be common among friends, and one's friend should be as oneself.' They especially exert themselves in this."[274]

[2] Valerius Maximus tells the story of two Pythagoreans—two disciples of Pythagoras—Damon and Pythias, who were such great friends that, when the tyrant Dionysius sentenced one of them to death, and he had obtained a grace period before he died to profit his house and ordain his domestic affairs, the other one did not hesitate to give himself to the tyrant as surety on behalf of the first. When the determined day approached and the first had not returned, the second proclaimed to anyone who censured his stupidity for being such an imprudent sponsor that he had no fears for the constancy of his friend. At the exact moment of the very hour established by Dionysius, the one who had undertaken to return arrived. The tyrant admired their spirit and remitted the penalty, and, since he wanted to be a part of such faith, asked to be received into the society of their friendship.[275]

---

272. Jerome, *Against Jovinian*, 1.42.
273. Aristotle, *Politics*, 3.9.1280b.5–11. See also *Ethics*, 2.1.1103b.3–6.
274. Jerome, *Apology against the Books of Rufinus*, 3.39.
275. Valerius Maximus, *Memorable Deeds and Sayings*, 4.7, ext. 1. See above 1.11.3, 3.7.2. For Dionysius, see note at 1.11.3.

[3] Jerome also writes about other lessons or laws which Pythagoras handed down in his polity about "two times when it is especially necessary to take care to worship the Truth, that is, God, which alone brings persons near to God. These times are the morning and the evening, that is, the time when we are about to act and the time when we have done acting."[276] Jerome also reports in *On Ecclesiastes* that it was a Pythagorian teaching that students should be silent for five years, but then speak as learned men.[277] Other lessons and laws attributed to Pythagoras are handed down in the form of enigmas, which Jerome relates in *Against Jovinian*:

> "Do not jump over a statera, he says," that is, do not go beyond justice. "Do not warm a fire with a sword," that is, do not provoke an angry and excited spirit with slanderous words. "Do not seize the crown," that is, observe the laws of the cities. "Do not eat your heart," that is, expel sorrow from your spirit. "Do not walk on a public road," that is, do not follow the errors of the many. "Do not keep a swallow in your home," that is, do not admit garrulous and verbose people into your society.[278]

This philosopher hands down many other lessons similar to these and other laws for his polity that are more ordained to spiritual than bodily government, but corporal things are more easily disposed of when a polity is regulated by them.

[4] What I have said about the various polities will suffice for the present. Now, in the following chapters, I must take up the true political life, as related by Aristotle and other wise ones.

Chapter 23

What the perfect polity consists of, from which it receives political happiness, namely when the parts of the polity are well disposed and mutually interrelated.

[1] Since, when I consider a polity, I refer to a city, the mode of proceeding to discuss a polity depends on the quality of the city. A city, as Augustine says,

276. Jerome, *Apology Against the Books of Rufinus*, 3.39.
277. Jerome, *Commentary on Ecclesiastes*, on Ecclesiastes 3.7.
278. Actually, Jerome, *Apology Against the Books of Rufinus*, 3.39, but the quotation is quite close, suggesting that the "Jovinian" in the text was a slip of the pen either of Ptolemy or an early copyist.

"is a multitude of human beings bound together by some chain of society, which is rendered blessed through true virtue."[279] This definition does not clash with Aristotle's opinion, which places political felicity in the perfect government of the polity.[280] For the virtue by which a political rector exercises governance over a city is the architect of all other virtues of the city, because the other civil virtues are ordained to that virtue, just as the equestrian virtue and that of archers are ordained to the military virtue. Therefore, political felicity consists in its operation, since it is the supreme virtue, as Aristotle seems to imply in the passage just cited. The true and perfect polity is like the well-disposed body, in which the organic strengths have perfect vigor. If the supreme virtue, which is reason, directs other inferior potencies and they are moved by its command, then a certain pleasantness and perfect pleasure of strengths arises in both, and this we call harmony. Augustine says that a well-disposed republic or city can be compared to a voice in a melody, in which, with diverse, mutually proportionate sounds, a song becomes pleasant and delectable to the ears.[281]

[2] This was characteristic of the State of Innocence, which was regulated by the virtue of original justice beyond the act of divine cognition. This causes contemplative felicity, and it is in this way that perfect men want nothing except that which the regulation of reason mandates and what pleases God, according to a certain participatory virtue found in them. For this reason the philosopher Plutarch was motivated to compare the republic or polity to a natural and organic body, in which motions depend on the movement of one or two parts, such as the heart and brain, and yet every part of the body has a proper function corresponding to the first motions and assisting in the ministry of the others.[282] Hence, this body shows itself to be animated through the benefit of the divine gift, and this happens with the greatest equity through the rudder of reason with the approval of God. Paul confirms this in 1 Corinthians, when he shows that the whole Church is one body distinguished in parts but united by the chain of charity.[283] Therefore, in a true civility or polity

---

279. Augustine, *The City of God*, 15.8. The second clause is not in 15.8.
280. Aristotle, *Ethics*, 1.9.1099b.30f.
281. Augustine, *The City of God*, 2.21, quoting Scipio Africanus quoted in Cicero, *On the Republic*.
282. (Pseudo)-Plutarch, "The Instruction of Trajan," as reported in John of Salisbury, *Policraticus*, 5.2, 5.9, 6.20, and passim. John may have manufactured this source himself. In this schema the ruler represents the head and soul; the senate the heart; the judges and provincial governors the ears, eyes, and mouth; the officials and soldiers the hands; the ruler's assistants the flanks; treasurers and record keepers the stomach and intestines; and the peasants the feet.
283. 1 Corinthians 12, especially 12–14.

it is required that the members be conformed to the head and not mutually discordant and that all things be disposed in civility, as I just said.

[3] Moreover, if we consider causes and the things caused and moving things and the things moved, we see that there is a necessary mutual proportion among them with regard to their influence, since the inferior are moved according to the motion of the superior, and, since nature does not fail in necessities, the superior move only to the extent suitable for the inferior. Therefore, if this is the order of superior things with respect to the inferior, and visa versa, in any created nature at all, it ought much more to be true in intellectual nature, and to the degree that this is more perfect in beings. If such a disposition leads to a pleasantness in contemplation, it should be that much stronger in operation. For this reason, as Aristotle says,[284] the Pythagoreans were motivated to place melody among the celestial bodies on account of their ordained and unfailing motions, from which arises the greatest pleasantness. And because they said that those bodies are animate, they endowed them with felicity. Therefore, to live politically makes life perfect and happy.

[4] Besides, order is "the disposition of equal and unequal things giving to each its due," as Augustine says.[285] According to this definition there are various ranks in a polity, with respect to the execution of offices as well as to the subjection or obedience of the subjects, so that there is a perfect social congregation when all are properly disposed and operate properly in their own states. Just as a building is stable when its parts are well laid down, so also a polity has firmness and perpetuity when all, whether rectors, officials, or subjects, work properly in their own ranks, as the action of their condition requires. Because there is nothing repugnant there, there will be the greatest pleasantness and perpetual firmness of state, which is characteristic of political felicity, as Aristotle tells us.

[5] In Exodus, Moses' relative Jethro describes for us just such rectors of the city or polity as those, for the purpose of preserving the people in peace: "Provide from the plebeians mighty men who fear the Lord, in whom there is truth, and who hate avarice, and constitute from them tribunes and centurions and ones set over fifty and over ten who may judge the people at all times." Afterward he adds, "If you do this, you will fulfill the command of the Lord; you will be able to sustain his precepts, and all the people will re-

---

284. Aristotle, *On the Heavens*, 2.9.290b.12–24.
285. Augustine, *The City of God*, 19.13.

turn in peace to their own place,"[286] as if all things would exist in the certain mental pleasantness and temporal peace from which human felicity arises, if such ones as are ordained here were governors of the republic. The Roman rectors were such as these, Sallust says, for which reason the Republic went from small to great, because they manifested: "industry at home, just command abroad, a free spirit in counseling, and were addicted neither to lust nor transgressions."[287] In these phrases Sallust shows us the acts of a virtuous government, from which comes the perfect and happy polity.

Chapter 24

A threefold division of the polity and a follow up of each part. First, how the integral parts are distinguished in Socrates and Plato's opinion.

[1] Now I must take up the species or parts into which the civility or polity is divided, and it is necessary to look at these either with regard to the whole city to which the integral parts belong, or with regard to its government, or with regard to how it is ordained to the activities of war, because different historians and authors of laws assign various designations according to this division.

[2] With regard to the first mode of making the division, a good example is the polity of Socrates and Plato that I touched on above.[288] They put the whole polity together from five parts: rectors, counselors, warriors, artisans, and farmers. In another polity, Romulus, the first ruler of the city of Rome, as the histories report, divided the multitude of his people into three parts: namely, senators, knights, and plebeians.[289] Hippodamus also constituted his polity from three kinds of persons: namely, warriors, artisans, and farmers, as I mentioned above.[290] All of these are defensible and reasonable.

[3] The first, which comprises five kinds of persons, seems suitable enough. If we consider our need for spiritual strengths, from which comes the necessity of constituting the city, it is apparent that this division is sufficient. Human beings experience need with regard to their intellective part so that they can live according to virtue.[291] Because of this they were provided with a direc-

---

286. Exodus 18.21–23. The quote is not exact.
287. Sallust, *The War with Cataline*, 52.21. See above 2.8.3, 3.4.3, 3.20.5.
288. 4.4–4.7, 4.10.5.
289. See above 4.19.5.
290. 4.11.1.
291. See Aristotle, *Ethics*, 2.1.1103b.3–6, *Politics*, 3.9.1280b.5–11.

tion for doing things, to which is ordained the consultative virtue, which is placed by Aristotle among the intellectual virtues.[292] As is said in Ecclesiasticus: "Son, do nothing without counsel, and you will not repent after the deed."[293] Therefore, counselors are the best part of a republic or polity, which is why Plutarch compares them to the eye, which is a very noble part of the body.[294] We also need something to rein in the concupiscent or the affective when it is inordinate, as Aristotle himself tells us, calling those things sicknesses.[295] So, rectors are necessary for correcting the evils of human beings, on account of which Paul says: "they do not bear the sword without cause . . . they are avengers in wrath against those who act badly."[296] For this reason, rulers and rectors instituted laws, as Aristotle makes clear, and Paul says in Galatians: "Law was put in place on account of transgressors,"[297] and also: "law was not put in place for one who is just."[298]

[4] There are also other needs of human life, such as covering, ornament, and nourishment, corresponding to the other potencies of the spirit.[299] The first two fulfill the need of the sensitive part of a person, which is the artisans' duty, that is, to delight or supplement the senses of sight, hearing, smell, or touch, whether they do this through buildings, clothes, shoes, or any other artificial thing. Farmers are ordained to fulfill the need of human life for nourishment, which corresponds to the vegetative part, whether they do this with bread, wine, fruit, flocks, cattle, or birds, all of which farmers transport to the cities and sell.

[5] Warriors are also a suitable part of the polity, ordained against those who incite the other parts and to defend the other parts. Knights are constituted in the city that they might oppose enemies on behalf of their fatherland, and they are bound by oath when they ascend to the military rank not to refuse to die on behalf of the republic, as the *Policraticus* tells us when it treats the sacrament of becoming a knight.[300] Therefore, the warrior is necessary in a republic and is a distinguished part of the polity, because the duty of a warrior

---

292. Aristotle, *Ethics*, 6.9.1142a32–1142b34 lists deliberation as an intellectual virtue.
293. Ecclesiasticus (Sirach) 32.24.
294. (Pseudo)-Plutarch, "The Instruction of Trajan," as reported in John of Salisbury, *Policraticus*, 5.2, 5.9, 5.11. Actually John identifies the eyes, ears, and mouth with judges and provincial governors. Although he stresses counseling, he does not identify counselors per se with any specific bodily part. He discusses them, however in a chapter on the senate (5.9), which he identifies with the heart, and speaks of both in terms of the wisdom of old age.
295. Aristotle, *Ethics*, 7.1.1145a.32.
296. Romans 13.4.
297. Galatians 3.19.
298. 1 Timothy 1.9.
299. See above 1.1.3, 4.2.3–4.
300. John of Salisbury, *Policraticus*, 6.4.

is to assist the ruler on behalf of the pursuit of justice, as the *Policraticus* says, and also to fight faithfully and constantly against enemies for the preservation of the fatherland. The warrior is thus singularly fruitful not only to part of the polity but also to the whole of the military rank in the polity.

[6] From all these things it is completely clear that Socrates and Plato provided their polity with a sufficiency of parts.

Chapter 25

Hippodamus and Romulus also handed down a sufficiency of integral parts.

[1] Going back to the two other ways of dividing a polity, we can validate them using the division already made, since these other ways are comprehended by the first, whose sufficiency has already been shown.

[2] In Romulus's division, we take the senators to be political rectors, as are the wise ones appended to them, whether they are assessors or others learned in the law, for political rulers take more counsel than regal or imperial rulers. 1 Maccabees says about the Romans: "They took daily counsel concerning the multitude so that they might do those things that were worthy."[301] The reason for this is that political government alone is strengthened by laws, as I said above.[302] Although regal or imperial government may be guided by laws, it consists of the will of the ruler manifested in suitable cases about any matter at all, because what pleases the ruler is held to be law,[303] as the rights of such a government delineate. Therefore, we must conclude that it is especially necessary in political lordship to have counselors, whom we include under the name of senators. For this reason, Isidore says in his *Etymologies* that a senator is so-called from counseling and considering, since he is one who places himself in a position to counsel but not harm anyone.[304] For this reason also, Augustine counts the old among the senators.[305] We also include rectors under

301. 1 Machabees (Maccabees) 8.15. The quote is not exact.
302. 2.8.1, 2.8.6, 3.21.7, 4.1.3, 4.16.3.
303. *The Body of Civil Law: Institutes* 1.2.6; *Digest* 1.4.1.
304. Isidore of Seville, *Etymologies*, 9.4. That is, from "*sinendo*," "placing." Isidore also says that it is from "*seniores*," that is, "elder ones."
305. Augustine, *On the Heptateuch*, 3.25, on Leviticus 9.1, where he connects the word for senate with that for the old and also with the Greek Gerousia. See also John of Salisbury, *Policraticus*, 5.9.

the name of senator, as Isidore tells us, citing the words of Sallust: "The senators are called fathers because of their diligent care of the government."[306] Just as fathers guide their children, so those ones guide the Republic.

[3] Therefore, it is clear that rectors and counselors, whom Socrates and Plato listed distinctly in their polity, are included under the name of senators, whom Romulus distinguished from knights and plebeians. We can also include artisans and farmers under the name of plebeian, since both kinds come from the plebeian nation. So it seems that the division of the multitude of the city according to these philosophers is not in conflict with the division that Romulus made.

[4] Hippodamus's distinction, which I have already treated thoroughly,[307] seems doubtful, since it makes no mention of counselors and rectors, nor can we reduce them to the parts he assigned, since these parts perform different acts and have different natures. If we attend to the things we hear about that civility, the question is more easily solved. He treats judges and assessors and makes distinctions about them, and from this we can understand him to be talking about counselors and rectors, whom he does not directly mention as being parts of a polity, because he is primarily interested only in those parts which have to do with the needs of corporal life. So, his position does not differ substantially from the first position, namely that of Socrates and Plato.

[5] What I have now said about the parts of the polity, and what constitute it, will suffice.

[6] Still, it seems that I have to consider one of the parts now, namely the warriors, because all polities mention it. In *On the Military*, Vegetius gives as a reason that warriors preserve the vigor of all regions.[308] The Roman Republic was diminished when it fell out of the practice of making war after the First Punic War, when the Romans led a life of peace for twenty years, which "so enervated the Romans, who were victors everywhere, that in the Second Punic War they were not Hannibal's equals. They achieved victory only after the loss of many consuls, leaders, and armies, and only after they were able thoroughly

306. Isidore of Seville *Etymologies*, 9.4; Sallust, *The War with Cataline*, 51–52. Isidore actually says: "They are called 'Fathers,' as Sallust says, from the similarity of their responsibilities. For just as fathers nourish their children, so also they nourish the Republic."
    307. 4.11.1.
    308. Vegetius, *On the Military*, 1.28. Vegetius actually says that the passion for war has not grown weak in men, nor is the law which produced such men unproductive, and he lists the martial regions now under Rome.

to learn again military practice and exercise." Afterward he concludes: "Therefore they are always engaged in gathering and exercising their youths, for it is more useful to educate them in arms than to hire foreigners for a wage.[309]

[7] Therefore, warriors are necessary at all times in a republic, both to preserve the citizens' peace and to avoid the enemies' incursions. In consideration of their profit to the republic, they receive a greater honor among the citizens, in as much as they are more necessary for the preservation of the polity and because they are obliged to expose themselves to danger on its behalf. For this reason the crown of the victorious is given to them alone. This is why the *Policraticus* compares them to the hand,[310] which, according to Aristotle, is the organ of organs.[311] By rights those knights are also adorned with greater privileges than other citizens in regard to testaments, donations, and other affairs, but especially when they are in their camps and exercising their office.

Chapter 26

*Other parts of the polity having to do with government and an
explanation of the words used for various officials.*

[1] When it comes to the parts of a polity having to do with government, I must especially use the Romans as exemplars, because the Roman Republic was very distinguished in its order, and because historians have described the hierarchy of officials after the expulsion of Tarquin from the kingdom. They relate that first the consuls were instituted, the earliest of whom were Brutus, who was instrumental in expelling Tarquin, and Tarquin Collatinus, Lucretia's husband, who was called this either because he counseled the citizens or because he governed with the counsel of all.[312] They changed these officials every year, as I said above,[313] so that no one could remain insolent for long

309. Vegetius, *On the Military*, 1.28. The quote is not exact.
310. John of Salisbury, *Policraticus*, 5.2, 6.1.
311. Aristotle, *On the Spirit*, 3.8.432a.1–2.
312. Eutropius, *A Brief History of Rome*, 1.1–9. Actually Tarquin Collatinus was called this since he lived in the town of Collatia near Rome. Lucius Tarquinius the Proud (r.534–510 B.C.E.) was, according to Roman legend, the last of the seven kings of early Roman history. Tarquin's son, Tarquinius Sextus, raped Lucretia, wife of another relative of the king, Lucius Tarquinius Collatinus. In response, Lucretia killed herself, for which reason she became an exemplar of the virtuous Roman woman. Her husband and Lucius Junius Brutus led an attack on the king, which resulted in his expulsion and their appointment as the first consuls of the Roman Republic (509 B.C.E.). Tarquin unsuccessfully tried to force his way back into power, and Brutus sentenced his own sons to death for their part in that conspiracy, making him another hero of Roman virtue.
313. 2.8.1, 3.6.6, 3.20.3, 3.21.4, 4.7.4, 4.16.3.

but would provide aid quickly and moderately. For this reason the two were made equal, one taking care of the civil situation, the other of the military.

[2] In the course of time—in the fifth year after the kings had been driven out—they devised the dictatorship, on the occasion of a reformation in Rome. When the son-in-law of Tarquin had gathered a great army against the city to avenge the great injury to the king, they instituted a new dignity, called the dictatorship, to greatly strengthen the nation, and it had a more extensive power and command than the consulate. Likewise, the term of office was longer, expiring after five years, whereas the consulate lasted only for one year. The people called the dictators "masters," and the histories report that Julius held this dignity. The histories also tell us that the Master of Equites, who attended the dictator, was instituted in the same year. The first dictator, as Eutropius writes, was Lartius, and the Master of Equites, Spurius Cassius.[314]

[3] In the sixth year, because the consuls excessively oppressed the plebeians, the peoples instituted the tribunes, who were called this, as Isidore tells us in the *Etymologies*, because they handed down rights to the people.[315] In the cities of Italy the *Anziani*, who are ordained to the defense of the plebeian nation, hold this position today. I must note here that the senators existed continuously from the time that Romulus instituted them, and the histories tell us that the tribunes were devised to favor the plebeians, since the senators and the consuls were attacked by the people.[316]

314. Eutropius, *A Brief History of Rome*, 1.12. Eutropius says that these officials were established nine years after the expulsion of the kings, in 501, and this agrees with Livy, *History of Rome*, 2.18. Ptolemy's mixup may be related to another error: dictators were limited to a maximum of six months, not five years and were expected to resign when their specific task had been accomplished and return power to the consuls. Later dictators, like Julius Caesar, had wider powers for more than one specific task. Eutropius mistakenly states that Augustus also was dictator, but Ptolemy may be aware from other sources that this is false; in any case, he does not repeat it. A consul chose the dictator, who then chose a Master of Equites (cavalry) to help him. I use the term "Master of Equites" instead of the more common "Master of Horse" because the "equites" were not simply mounted fighters but members of an official order of ancient Rome with a rank higher than the plebeian but lower than the senatorial.

315. Isidore of Seville, *Etymologies*, 9.3–4. "hand down" is *"tribuo"* in Latin. Isidore says that they hand down rights to the people or knights. Eutropius, *A Brief History of Rome*, 1.13, says tribunes were established sixteen years after the kings' expulsion, in 494, which again agrees with Livy, *History of Rome*, 2.32.

316. Eutropius, *A Brief History of Rome*, 1.13. One might think that Ptolemy would say the reverse—that the tribunes were instituted because the consuls and senators attacked the people. But what I think he means here is that because they oppressed the people, the people protested and attacked them, as a result of which the tribunate was established. Eutropius, 1.2, says that Romulus chose 100 older men to advise him and made them senators.

[4] The histories, especially Isidore in his *Etymologies*,[317] also mention the titles of other Roman officials, namely the censors, patricians, praefects, praetors, enrolled fathers, proconsuls, exconsuls, censorini, decurions, magistrates, and notaries. I can only give a summary of these.

[5] The censorial dignity was that among the Romans of old which among the moderns is the judicial dignity, for it pertains to a judge to act as a censor.[318] They are also called "censors of patrimonies," who, as Isidore also tells us "are called this from the monetary census." This is an office of especial responsibility in the city in appointing guardians, administrators, and caretakers, in all cases or business affairs involving orphans or widows, and in dividing patrimonial estates.

[6] The patricians are called this because these citizens take care of the Roman Republic in the same way as fathers act toward their children. The Fabian home, which I discussed above,[319] was of this sort. The patriciate was therefore not an office in the Republic but rather some of the city's offspring whom the people revered as fathers because of the zeal which they had for the Roman polity. For this reason the law[320] of nations preferred the patriciate to any eminence or rule, just as a father is preferred to any tutorial care.

[7] Praefects are called this because they have precedence in praetorial power, for which reason praetors are also called praefects. Such an office brings about whatever happens, as if the prefect were especially the operator and executor of justice. Nevertheless, Sacred Scripture refers to exterior actions, as is written at the beginning of Exodus: "Pharaoh ordered the praefects of works and the superintendents of the people, saying: 'No longer will you give straw to the people for making bricks.'"[321] These are also called praetors from their pursuit of justice.

[8] Senators are called "enrolled fathers" by reason of their office. As Isidore reports, when Romulus instituted them in ten *curiae*, he chose them and "with the people present placed their names together on golden tablets, and so they

---

317. Isidore of Seville, *Etymologies*, 9.4.
318. Isidore of Seville, *Etymologies*, 9.4. "To act as a censor" is a bad choice to translate "*censere*," perhaps, but other choices would be worse since the word "*censor*" had a much wider range of meaning in Latin, from appraise to tax to consider to judge. It did not usually refer specifically to the activity of a censor.
319. 3.20.3, 4.7.7.
320. *Ius.*
321. Exodus 5.6–7.

were called 'enrolled fathers.'"[322] He also distinguished three orders among them: "the first were called 'Illustrious Ones,' the second 'Notable Ones,' and the third 'Most Glorious Ones.'" It would take a long time to expound all these words.

[9] Proconsuls were called coadjutors of the consuls,[323] as it were additions to or extensions of the consuls. Like the procurator of managers or administrators, they did not perform in the consulate simply speaking. Alternatively, a proconsul is called an "assessor," who judged in the place of consuls.

[10] An exconsul is a former consul, out of office when the year of office has been completed, so that an exconsul, as it were, exists outside the consulate. Nevertheless, exconsuls retained some rank from their consulate, or some immunity or sign of their eminence, through which they were recognized as having been consuls.

[11] Censorini are said to be minor judges involved with acts of censorial care, or they are deputies of the government about which I wrote above,[324] inferior censors, as it were.

[12] Decurions are so-called from the acts of the curial office, as Isidore says,[325] because they are "of the order of the curia and because they administer the office of the curia." Joseph of Arimathia was so-styled—a noble "decurion and a just and good man"[326]—who bought a piece of muslin on behalf of our Lord and conferred a most obliging and most reverent burial on him. I said enough at the end of the book above about this magistracy.[327]

[13] Now I must treat the last and lowest office of any government at all, which is the notary, so-called, as Isidore tells us, since "such a one is a carrier of tablets"[328] and one who undertakes to write on them. Through them acts

322. Isidore of Seville, *Etymologies*, 9.4. According to legend Romulus divided each of the three Roman tribes into ten *curiae*. There were ten *gentes* in each *curia*. See also John of Salisbury, *Policraticus*, 5.9.
323. Isidore of Seville, *Etymologies*, 9.3.
324. 4.26.5, assuming that Ptolemy is referring to censors by "the government." Isidore does not mention this official.
325. Isidore of Seville, *Etymologies*, 9.4.
326. Luke 23.50.
327. Ptolemy mentions, but only mentions, decurians at 3.21.1, but not as Roman officials, even though he lists Roman officials in the same paragraph. Rather, he says they were established by Judas Maccabeus.
328. Isidore of Seville, *Etymologies*, 9.4. "*Tabellio*" is "notary"; "*tabella*" is "tablet."

of the republic or of private personages are accomplished. They are also called "public scribes," because they alone write down public deeds, and the laws[329] of nations also call them "public servants."

[14] It remains to define one last name of a dignity having to do with the government of a polity, and this is the "scipio," which properly designates a "staff,"[330] which, as it were, supports and sustains one's leadership, and which Cornelius Scipio's father needed. The histories tell us that this father was blind, so that he came into the forum with a staff or a scipio. Because his son, Publius Cornelius, sustained the Republic against Hannibal and the Carthaginians, he was called "Scipio" by way of analogy, and because he subjugated all Africa to the Romans he was called "Scipio Africanus." This served to differentiate him from the other Scipio, his nephew, who conquered Spain and was called Lucius Cornelius Numantinus, from Numantia, which he subjected and prostrated. Augustine also writes that there was a third Scipio, called Nasica, brother of Scipio the Elder,[331] who forbade the destruction of Carthage, asserting that it was good medicine for the Romans. Therefore, on account of the probity of these great men and considering the origin of the name of Scipio, the legislators called the rod that rulers carry in their hand with the sceptre a scipio, as if to say that they would always be victorious, as the great Scipio was. Isidore says in his *Etymologies* that "triumphant ones wore a purple pallium and were clad in a toga and bore a scipio and the sceptre in their hands in imitation of Scipio's victory."[332]

[15] I have said these things about the names of dignities involved in government.

---

329. *Iura.*

330. Isidore of Seville, *Etymologies*, 18.2.

331. Augustine, *The City of God*, 1.30. Scipio the Elder is Publius Cornelius Scipio Africanus (237–183 B.C.E.), who defeated Hannibal; his father was Publius Cornelius Scipio (d.211). Publius Cornelius Scipio Aemelianus Africanus Numantinus (185–129 B.C.E.), known as Scipio the Younger, was the adopted grandson of Scipio the Elder. Publius Cornelius Scipio Nasica was consul in 138 and not Scipio the Elder's brother.

332. Isidore of Seville, *Etymologies*, 18.2. The pallium was first of all a Greek philosopher's cloak, and later a toga, but in the Middle Ages it normally referred to a white vestment worn by the pope and conferred by him on archbishops as a symbol of their power. Purple was, of course, the imperial color. What Isidore actually wrote was that they were clothed in a tunic embroidered with palm-branches (*palmata*), something worn by generals in their triumphant processions.

Chapter 27

The parts of a polity having to do with warriors, who are distin-
guished in three ways.

[1] It also seems suitable for me to discuss the parts of a polity ordained to war, since these are necessary to it, as I proved above.[333] Indeed, if they are well disposed they produce beauty and charm and generate pleasure and thereby increase the vigor of the heart and render persons bold when adversaries attack. When Solomon in the Canticles has disposed his army for war, he compares it to the beauty and charm of his wife: "You are beautiful and charming, daughter of Jerusalem, terrible as an ordered battle line from the camps."[334] For beauty is so attractive that, in the face of terror, one neither fears nor dreads attacking anything, and this is especially apparent in those who love excessively. This also happens with the well-ordered battle line, and therefore Solomon uses the word "terrible," to refer either to his wife's beauty or to the battle line. Therefore, I not inappropriately take up these parts here, because they contribute to the adornment of the polity, and because persons in war especially need government on account of their exercise of a difficult and terrible act.

[2] It seems suitable to divide the army in camps into groups with fixed numbers, by assigning leadership to someone to govern each and direct it in fighting enemies. We can find this in Vegetius's *On the Military*, in which the army is divided into legions, and he says that two legions are sufficient for any leader or consul.[335] He divides a legion into ten cohorts, but the first cohort takes precedence both in number and merit. As Vegetius tells us: "It recruited the most eligible men, both by birth and in literacy."[336] He says that this is done since camps are more confident if such great men are exposed on the first battle line, and because wisdom is especially required where there is danger to the whole army.

[3] This cohort carries the eagle, the special sign of the Roman camps and the insignia of the whole legion, which was abandoned by the later Roman Emperors. Perhaps I can give the reason for this insignia. Vegetius says that the Roman's military discipline put the first battle lines on the wing of the battle formation,[337] but among all birds' wings those of the eagle are the strongest.

333. 4.24.5, 4.25.6–7.
334. Canticle of Canticles (Song of Songs) 6.3.
335. Vegetius, *On the Military*, 2.4.
336. Vegetius, *On the Military*, 2.6.
337. Vegetius, *On the Military*, 3.20.

Alternately, it could be said that the sign of the eagle was handed down to them because of their preeminence in the world in lordship, because of the celestial and divine influence which they ought continuously to invoke, as the ruler Judas Maccabeus did when he asked for aid from heaven in fighting.[338] This is especially appropriate for them on account of the danger to which they committed themselves, or because they deserved to be victorious in the presence of God because they exposed themselves to death on behalf of their people. This eagle is mentioned in Ezekiel in reference to Nebuchadnezzar, monarch of the east: "A large eagle with great wings and long limbs, with thick and multicolored feathers, came to Lebanon and took away the pith of the cedar."[339]

[4] After this Vegetius mentions the size of the prime cohort, which he calls the "millarian cohort" because there are 1105 foot soldiers in it and 135 equestrians. And he calls the other cohorts "quinquagenarian cohorts," because he numbers 555 foot soldiers in each of them and 61 equestrians, so that each equite has a fixed number of foot soldiers. He also placed the stronger ones in the fifth cohort, because the fifth is responsible for the left wing, as the first is for the right wing.[340] Vegetius says many other things in this regard and goes on extensively with such enumerations, and his extraordinary words may well need a more full exposition in modern times. But what I have said will suffice for the present.

[5] If for its direction the multitude of people in a polity should be disposed within fixed boundaries of rank and number, how much more should this be done in camps, in which the difficulty of government is greatest and most dangerous, both because of the work that is incumbent on them, which is ordained to the end of the terrible event of death, and because of the enemies that attack them. As in Exodus when his relative Jethro counseled Moses to divide his burdens by means of various offices for judging the people: "Provide mighty men who hate avarice, and constitute from them tribunes and centurions and ones set over fifty and over ten who may judge the people";[341] so also when his enemies attacked him Judas Maccabeus divided his camp, by constituting leaders over groups of the same number, namely "tribunes, cen-

---

338. I Machabees (Maccabees) 3.44–54, 4.10–11, 30–32, and passim.
339. Ezechiel (Ezekiel) 17.3.
340. Vegetius, *On the Military*, 2.6. Obviously "*quinquagenarian*," "consisting of fifty," should be "*quingentarian*," "consisting of five hundred," and it is in Vegetius. Vegetius also places 132 (instead of 135) armored equestrians in the millarian cohort.
341. Exodus 18.21–22. The quote is not exact.

turions, pentacontarchs, and decurions."³⁴² This number is sufficiently proportionate in its limits for the distinction of the army, and for this reason each is contained in another to make it easier to bring them together when the necessity of making war requires this. The distinction that Vegetius makes of the disposition of the battle lines is attended to when a field war is ordained, although he also reduces the cohorts to centuries and decades for certain causes and reasons.

Chapter 28

The titles of leaders and of the number of the cohorts, and what each signifies.

[1] Because we have treated the titles of leaders, we must see what Sacred Scripture names them and how the Roman Republic and the moderns describe them.

[2] First, the tribune, which title Vegetius says came from "tribe," because the tribune was in charge of the knights whom Romulus had chosen, and these came from a tribe.³⁴³ But Isidore says that the tribunes are called that because they hand down rights to the plebeians,³⁴⁴ since they were instituted after the consuls to favor the plebeians. It is written elsewhere that those who had charge over one thousand knights were called tribunes, whom the Greeks call "chiliarchs," just as the centurions get their name for having charge over one hundred knights.³⁴⁵ The same thing is true concerning the quinquagenaries and the pentacontarchs.³⁴⁶ Vegetius does not mention pentacontarchs, but Sacred Scripture does, in the books that I have already mentioned,³⁴⁷ and in 4 Kings, the flames deservedly burned up those quinquagenaries and pentacontarchs who came to curse Elijah.³⁴⁸ The decans and decurions are called that

---

342. 1 Machabees (Maccabees) 3.55.
343. Vegetius, *On the Military*, 2.7.
344. Isidore of Seville, *Etymologies*, 9.3. "Hand down" is *"tribuere"* in Latin.
345. Isidore of Seville, *Etymologies*, 9.3. Isidore does not relate the chiliarchs specifically to the tribunes.
346. Isidore of Seville, *Etymologies*, 9.3. Isidore mentions only the quingentarians.
347. 3.21.1, 4.27.5, citing 1 Machabees (Maccabees) 3.55.
348. 4 Kings (2 Kings) 1. 9–15. The three quinquagenariae (groups of fifty) under their "ruler of the quinquagenariae" (4 Kings [2 Kings] does not use the title "pentacontarch") came to Elijah to give the king's orders that he come down from the mountain. Elijah called for fire from heaven to consume the first two groups, but spared and obeyed the third.

because they have responsibility for ten knights in the camps, and Vegetius places each group in one squad and one tent.[349]

[3] The general names of the well-ordered multitude of those armed for fighting are as follows. "Army" is said to come from the word for exercise or practising,[350] for this multitude requires both. "Camps" are so-called from chastity, as Isidore tells us, "because lust ought to be restrained there."[351] Delights were kept out of the camps, since fighting the enemies should be incumbent on them, as Vegetius writes.[352] It is for this reason that the Midianites vanquished the camps of the children of Israel, who had committed fornication with their daughters, as is written in Numbers.[353] On this account it is written in Deuteronomy that the Lord walked in the midst of the camps of the people of Israel, so that their camps might appear holy and there be no foulness among them.[354] Alternately, they are called "camps" on account of the fortification of the army within ramparts, palisades, and other strong forts, which the Roman rulers did when enemies invaded.[355] For this reason, diggers, carpenters, and stone-cutters were brought under military discipline, so that the necessary artisans might be at hand to protect the army.

[4] There is another name that indicates the multitude of fighters, namely "legion," so-called from how they are chosen, as Isidore tells us, because the knights comprising it were gathered or chosen by others who were very experienced.[356]

[5] Vegetius and Isidore also tell us certain other names for parts of the legion or army, such as the maniple, which is a group numbering two hundred knights, so-called because they assault their enemies in war in the morning, or

349. Vegetius, *On the Military*, 2.8, 13, 14. According to Vegetius, the decurian is the head of the turma (squadron) of calvary; the decan of a squadron of infantry, which have thirty-two men.

350. Isidore of Seville, *Etymologies*, 9.3. "Army" is "*exercitus*"; "exercise" is "*exercitium*"; and "to practice" or "exercise" is "*exercito*."

351. Isidore of Seville, *Etymologies*, 9.3. "Camp is "*castra*"; "chastity" is "*castitas*"; and "restrain" is "*castro*."

352. Vegetius, *On the Military*, 1.3, 1.7.

353. Numbers 25.1–9. Actually Numbers reports that the fornication occurred with Moabite women, who then seduced the men into worshipping their god, for which reason Moses executed 24,000 of his own people. It was because Phinehas killed a newly fornicating couple, the woman of whom was a Midianite, that Moses was satisfied with a moderate number of deaths.

354. Deuteronomy 23.14.

355. "*Vallibus*," translated here by "within palisades" is actually a part of "*vallis*," that is, "valley," not "*vallus*" or "*vallum*," "palisade." The etymological claim is not clear; perhaps Ptolemy is saying that "*castrum*," "camp" comes from another use of the same word, that is, for any fortified place, such as a castle.

356. Isidore of Seville, *Etymologies*, 9.3. "*Legio*" is "legion"; "*lego*" is "to gather."

because they bring bundles of straw or grass with them for use in signaling.[357] About this Lucan writes: "he assembles the armed maniples for giving signals quickly."[358] Others are called velites on account of their agility, from a word for "flying about."[359] The Roman Republic had certain agile youths in the military service of the legions who, when the enemies attacked, sat together behind the backs of the equites, then suddenly leaped down from their horses and threw the enemies into confusion. Such knights, as Isidore writes, were very troublesome to Hannibal;[360] it was because of them that most of his elephants were slain. Eleazar was one of them, and 1 Maccabees tells us that he sprang up in the midst of the legion attacking the camps of the king of Antioch and attacked an elephantine beast clad in armor with the corselets of the king and killed the beast.[361]

[6] There is another kind of those who are armed, called the "battle line," from the word for "acuity,"[362] so-called as Isidore says, because it uses boldness to attack enemies. Sacred Scripture often mentions this; in 1 Paralipomenon it is written about one tribe of the Israelite people that they went out to the fight in a battle line, calling out against their enemies.[363]

[7] There is yet another name called the "wedge," as Isidore tells us, which is, as it were, an assemblage, that is, a multitude, gathered together as one for fighting,[364] and it is especially necessary in making war. In Deuteronomy it is said of it that, "everyone will prepare their wedge for war."[365] It is perhaps from this that the title of "constable" derives its usage among the moderns, one who is, as it were, the head of a stable wedge, that is, of a constant and strong one.[366]

[8] There is another new name among the Tuscans for the first cohort, in analogy to the first Roman cohort, as Vegetius says, "into which knights powerful according to the census and through their stock, literacy, form, and

---

357. Vegetius, *On the Military*, 2.7–8; Isidore of Seville, *Etymologies*, 9.3. "*Mane bello*" is "in the morning in war"; "*manipulus*" is "bundle."
358. Ptolemy takes this quote from Lucan from Isidore of Seville, *Etymologies*, 9.3.
359. "*Volito*" is "fly about."
360. Isidore of Seville, *Etymologies*, 9.3.
361. 1 Machabees (Maccabees) 6.43–46.
362. Isidore of Seville, *Etymologies*, 9.3. "*Acies*" is "battle line"; "*acuitas*" is "acuity" or "sharpness."
363. 1 Paralipomenon (1 Chronicles) 12.36.
364. Isidore of Seville, *Etymologies*, 9.3.
365. Deuteronomy 20.9.
366. "Constable" is "*conestabulus*"; "stable wedge" is "*cuneus stabilis*." Actually "constable," in medieval times a high military leader, comes from "*comes stabuli*," "count of the stable."

virtue were sent, and over which a special tribune has charge because of his knowledge of arms, virtue of body, and honorable morality."[367] They call this cohort a "trapelo," so-called since it breaks through the battle lines of the enemies, for the word "trapellation" means this.

[9] Vegetius tells us many things about the officials of the camps,[368] but this summary will suffice for the present, in so far as it pertains to my treatise on the polity in this fourth book.

[10] It remains further to treat the rule of household management, that is the government of the home, which is that of the paterfamilias, whose rule has an altogether distinct matter from other rules. Therefore, it seems to be suitable for me to compose this work separately, and divide it into books or treatises and their chapters according to the requirements of the nature of the facts, which mode Aristotle also follows in this matter.[369] The same holds for the virtues which are required for the parts of any government, whether of subjects, rectors, rulers, or faithful subjects, because the order of teaching the art of living requires this, and not that I should treat them at the same time and in a mixed fashion as some have done, because this would impede the understanding of learning and oppose the norm of teaching.

367. Vegetius, *On the Military*, 2.12.
368. Vegetius, *On the Military*, 2.9–14.
369. A reference to Aristotle's *Oeconomica*, or *Household Management*, now usually considered to be spurious.

Bibliography

This bibliography makes no attempt to be a comprehensive bibliography for medieval political thought, Thomas Aquinas, or Ptolemy of Lucca. It is simply a convenient listing of the sources cited in this book. I have not listed sources that exist in many editions with standard divisions that I use in the notes, but I have cited some recent translations that may not be well known. I have also listed some of the pre-modern sources that can only be found in obscure editions.

Aristotle. *Politicorum Libri Octo cum vetusta translatione Guilelmi de Moerbeke*. Edited by Franciscus Susemihl. Leipzig, 1872.

Baron, Hans. *The Crisis of the Early Italian Renaissance*. Princeton, N.J.: Princeton University Press, 1966.

——. "A Defense of the View of the Quattrocento First Offered in *The Crisis of the Early Italian Renaissance*." In Baron, *In Search of Florentine Civic Humanism*. 2 vols. Princeton, N.J.: Princeton University Press, 1988, 195–211.

Bisson, Thomas N. " 'Quanto personam tuam' (X 2.24.18): Its Original Significance." *Proceedings of the Fourth International Congress of Medieval Canon Law*. Vatican: Biblioteca Apostolica Vaticana, 1976, 229–49.

Black, Antony. *Political Thought in Europe, 1250–1450*. Cambridge Medieval Textbooks. Cambridge: Cambridge University Press, 1992.

Blythe, James. " 'Civic Humanism' and Medieval Political Thought." Paper presented at the Harvard and University of Colorado Conference on Civic Humanism. In press.

——. "Family, Government, and the Medieval Aristotelians." *History of Political Thought* 10 (1989): 1–16.

——. *Ideal Government and the Mixed Constitution in the Middle Ages*. Princeton, N.J.: Princeton University Press, 1992.

——. "Women in the Military: A Medieval Debate." Paper presented at the 30th International Congress on Medieval Studies, Kalamazoo, Michigan, 1995.

Cohn, Norman. *The Pursuit of the Millennium*. Rev. ed. New York: Oxford University Press, 1970.

Davis, Charles Till. "Ptolemy of Lucca and the Roman Republic." *Proceedings of the American Philosophical Society* 118 (1974): 30–50.

——. "Roman Patriotism and Republican Propaganda: Ptolemy of Lucca and Pope Nicholas III." *Speculum* 50 (1975): 411–33.

Demongeot, Marcel. *Le meilleur régime politique selon saint Thomas*. Paris: Ancienne Librairie Roger et Chernoviz, 1928.

Engelbert of Admont. *De Regimine Principum*. Regensberg, 1724.

Eutropius. *Brevarium (A Brief History of Rome)*. Translated by H. W. Bird. Liverpool: Liverpool University Press, 1993.

Friedberg, Emil, ed. *Corpus Iuris Canonici*. 2 vols. Leipzig: Tauchnitz, 1879; reprinted Graz: Akademische Druck- und Verlagsanstalt, 1959.

Gewirth, Alan. *Marsilius of Padua, the Defender of Peace*. 2 vols. Records of Civilization: Sources and Studies 46. New York: Columbia University Press, 1951–1956; reprinted New York: Harper and Row, 1967.

Gilbert, Felix. "Sir John Fortescue's 'Dominium Regale et Politicum.'" *Mediaevalia et Humanistica* 2 (1943): 88–97.

Giles of Rome. *De Regimine Principum Libri III (On the Government of Rulers)*. Frankfort: Minerva, 1968 (reprint of the Rome, 1556 edition).

Gratian. *The Treatise on Laws. Decretum DD. 1-20*. Translated by Augustine Thompson. Washington, D.C.: Catholic University Press, 1993.

John of Paris. *On Royal and Papal Power*. Translated by John A. Watt. Toronto: Pontifical Institute of Mediaeval Studies, 1971.

———. *Tractatus de Potestate Regia et Papali*. In *Johannes Quidort von Paris: Über königliche und päpstliche Gewalt*. Edited by F. Bleienstein. Stuttgart: E. Klett, 1969.

John of Salisbury. *Policraticus*. Translated by Cary Nederman. Cambridge: Cambridge University Press, 1990.

Kuttner, Stefan. "Cardinalis: The History of a Canonical Concept." *Traditio* 3 (1945): 129–214.

———. "Gratian and Plato." In *Church and Government in the Middle Ages*. Edited by C.N.L. Brooke et al. Cambridge: Cambridge University Press, 1976, 93–118.

McGinn, Bernard. *Visions of the End: Apocalyptic Traditions in the Middle Ages*. New York: Columbia University Press, 1979.

Markus, R. A. "Two Conceptions of Political Authority: Augustine's *De Civitate Dei*, XIX, 14–15, and Some Thirteenth Century Interpretations." *Journal of Theological Studies* N.S. 16 (1965): 68–100.

Mohr, Walter. "Bemerkungen zur Verfasserschaft von *De Regimine Principum*." In *Virtus Politica*. Edited by Joseph Müller and Helmut Koblenberger. Stuttgart and Bad Cannestatt: Frommann Verlag and Günther Holzboog, KG, 1974, 127–45.

Nederman, Cary. *Community and Consent: The Secular Political Theory of Marsiglio of Padua's "Defensor Pacis."* New York: Rowman and Littlefield, 1994.

———. "Nature, Sin, and the Origins of Society: The Ciceronian Tradition in Medieval Political Thought." *Journal of the History of Ideas* 49 (1988): 3–26.

———. "The Union of Wisdom and Eloquence Before the Renaissance: The Ciceronian Orator in Medieval Thought." *Journal of Medieval History* 18 (1992): 75–95.

O'Rahilly, A. "Notes on St. Thomas: IV. *De Regimine Principum*"; "V. Tholomeo of Lucca, Continuator of the *De Regimine Principum*." *Irish Ecclesiastical Record* 31 (1929): 396–410; 31 (1929): 606–14.

Peter John Olivi. *De renuntiatione papae Coelestini (On the Resignation of Pope Celestine)*. Edited by V. P. Livarius Oliger. *Archivum Franciscanum Historicum* 11 (1918): 354–57.

Pocock, J. G . E. *The Machiavellian Moment: Florentine Political Theory and the Atlantic Republican Tradition*. Princeton, N.J.: Princeton University Press, 1975.

Ptolemy of Lucca. *De Regimine Principum (On the Government of Rulers)*. Edited by R. P. Joannes Perrier. In Thomas Aquinas, *Opuscula Omnia necnon Opera Minora*. Tomus Primus: *Opuscula Philosophica*. Paris: P. Lethielleux, 1949.

———. *Determinatio Compendiosa de juribus imperii (A Short Determination of the Jurisdiction of the Roman Empire)*. Edited by Marius Kramer. In *Fontes Iuris Germanici Antiqui*. Hanover and Leipzig: Bibliopolius Hahnianus, 1909.

———. *Die Annalen des Tholomeus von Lucca (Tuscan Annals)*. Edited by B. Schmeidler. Monumenta Germania Historia. Scriptores rerum Germanicarum, N.S.8. Berlin, 1930.

———. *Exameron (Hexameron)*. Edited by T. Masetti. Siena, 1880.

———. *Historia Ecclesiastica (Ecclesiastical History)*. Edited by L. A. Muratori. In *Rerum Italicarum Scriptores*, vol. 11. Milan, 1727.

Savonarola, Girolamo. *Treatise on the Constitution and Government of Florence*. In *Humanism and Liberty*. Edited by R. N. Watkins. Columbia: University of South Carolina Press, 1978.

Stephenson, Carl and Frederick Marcham, eds. *Sources of English Constitutional History*. New York: Harper, 1937.

Thomas Aquinas. *Opera Omnia*. Edited by Robertus Busa. Stuttgart-Bad Cannstatt: Frommann Verlag and Günther Holzboog, KG, 1980.

Tierney, Brian. "A Conciliar Theory of the Thirteenth Century." *Catholic Historical Review* 36 (1950–1951): 415–40.

———. *The Crisis of Church and State, 1050–1300*. Toronto: University of Toronto Press, 1988.

———. "Origins of Natural Rights Language: Texts and Contexts, 1150–1250." *History of Political Thought* 10 (1989): 615–46.

———. *Religion, Law, and the Growth of Constitutional Thought*. Cambridge: Cambridge University Press, 1982.

Ullmann, Walter. *A History of Political Thought: The Middle Ages*. Baltimore: Penguin Books, 1965.

Vegetius. *Epitome of Military Science (On the Military)*. Translated by N. P. Milner. Liverpool: Liverpool University Press, 1993.

Weinstein, Donald. *Savonarola and Florence: Prophecy and Patriotism in the Renaissance*. Princeton, N.J.: Princeton University Press, 1970.

Witt, Ronald. "The *De Tyranno* and Coluccio Salutati's View of Politics and Roman History." *Nuova Rivista Storica* 53 (1969): 434–74.

———. "The Rebirth of the Concept of Republican Liberty in Italy." In *Renaissance Studies in Honor of Hans Baron*. Edited by Anthony Mohlo and John A. Tedeschi. Dekalb: Northern Illinois University Press, 1971, 173–99.

Index to Aristotle Citations

Index to Augustine Citations

Index to Biblical Citations

General Index

This index is primarily intended as a guide to the text of Ptolemy's work. As such, it includes all proper names and many significant topics in the text. It does not include names or topics found only in the footnotes. It includes items found in the introduction only if they are also in the text, if they are modern scholars, or if I felt it would be helpful to include them. I do not include citations of Aristotle, Augustine, or the Bible, since these can be found in separate indices.